New Map
of the
CITY of DUBLIN

Scale of half a Mile Irish

JOYCE-AGAIN'S WAKE
An Analysis of Finnegans Wake

JOYCE-AGAIN'S WAKE

An Analysis of Finnegans Wake

BERNARD BENSTOCK

UNIVERSITY OF WASHINGTON PRESS

SEATTLE AND LONDON

THIS BOOK IS DEDICATED TO MY FATHER

Preface

It is hoped that *Joyce-again's Wake* will be many things to many people, but most important that it will serve the increasing number of "middle-range" readers (those with enough patience to be willing to participate in the work necessary for an understanding of Joyce's masterpiece, but without that ideal insomnia being simulated by Joycean scholars). As such this "analysis" hopes to bridge the specialized and vital work being done by Joyceans and the boundless country of Joyce's *Wake*. I have leaned heavily upon the indispensable handful of books hitherto available, especially those which have miraculously reduced every Joycean's work from a matter of decades to a matter of years: Mrs. Glasheen's *Census*, Atherton's *The Books at the Wake*, the Campbell-Robinson *Skeleton Key* (despite my reservations it has been highly important in opening many doors, especially at a time when no other keys were available), the Hodgart-Worthington *Song in the Works of James Joyce*, Harry Levin's *James Joyce*, and more recently the two Clive Hart books, *Structure and Motif in Finnegans Wake* and *A Concordance to Finnegans Wake*. And Richard Ellmann's definitive biography of Joyce has proved itself vital to any work on any aspect of James Joyce.

I have endeavored to quote copiously from *Finnegans Wake*, in the belief that it is essentially the sound and sense of Joyce's own words that work the necessary magic for the reader of the *Wake*, and that the greater the familiarity the reader has with those words the closer he comes to understanding for himself much more than any commentator can offer in explication. In some instances I have even attempted to be exhaustive in tracking down echoes in the *Wake*, and in these instances any missing item is due to ignorance rather than reticence. I have taken the liberty of eliminating opening and closing ellipses in these quotations for easier readability. Inclusive page-and-line numbers are given from the 1939 Viking Press edition of *Finnegans Wake* with corrections made from Joyce's list of "Corrections of Misprints in *Finnegans Wake*." Line references are counted from the top of each page and follow the period; thus 101.6-9 means page 101, lines 6 to 9. In chapter 10, marginal notes are designated by the letters R and L, indicating right and left on the page, and footnotes are numbered and noted by a lower-case "n." Other Joyce books from which I quote are also listed by page in parentheses and indicated with D for *Dubliners* (Compass edition), AP for *A Portrait of the Artist as a Young Man* (Compass edition), and U for *Ulysses* (Bodley Head edition, 1937).

The "working outline" that follows is included here for easy reference for the reader. It is not intended as a synopsis of the *Wake* (I have very definite prejudices against synopses), but is merely a guide which I used while working on this volume in order to remind myself of the context of a particular quotation, and which may be profitably used by the reader for just such a purpose. It gives no more than a surface suggestion of what may be happening in a particular portion of the *Wake*, or even just a heading for one of the more self-contained sections.

Acknowledgments

I am indebted to several learned Joyceans for their assistance, particularly Fritz Senn of Zurich and Clive Hart of Newcastle, co-editors of *A Wake Newslitter,* and Thomas F. Staley, editor of the *James Joyce Quarterly,* all three of whom have read through the manuscript and raised suspicious eyebrows at necessary instances. Mrs. Adaline Glasheen, the *Wake* census-taker, will find that some of the elements of our correspondence has crept into the text, and I am grateful for her opinions.

An important service was graciously rendered by Lawrence A. Wiggin, who donated the product of his knowledge and close reading of the *Wake* to the analysis of the Prankquean portion found in the Appendix. Prof. Laura Jepsen of the Department of English at Florida State University was instrumental in getting me started on all this many years ago and Michel T. Blouin of the Department of English at Louisiana State University helped me proofread when it was all finished, while special thanks goes to the Graduate School of Louisiana State University for typing the manuscript.

Portions of this book have appeared in the following places, and I am indebted accordingly for permission to re-use the material: aspects of Chapters 3 and 5 appeared in the *Bucknell Review* as "A Portrait of the Artist in *Finnegans Wake*"; a segment of Chapter 1 was printed in the *James Joyce Quarterly* (University of Tulsa Press) as "The Quiddity of Shem and the Whatness of Shaun"; a draft of the second part of Chapter 2 was titled "The Final Apostasy: James Joyce and Religion" in *ELH, A Journal of English Literary History;* and an abbreviated version of Chapter 4 was included as "Here Comes Everybody: *Finnegans Wake* as Epic" by editor Donald E. Stanford in *Nine Essays in Modern Lit-*

erature (Louisiana State University Press). The Viking Press has granted permission for the extensive quotations from James Joyce's *Finnegans Wake,* and I am also indebted to the numerous publishers from whose works I have included quotations to a lesser extent, and I acknowledge these in initial footnotes.

Contents

List of Illustrations

A Working Outline of Finnegans Wake

CHAPTER 1 (pp. 3-29)

CHAPTER 2 (pp. 30-47)

CHAPTER 7 (169-95)

JOYCE-AGAIN'S WAKE

An Analysis of Finnegans Wake

CHAPTER ONE

What We Still Don't Know About Finnegans Wake

More than three decades have elapsed since the twelve disciples were gathered together by James Joyce and commissioned to produce their *Exagmination Round his Factification for Incamination of Work in Progress* in an attempt to open the floodgates of critical understanding in advance of Joyce's last and most difficult work. More than two decades have passed since the finished bulk of *Finnegans Wake*'s 628 pages was made available to readers and critics. Despite Joyce's disappointment during his last years concerning the amount and caliber of critical comment, the years after his death have produced a tidal wave from the initial trickle. Already available to the lay reader and the scholar are a "skeleton key," a "census," a "reading" of *Finnegans Wake,* a "concordance" (and a "dictionary" is in the offing), as well as book-length studies of literary allusions, religious significance, songs, and "structure and motif" in the *Wake.*[1] Articles in scholarly publications and commentaries in popular periodicals abound, and it is not unknown for a commentator to have the same article rejected as too specialized by one periodical and too general by another, only to have it accepted by a third—the gamut is wide, the quantity abundant. Yet many of the most basic questions (especially that nagging all-inclusive one asked by the layest of lay readers : "But what is it all about exactly?") remain unanswered.

The "basic" question can well remain unanswered. William York Tindall contends that *"Finnegans Wake* is about *Finnegans Wake,"*[2] and I for one am content to let it go at that. It seems preferable to beg the question rather than beggar the work. The horror of the plea is that it calls for an answer in the proverbial "25 words

or less"! Here in the flesh is that digest reader who pathetically re-
quests a paraphrase of *Finnegans Wake,* and it is equally pathetic
to note how many critics and commentators seem perfectly willing
to provide some sort of "pony." When the mutilated version of
Ulysses was being pirated in the United States in 1927, some 167
international literary personages banded together to protest vigor-
ously. Perhaps some such group should now assemble to attest once
for always that a work of literary art *cannot be paraphrased,* since
paraphrase is a method of reducing a work into something else,
and, in the case of the *Wake,* it most often proves to be reducing
toward absurdity.

The only worthwhile method of explicating the *Wake* is
through augmentation, not diminution. A comparison of pages 24
through 37 of *A Skeleton Key to Finnegans Wake* with the rest of
that volume is an apt case in point: these "demonstration" pages,
analyzing the first four paragraphs of the *Wake,* are highly valuable to the intelligent reader in their rather full examination of
those paragraphs. The rest of the *Key* is usually slapdash scholarship, "boiling down" Joyce's work into insipid pap, and leaving
the lazy reader with a predigested mess of generalizations and
catch phrases. When otherwise competent Joyceans like Wilder
and Tindall quibble about how many hours of *Finnegans Wake*
reading (one thousand or one hundred) make a real *Finnegans
Wake* reader, they are taking away valuable time from the "angels
dancing on the head of a pin" controversy. A *Finnegans Wake*
"reader" is not measured by time spent but by intelligence and information contributed toward an understanding of the work.

One of the minor irritations of *Wake* scholarship results from
the chapter-title confusion indicated by the chart below. It is apparent that the book is divided into four basic parts, the first three
being further subdivided into chapters (eight for the first part,
four each for the second and third). That Joyce preferred to leave
all these parts untitled is an author's prerogative, although he referred to them at various times in his letters and in conversation by
general names (the third book he called "the four watches of

Shaun," chapter 8 he called "Anna Livia Plurabelle," etc.) and gave portions of the work various titles when they were published separately. Any commentator would concede that it is preferable to have a title name rather than merely call a section "Book II, chapter iii" or "chapter 11," yet the chart below indicates vast liberties taken by critics of renaming (hence "rewriting") Joyce's work.[3] Of the three sets, Mrs. Glasheen's is obviously the purest since almost all of her suggested titles are taken from Joyce's indications for titles. They are basic and succinct, although one or two seem mysterious to me; the list offered by Campbell and Robinson in their *Key* seems pompous and overblown, although they attempted to extract actual phrases from the chapters they were titling; Tindall, coming last, like Johnny MacDougall, is most intent on being clever and original. The vast variety of suggested titles (only chapters 7, 13, and 15 indicate any possible collusion) demonstrates a critical tendency among Joyceans of "I'd rather be original than right." Titles for the four "books" (Mrs. Glasheen abstaining in this area) are:

	Campbell and Robinson	*Tindall*
Book I	The Book of the Parents	The Fall of Man
Book II	The Book of the Sons	Conflict
Book III	The Book of the People	Humanity
Book IV	Recorso	Renewal

The chapter titles are:

		Campbell and Robinson	*Glasheen*	*Tindall*
Ch.	1	Finnegan's Fall	The Wake	The Fall of Man
Ch.	2	H.C.E.—His Agnomen and Reputation	The Ballad	The Cad
Ch.	3	H.C.E.—His Trial and Incarceration	Gossip	Gossip and the Knocking at the Gate
Ch.	4	H.C.E.—His Demise and Resurrection	The Lion	The Trial
Ch.	5	The Manifesto of A.L.P.	The Hen	The Letter
Ch.	6	Riddles—The Personages of the Manifesto	Twelve Questions	The Quiz

Ch. 7	Shem the Penman	Shem the Penman	Shem
Ch. 8	The Washers at the Ford	Anna Livia Plurabelle	A.L.P.
Ch. 9	The Children's Hour	The Mime of Mick, Nick and the Maggies	Children at Play
Ch. 10	The Study Period—Triv and Quad	Lessons	Homework
Ch. 11	Tavernry in Feast	The Tavern	The Tale of a Pub
Ch. 12	Bride-Ship and Gulls	Mamalujo	Tristan
Ch. 13	Shaun before the People	Shaun the Post	Shaun the Post
Ch. 14	Jaun before St. Bride's	Jaun	Jaun's Sermon
Ch. 15	Yawn under Inquest	Yawn	Yawn
Ch. 16	H.C.E. and A.L.P.— Their Bed of Trial	Parents	The Bedroom
Ch. 17	Recorso	Dawn	New Day

I reproduce this chart here not for the sake of petty quibbling, but because this mix-up seems symptomatic of a larger confusion present in the "synopses" offered with each of these three books on the subject. These short "digests" of the most important events of each chapter have the pitiful quality of giving us the impression that the commentators, like Aesopian blindmen, were reading three different books, all oddly enough entitled *Finnegans Wake*. The fault lies not with the commentators, each of whom seems to have honestly offered what he saw as the major aspects of each chapter, but with the basic nature of "synopses." In a work where every sentence opens a variety of possible interpretations, any synopsis of a chapter is bound to be incomplete. This tendency to offer titles and synopses is a natural one, stemming from the nature of the work itself: having to handle a vast panorama of events and personages and allusions, the working analyst attempts to offer some sort of guidelines both for himself and the reader, lest concentration on any particular part obscure its significance within the framework of the whole.

Although it is comforting to note how many new vistas into the *Wake* have been opened in recent years and how many misconceptions have been logically destroyed, it is also disconcerting to realize how slow certain erroneous concepts are to die or fade away. We are involved in an area where errors have an uncanny tenacity of their own, despite the number of times *requiescat in pace* has been said over them. Even errors made immediately after publication and corrected by Joyce himself still crop up over twenty years later. One such is the contention made by both Harry Levin and Edmund Wilson[4] that the laggard among the four old men, Johnny MacDougall, represents the province of Ulster, an error made on the basis that Ulster has been "slow" to join the rest of Ireland in breaking away from British rule. It was an intelligent error in 1939, and Joyce lauded these American critics who leaped into print with critical reviews where more angelic members of their profession feared to tread. But Joyce was quick to discredit the contention of "Ulsterman MacDougall,"[5] and it now seems obvious to us that the rearguardsman should be identified with Connaught (as witness Joyce's story "The Dead"), and that the author's concern would be about intellectual and cultural backwardness to a far greater extent than political. Yet many subsequent reviewers and commentators, unheeding or unaware of the corrective, continue to refer to old Johnny as Ulster. Even the 1960 revised and augmented edition of Levin's *James Joyce* perpetuates its initial error.[6]

Another early error of long duration was to refer to Anna Livia Plurabelle as "Maggie." This error arose from the repeated use of the name and its variants in the *Wake,* and the attempts of critics like Wilson to arrive at the plot line of the book.[7] Since Anna Livia is married to H. C. Earwicker it seems logical that she is Mrs. Earwicker (and indeed Mrs. Glasheen often refers to her as Mrs. E.). But, as Mrs. Earwicker, what is her given name? It is absurd to call her Anna Livia Earwicker; nowhere in the text is any such hybrid to be found, although manuscript draft Add MS 47473 has her sign her final letter as "Dame Anna Livia Plurabelle Earwicker." In fact Joyce seems particularly careful to keep his H.C.E. and A.L.P. characters separate and individual as such: when the *prænomen* and *nomen* are Anna and Livia, the logical *cognomen* is always Plurabelle (although the full appellation of "Anna Livia Plurabelle" is not to be found as such in the final text). This has led to the speculation that since "Mr. and Mrs. Earwicker" seems foreign as a domestic name, and since H.C.E. and A.L.P. exist as such on an archetypal level primarily, perhaps the family name of this married couple who are the "real" twentieth-century citizens of Chapelizod is in actuality Porter. This supposition is based on the common use of this name in various places throughout the *Wake* (72.3, 91.15, 104.18, 106.32, 135.7, 186.35-36, 276.L, 388.15, 560.22, 561.3, 563.24), but most often during the next-to-last chapter, where we see the Earwickers partially and perhaps fully awake in their bedroom above the pub. But this supposition carries little weight (although it seems destined to keep reappearing in articles for the next decade or so) since it presupposes accepting chapter 16 as outside the dream framework of the *Wake,* whereas it is actually still part of the dream—as witness the continuation of Joyce's "dream language"—and is merely a part of the dream closest to reality (nearest to the waking state) in the form of a cinematic scenario retelling the Earwicker story. As such it is in contradistinction to the Honuphrius* and Anita portion which succeeds it and manages to delve into the deepest part of the dream.

This still leaves us with the problem of Wilson's name of Maggie for the wife of H. C. Earwicker. If Maggie is not Mrs. E., who is she? The problem hinges on the all-important letter that has been dug up from the midden heap by the neighbor's hen, since this is where the name most often occurs (11.24, 66.19, 67.31-32, 94.16, 106.11, 23, 111.11, 15, 16, 112.28, 113.10, 116.8, 24, 120.17, 142.30, 145.2, 273.n6, 278.n6, 280.14, 20, 281.6, 14, 301. 15, 302.7-8, 420.7, 458.10, 18, 459.4, 460.26, 461.28, 528.12, 615.3, 13, 31). The significance of the letter exists on various levels

---

* This is the spelling Joyce uses nine times in the paragraph; its alternate, Honophrius, is used twice. The inconsistency is intended to reflect the controversy between the Semi-Arians and the accepters of the fourth-century Nicene Creed, Homoiousians and Homoousians.

(although it can safely be stated that each one is a manifestation of history: personal, political, romantic), and on a literal level the letter was apparently sent by someone in Boston named Maggie, probably a relative of the Earwickers, and addressed to them. Once read by the recipients (sometime in the past) it was discarded, only to be dug up accidentally by the hen and found by the neighbors. Thus the letter is said to contain information concerning Earwicker's monumental indiscretion (or at least this is the interpretation placed upon it by the vindictive neighbors, the sinister Magrath and his none-too-innocent wife, Lily Kinsella). In actuality it is merely a chatty, newsy sort of family letter written by the American cousin, containing either news of or a reference to the Boston Tea Party. That historic act then becomes an aspect of Earwicker's misdemeanor: it was illegal, performed under cover of night, and employed disguises, although rather transparent ones to all concerned; it involved tea, a shibboleth in the *Wake* for love and sex (particularly "wetting the tea"). As such the evidence is there to accuse if not convict the suspicious publican.

On an allegorical level, the letter is a record of universal history, written by the artist-prophet Shem (apparently at the behest of the archetypal woman A.L.P., the source of the secrets of the creation, procreation, and perpetuation of the species) and stolen by the bourgeois politician brother Shaun for the purpose of passing it off as his own in order to reap the reward of making the universal secrets accessible to and palatable for his constituents and followers. It is the final form of the letter which best demonstrates this function (615-19); here Anna Livia vindicates the archetypal man H.C.E., and the letter serves like those of Paul and Peter in the New Testament to deify the Son of Man. In this context Maggie is seen in her role as Mary Magdalene, and her two personalities (before and after salvation) provide the split personalities of the Earwicker daughter, Issy.

It is on the third level, therefore, that Maggie is most important, since the letter-writer is Issy; the recipient varies often from the "aged" lover who is in reality her father, to either the Shem-figure or the Shaun-figure (or both), to her mirror image. When she is writing to her "lover" (either the Mark-Finn-Swift-Dodgson-Noah personification of H.C.E. or her Tristram-Dermot-young Swift brother), the tone is borrowed from Swift's "little language" in the *Journal to Stella*. When the receiver is Issy herself or her other self, the split mirrors the rivalry of the two girls (whether actual or Joyce-invented): Stella vs. Vanessa, Alice Liddell vs. Isa Bowman, Iseult of Ireland vs. Iseult of Brittany. But it is apparent that the Maggie of the *Wake* is not mother but daughter, except in the flashbacks when A.L.P. remembers herself as her young self—"just a young thin pale soft shy slim slip of a thing then" (202.27) and "Just a whisk brisk sly spry spink spank sprint of a thing theresomere" (627.4-5). As the *Census of Finnegans Wake* correctly maintains, the "Maggies" of "The Mime of Mick, Nick and the Maggies" (215-59) are the plural form of Issy, and are the temptresses who lurk throughout, especially as the Raven and the Dove, the "Magdalenes," the first two parts of the Sally-Christine split personality found in Morton Prince's *The Dissociation of a Personality*.[8] When multiplied into the Maggies of the Mime, playing the children's game of "Colours," they shift from two to seven, in the same relationship between the rainbow of *seven* colors that appeared to Noah as an omen and the *two* birds that he sent out from the ark, the raven and the dove.

Maggie is thus Issy, and the Maggies are the "Iseults"; Anna Livia (except in the nonliteral sense that her daughter succeeds her) is not Maggie, and the name "Maggie Earwicker" is a misnomer for her.* When Wilson first made this error in "The Dream of H. C. Earwicker" in June, 1939, it was certainly a venial one, but its continued repetition in so many critical commentaries since indicates the existence of plagiarized ideas without original thought, and a basic ignorance of *Finnegans Wake* and the prodigious amount of work by varied hands performed during the past two decades.

---

* At the risk of flailing a dead horse, attention might be called to Mrs. Antrobus in Thornton Wilder's *The Skin of Our Teeth:* her name is Maggie.

Many problems exist in the nebulous area which Mrs. Glasheen delightfully calls "Who is who when everybody is somebody else."[9] The publication of the first volume of Joyce's letters in 1957 seems to have done more to compound rather than simplify these problems. In discussing the embryonic *Wake* he refers to his "Shem-Ham-Cain-Egan"[10] character; whereas Cain and Ham are obvious prototypes for the accursed Shem, Egan seems to be a startling inclusion. There is no quarreling with the identification in the *Census* of the "Pierce Egan" who appears at 447.23 of the *Wake* as the author of "Compost liffe in Dufblin" as a nineteenth-century "English sporting writer, whose works include *Real Life in Ireland by a Real Paddy*."[11] That this "sham" writer is a fitting mask for Shem is also obvious, but somehow this single allusion to Egan hardly seems to justify Joyce's coupling him with Cain and Ham.

Even more perplexing is Joyce's reference to "Cain-Shem-Tristan-Patrick" in a letter to Harriet Weaver dated 16 August 1924.[12] Although all critics agree that Shem is Cain, many from Campbell and Robinson on down through the post-*Key* years have assumed that it is Shaun who is both Tristan and Patrick. The *Key* had unequivocally listed Tristan as Shaun,[13] and labeled the St. Patrick of the *ricorso* as "Shaunish"[14]—judgments which remained fairly standard and were reiterated often; e.g., M. J. C. Hodgart: "St. Patrick (who like St. Kevin represents Shaun) refuses to follow the sophistries of the druid (Shem)."[15] The *Census,* appearing twelve years after the *Key,* also accepted Shaun-Patrick, but insisted that Shem was Tristram.[16] When the Joyce letters were published a year after, the *Census*-taker had some very serious second thoughts, offering a corrigendum in "Out of My Census" (dated 1959). Accepting the hint that Shem was St. Patrick, Mrs. Glasheen went on to recognize Shem as Taff and Shaun as Butt (with various pieces of evidence offered: "Taffy Was a Welshman" identifying Shem, while Billy Budd, butter, Burrus, Buck Mulligan, and a barrel produce Shaun), but cautioned: "I am understandably leery of the confident statement and here say firmly that I cannot really read 'Buckley and the Russian General' or 'The Archdruid and St. Patrick'."[17]

One's first temptation is to turn a leery eye at Joyce himself and attempt to pass off his casual comment of "my one bedazzled eye searched the sea like Cain-Shem-Tristan-Patrick"[18] as a wholly personal one, Joyce visualizing himself in these various roles without intending that Miss Weaver (the letter's recipient) should transfer the allusion to the embryonic *Wake,* but this seems hardly likely to anyone who has retrospectively followed Joyce's self-involvement in his work. Nor would an attempt to devalue the postulation as being premature (1924 being only the second year of Joyce's efforts on the book) be plausible, since dated evidence indicates that by the time this remark was written, Books One and Three were already in rough draft. But it is still conceivable that there exists in the *Wake* a corresponding composite to the Shem-Cain-Tristan-Patrick mentioned—in the form of a Shaun-Abel-Tristan-Patrick counterpart.

The recent publication of Clive Hart's *Structure and Motif in Finnegans Wake* may well prove to be a timely aid in unscrambling the confusing conglomeration of Butts and Taffs and Tristrams and Patricks, since Mr. Hart does much to establish a concept of time-and-space in the *Wake,* the movements, changes and reversals of which may offer a guide to the confused and a beacon to the lost. In discussing the Shem-Shaun polarity, Mr. Hart notes

> . . . two extremes to the function of this polarity, between which the line of development swings to and fro: when their orbits are in close proximity they war with each other and—at a moment of exact equilibrium—even manage to amalgamate, while at the other extreme there is total incomprehension and a failure to communicate, symbolised by the point of farthest separation of the orbits.[19]

The meeting points, therefore, are in chapters 1, 11, and 17 (at beginning, middle, and end), so that the structure overlapping the *Wake* is the figure that symbolizes infinity. Thus, the couplings of Mutt-Jute and Muta-Juva ("the same event looked at from opposite sides"[20]) as well as Butt-Taff, involve interchangeability and identity rather than antagonism and dissimilarity. This is corroborated by internal evidence in the case of Butt and Taff. The open-

ing cry of "We want Bud" (337.32) indicates the popularity of
the hero and suggests Shaun, while the *Skeleton Key* maintains that
the Butt-Shem figure has the characteristics of invader, and Taff
those of the native defender.[21] Also, whereas Taff is described as
"a smart boy" (338.5), Butt is a *"mottledged youth"* (338.11),
suggesting the descriptions in the Mime program of Shem as "the
bold bad bleak boy" (219.24) and Shaun as "the fine frank fairhaired fellow" (200.12)—the extremity of the earlier description is
certainly greatly tempered by the time the pair reach the middle
chapter, but a touch of Shem is nonetheless present in Butt, and an
element of Shaun in Taff. Both, incidentally, share a clerical
affinity, Butt being of *"clergical appealance"* (338.11), while Taff
is *"of the peat freers"* and *"the karmalife order"* (338.5-6). At
least one key to their reconciled personalities is available in another
pair mentioned just before the Butt-Taff scene, the Saxon chiefs
Horsa and Hengest, both sons of the same father and therefore
"hunguest and horasa, jonjemsums both" (325.17), elsewhere
codified as "but Heng's got a bit of Horsa's nose and Jeff's got the
signs of Ham round his mouth" (143.22-24), so that not even
such opponents as Ham and Japhet are incapable of Joycean reconciliation.

Does a neutralized Butt-Taff, however, necessarily lead to a neutral St. Patrick? It becomes apparent from internal evidence in the
Wake that both Shem and Shaun share aspects of the Irish saint,
whose existence in the book, like that of St. Kevin, remains somewhat nebulous until the final chapter. It may be noted that Shem
has "an adze of a skull" (169.11), while Shaun calls upon the
blessings of "Haggispatrick" (404.35); Shem is identified as
being in "his pawdry's purgatory" (177.4), but at another instance
"Shaun replied patly, with tootlepick tact" (410.24); Shem is
heard to "squeal like holy Trichepatte" (228.6), while Shaun is
addressed as "Mr Trickpat" (487.23). Numerically, the Shaun-as-
Patrick pattern is slightly greater (91.6, 404.35, 410.24, 411.20,
425.28, 442.36, 447.29, 472.1-2, 478.26, 484.1, 485.7-8, 486.2,
487.23, 490.14), but the Shem references seem stronger and more

apt (169.11, 177.4, 228.6, 301.30, 352.36-353.1, 424.34, 425.30, 463.1, 464.16, 479.12, 490.8-10, 564.32). Nonetheless, it should be apparent that, even with a handful of these correspondences in doubt, there seems to be a fairly well-balanced number of Patricks in Shem and Shaun.

And what of Tristram?* Of the many allusions to the name in the *Wake,* only five can be interpreted to apply to either one of the Earwicker sons with any degree of assurance. Of the four that allude to Shaun, "fairescapading in his natsirt" (388.3) links Tristan (a reversed *natsirt*) with Parnell (Shaun) since the Irish leader is reputed by a scrap of apocrypha to have escaped down a fire escape in his nightshirt when almost apprehended in a Tristan situation with his Isolde, Kitty O'Shea. A more substantial reference identifies "Trinathan partnick dieudonnay" (478.26), coupling Shaun with Patrick, Swift, and Tristan (but also with Nick, the Devil, indicating perhaps that Shaun is part Nick and part Mick). The two other allusions are to "toppling Humphrey hugging Nephew" (484.9), Tristan being Earwicker-Mark's nephew, and "Tantris, hattrick, tryst" (486.7), which again groups Tristan and Patrick with Shaun. Shem, on the other hand, is linked with Tristan and Wagner's *Liebestod* when Shaun refers to Shem swigging "a slug of Jon Jacobsen from his treestem sucker cane. Mildbut likesome!" (424.27-28); again Patrick's shamrock in *treestem* and his British name (Sucat) in *sucker* indicate that Tristan and Patrick share a duality all their own in the *Wake.* In the Yawn scene the Interrogators (as much befuddled as most critics) investigate the disintegrating corpus with every intention of finding out its identity. Aware of the Jacob-Esau switch which fooled blind Isaac, these four Aesopian blindmen are understandably suspicious: "Hood maketh not frere," they assert; "The voice is the voice of jokeup, I fear" (487.21-22). "Are you imitation Roma now or Amor now" (487.22-23), they wonder, addressing Yawn as "Mr Trickpat"

---

* A recent mining of Tristram information can be found in David Hayman's "Tristran and Isolde in *Finnegans Wake:* A Study of the Sources and Evolution of a Theme," *Comparative Literature Studies,* I, No. 2 (1964), 93-112.

(487.23), indicating that the body belongs to a composite Patrick-Tristan, but contains an internal dichotomy as well: between *Roma* (the Church of Rome represented in Ireland by St. Patrick) and *Amor* (the concept of chivalric love associated with Tristram).

If anyone is expected to recognize Tristram it is certainly Iseult, yet she seems no more certain than more objective observers. On at least two occasions Shaun claims that her letters are addressed to him: "you, sis, that used to write to us the exceeding nice letters" (431.29), and in reply to the comment: "you have your letters": "Throsends. For my darling. Typette!" (478.1-3). We should, however, remember that Shaun is a purloiner of other people's mail. Yet, one version of Iseult's love letter addresses her lover variously as "Jaunick"* (457.36), "Joke" (458.13), "Jer" (458.15), "Jack" twice (459.27, 460.27), "joey" (460.36), "Shane" (461.25), "Jaime" (461.31), and "Juan" (461.31). *Jack* and *Juan* are obviously John (therefore Shaun), while *Jaime* and *Jer* are James and Jerry (therefore Shem); *Shane* can be either Shem or Shaun (but certainly implies St. Patrick since Slane was the scene of Patrick's conversion of the druid). *Joke* could be either Jake-Jacob-Shem or Jack-John-Shaun. *Joey* fails to unlock either door, while *Jaunick* combines John-Shaun with Nick-Shem. The confusion is compounded in Iseult's closing "Hymn" to the Tristram-Iseult chapter: *"By the cross of Cong, says she, rising up Saturday in the twilight from under me, Mick, Nick the Maggot or whatever your name is, you're the mose likable lad that's come my ways yet from the barony of Bohermore"* (399.25-28). And the last line of the chapter reads: "So, to john for a john, johnajeams, led it be!" (399.34), *johnajeams* echoing "John a'Dream's" (61.4) and coupling John and James, Shaun and Shem.

This ambivalent Tristram, then, indicates a basic pattern in *Finnegans Wake* somewhat more complex—but no less patterned—than that described by Mr. Hart's infinity shape. The *Wake* actually forms three arcs instead of two, as Shem and Shaun come together at four points: the opening chapters, the end of the first book, the

---

* Pronounced "yonic," this suggests sexual ambivalence as well.

last two chapters of the second book, and throughout the final chapter. The pattern is formed in this way: all is chaos at the opening of the cycle into which the twins are born: "A.D. 1132. Two sons at an hour were born until a goodman and his hag. These sons called themselves Caddy and Primas. Primas was a santryman and drilled all decent people. Caddy went to Winehouse and wrote o peace a farce. Blotty words for Dublin" (14.11-15). Clearly defined as Cain and Abel, the two brothers have not yet fought, and although easily differentiated between they are as innocent of conflict as the nursery rhyme rhythms of this piece indicate. In short, they are at *peace,* although that peace is merely *a farce.*

Soon after, Mutt confronts Jute, but a significant switch in roles takes place before they ever speak to each other. The Jute who is the defender is identified as a Shaun-surrogate, since he is "Comestipple Sacksoun" (15.35), and the Earwicker handyman, Mahan ("What a quhare soort of a mahan"—16.1), and Mick ("michindaddy"—16.1-2). Yet, by the time the conversation begins, this same Jute is the invader approaching the defender, Mutt; the switch is apparent from "Let us swop hats and excheck a few strong verbs weak oach eather yapyazzard" (16.8-9). Which son plays Mutt and which plays Jute is of no significance at this stage, and the confusion of roles carries over into the Jarl van Hoother episode in which Tristopher and Hilary are indeed interchangeable and indeed interchanged by the kidnaping Prankquean (although a member of the Joyce family might insist that they are "Bile Beans" and "Sunny Jim" respectively). Chapter 1 ends with no clear Shem-Shaun differentiation, nor is there one in the second chapter either. We may strongly suspect that the Cad who accosts Father Earwicker in the park is cadet Shem, and that the balladmonger Hosty is Shem the Holy Ghost, but Clive Hart's assertion that the first half of the book is Shem-oriented while the second half is Shaun-oriented[22] explains the greater emphasis on Shemmishness for these two anti-Earwickerians. It is only when the fourth chapter brings us to the trial of Festy King that an apparent split is evident between the brothers, but even here the visual similarities are emphasized. No conviction is possible because no one can distinguish between Festy King and Pegger Festy, and the existence of a third force, the Wet Pinter, advances the confusion caused in attempting to identify the three soldiers in Phoenix Park in any mathematical way with Shem and Shaun.

By chapter 6, however, the battle lines are drawn with certainty: apparently the twelve questions are asked by Shem ("set by Jockit Mic Ereweak"—126.7) and answered by Shaun, and question 11 involves Shaun in his self-defense through his surrogates, the Mookse and Burrus, against Shem's personification as the Gripes and Caseous. The next chapter also ends with the conflict at high gear between Shaun-Justius and Shem-Mercius, but with the final chapter of Book I, night falls on the gossiping of the washerwomen, who merge into a tree and a stone while invoking the "tale told of Shaun or Shem" (215.35), which becomes a tale of "stem or stone" (216.3-4), but indistinguishable from each other in the darkness. Although very different sorts of things, the tree and the stone unite into "tree-stone" or "Treestone" (113.19) or *"Treestam"* (104.10) or finally "Tristan" (398.29). And we shall soon see that this single figure will again become the unified form of Shem and Shaun.

But Book Two opens with open conflict again: "the Brothers Bratislavoff" (219.14) are pitted against each other in the Mime, with the Nick figure as "GLUGG" played by "Mr Seumas McQuillad" (219.22), and the Mick protagonist portrayed as "CHUFF" by "Mr Sean O'Mailey" (220.11). The battle continues on into the next chapter where Kev and Dolph are at their lessons and at each other's throats. And, although the third chapter abandons the Earwicker children for the tavern scene, the Tale of the Norwegian Captain and Kersse the Tailor presents another set of opposing forces, most often identified with Earwicker confronted by his Cadversary. But the tale ends in the assimilation of the roving pirate, and the ensuing television skit offers Butt and Taff, interchangeable opponents who finally merge in Buckley to shoot the Earwickerian Russian General. Not only have the antagonistic sons

become *"now one and the same person"* (354.8), but they have
been turned inside out and backward and upside down as well, so
"till butagain budly shoots thon rising germinal let bodley chow
the fatt of his anger and badley bide the toil of his tubb"
(354.34-36). Thus the last chapter of this book deals with the
combined tree-stone again, in the chapter involving the bridal ship
of "Trustan with Usolde" (383.18).

Book Three then begins the battle over again on a new level:
dealing with what Joyce called "the four watches of Shaun," the
first three chapters of this book at least keep Shaun in the fore-
ground, as he is transmuted from Shaun to Jaun via Haun to Yawn.
At each stage he is faced with his brother-antagonist: as he tells the
tale of himself as Ondt confronted by Shem as Gracehoper, as he
attacks Shem for "his root language" (424.17), as he berates Shem
for his sexual liberties ("we'll go a long way towards breaking his
outsider's face for him for making up to you"—442.22-24—), and
as he departs as Jaun and introduces his successor, "lost Dave the
Dancekerl" (462.17). The disintegration of Jaun as Haun results
in the Yawn-corpus of the next chapter, where so many of the
Tristram and Patrick allusions are encrusted, until the last chapter
of Book III brings us by the backward progress of *Wake*-time to the
infancy of Jerry and Kevin. The St. Kevin who comes into prominence in the final book is thus a composite figure like Tristan, and
is the result of the final pre-birth harmony of Shem-and-Shaun elements, but before the book ends, Muta and Juva (mutated and rejuvenated)* face each other at the new battlefield of Slane for the
encounter of St. Patrick and the Archdruid.

In the previous two instances at which harmony concludes the
brother conflict, the part of harmonizing agent was played by
women: the washerwomen created the tree-stone (chapter 8);
Iseult's hymn celebrated the combined Tristram (chapter 12); and
now Mamalujo, "four dear old heladies" (386.14-15), usher in

---

* Regarding the problem of the chicken and the egg: an examination of
Biddy the hen tells us about her "volucrine auto*muta*tiveness" (112.12), while
"Ague will be re*juve*nated" (112.20) (italics mine).

the final harmony, established finally by Anna Livia in the *ricorso*. The implications in the last two chapters are that the twin sons cannot be accepted at face value since they have reversed roles again. The suspicion that they were changed in their cradles as infants is beginning to develop: "The coeds, boytom thwackers and timbuy teaser. Here is onething you owed two noe. This one once upon awhile was the other but this is the other one nighadays" (561.4-6). In the last chapter, the final version of Anna Livia's letter corroborates this reversal: 'both are Timsons now they've changed their characticuls during their blackout" (617.13-14), and her final soliloquy adds to the idea that their identities were never very certain:

> Them boys is so contrairy. The Head does be worrying himself. Heel trouble and heal travel. Galliver and Gellover. Unless they changes by mistake. I seen the likes in the twinngling of an aye. Som. So oft. Sim. Time after time. The sehm asnuh. Two bredder as doffered as nors in soun [620.12-16].

It logically then follows that the sons in the *Wake* are at various instances unified into a single figure, are themselves as a pair, and are multiplied by Joyce's "inflationary" process into a trio. In the last group they are most often the Three Soldiers, therefore Tom, Dick, and Harry (an obvious threesome in "thump, kick and hurry" [285.6], but disguised as two in "tomthick and tarry" —291.7); Shem, Ham, and Japhet ("shame, humbug and profit" —582.10); the Roman triumvirate ("Oxthievious, Lapidous and Malthouse Anthemy"—271.5-6); the three "musketeers" (64.22); the brothers in Swift's *Tale of a Tub* ("padderjagmartin"—86.2); perhaps Pegger Festy, Festy King, and the Wet Pinter; or just A.B.C. ("Arty, Bert or possibly Charley Chance" —65.16).* As two they are the well-defined pair of hostile oppo-

---

* At various instances Joyce seems to be interrupting to allow the weary reader to plead for a halt. This literal-minded reader is called "abcedminded" (18.17)—"abecedeed" (140.14), "a B.C. minding" (272.12-13), "absedes" (552.7), "Abbreciades" (534.2), and even "antiabecedarian" (198.20). Joyce is tampering with language here at its most basic level, the "alphabites" (263.n1), the "A.B.C." (65.28). The Greek equivalent is found in "alfi byrni gamman

sites, too long considered to be always in opposition, whereas there
are many instances in which they are not in conflict necessarily, nor
even distinguishable from each other. Horsa and Hengest have already been mentioned in this context, and so might be: Tim and
Tom; Olaf and Ivor ("an Ivor the Boneless or an Olaf the Hide"
—100.25-26; with Sitric they form a threesome: "Olaf's on the
rise and Ivor's on the lift and Sitric's place's between them"—
12.31-32); Romulus and Remus ("robulous rebus"—12.34);

---

dealter etcera zezera eacla treacla youghta kaptor lomdom noo" (568.32-33)
and "ardent Ares, brusque Boreas and glib Ganymede like zealous Zeus" (269.
17-18), while the Hebrew version, the "allaphbed" (18.18), is seen in
"allaughed . . . baited . . . gammat" (492.4) and "Mac Auliffe . . . MacBeth
. . . MacGhimley . . . MacDollett" (290.6-9). Since the third Hebrew letter
stands for camel, we find "alphabeater cameltemper" (553.2-3) and a fully
translated "oxhousehumper" (107.34). "Olives, beets, kimmells, dollies"
(19.8-9) become irished as "alfrids, beatties, cormacks and daltons" (19.9).
The alphabet also serves as a personification of the three soldiers, "Arty, Bert
or possibly Charley Chance" (65.16), and when the girl is Margareena, the
rivals are "Antonius-Burrus-Caseous" (167.4). Three become one in the person
of "A. Briggs Carlisle" (514.26), Dublin's Carlisle Bridge, or "Abraham
Bradley King" (294.24), a former lord mayor of Dublin, also seen in "Abraham Badly's King" (421.5-6). Two instances at which the entire alphabet is
paraded (plus two Greek extras to produce the monthly number of 28) are
"Ada, Bett, Celia, Delia, Ena, Fretta, Gilda, Hilda, Ita, Jess, Katty, Lou, (they
make me cough as sure as I read them), Mina, Nippa, Opsy, Poll, Queeniee,
Ruth, Saucy, Trix, Una, Vela, Wanda, Xenia, Yva, Zulma, Phoebe, Thelma"
(147.11-15) and "apple, bacchante, custard, dove, eskimo, feldgrau, hematite,
isingglass, jet, kipper, lucile, mimosa, nut, oysterette, prune, quasimodo, royal,
sago, tango, umber, vanilla, wisteria, xray, yesplease, zaza, philomel, theerose"
(247.35-248.2). Other listings may not run the gamut "from aab to zoo"
(263.n1), but include "Arm bird colour defdum ethnic fort perhaps? Sure and
glomsk handy jotalpheson as well" (89.33-34); "aiden bay scye and dye"
(327.34); "amreeta beaker coddling doom" (91.22); "ach beth cac duff"
(250.34); "adder's badder cadder" (303.29); "aped one . . . based two . . .
seed three" (314.10-12); and even "a boer constructor" (180.35). Backward
they are "Carrageen moss and blaster of Barry's and Asther's mess" (184.21-
22) and "this Calumnious Column of Cloaxity, this Bengalese Beacon of
Biloxity, this Annamite Aper of Atroxity . . . a badbad case" (179.13-16);
and a slightly scrambled "and oubworn buyings, dolings and chafferings"
(597.18). Even single words like *"Abbrace"* (106.32) and "abracadabra"
(184.26) are suspect, while the anagram of "bloody antichill cloak" (99.12)
may imply Bailé-átha-Cliath, the old Irish name for Dublin.

and Saints Peter and Paul ("Sinner Pitre and Sinner Poule"—
192.13). On the individual level, they unify harmoniously for a
joint purpose (usually the same one that creates *three* out of *two*:
to plague the father) as Buckley, Tristram, St. Patrick, St. Kevin,
Hosty, and the Cad. A single-minded view of Shem and Shaun exclusively as antagonists, therefore, dismisses various important layers of significance in Joyce's scheme in the *Wake,* two of which are
probably as significant as the Bruno theme: the overthrow of the
father figure and the cyclical evolution of historical patterns.

In all, the problem of identifying a *Wake* character by his associated historical or mythical prototype is often oversimplified and
can be rather misleading. As Mrs. Glasheen's chart shows, very
often two of Joyce's characters are served by a single prototype or
share the characteristics of a single personage. For example, when
Earwicker is the patriarch Abraham, Shaun is Isaac, the son who
is chosen to inherit from his father; when Earwicker is the old
Isaac, the same Shaun is the Esau who is disinherited (conversely,
Shem is the disinherited Ishmael and the Blessed Jacob). The parallels in *Finnegans Wake* are never simple because Joyce's capri-
ciousness (intentional and logically supported) and his sense of
the real complications of things always lead him to prove that parallel lines eventually meet. With this concept in mind one can answer many questions posed by Mrs. Glasheen in her chart and correct some of the answers there. Although H.C.E. is Oscar Wilde
when the Irish author is the "fallen hero," it is Shem who personifies Wilde when we think of Wilde as the aesthete who mocks
convention and propriety. When Earwicker is being maligned
early in chapter 2, he is conceived of as "a great white caterpillar
capable of any and every enormity in the calendar" (33.23-34),
and the ballad that concludes the chapter labels him "Fingal Mac
Oscar Onesine Bargearse Boniface" (46.20). Shem, on the other
hand, is identified with the mocker and the fugitive, and as Glugg
threatens to "fire off, gheol ghiornal, foull subustioned mullmud,
his farced epistol to the hibruws" (228.32-34)—using Wilde's
adopted name of Sebastian Melmoth. But if Shem is author Wilde

then it is logical to assume that Shaun the Boast will claim the title also: he quotes Wilde at the beginning of chapter 13, "which bit his mirth too early or met his birth too late" (408.16-17), and soon lays claim to the title and position: "I am, thing Sing Larynx, letter potent to play the sem backwards like Oscan wild or in shunt Persse transluding from the Otherman or off the Toptic" (419.23-25). Thus all three principal male participants in the *Wake* can be seen masquerading as Oscar Fingall O'Flahertie Wills Wilde.

Another question of identity concerns the music hall pair (at least in Joyce's eyes) of Pigott and Parnell. It is apparent, as the "Who is who" chart states, that Shem is Richard Pigott to Shaun's Charles Stewart Parnell (when we think in terms of Shem as the scoundrel and "forger" and Shaun as the political figure beloved by his people). Who then is Gladstone? asks the chart's author. Here we pose a new situation. It is certainly Earwicker who is the "Grand Old Man" and Shem and Shaun are then a combined Parnell, a thorn in his thick hide as they were in Isaac Butt's. It is in this sense that Shem and Shaun as Taff and Butt combined as Buckley to shoot the Russian General, H.C.E., and also combined as Napoleon to plague the hero on the white horse, Wellington, the Iron Duke. But when Kitty O'Shea enters the Parnell picture, it is Earwicker who is Parnell, the hero destroyed by the temptress (interestingly enough both Parnell and H.C.E. are Protestants). Then again when Shaun becomes Tim Healy to betray Parnell, that Parnell seems to be Shem; Shaun's role is then a dual one as the betraying politician and the Roman Catholic clergy hounding the uncrowned king. In this context much of Jaun's vicious sermonizing takes on an added significance, particularly in the section which rails against the "lecherous" Shem:

> Divulge . . . divorce into me and say the curname in undress . . . of any lapwhelp or sleevemongrel who talks to you upon the road . . . and volunteers to trifle with your roundlings for proffered glass and dough . . . without taking out his proper password from the eligible ministriss for affairs with the black fremdling, that enemy of our coun-

try, in a cleanlooking light and I don't care a tongser's tammany hang who the mucky is. . . . He's a markt man from that hour [441.24-442.18].

It is therefore equally true that, depending upon the context, if the motif is that of the brother conflict, Shem and Shaun are Pigott and Parnell, Parnell and Healy, Parnell and Gladstone, as well as Gladstone and Disraeli.

The coincidence of names is thus of great importance. Joyce obviously delighted in every such coincidence, but, since he selected his material, we must assume that no name finds its way into the *Wake* by accident, without first having passed through the author. The existence of *two* Iseults was apparent grist for Joyce's multiple-level mill and fits his scheme of things perfectly. But two Tristrams required searching, and the existence of Sir Almeric Tristram in Irish history, particularly in connection with Howth, offered Joyce a second level for many allusions involving the interaction of political invasion with "amorous" invasions—the marrying and settling down of the invader, planting roots and defending his new homeland. Time after time in the *Wake* a single name opens two or more possibilities: Oscar can mean the grandson of Finn MacCool or the famous literary son of "Speranza," Lady Wilde; Noah is both the Biblical figure, whose night of drunkenness provides an important parallel for the division of the sons, and Sir Noah Guinness, the brewer of nineteenth-century Dublin; Arthur implies both the legendary king who is a parallel for both Finn and Mark of Cornwall and the Duke of Wellington, as well as another Guinness; Mark is the gospeler, hence Marcus Lyons, the uncle of the amorous Tristram, and Mark Twain; Oliver is both the friend of Roland and the Cromwell who invaded Ireland; Isaac is the Biblical patriarch, Parnell's predecessor Butt, and Swift's pseudonym Bickerstaff. And so the list develops and expands, until the reader realizes that even Michael offers a set of possibilities, that the Archangel who is the Mick-prototype for Shaun is not the same character as the "Father Michael" who figures in the Letter, and may well have been an early lover of Anna Livia, although only two overt indications are apparent and neither indicates that the Michael in question is actually "Father" Michael, but "Michael Arklow" (203.18) and "Michael *vulgo* Cerularius" (573.4). That Earwicker may be his own predecessor as Anna Livia's lover is suggested by his characterization as "Mr Makeall Gone" (220.24), another Michael to contend with. It has been noted in many critiques of the *Wake* that the Gaiety Theatre impresario of Joyce's day, Michael Gunn, provides an important model for Earwicker, but most important because the various versions of his name in the *Wake* underscore him as God (the one above suggests creator and destroyer): *"Duddy Gunne"* (104.8), suggesting God the Father, also "dead and gone"; "gunnfodder" (242.10); "Gonn the gawds" (257.34); "Master's gunne" (531.4-5); "Diu! The has goning at gone" (598.9). The Michael Gunn who is God the Father would logically produce the Archangel Michael to fight his battle in heaven against Lucifer.

The greatest confusion in this area concerns characters named Tim and Tom, since both names offer a variety of echoes separate from each other and related to each other. That "Thomas" means "twin" in Hebrew is significant in relation to Shem and Shaun, but hardly serves to differentiate between them. The "Tom" of "Tom, Dick and Harry" (at least a score of these are apparent in the *Wake*—8.26-27, 19.27-28, 55.15, 90.3-4, 285.6, 291.7, 313.26-27, 316.5, 322.9, 325.34, 329.3, 337.30, 351.1-2, 354.32, 376.26, 410.35-36, 425.25, 485.11, 506.1-2, 575.26, 578.6-7, 597.6—not including those closer to "Shem, Ham and Japhet") again indicates one of the brothers when they expand into the trio of soldiers who spy on Earwicker and the girls in the park. As such this Tom is Kipling's soldier, Tommy Atkins, as well as Twain's Tom Sawyer, the pun on whose surname also reveals the proverbial "peeping Tom" of Godiva fame. To this list may also be added "doubting Thomas," although I can find no specific reference to him in the *Wake*. All of these Toms and Thomases fit one or both of the sons of Earwicker, but do not cover Joyce's own characters, Treacle Tom and Toucher Tom (the two may well be one and the same person), although their nefarious personalities may also disclose them to be Shemites of a sort.

Tim, on the other hand, more often seems to identify Earwicker, since Tim Finnegan is a predecessor or prototype of H.C.E., but Tim Healy, who also figures occasionally in the *Wake* ("Healiopolis," 24.18; "timocracy," 291.8; etc.), may indicate either Shaun in his conflict with Parnell, or more often Earwicker as the successful politician and head of the household ("Uncle Tim's Caubeen"— 622.7). But most often I suspect both Tim and Tom to imply the Egyptian God-Creator, Atem or Tem or Mut, whose expectoration on the dunghill created Man; thus: "he could call himself Tem, too, if he had time to? You butt he could anytom" (88.35-36). This leads to the conjecture that Earwicker as master-builder Tim Finnegan and mankind-creator Atem and Father Time or Cronos subdivides himself into his children, the "anytoms," who as "Tom, Dick and Harry" expand into Everyone. This is borne out in

> Length Withought Breath, of him, a chump of the evums, upshoot of picnic or stupor out of sopor, Cave of Kids or Hymanian Glattstoneburg, denary, danery, donnery, domm, who, entiringly as he continues highlyfictional, tumulous under his chthonic exterior but plain Mr Tumulty in muftilife, in his antisipiences as in his recognisances, is, [Dominic Directus] a manyfeast munificent more mob than man [261.13-22].

The danger, therefore, of thinking in terms of a single Tim-Tom figure, or even separate but clearly defined Tim and Tom, becomes manifold as we realize the multiplicity of allusions these names conjure up and the variety of possibilities that can result from them. A remote clue to the sameness of Tim and Tom may be extracted from *A Portrait of the Artist* where Simon Dedalus calls the curate with, "Tim or Tom or whatever your name is" (AP 95).*

When dealing with the Earwicker children it is important to appreciate what appears to be an "inflationary" or "augmentation" or "exaggeration" approach taken by the author. On the largest scale

---

* Echoes: *"Mick, Nick the Maggot or whatever your name is"* (399.26-27); "Pat Whateveryournameis" (479.12).

the two boys and a single girl ("little Porter babes . . . The coeds, boytom thwackers and timbuy teaser"—561.3-4) are as much indicative of all children ("all the chippy young cuppinjars cluttering round us, clottering for their creams"—621.15-16) as their parents are of all men and women. The three individuals when placed side by side for a series of ones become "the one one oneth of the propecies, *Amnis Limina Permanent*" (153.1-2), and are thus compounded into 111 children to whom Anna Livia distributes presents in chapter 8: elsewhere they are found as "one one and one ten and one hundred again" (101.34-35) and "a hundred and eleven others" (38.13) and even *"Twenty of Chambers, Weighty Ten Beds and a Wan Ceteroom"* (105.3-4).

As much as Earwicker is both a single promontory and a range of mountains, and Anna Livia is a river in its full state of fulfillment from source to sea, the three children expand to become all-inclusive. The inflationary process begins with the five characters with whom Earwicker is involved in Phoenix Park, the two girls and the three soldiers, apparently personifications of Issy, Shem, and Shaun. (It should not be overlooked, in order fully to appreciate the "inflation" here, that the five characters besetting H.C.E. are themselves the five members of the Earwicker family: thus Anna Livia and Issy are the Temptresses, and Earwicker is one of the soldiers along with Shem and Shaun.)

In the same sense that the two sons are eventually reconciled as one and had initially been offshoots of the single Father, they are also capable of subdividing from two into three. They begin as the two base points (as when Earwicker's "rocks . . . exaggerated themselse . . . while they went doublin their mumper"—3.7-8), and are so represented in the triangle in construction in the "riddles" chapter ("the climactogram up which B and C may fondly be imagined ascending"—165.23-24)* where C equals Caseous (a

---

* It seems consistent with *Wake* logic to assume that one triangle in the book suggests another, and a comparison with the pair of triangles constructed within the suggestive confines of Anna Livia's buttocks (293) reveals much of interest to Freudian-oriented *Finnegans Wake* enthusiasts. The "masculine" construction in chapter 6 not only foreshadows, but progresses hand-in-glove

cheesy type of Cassius who as Shem is Caesar-Earwicker's prime
nemesis) and B represents Burrus (a buttered version of Brutus
who as Shaun contributes to the downfall of the father figure and
probably resembles the *burro* who accompanies the Four Old
Men). (By the time we reach the Lessons chapter, the triumvirate
is complete and "Sire Jeallyous Seizer" is confronted by "the
tryonfroit of Oxthievious, Lapidous and Malthouse Anthemy"—
271.3, 5-6.) But who is Antonius then? asks Mrs. Glasheen's

---

with the feminine complex of chapter 10. The first triangle is actually "in
erection" as it ascends toward the completed form which is the mother's sexual
parts. Thus the incest motif which is concerned with Earwicker's licentious
desires for his daughter Isobel is complemented by the Oedipal lusts of the
sons for Anna Livia. Joyce's description of the evolving figure can then be
read for its multitude of double meanings: "The hatboxes which composed
Rhomba, lady Trabezond (Marge in her *excelsis*), also comprised the climactogram up which B and C may fondly be imagined ascending and are suggestive
of their true crust by even the youngest of Margees if she will take plase to
layers of eocene and pleastoseen formation and the gradual morphological
changes in our body politic which Professor Ebahi-Ahuri of Philadespoinis
(Ill)—whose bluebutterbust I have just given his coupe de grass to—neatly
names a *boîte à surprises*. The boxes, if I may break the subject gently, are
worth about fourpence pourbox but I am inventing a more patent process,
foolproof and pryperfect . . . after which they can be reduced to a fragment
of their true crust by even the youngest of Margees if she will take place to
be seated and smile if I please" (165.21-166.2). The subject here (besides
quantum mechanics) is seduction, particularly defloration of virgins, as *boxes*
suggest vaginas in vulgar slang and *hatboxes* the figleaflike concealment offered
by clothing (a motif involving the concept of the "outer shield" hiding what
is real and basic; *gentlemen's spring modes,* Wyndham Lewis would be cha-
grined to learn, means both sartorial fashions and methods of sexual attack).
The vagina is a *climactogram* since it is the source of passion and sexual climax.
The mother (*lady Trabezond*) is best represented in most ideal sexual form
during the present age by her virginal daughter (*Marge in her excelsis*),
whose hymen the lecherous brothers are ingeniously scheming to destroy
(*if I may break the subject gently*) by a *coup de grâce* in the grass (*coupe de
grass*), a method quite familiar to the Lynch of *Ulysses.* They are indeed
loving brothers of the penis (*Philadespoinis*). The sexual connotations of still
another geometric problem in the *Wake* ("Show that the median, hce che ech,
interecting at royde angles the parilegs of a given obtuse one biscuts both the
arcs that are in curveachord behind"—283.32-284.4) are investigated by Diana
and Paul Thompson, "A Geometry Problem in *Finnegans Wake,*" *Analyst,*
No. 20 (September, 1961), pp. 2-4.

chart. He is apparently a synthesis of the opposing pair in the He-
gelian scheme of things, described by Joyce as

> an elusive Antonius, a wop who would appear to hug a personal in-
> terest in refined chees of all chades at the same time as he wags an
> antomine art of being rude like the boor. This Antonius-Burrus-Case-
> ous grouptriad may be said to equate the *qualis* equivalent with the
> older socalled *talis* on *talis* one just as quantly as in the hyperchemical
> economantarchy the tantum ergons irruminate the quantum urge so
> that eggs is to whey as whay is to zeed like your golfchild's abe boob
> caddy [167.1-8].

Antonius-Burrus-Caseous and *abe boob caddy* ("Et tu, Brute"
becomes "Et tu, Cassius") suggest the A.B.C. configuration often
found in *Finnegans Wake* (from "Arty, Bert or possibly Charley
Chance" [65.16] to "alphabeater cameltemper"—553.2-3), representing the entire alphabet in the same sense that Tom, Dick,
and Harry (from "Tob, Dilke and Halley" [90.3-4] to "tomb,
dyke and hollow"—597.6) are accepted in popular parlance to
signify just about everybody. (As seen in the quotation above, the
alphabet runs its course from A to *eggs, whey, zeed* or, as found
elsewhere in the *Wake,* from "Ada, Bett, Celia" to "Xenia, Yva,
Zulma" [147.11-14] and from "apple, bacchante, custard" to
"xray, yesplease, zaza" [247.35–248.2] *and beyond*.) Issy may
have her mirror image with which to double herself into two
temptresses or split herself into opposing halves; Shem and Shaun
are coalesced into a unified figure or add a third dimension to become the three soldiers who plague Earwicker. "It's as simple as
A.B.C." (65.27-28), comments Joyce.

But what is as simple as A.B.C. can also be "as semper as oxhousehumper" (107.34), indicating that since it is as eternal as the
progression of the alphabet (used here as a translation of the
words that stand for the first three letters of the Hebrew alphabet), it is also as complex as life itself. Simplicity can be a decep-
tive danger where *Finnegans Wake* is concerned, and even the best
analyses of parallel situations suggested in the *Wake* must by Joycean necessity run aground if too literally translated. No parallel

can be carried too far, and none is without its exceptions. Since opposites must by Bruno's concepts eventually be reconciled, and since every rule presumably has its exceptions, Joyce delights in planting an inherent inconsistency in every logical development he constructs. As Professor Morse thoroughly states the case,[23] Shem is Jacob to Shaun's Esau (they are "Jakob van der Bethel" and "Essav of Messagepostumia"—607.8-9), which on the surface looks to be a reversal of the case of Shem-Cain-Ham and Shaun-Abel-Japhet. But Morse proves that, although the accursed in two instances, Shem is the blessed in the third, and we are now that much better equipped to appreciate the subtleties by which Joyce chose his parallels. The dichotomies of Good and Evil are not always clearly divisible, either between Archangel Michael ("Michael Engels"—533.29) and Lucifer ("Lousyfear"—439.7) or Ahura Mazda ("ormuzd"—163.2) and Ahriman ("arimaining lucisphere"—239.34), despite the single-mindedness of Judeo-Christian scriptures and the Zoroastrian *Avesta.* Joyce was aware that the "prince of darkness" and the Persian "god of light" had something in common, at least in the etymologies of their names, that a Lucifer match ("he strikes a lousaforitch"—69.12) could give off light in the same manner as does a Mazda bulb. There is a patent irony in the fact that the Cain who struck the murderous blow in Genesis is the Shem who is repeatedly struck by Shaun (247, 300-3) in the *Wake;* that whereas it was Cain who "was very wroth and his countenance fell" (Gen. 4:5), it is Shaun who "was wreathed with his pother" (303.15) and "his countinghands rose" (304.1-2). Further to equate the justification of each of the brothers, another reference in the *Wake* informs us that "each was wrought with his other" (252.14). Though the battle lines are usually clearly drawn by Joyce, they are sometimes purposefully confused.

Shem as Ham is also a logical construction. It is Shem who spies upon his father's nakedness (566-67) and thus learns his father's secret (the penis in erection which is the key to procreation).[24] Once the secret is out, Shem has the knowledge necessary to supplant the old man. Like the Ham of the nakedness incident (Gen. 9:20-27) he too is a mocker, but there is a fine coincidence that Shem should bear the name of one of the "good" brothers who did not mock. If Shem is Ham and Shaun is Japhet, who then is the Biblical Shem? This question (also asked by the Glasheen chart) again answers itself in the "inflationary" sense of the two sons becoming the three soldiers, all three of whom mock the old Earwicker.* All three (meaning both sons and their mysterious third personification) are guilty of "shame, humbug and profit" (582.10), a legacy inherited from their bourgeois father.

Nor is the "blessed" Jacob free of guilt. His role in Genesis is often suspect, and only a far more literal reader of the Bible than Joyce can fully accept God's arbitrary decision to honor Jacob's claim to Esau's birthright through deception and connivance. Craftiness is not necessarily to be equated with "goodness," nor is Esau's readiness to sell his birthright for a serving of "red pottage" a particularly "evil" act, despite the obvious indication that he cared little for the sacredness of God's covenant with his father and grandfather. Joyce's Shem cares just as little, for that matter,

---

* An interesting parallel to Earwicker's Phoenix Park involvement can be found in a 1933 disclosure of a tablet bearing the text of a pre-Hebraic Canaanite spring festival which anticipates the Pentecost: "The sacred drama then begins on the reverse side of the tablet with a prologue invoking the 'Gracious Gods' and the sun [Cf. *FW*, 237 ff.], and the greeting of the worshippers assembled with their offerings (23-27). The action of the play, it is explained, opens with a scene on the seashore before the house of El where the aged supreme deity demonstrates his virility to two girls, identified with Anat and Asherah, who watched him carrying water into his house, and with accurate marksmanship shoot an arrow into the air and bring down a bird, which he then plucks and boils for his meal. As these events are recorded in the text, so impressed were they with his youthful strength and adroitness that they offered him their devoted service as either his brides or his daughters (30-36). It was as wives that he accepted them, and an erotic scene follows in which after passionate intercourse they conceive and bring forth the two gods, Dawn (Shr) and Sunset (Slm) (49-52a). This episode is repeated with the offspring called the 'Gracious Gods' (55-61a), the children and their mothers feeding voraciously for seven years on the fruitful earth (61b-76)" (E. O. James, *Seasonal Feasts and Festivals* [London: Thames and Hudson, 1961], p. 99).

and at times indicates that Esau's characteristics are his as well. "Do you hold yourself then for some god in the manger, Shehohem, that you will neither serve not let serve, pray nor let pray?" (188.18-19), demands Shaun in his Christlike personification, echoing the Christ of Matthew 23:13: "But woe to you, scribes and Pharisees, hypocrites! because you shut the kingdom of heaven against men; for you neither enter yourselves, nor allow those who would enter to go in." The irony lies in the Shaun-Christ's pose as "Justius" berating Shem-Mercius, the latter being a far better example of Christian mercy at this instant—and at many others in the *Wake*. It is also possible, of course, that the irony is twofold, and Joyce is commenting on the lack of "mercy" so often demonstrated by the irate, hot-tempered Christ depicted in the Gospels.

Nonetheless, Shem is Jacob and Shaun is Esau only when this arrangement serves Joyce's greater purpose, and he in no way feels bound by consistency to insist that Shem always behave like Jacob and Shaun always like Esau. As the natural man, as the hairy man, as the glutton, Shaun is obviously Esau, while as the smooth urbanite and the outcast, Shem is Jacob. But Jacob's successful wooing of the Maggies (Rachel intentionally and Leah inadvertently) is closer to Shaun's successes with the young girls of the *Wake*, while Shaun's unjustified claim to the letter as his own coincides with Jacob's claim to Esau's birthright. Nor is it always clear which twin is the older, a point about which Genesis is quite unequivocal. At the clearest instance Shem is indicated as the younger twin in a definite echo of the original; in the "bedroom" chapter we find: "Jerry Jehu. You will know him by name in the capers but you cannot see whose heel he sheepfolds in his wrought hand because I have not told it to you" (563.7-9), while Genesis 25:26 reads: "Afterward his brother came forth and his hand had taken hold of Esau's heel; so his name was called Jacob." (Note that Joyce separates the "sheep" from the "goats" when he identifies Shem with *capers* and Shaun with *sheepfold*, reiterating that Shem is satyrlike compared to Shaun's pose as the Lamb, but the significance is much greater still when we realize that this gives Shem a claim as the

natural heir of H. C. Earwicker, who has often been identified as
the "goat" [particularly the scapegoat]: "*Hircus Civis Elbanensis!*
He had buckgoat paps on him" [215.27-28], although his hirsute-
ness is transmitted to Shaun.)

There are indications in the book, however, which seem to point
to Shem as the older: in the closing portion of the Shem chapter,
the Penman as Mercius addresses himself as "firstborn and
firstfruit of woe" (194.12), and, during Shaun's first chapter, the
Post says: "Weh is me, yeh is ye! I, the mightif beam maircanny,
which bit his mirth too early or met his birth too late! It should of
been my other with his leickname for he's the head and I'm an ev-
erdevoting fiend of his" (408.15-18). But neither of these two
quotations definitely points to Shem as the older, and both can be
interpreted to mean Shaun. What is unequivocal, however, is a reference to Shem as "this Esuan Menschavik" (185.34), which
seems to label him as Esau as well as the "minor" (Russian, *men-
shevik*) brother.* And it is nonetheless most important that Jacob
and Esau together bury their father as Shem and Shaun combine as
Buckley to shoot the Russian General. Should external evidence be
of any help in deciding the relative age of the mismatched twins, it
may be noted that James Joyce was almost four years older than his
brother, John Stanislaus (still the major model for Shaun), and
that of the brother apostles, James and John, dubbed "sons of
thunder"† by Jesus, James was the older, John the younger.

Also uncertain is the name Joyce has given to Earwicker's public
house in Chapelizod. If we accept the judgment of the *Skeleton
Key,* the pub is simply called the Bristol Tavern,[25] without any
further elucidation offered. And indeed there is ample reason to
accept the name without further quibbling. Some seventeen allusions seem to corroborate the Bristol, although only three are in
"pure" form as such: "the house the once queen of Bristol and
Balrothery twice admired because her frumped door looked up Da-
cent Street" (405.26-28); "Step out to Hall out of that, Ereweak-

---

* To compound the confusion, Shem is also labeled "aboleshqvick" (302.18).
† "Boanerges" (22.32).

er, with your Bloody Big Bristol" (421.12-13); "They were
erected in a purvious century, as a hen fine coops and, if you know
your Bristol and have trudged the trolly ways and elventurns of that
old cobbold city, you will sortofficially scribble a mental Peny-
Knox-Gore" (606.16-19). Yet none of these definitely identifies
Earwicker's tavern (the second one in fact seems rather to refer to
his penis). The reference that leads Campbell and Robinson to
refer to the "Bristol Tavern" occurs during Luke Tarpey's comments on Matt Gregory:

> she due to kid by sweetpea time, with her face to the wall, in view of
> the poorhouse, and taking his rust in the oxsight of Iren, under all the
> auspices, amid the rattle of hailstorms, kalospintheochromatokreening,
> with her ivyclad hood, and gripping an old pair of curling tongs, be-
> longing to Mrs Duna O'Cannell, to blow his brains with, till the
> heights of Newhigherland heard the Bristolhut, with his can of tea and
> a purse of alfred cakes from Anne Lynch and two cuts of Shackleton's
> brown loaf and dilisk, waiting for the end to come [392.25-33].

The *Key* translated *the Bristolhut* as the "Bristol Tavern,"[26] but
without ever actually asserting that this is H.C.E.'s pub.

Of the other "Bristol" references, those that do seem to imply
Earwicker's establishment more precisely include the mention in
the Prankquean Tale of the piratess returning to van Hoother's
"keep of his inn" (21.14), now called "the bar of his bristolry"
(21.34); the answer given by Yawn's "ghost voice" to the question "And Drysalter, father of Izod, how was he now?": "—To
the pink, man, like an allmanox in his shirt and stickup, brustall to
the bear, the Megalomagellan of our winevatswaterway, squeezing
the life out of the liffey" (512.2-6); and Earwicker's own statement through the body of the prostrate Yawn:

> The amusin part is, I will say, hotelmen, that since I, over the deep
> drowner Athacleeath to seek again Irrlanding, shamed in mind, with
> three plunges of my ruddertail, yet not a bottlenim, vanced imperial
> standard by weaponright and platzed mine residenze, taking bourd and
> burgage under starrymisty and ran and operated my brixtol selection
> here at thollstall, for mean straits male with evorage fimmel [539.16-
> 22].

(It is interesting to notice that in each of these three selections
there exists a phallic reference to the erected penis—*bar, stickup,*
and *straits male*—in support of the previous *Bloody Big Bristol,*
hinting that the pub may well have gotten its name from being
identified with the "erection" raised by the male hero.*)

The remaining allusions are vague at best: "indanified himself
with boro tribute and was schenkt publicly to brigstoll"
(133.28-29); *"the birstol boys artheynes"* (353.34); Patrick
Thistle agen S. Megan's versus Brystal Palace agus the Walsall!"
(378.18-19); "he was so slow to borstel her schoon for her"
(391.8-9); "about their bristelings" (442.10); "culprines of Eras-
mus Smith's burstall boys with their underhand leadpencils climb-
ing to her crotch for the origin of spices" (504.26-28); "Blaw-
lawnd-via-Brigstow" (537.24-25); "best Brixton high yellow"
(538.9); and "you were bragged up by Brostal" (624.32-33).
The numerous instances in which these "Bristols" are connected
with Borstal and Brixton, junior and senior houses of correction
(and "brigs" in general), may well add a curious note to the name
of the Chapelizod tavern. But the strongest reason for accepting
Bristol as the name comes from the charter that King Henry II
gave to the city of Bristol, presenting that British town with the
city of Dublin in 1172. This historic event is celebrated in the
Wake (where Earwicker serves as a personification of the British
monarch). The Dublin charter is therefore parodied during Earwicker's boastful recording of his "era of progress":

> Wherfor I will and firmly command, as I willed and firmly com-
> manded, upon my royal word and cause the great seal now to be
> affixed, that from the farthest of the farther of their fathers to their
> children's children's children they do inhabit it and hold it for me un-
> encumbered and my heirs, firmly and quietly, amply and honestly, and
> with all the liberties and free customs which the men of Tolbris, a
> city of Tolbris, have at Tolbris, in the county, of their city and through
> whole my land. Hereto my vouchers, knive and snuffbuchs. Fee for
> farm. Enwreak us wrecks [545.14-23].

---

* Various puns overlap in "the penic walls and the ind" (156.3), including punkah wallah, Punic Wars, penal walls, the pen and the penis, the inn,
India, and indigo.

A second possibility more recently advanced is that the pub is called the Mullingar, since a public house of that name actually exists in Chapelizod. Several uses of the name in the *Wake* indicate that Mullingar is a more accurate choice than Bristol, and, although it is not as frequently mentioned, the references are far stronger. One or two may refer actually to the Westmeath County town of Mullingar, but even these seem to incorporate drinking allusions: "the Mullingcan Inn" (64.9); "the Mullingar Inn" (138.19-20); *"The boss's bess bass is the browd of Mullingar"* (286.L); "that mulligar scrub" (321.33); *"the Mullingaria"* (345.34); "the porlarbaar of the marringaar of the Lochlunn gonlannludder of the feof of the foef of forfummed Ship-le-Zoyd" (370.27-29); "those Mullinguard minstrelsers" (371.34); "Mocked Majesty in the Malincurred Mansion" (380.4-5); and "Mallinger parish, to a mead that was not far" (475.22-23). The "coincidence" of *fee for farm* in the Bristol allusion (545.23) and *foef of forfummed* again suggests that possibly both names are intended for the tavern, the Mullingar existing on the literal level of the plot, while the Bristol again involves Earwicker historically as an invading Anglo-Norman, thus lending further weight to the duality of his existence as both native and foreigner, defender and invader. Professor Tindall, who seems to prefer "Mullingar" as the pub name, finds eight of the nine Mullingar allusions listed above, but misses—or dismisses—eleven of the Bristol references.[27]

But even a compromise decision of allowing both possibilities within certain limits does not end speculation on the subject of the pub's name. Knowing as we do that Sheridan Le Fanu's *The House by the Churchyard* offered so much basic landscape and situation for Joyce's *Wake*, it is difficult not to wonder aloud why so fitting a name as the Phoenix, another real pub in Chapelizod mentioned by Le Fanu, did not determine Joyce's decision in naming Earwicker's place. Although the word "phoenix" plays a vital role in *Finnegans Wake,* both as the place name of the Dublin park and for the mythological symbolism of the bird of resurrection, there seem to be no definite instances in Joyce's book where it is employed as a name for the pub. The reason may be twofold: that

Joyce's recollection of details from Le Fanu was not exact (see his letter to Budgen,[28] which as late as 1937 asks for information regarding names)—although he certainly might have remembered so cogent a point—but more important that he never depended upon slavish imitation of the materials he used, and would probably have been well content to do his own naming, the phoenix having already been well pressed into service. The double significance of the park's naming already adds two important ideas, the original Irish name of *fiunishgue* (clear water) and the English misreading into Phoenix.[29] It is just by this sort of process of "misreading" (although not accidental any longer, but controlled by Joyce) that significances multiply in the *Wake*.*

And yet even the pub called The Mullingar or The Bristol (with The Phoenix understood) has surrogates galore in *Finnegans Wake,* since *the* pub is also *all* pubs. Like everything else in the book, the array of pubs includes two varieties: *real* Dublin pubs of Joyce's era, and those he "invents," and, since Dublin imagination is so potent, a list like "the House of Blazes, the Parrot in Hell, the Orange Tree, the Glibt, the Sun, the Holy Lamb" (63.23-24) is no less imaginative for being actual Dublin drinking houses than Joyce's compound of "the Duck and Doggies, the Galopping Primrose, Brigid Brewster's, the Cock, the Postboy's Horn, the Little Old Man's and All Swell That Aimswell, the Cup and the Stirrup" (39.35-40.2), or "Byrne's and Flamming's and Furniss's and Bill Hayses's and Ellishly Haught's" (289.13-14). In other incarnations Earwicker's pub could be any of the following: "The Inns of Dungtarf" (16.22), "the Rum and Puncheon" (69.33), *"L'Auberge du Père Adam"* (124.34), "The Goat and Compasses" (275.16), "the snug saloon seanad of our Café Béranger" (372.11-12), "the Wheel of Fortune" (405.24), "the Cat and Coney or the Spotted Dog" (436.23), "the Beer and Belly and the Boot and Ball" (464.28), "the Tower of Balbus"

* In evaluating the debt to Le Fanu, Aneiran Talfan Davies comments that "it is here that HCE keeps his pub, under the sign of the phoenix" ("A Note on *Finnegans Wake," Welsh Review,* VII [Summer, 1948], 142).

(467.16), "the Anchor on the Mountain" (479.11), "Nile Lodge" (494.34), "the Heaven and Covenant" (510.25-26), "Toot and Come-Inn by the bridge called Tiltass" (512.34-35), "Eccles's hostel" (514.15), "the Bar Ptolomei" (529.34), "the Morgue and Cruses" (530.13), "his hostel of the Wodin Man" (535.5-6), "Oscarshal's winetavern" (536.21), "the Cat and Cage" (563.19), "the snug at the Cambridge Arms of Teddy Ales" (587.8-9), "Wynn's Hotel" (609.15-16)—or any one of scores of others.*

An examination of these surface problems indicates something basic in the dilemmas confronting the *Wake* scholar: that the years following publication have produced a wealth of exegetical material, but also a far greater wealth of unsolved questions and untapped resources. That the plot of *Finnegans Wake* is crucial to an understanding of the book has begun to obsess commentators, yet the few questions treated here should indicate that they are far from agreement on what happens, to whom it happens, and why it happens. The various substrata characters remain an enigma, although the five principals have been well described and individualized by now. Even the Four Old Men have received fairly thorough treatment, but such personages as Kate the Charwoman, the Cad, Lily Kinsella, Old Joe the Curate, Constable Lally Tomkins, and Constable Sackerson are far from clear. The last three, for example, may not be three distinct characters at all, but only two, for there is reason to believe, as Mrs. Glasheen does, that Sackerson is another name for the Man Servant,[30] since as a policeman he comes to close the pub (370). But, since policeman equals policeman, this may well mean, as Campbell and Robinson seem to think it does, that Lally is Sackerson,[31] and that possibly all three are one person.

Since Sackerson at the beginning of Jaun's chapter is a petrified pillar of sorts, indicating Earwicker interred in the landscape, we

---

* Mrs. Glasheen believes that the third riddle in chapter 6 holds the key to the pub name. If so, then the answer, "Thine obesity, O civilian, hits the felicitude of our orb!" (140.6-7), which parodies the Dublin motto, indicates that Dublin itself is H.C.E.'s tavern (The Dublin Inn, Dubl Inn, Double Inn?).

are now faced with the possibility that all the male characters in
the book are H.C.E.; this is true on the symbolic level of the
Wake, but if carried too far negates the underlying literal level on
which everything is constructed. It is sheer *reductio ad absurdum*
to maintain that Earwicker is Lally, since that policeman is identified with the Four Old Men who plague Earwicker (94-96), nor
is it too safe to assume that Earwicker is Sackerson (despite that
policeman's efforts to close the pub and rescue the publican from
his hostile customers), since he testifies about Earwicker's Phoenix
Park activities during the Yawn seance (511).

The only way out of such dilemmas is to realize that the shifting
perspectives of the dream create changes that are internally logical
only in relation to the new situations created. As we have seen in
investigating previous material, one possibility is never sufficient.
The question is not so much "who is who when everybody is somebody else," but who is who in each particular situation. We have
seen, for example, that all three principal males have taken turns
being Jonathan Swift. The identity of the Cad, then, must be multiplied threefold, if we accept the name as derived from Swift's
Cadenus. When we first meet the Cad, he has confronted Earwicker in the park with a request for the time, inadvertently tricking
Earwicker into a confession-denial of his guilt (36). The Cad thus
presents himself as Earwicker's opposite, his enemy; and, if both
Earwicker and the Cad are incarnations of Swift, we are faced with
the very logical realization that Earwicker is his own enemy—as
indeed he is.

The Cad's wife ("knee Bareniece Maxwelton"—38.9) is the
original instrument broadcasting H.C.E.'s misdemeanor, but a
careful examination of her name indicates that she is already
known to us: *Maxwelton* suggests "Annie Laurie" (hence,
A.L.P.), while *niece* indicates Issy, the daughter-disguised-as-niece
in Earwicker's dream (21.14-15, 312.24, 314.22, 348.23, 349.28,
373.26, 532.24, 558.21, 608.8). Thus the two women of Earwicker's household combine as his enemy's wife to defame him.

That the Cad is also Earwicker's sons then becomes obvious: in a

review of the events of the encounter and subsequent trial, we hear
of "that same snob of the dunhill, fully several yearschaums riper,
encountered by the General on that redletter morning or maynoon
jovesday" (50.30-32). The *dunhill* and *yearschaums* references
indicate the pipe the Cad was carrying ("he met a cad with a pipe"
—35.10-11), while *General* Earwicker prefigures the shooting of
the Russian General (H.C.E.) by Buckley. During the "shooting"
chapter, it is Taff who is identified with the Cad ("Piff paff for
puffpuff and my pife for his cgar"—341.16-17), which reminds us
that Earwicker is identified by the cigar symbol (phallic, of course)
since the instance in which he gave a cigar away ("he tips un a
topping swank cheroot . . . suck that brown boyo, my son, and
spend a whole half hour in Havana"—53.22-26). At another instance Shem is identified with the Cad since he is "Jakob van der
Bethel, smolking behing his pipe" (607.8), while Shaun gets the
nod when he describes himself with "my g.b.d. in my f.a.c.e., solfanelly in my shellyholders and lov'd latakia, the benuvolent, for
my nosethrills" (450.10-11); since *g.b.d.* refers to "pipe notes,"
and *solfanelly* is not just musical but also sulphurous, we can add
these to *latakia* to picture Shaun as the pipe-smoking Cad. Other
origins of Joyce's Cad can be found in *cadet,* the youngest son; in
Cadmus, the founder of Thebes; and the most important in the Ca-
duceus of Hermes, whose interlocked serpents return the encounter
in Phoenix Park to the Garden of Eden and strongly identify the
Cad with Satan.

All roads in *Finnegans Wake* lead back to home, and all characters return to the interrelated five (and even the basic two). Since
Earwicker is both Swift, the old man in love with young Vanessa,
and Bartholomew Van Homrigh ("Barthalamou, where their dutchuncler mynhosts and serves them dram well right for a boors'
interior (homereek van hohmryk)"—314.22-24), Vanessa's father, he finds himself in the ticklish position of pursuing his own
daughter. But *dutchuncler*—and "ungkerls" (314.31) in the next
paragraph—indicates the way out of the dilemma for the dreaming
Earwicker, as daughter becomes safely transformed into niece. The

complicated tale of Earwicker's long nightmare defies any sort of synoptic treatment, since a synopsis is a single retelling of the events, while no single event actually exists unaltered for very long. Time and space and the vagaries of the psychology of dreams work their wonders on the material of the *Wake,* leaving a dozen questions newly unearthed for every answer miraculously found.

There remains, then, only the cold, logical realization that *Finnegans Wake* as an enigma may well go unsolved. Time, which was expected to bring all evidence eventually to the surface in an ordered pattern, so far has had the opposite effect. We are moving further and further away from the period of the book's genesis, and certain doors have now shut, to remain shut permanently. Joyce's death less than two years after publication must be acknowledged as the greatest blow to any expectation of a full explication. The author's own willingness during his lifetime to provide "the keys to" had been instrumental in bringing *Ulysses* so clearly into focus in so short a time. His method of distributing the hints necessary for individual interpretations leading toward a totality of explication is well known, as is his suspicion of artists who are unwilling to aid in achieving an understanding of their work (of Brancusi he said: "But I wish he or Antheil, say, could or would be as explicit as I try to be when people ask me: And what's this here, Guvnor?"[32]). Joyce's willingness to assist at the probing operation is indicated by the "marshalling" of the twelve "exagminers" in 1929 while the work was still in progress, and his plan for "a book of only 4 *long* essays by 4 contributors . . . the subjects to be the treatment of night . . . the mechanics and chemistry, the humour, and I have not yet fixed on the fourth subject."[33]

Much happened during the 1930's to prevent Joyce from mapping out the exegetical attack on the bastion he has built; it is obvious that he did not expect to die without providing many further hints and suggestions for understanding *Finnegans Wake.* That "ideal reader suffering from an ideal insomnia" (120.13-14), if he ideally exists, finds himself tunneling in the dark without the headlamp usually provided for such work. It does not seem too soon to predict that *Finnegans Wake* will never be fully read by any reader (no matter how ideal he may otherwise be). Fragments will be chipped away, brought into the glare of the sun, polished to a high gloss and admired. Conversely, generalities and broad statements will be made about the *Wake,* and in many cases fairly well documented. But the replacement of piece after piece into a reconstructed mosaic fully indicating the lines of the book's ideas and material will probably never take place.

What Joyce said of Ezra Pound and his interpretation of *Ulysses* will be said of many critics for years to come: there will be "brilliant discoveries and howling blunders."[34] But it is naïve to expect, in the foreseeable future, that the mountain will come to Mohammed. Joyce, who apparently delighted in creating his own facsimile of previous "bibles," may have provided for many centuries of new "Talmudic" scholarship. The number of words already printed explaining the *Wake* far exceeds the number of words in the *Wake* itself. The role of the contemporary commentator of *Finnegans Wake* is not to pontificate on "what it is all about exactly," but humbly to attempt to show, while pausing along the route of his reading, "what's this here, Guvnor?"

CHAPTER TWO

Forty Ways of Looking at a White Elephant

I: POLITICAL MIASMA

In one of the first comprehensive analyses of the completed *Finnegans Wake*, Harry Levin, cautioning critics against the myriad confusions inherent in the *Wake*, accurately likened the commentator's task to that of the Aesopian blindmen who investigated the elephant. Levin prophesied that many inaccurate judgments would be made of Joyce's literary "white elephant"[1]—"What a lubberly whide elephant for the men-in-the-straits!" (300.n4), comments Issy in a footnote. The two decades since Levin's prophecy have witnessed many attempts by critics to "place" Joyce's book in preconceived pigeonholes, with strange and disastrous results at times. Early commentators have suffered from a dearth of available exegetical and analytical material; succeeding commentators now find it necessary to correct the inaccurate interpretations that have adhered to the work before continuing the tortuous process of gleaning the ideas that are basic in the *Wake*. Political and religious prejudices in particular have been instrumental in obfuscating the already murky environs, so much so that it has become necessary for each annotator to initiate his own campaign to cleanse the enigmatic surface of non-Joycean coatings. No critic, however, can be certain that his efforts are any the less blind than those of preceding Aesopians, or that his whitewashing will not leave just another dark coat. He must nonetheless make his original efforts in an area where trial-and-error criticism is the prescribed if precarious method.

The problem of begetting an unprejudiced but individual critique is manifold: Joyce managed during a full literary career to attract many strange adherents to his various causes and apostasies; he also managed to make enemies in the various facets of the political, religious, and literary worlds. His untimely death prevented his being able to protect himself and his work from a host of avenging angels who have rushed in and claimed discipleship or made claims upon Joyce which only he himself could have unequivocally disavowed. Since the *Wake* serves to investigate contemporary man in terms of his history, religious and political claims in particular have been made which must be closely scrutinized.

History in *Finnegans Wake* is a world of its own. The entire history of the human race flows past with the waters of the Liffey in an order logically concomitant with Joyce's structural plan, though contemptuous of mundane concepts of chronology—"riverrun, past Eve and Adam's, from swerve of shore to bend of bay" (3.1-2)—in a Viconian circle that Joyce the Artificer has successfully squared: "eggburst, eggblend, eggburial and hatch-as-hatch can" (614.32-33). Thus the flow of comprehensive but inarticulate history courses through all levels of the book like Anna Livia herself: "babbling, bubbling, chattering to herself, deloothering the fields on their elbows leaning with the sloothering slide of her, giddygaddy, grannyma, gossipaceous Anna Livia" (195.1-4).

The history of man's globe is mirrored in the history of Ireland, the microcosm reflecting the cosmos, in whose invasions, defenses, struggles, absorptions, and metamorphoses Joyce saw universalities, "Simply because as Taciturn pretells, our wrongstoryshortener, he dumptied the wholeborrow of rubbages on to soil here" (17.3-5). On the nearest level, the nation that represents all nations becomes the city that is all cities, since the erecting of the city comprises the evolution of the developing human animal into the rival of the God of the Creation: "And that was how framm Sin fromm Son, acity arose" (94.18). Thus, on the lowest level of Joyce's creation, arises Earwicker, the mortal publican of Chapelizod, hovering in time between the nineteenth and twentieth centuries, representative of present man and his immediate heritage, with the ghost of the eternal Finn as his perpetual shadow. "Is that the great Finnleader himself in his joakimono on his statue riding the high horse there forehengist?" (214.11-12), asks the washerwoman on the banks of the Liffey, but it is only "the quare old buntz too, Dear Dirty Dumpling, foostherfather of fingalls and dotthergills" (215.13-14).

With Earwicker, the specter of history appears in the present age like the uninvited relative at the wedding. Even for Joyce, for whom the past was fluid not fixed, the chaos of the present (the core and continuum of his work) suggested hazards that required careful handling and complete control. The years during which he wrote his *Wake,* the precarious twenties and thirties, when thousands of authors of various stripes and shades concerned themselves passionately with the *here* and the *now,* existed for Joyce the artist only on the peripheral edge of his circled square of history.* Except for contemporary events in Ireland (which for Joyce were a logical development of the events of the previous century, and which he had prognosticated with scientific accuracy), much of what transpired in the world at the time was of no interest to him. Despite the all-inclusive dream pattern that allowed him to compress historical, mythological, and legendary events of all times and places within his work, Joyce carefully avoided much of contemporary European political events, apparently because they had not yet become history and still lacked universality. Political names that were on everyone's lips at the time, and on many of the pages of literature of the day, rarely found their way into *Finnegans Wake.*

Joyce's nonpolitical approach deserves a certain amount of clarification. Louis Gillet seems to have found Joyce without a shred of concern for what was happening politically about him:

> In fact, I don't recall once, during all those years, having heard Joyce say a word about public events, pronounce the names of Poincaré, Roosevelt, Franco, Baldwin, Valera, Stalin, or make an allusion to Geneva, Locarno, Abyssinia, Spain, China, Japan, the Negus or the Mikado, the Stavisky affair, Violette Nozières, armament or disarmament, oil, the

---

* Thomas Mann, with whom critics so often couple Joyce, had published his *Betrachtungen eines Unpolitischen* ("Notes of a Non-Political Man") in 1918, but his later *engagement* was of course never paralleled by Joyce.

stock-exchange, the races at Auteuil, Gorgouloff, Doumer's assassination, Dolfuss, King Alexander, the Rhineland, Austria, Morocco, the Congo or Gerolstein, or anything else that may be found in the headlines of the newspapers; all that was for him as if it didn't exist.[2]

Yet both comments in Joyce's letters and statements made by other friends at the time (as reported in Ellmann's biography) belie Gillet's recollection. The possibility of world war weighed heavily upon him during the thirties with no pollyannaism on his part to disguise the obvious forebodings. Wars in Ethiopia, Spain, and China are mentioned in his letters, as is the prospect of war between Japan and the United States, not to mention the European prospects. His disdain for both Mussolini and Hitler was unhidden, and his attitude toward Communist Russia combined sympathy and suspicion.

The extent to which he was able to rise above contemporary events and take a long historical look at what was happening (vitally important for his approach to the *Wake*) is indicated in his 1936 "interview" with Ole Vinding; Vinding asked: "Do you like Italy now that Mussolini is there?" Joyce replied: "Naturally. Now as always. Italy is Italy. Not to like it because of Mussolini would be just as absurd as to hate England because of Henry the Eighth."[3] Yet the pro-Fascist attitudes of Pound and Wyndham Lewis he treated with scorn,[4] nor were his political beliefs, such as they were, at all naïve: he was as much aware of the subtleties of official British hypocrisy as he was of the obviously pernicious motives of official Germany: "And any time I turn on the radio I hear some British politician mumbling inanities or his German cousin shouting and yelling like a madman."[5]

Neither is the absence of contemporary political allusions in the *Wake* as complete as that claimed by Gillet in Joyce's personal conversations. Levin, in fact, finds a rather interesting collection of the flotsam and jetsam of the thirties among the carefully sifted debris of the *Wake:* "Joyce alludes glibly and impartially to such concerns as left-wing literature,[116] Whitman and democracy,[263] Lenin and Marxism,[271] the Gestapo,[332] the

Nazis,[375] the Soviets,[414] and the 'braintrust.'[529]''[6] (Levin's numerals refer to pages in *Finnegans Wake*.) Again it is important to stress that the appearance of these elements does not constitute a commitment by Joyce to a point of view, but it does indicate his awareness of their importance in the times in which he lived.

"Left-wing literature" is introduced in a mock-Marxist reading of the "mamafesta" of chapter 5 in conjunction with other attempts to interpret its significance: "we have perused from the pages of *I Was a Gemral,* that Showting up of Bulsklivism by 'Schottenboum', that Father Michael about this red time of the white terror equals the old regime and Margaret is the social revolution while cakes mean the party funds and dear thank you signifies national gratitude" (116.5-10)—a dig at G. B. Shaw is also intended. On "Whitman and democracy" we have the enigmatic comment during the Lessons: "And old Whiteman self, the blighty blotchy, beyond the bays, hope of ostrogothic and ottomanic faith converters, despair of Pandemia's postwartem plastic surgeons? But is was all so long ago" (263.8-13), an aspect of the History being studied by the children. "Lenin and Marxism" are found buried in a Shem marginal note during the lessons: *"Ulstria, Monastir, Leninstar and Connecticut"* (270-271.L), which transfers the four provinces of Ireland to international settings (Geography now being taught), so that *Leninstar* is probably dependent upon Leningrad rather than Lenin himself. The "Gestapo" is contrasted with the Cheka in "Gestapose to parry off cheekars" (332.7-8), as the radio in Earwicker's tavern blares forth the news of impending war prior to the Crimean episode; the conflict itself is of course fraternal, so "One bully son growing the goff and his twinger read out by the Nazi Priers" (375.17-18) is another contrast of opposing forces, although *Nazi Priers* has a strange echo in "noisy priors"* (422.36) and "nicies and priers" (196.21). "So vi et (414.14)—echo of a simple "So be yet!" (27.30)—signifies both resurrection and resignation. "Bright young chaps of the

---

* Actually the Latin *nisi prius,* notes Clive Hart in "An Index of Motifs in *Finnegans Wake*" (*Structure and Motif,* p. 235).

brandnew braintrust" (529.5) might suggest the New Deal, but it hardly seems likely.

To Levin's grouping Mrs. Glasheen adds a few personalities in the *Wake,* including a second reference to Nikolai Lenin:[7] "reptrograd leanins" (351.27-28) refers to both Leningrad and Leninist leanings. The city and the Russian milieu in general for the Crimean War interlude here are both significant, but the fact that Lenin was a fellow exile of Joyce's in Zurich during the World War I years should not be overlooked as the sort of coincidence that delighted Joyce. Mrs. Glasheen's reference to Stalin,[8] however, is not as certain; the passage, occurring during the History portion of the studies, informs us that "the same Messherrn the grinning statesmen, Brock and Leon, have shunted the grumbling coundedtouts, Starlin and Ser Artur Ghinis" (272.24-27), but Ellmann points out that this refers to the victory in 1880 in Dublin of Liberal candidates Brooks and Lyons over Conservatives Stirling and Arthur Guinness,[9] although the augmented title of *statesmen* and the French-German form of address in *Messherrn* for Dublin politicos may indicate an international level as well. Adolph Hitler is also alluded to in "new hikler's highways" (410.8), but, except for Hitler's building of the *Autobahnen* (for hikers?), there is nothing of political importance here.

Contemporary Irish politics, on the other hand, forms a more coherent part of the *Wake.* Politically Ireland represents the world at large, and its capital city, once "The seventh city" (61.36) of Christendom, now becomes the world center, "Healiopolis" (24.18), the sun city around which the world revolves. Here is the land that is constantly being invaded, constantly rebelling against its conquerors, constantly absorbing the strangers who settle in it, and constantly unable to unite in a common cause. Religious turmoil, economic poverty, contrasts of Georgian pomp and contemporary slums, two languages, of which one is indigenous and unused and the other foreign and dominant—all these contribute to its universality. It is a country which exiles its artists and in which strangers and artists find themselves exiles: Stephen the heretic,

Bloom the Jew, Earwicker the "Skand" (157.16) and "episcopalian" (559.26).

The events of the Easter Rebellion of 1916, when "the grim white and cold bet the black fighting tans" (176.24-25), through the creation of the Free State with de Valera's two documents, "ducomans nonbar one" (358.30; also 386.20-21, 482.20, 528.32-33) and "decumans numbered too" (369.24-25; also 390.29, 619.19), represented not only the chaos of the present age, but a shift with the new Catholic domain of Eire to a theocracy, a change concomitant with the Viconian cycles that govern the *Wake's* structure. Significantly enough, the political events are presented primarily in terms of personages, as the leadership of the Irish nationalist factions moved from "Isaac's Butt" (421.4) to "parnella" (173.11) to "Healy Mealy" (329.34) to *"Da Valorem's Dominical Brayers"* (342.11). It is Eamon de Valera who emerges from the *Wake* as the personification of the contemporary Irish political scene, and, although Gillet claims he never heard Joyce mention his name, Joyce included copious references to the Irish leader (4.4, 9.36, 51.13, 72.11, 261.n2, 342.11, 473.8, 543.2, 626.31), and many commentators have been alert to notice the de Valera-like personality of the bourgeois politician, Shaun the Post, while Kenner also sees similarities between the "Longfella" and the author of *Finnegans Wake* (birthyear, near-blindness, physical stature, even aspects of personality).[10] And thus Joyce's "alter ego" becomes an aspect of Shem as well, and again we find that the antagonist brothers strangely share still another prototype.

The event that most cogently brings the *Wake* into contemporary focus is the Wall Street Crash of 1929 (or any of the numerous depressions that preceded it—another aspect of the recurring pattern of history), and it is most surprising that Gillet should list "the stock-exchange" among the missing topics of Joyce's conversation, since Joyce's letters indicate that he was concerned about the Depression and its effect on many of his friends. Symbolic of the Fall motif (it is listed in a series of falls that follow the initial thunderclap), the economic bust is referred to as the "wallstrait oldparr . . . retaled" (3.17). It is identified with H.C.E. of course: "he pours into the softclad shellborn the hard cash earned in Watling Street" (134.19-20) and compounded with Satan, Adam, and Humpty Dumpty:

> *Cleftfoot from Hempal must tumpel, Blamefool Gardener's bound to fall;*
> *Broken Eggs will poursuive bitten Apples for where theirs is Will there's his Wall* [175.17-20].

And the doggerel ballad culminates in "O fortunous casualitas!" (175.29), one of the twenty-eight versions of *"O felix culpa!"* to be found in the *Wake,** here also signifying the casualty of many fortunes in the Wall Street debacle. Various versions of Earwicker's downfall in Phoenix Park are couched in economic terminology, linking his fall with the Stock Market Crash; for example:

> Or to have ochtroyed to resolde or borrough by exchange same super melkkaart, means help; best Brixton high yellow, no outings: cent for cent on Auction's Bridge. . . . Not for old Crusos or white soul of gold! A pipple on the panis, two claps on the cansill, or three pock pocks cassey knocked on the postern! Not for one testey tickey culprik's coynds ore for all ecus in cunziehowffse! So hemp me Cash! [538.7-16].

Here both the fall of the great city and the fall of the hero through sexual temptation are mirrored in the "selling out." Other Wall Street terms are heard in the repetition of the "bull-bear" phrases which denote a selling market and a buying market; since these follow each other in cyclical form and are opposites, Joyce is able to utilize them for both Vico and Bruno, and bull versus bear often becomes bull-again versus bear-again: "Bull igien bear and then

---

* Niall Montgomery has listed twenty puns ("The Pervigilium Phoenicis," *New Mexico Quarterly*, XXIII [Winter, 1953], 470-71), to which should be added: "on Felix Day" (27.13-14), *"O'Phelim's Cutprice"* (72.4), *"Ophelia's Culpreints"* (105.18), "old phoenix portar" (406.10), "more freudful mistake" (411.35-36), "prof. kuvertly falted" (606.27), "a grandfallar" (29.6-7), and "of fallen griefs" (207.3).

bearagain bulligan" (272.29-30; also 87.21, 358.30-31, 464.28, 522.15, 583.4).

The significance of the Crash is essentially Viconian, ending the last era of the cycle and creating the chaos that precedes the birth of the new era. As such the importance is unmistakably Marxian as well: the downfall of capitalist economy heralds the social revolution which so many of Joyce's contemporaries were expecting during the thirties. A Marxian view is of course not incongruous with the Viconian precepts Joyce used, nor is his youthful preoccupation with socialism to be completely disregarded. Stanislaus Joyce notes that Joyce, even in his Trieste days, "called himself a socialist,"[11] and indeed Shem is often called a "sposhialiste" (240.3) and a "Menschavik" (185.34); "aboleshqvick" (302.18), since Bolsheviks sought to abolish the existing order quickly; "that bogus bolshy of a shame" (425.22); and he is accused of "making friends with everybody red in Rossya" (463.23-24)—of course by Shaun, who himself is suspect for wearing buttons of "krasnapoppsky red" (404.24-25). "Rooskayman kamerad?" (89.7) the trial witness is asked. As the Gracehoper Shem is denied even "one pickopeck of muscowmoney" (416.17-18) by the Ondt, and Shaun threatens his brother with: "Tiberia is waiting on you, arestocrank! Chaka a seagull ticket" (424.9-10). Cheka, the first form of the Soviet Secret Police (here punned with Anton Chekhov and his play *The Sea Gull* *), has been encountered before, and is teamed with its successor, the O.G.P.U., in "hogpew and cheekas" (442.35), which Shaun intends employing (as detectives, although hog jowls, as delicacies, interest him also) to track down Shem.

Far from being a confirmed socialist, however, Shem confesses that he is not actually committed, but "could neither swuck in nonneither swimp in the flood of cecialism" (230.8-9). Earwicker, on the other hand, combines all shades of political opinion in his all-inclusiveness, being "whugamore, tradertory, socianist, commoniser" (132.19-20).[12] The conflict between Bolsheviks and Czarists

---

* Joyce's triple pun includes the Russian word for seagull, *chaika.*

in Russia is seen by Joyce as an aspect of the fraternal battle, suggesting to him a synthesis of conflicting opposites: "White monothoid? Red theatrocrat? And all the pinkprophets cohalething?" (29.15-16)—it all took place a long time ago in the War of the Roses and has long since been resolved. But, for a writer accused of being antiseptically nonpolitical, Joyce manages to incorporate into his work many allusions to the "socialights" (32.9), "sowsealist potty" (72.23), "the sociationist party" (144.5-6), "cummanisht" (320.5), "socializing and communicanting" (498.20-21)—which seems harmless enough—and "yon socialist sun" (524.25). Even Shaun confuses communism with Holy Communion and arrives at "communionistically" (453.32).* The *Census,* incidentally, lists three mentions of Karl Marx and four of Friedrich Engels (one dubious).

Much of Joyce's preoccupation with Russia in the *Wake* is historical rather than ideological, since the Crimean War is used as an important conflict. In a plan where all history is simultaneous, Czarist Russia and the U.S.S.R. share the spotlight during the Butt-Taff episode. Therefore, Taff's cry of "Trovatarovitch!" (341.9) brands Butt as the son of thunder, the son of a comrade, and the son of a troubador (as well as some sort of avatar),† so that when he next appears, it is *"with the sickle of a scygthe but the humour of a hummer"* (341.10). Thereafter, Butt is called "commeylad" (343.8), and when Butt and Taff are united against the General, they form a *"commonturn"* (354.19). Such dabbling in jargon hardly commits Joyce, whose authorized biographer records his early readings in socialist works but comments that Joyce's "own socialism was thin and unsteady and ill-informed and he knew it to be so. Indeed, it was more of a sympathy than a conviction, a feeling that the perfect freedom in life with the absolute minimum of restraining laws was an ideal devoutly to be desired."[13] This seems

---

* The second edition of Joyce letters, in the process of being edited by Richard Ellmann, will contain several other references by Joyce to the extents and limitations of his youthful socialism.

† Perhaps also Tvashtar, the divine artificer of Vedic myth.

to be as far as his interest in revolutionary socialism went. Admittedly unable to suffer past the first sentence of *Das Kapital*,[14] he went on to write his own unreadable history of mankind, arriving at his own dialectics, presumably through Vico. Nevertheless, the *Wake* deals with the self-destruction of existing society and the heralding of a new era with promising call:

> Sandhyas! Sandhyas! Sandhyas!
> Calling all downs. Calling all downs to dayne. Array! Surrection! Eireweeker to the wohld bludyn world. O rally, O rally, O rally! Phlenxty, O rally! To what lifelike thyne of the bird can be. Seek you somany matters. Haze sea east to Osseania. Here! Here! Tass, Patt, Staff, Woff, Havv, Bluvv, and Rutter. The smog is lofting. And already the olduman's olduman has godden up on othertimes to litanate the bonnamours [593.1-8].

But, whatever the actual tenor of this political message, which combines a cry for peace (*shanti*—Sanskrit) and holiness (*sanctus*—Latin) with the Sanskrit word for the twilight between eons, as well as a resurrection and a bloody insurrection, it obviously remains an individually Joycean call which could not easily be shaped to fit a preconceived political concept. Nonetheless, political critics have sought a "doctrine" from Joyce and have been particularly interested in determining where Joyce's final work placed him politically. This approach has been codified in succinct form by David Daiches in *The Novel and the Modern World*:

> In *Dubliners*, Joyce is the artist observing his environment; in *A Portrait of the Artist*, he is the artist rejecting his environment; in *Ulysses*, he is the artist re-creating from a distance the world he has rejected. Unlike some of his contemporaries—and contrary to what we might deem to be the natural development of an artist of his generation— Joyce has not moved to a final stage where he reaccepts his environment with a new understanding of its deficiencies and a new consciousness of the difference between its deficiencies as a particular environment which can be changed and its deficiencies as a microcosm of life.[15]

Such is Daiches' formula for what he considers a mature artist of Joyce's generation (the inherent fallacy here is that a writer's societal obligations vary from generation to generation, rather than remaining consistent in relation to the rationale of that particular era): he expects the sort of political consciousness which can reverse the direction of a three-part initiation away from an acceptance of mankind, achieving a metamorphosis that leaves the writer a rational advocate of the perfectibility of man. But Joyce, Daiches maintains, never arrived at the final political position of reacceptance:

> It might be argued that *Finnegans Wake* is what it is because it represents a repetition of the third stage instead of progress to a fourth. Perhaps a political analogy might be helpful. What one might call the "four ages of a young man" of the present generation are: first, the observer; second, the liberal; third, the cynic or disillusioned individualist; fourth, the Marxist, using the term symbolically to denote a reacceptance of the necessity of purposive action at a new level.[16]

Already rather narrow in the earlier statement,* Daiches' formula now becomes complicated by such semantically suspect words as "liberal" and "cynic," as well as a definition of "Marxist" (using the term "symbolically" does not help) which defines it somewhat out of existence. But the more serious error is to straitjacket all authors within the same limits of responsibility, and thus expect Joyce to behave artistically toward his literary material as, say, John Dos Passos or John Steinbeck did toward theirs. (It must have come as rather lukewarm comfort for Joyce to have been defended by a Soviet critic for his influence on Dos Passos.[17]) Thus having codified within his own concepts the terms under which Joyce must surrender his "cynicism" and "reaccept his environ-

---

* If Daiches' prescription is a bit leaden for easy digestion in its initial presentation, it is hardly lightened when parroted over a decade later. Yet, in an article describing "The Catholicism of James Joyce," Sam Hynes asserts: "We may generalize about Joyce's first three works (excluding the trivial *Chamber Music*) and say that *Dubliners* represents the artist's Irish-Catholic environment, *The* [*sic*] *Portrait of the Artist as a Young Man* his struggle against that environment, and *Ulysses* the fruit of that struggle—and the price. *Finnegans Wake,* in so far as I am able to penetrate it, seems for our purposes simply an extension of *Ulysses*"—*Commonweal,* LV (February 22, 1952), 487.

ment," Daiches concludes that in the *Wake* Joyce does not concede to these terms: "Joyce's exile has been final: to the end he has denied any stake in the rejected world that is the subject matter of his art."[18]

It is this statement* which indicates the necessity for a review of the *Wake* in terms of Joyce's final attitudes, investigating his own terms for reacceptance and his efforts in regard to those terms. In the place of this sort of analysis we have been treated to the attitudes of others, of the critics themselves who have sought to claim or reject Joyce in view of their own ideals. Thus Joyce has been lauded or denigrated in the name of such ideals as Marxism and democracy, "progress" and *status quo*.

Marxists and near-Marxists in particular have been responsible for a certain amount of political criticism of James Joyce, but little of this has been carried over from *Ulysses* to *Finnegans Wake*, partly because of the difficult nature of the last book (which has caused even the most audacious commentators to display a certain degree of caution) and partly because the rigidity of such political commentaries on art has been decidedly tempered since the politically disastrous days of 1939. Some of the pre-*Wake* criticism remains quite interesting, however, particularly the controversy that raged at the All-Union Writers' Congress in Moscow in 1934.† Little information is available, but enough for us to realize that Karl Radek's denunciation of Joyce on political grounds did not constitute a unanimous Marxist view, and that better balanced opinions were certainly forthcoming, among them V. Gertsfelde's:

> The power of the bourgeoisie to-day is largely dependent on its ability to hide behind a screen of pseudo-democracy, religion, and mysticism.

* In the second edition (1960) of *The Novel and the Modern World*, Professor Daiches has carefully reworded these comments on Joyce: the phraseology is far more subtle, but the ideas remain essentially the same.

† For excerpts from the Karl Radek—Wieland Herzfelde [*sic*] controversy— with a postscript by Sergei Tretiakow ("A word on the subject of Joyce. There is heated discussion around his name. Some defend him, others abuse him. Vychnevsky says—wonderful. Radek replies—putrefaction. The fight continues. But who has read this book?")—see the quotations from the *Neue Deutsche Blätter* of September, 1934, reprinted in *A James Joyce Yearbook*, pp. 184-86.

In the realm of ideas this smoke-screening is carried out to a high degree of perfection. The bourgeoisie succeeded in transforming science and art into a mystery; consequently, scientists and artists become "neutral" people whose mysterious and spiritual depths no ordinary mortal can fathom. These men were placed above the slings and arrows of the populace. . . .[19]

(Thus we have the image of Shem, the "Esuan Menschavik and the first till last alshemist" [185.34-35] who "squirtscreened from the crystalline world waned chagreenold and doriangrayer in its dudhud"—186.7-8.)

Gertsfelde's description of the artist in middle-class society might well have interested Joyce, an artist well aware of his own exile from his class. We hardly need Gorman's statement to remind us that Joyce "despised the bourgeois class as a class,"[20] since so much of Joyce's work echoes his condemnation of the middle class, their hypocritical morality, their mediocrity of taste and thought, their book banning and burning, and their insistence on compromise and conformity. Stephen Dedalus's oft-quoted assertion, "I will not serve that in which I no longer believe, whether it call itself my home, my fatherland, or my church" (AP 247), despite its flamboyance, remained for Joyce a serious statement of defiance throughout his work. Even if we find, as Daiches insists, that *Finnegans Wake* is a recreation of Joyce's rejected world on his own terms, Joyce's antipathy for the basic concepts of middle-class ideals will be found to remain intact. Thus, the Marxian qualifications cited by Gertsfelde apply quite well to Joyce, who existed as an artist outside of the bourgeois orbit, lamenting in personal terms, as the Marxist does in political terms, the situation of the creative individual in bourgeois society.*

---

* The obituary on Joyce that appeared in the *New Masses* proves to be an interesting document and an obituary on more than just Joyce; in its entirety it reads: "James Joyce's influence on younger writers had begun to decline long before his death in Zurich last week. To disillusioned novelists of the post-war decade, the author of ULYSSES appeared as the prophet of a new and liberated literature. At the end of the thirties one can look back and see that Joyce was merely the most brilliant expression of an older literature which had lost its vitality and its capacity for hope. For Joyce was essentially the

Nor does the bourgeois screen of "pseudo-democracy, religion, and mysticism" apply to Joyce. His *non serviam* rejects the religion of his youth (and leads to rejection of all religion), and applies equally well to the political scheme of the "democracy" sponsored by his social class. He remained at all times suspicious of political causes that waved the banner of democracy: the First World War (the war ballyhooed to make the world "safe for democracy") found him in neutral exile in Zurich. It seems apparent that Joyce allied such pseudo-democracy with the political motives of the middle class. His upbringing had taught him that imperialist Britain represented politically those ideals, and his brother tells us that Joyce "considered well founded Newman's criticism, which charged English liberalism with being a composite of intellectual nebulosity and indifferentism."[21] Of William Ewart Gladstone ("whilom eweheart"—336.34), that grand champion of nineteenth-century English liberalism, Earwicker says, in a prologue to the radio broadcast of the Crimean War incidents:

—It was of The Grant, old gartener, *qua* golden meddlist, Publius Manlius, fuderal private, (his place is his poster, sure, they said, and we're going to mark it, sore, they said, with a carbon caustick manner) bequother the liberaloider at his petty corporelezzo that hung caughtnapping from his baited breath, it was of him, my wife and I thinks, to feel to every of the younging fruits, tenderosed like an atalantic's breastwells or, on a second wreathing, a bright tauth bight

philosopher of social pessimism, doom, and bitter negation. He had cut the lines of communication with the outside world, living in voluntary exile not only from his native Ireland but from the masses of mankind. A man of encyclopedic learning, great technical dexterity, and unusual sensitivity to the sound and color of words, James Joyce seemed intent on perverting his talent as a gesture of revolt against a world which he despised. But like all nihilists he failed to conquer the world; he was conquered by it. His rejection of logical consciousness, his contempt for humanity, his disintegration of social language was the literary reflection of the anarchic and destructive impulses of capitalist society. Joyce led to the brink of moral and intellectual self-annihilation. It is little wonder that so many of the younger generation of writers, turning to the working classes for courage and creativity, have repudiated Joyce's outlook and the decadent bourgeois order which distorted his great gifts."—"James Joyce," *New Masses*, XXXVIII, No. 5 (January 21, 1941), 19.

shimmeryshaking for the welt of his plow. And where the peckadillies at his wristsends meetings be loving so lightly dovessoild the candidacy, me wipin eye sinks, of his softboiled bosom should be apparient even to our illicterate of nullatinenties [336.21-32].

This convicts not only Gladstone, the "Grand Old Man" (*Grant, old . . . Manlius*), of expansionism in the name of liberalism, but also U. S. Grant (*The Grant . . . fuderal private*), another *liberaloider* who *dovessoild the candidacy,* as well as Napoleon Bonaparte (*petty corporelezzo*) who conquered in the name of the ideals of the French Revolution.

It has remained for a recent Italian translator of *Ulysses* to transpose Stanislaus Joyce's statement about Joyce's rebellious attitudes to Joyce's work: in an interview Giulio de Angelis commented that he "reads Joyce's book as a heretic Irishman's attack against all the established institutions: the Church, the British Empire, the language of the British."[22] Here is a most succinct comment on the Joycean point of view, on the attitudes toward the heritage of the nineteenth century which the foster country left for Joyce, whose *Wake* is an annotated commentary on that heritage, his "victuum gleaner" (364.33-34) of the debris of the Victorian Age. Where Ireland represented the victimized nation, Great Britain represents the victor and oppressor. The Duke of Wellington, of Irish ancestry, ironically, and a national hero of the Irish, is the figure of the British conqueror, and the trip to the "Willingdone Museyroom" (8-10) shows us England's colonial wars of the nineteenth century, while the most symbolic of the wars in the *Wake* is the Crimean conflict (337-355), again famous in Irish story and song because of the participation of Irish recruits in the British contingent: "with his drums and bones and hums in drones your innereer'd heerdly heer he" (485.26-28).

An echo of the visit to the Museyroom conducted by Kate, "Mind your hats goan in!" (8.9) and "Mind your boots goan out" (10.22-23), is heard preceding the Crimean events: "katekattershin clopped, clopped, clopped . . . as she was going to pimpim him, way boy wally . . . band your hands going in, bind your heads

coming out. . . . And the Bullingdong caught the wind up. Dip"
(333.7-18). Not only a full treatment of the Battle of Sevastopol
and the constant references to Wellington's war with Napoleon
("the petty lipoleum boy"—8.25), but an entire history of the
march of Imperial Britannia culminating in the Victorian Empire
of the liberal nineteenth century passes before the reader of *Finnegans Wake*. Every outrage against the Irish is certainly included,
from the landing of Strongbow in 1170 ("strongbowed launch"—
288.15) to the campaigns of Cromwell and King William III
("Upkingbilly and crow cru cramwells"—53.36) to the campaign
of terror conducted by the Black and Tans ("black fighting tans"
—176.24-25) during the "Troubles." Not only Irish struggles
against the British, but also the American ("don't you let flyfire till
you see their whites of the bunkers' eyes!"—542.25-26), the Chinese ("why this hankowchaff and whence this second tone, son-
yet-sun? He had the cowtaw in his buxers flay of face"—
89.36-90.2), the Indian ("saxy luters in their back haul of Coal-
cutter . . . confined to guardroom, I hindustand . . . Zenaphiah
Holwell . . . Surager Dowling . . . Kavanagh Djanaral"—
492.14-29), and others, are recorded in the *Wake*. "Boxerising
and coxerusing" (347.29) are part of the Crimean War scene, and
the extent of the Empire is realized in: "the turtling of a London's
alderman is ladled out by the waggerful to the regionals of pigmy-
land" (253.9-11).

It becomes the function of H. C. Earwicker in the *Wake* to represent the paternal figure of the British imperialist, since as the
outlander he is identified (as in the Ballad of Persse O'Reilly)
with all the ills visited upon Ireland ("He was fafafather of all
schemes for to bother us"—45.13). And since, as every schoolboy
is taught, flag followed trade in establishing the Empire, Earwicker
the publican becomes the tradesman (as in the Ballad: "this
soffsoaping salesman. Small wonder He'll Cheat E'erawan our
local lads nicknamed him"—45.31-46.1) who initiates the expansion. In the Yawn inquest, the voice of Anna Livia is heard

through the corpse discussing "that fluctuous neck merchamtur" (496.26) and the extent of his spheres of interest:

> and in the licensed boosiness primises of his delhightful bazar and re-
> united magazine hall, by the magazine wall, Hosty's and Co, Exports,
> for his five hundredth and sixtysixth borthday, the grand old Magen-
> nis Mor, Persee and Rahli, taker of the tributes, their Rinseky Pop-
> pakork and Piowtor the Grape, holding Dunker's durbar, boot kings
> and indiarubber umpires and shawhs from paisley and muftis in mus-
> lim and sultana reiseines and jordan almonders and a row of jam sa-
> hibs and a odd principeza in her pettedcoat and the queen of knight's
> clubs and the claddagh ringleaders and the two salaames and the
> Halfa Ham and the Hanzas Khan with two fat Maharashers and the
> German selver geyser and he polished up, protemptible, tintanambu-
> lating to himsilf so silfrich, and there was J. B. Dunlop, the best ty-
> rent of ourish times, and a swanks of French wine stuarts and Tudor
> keepsakes and the Cesarevitch for the current counter Leodegarius
> Sant Legerleger [etc.] [497.24-498.3].

The buying up of foodstuffs from the exotic lands beyond soon becomes the simple expedient of purchasing the corrupt rulers of those lands or conquering those not easily bought. Under the guise of benevolence and progress and enlightenment and the journeys of missionaries ("alliving stone"—283.17-18) and explorers ("fungopark"—51.20) can easily be discovered the face of imperialism, and Earwicker himself, defending his era of "benevolence, progress and enlightenment," reveals the reality of exploitation:

> Round the musky moved a murmel but mewses whinninaird and bel-
> luas zoomed: tendulcis tunes like water parted fluted up from the
> westinders while from gorges in the east came the strife of ourangoon-
> tangues. All in my thicville Escuterre ofen was thorough fear but in
> the meckling of my burgh Belvaros was the site forbed: tuberclerosies
> I reized spudfully from the murphyplantz Hawkinsonia and berriber-
> ries from the pletoras of the Irish shou. I heard my libertilands mak-
> ing free through their curraghcoombs, my trueblues hurusalaming be-
> fore Wailingtone's Wall [541.31-542.4].

In the wake of imperialism, despite the pseudo-democratic pretense, lie disease, war, famine, and religious persecution, and Earwicker's naïve boasting is too thin to hide the truth. Here is embodied the concept of "progress" that cloaked the miseries of the Victorian Age, the concept of industrial progress through colonialization, material advantages, and *laissez faire*. In Earwicker's shoddy defense of the system the obvious fallacies are discoverable: because the British Navy sailed into the Indies and up the Ganges (*gorges*) for the various kings named George and defeated the natives of Malaya (*ourangoontangues*), the result has been anything but progress for Ireland (*tuberclerosies* and *berriberries* as illnesses). Sir John Hawkins (*hawkinsonia*) introduced the potato to Ireland (the tuber, the spud, the murphy, the buried "berry"), but English policy induced the potato blight just as readily.

Two such statements of British liberalism are presented in the *Wake,* one for each of the professional politicians, Earwicker and his thoroughly bourgeois favorite son, Shaun. On one level we have Earwicker attempting to justify his guilty position, while on the other we have Shaun coupling his religious immunity from criticism with his political zeal and ideals. Shaun, who as priest should be a man of honor, concludes his amorous speech to Issy, after asserting, "I'm a man of Armor" (446.6), and announces his civic campaign, thereby admitting that poor living conditions exist under his jurisdiction: "Slim ye, come slum with me and rally rats' roundup! 'Tis post purification we will, sales of work and social service, missus, completing our Abelite union by the adoptation of fosterlings. Embark for Euphonia!" (446.27-30). Echoing the romantic "Come live with me and be my love" of Marlowe, as well as the religious "Abide with me" of the Protestants, Shaun's version invites Issy to come slumming and see the slums of Victorian Dublin, similar to the "rats' alley" of Eliot's London. These slums exist *post purification,* suggesting both an unsuccessful attempt to clean them up and a realization that they are beyond redemption.

Shaun's allusions stress the ineffectual efforts of the reform-minded social workers of the day to stem the tide of urban blight in the face of bourgeois aspirations for business success (*sales of work and social service*). Their ineffectuality is echoed in *Abelite union* (at least a fourfold pun containing the Abelites of fourth-century Africa who married but remained celibate; Peter Abelard, the emasculated lover of Heloise; the unionism of the innocent Abels of the world destined for destruction; and the explosive called abelite, hardly a symbol for unification). A typical slogan for the era might well be *Embark for Euphonia,* a promise of both harmony and happiness, but in this case it is essentially *phony.* Thus, in terms that are at once amorous, sexually suggestive, pompously civic-minded, and obviously insincere, Shaun's declaration of intentions continues:

> I'll put in a shirt time if you'll get through your shift and between us in our shared slaves, brace to brassiere and shouter to shunter, we'll pull off our working programme. Come into the garden guild and be free of the gape athome! We'll circumcivicise all Dublin country. Let us, the real Us, all ignite in our prepurgatory grade as aposcals and be instrumental to utensilise, help our Jakeline sisters clean out the hogshole and generally ginger things up. Meliorism in massquantities, raffling receipts and sharing sweepstakes till navel, spokes and felloes hum like hymn. Burn only what's Irish, accepting their coals. You will soothe the cokeblack bile that's Anglia's and touch Armourican's iron core [446.31-447.6].

Shaun's trade unionism smacks suspiciously of patronizing, and his patriotic echo of Swift's "Burn everything English, except their coal" sounds like the real thing, but actually is just the opposite. Shaun's unconscious slips, like Earwicker's and Shem's and Issy's and Anna Livia's, always reveal his true motivation when the actual words are investigated and not merely accepted at sound value. Shaun goes on to praise his father, whom he intends replacing, labeling him "priest-mayor-king-merchant" (447.15), and contrasting himself ("Jno Citizen"—447.22) with his outcast brother ("Jas Pagan"—447.22). But, as a Dublin politician, Shaun is quick to decry the filth of "dear dirty Dublin" when British cities are prospering: "When will the W.D. face of our sow muckloved d'lin, the Troia of towns and Carmen of cities,

crawling with mendiants in perforated clothing, get its wellbelav-
ered white like l'pool and m'chester?" (448.11-14). Shaun's
choice of Liverpool and Manchester as clean cities is ironic, nor is
his request for mere whitewashing far below the surface.

The second "defense" of British liberalism, Earwicker's, underscores the irony of Shaun's comparison between the effect of British policy at home and in subjugated Ireland, for it reveals that the
situation is not much better in *l'pool* and *m'chester* than in *d'lin*.
The gist of H.C.E.'s political sermon is that progress has wrought
wonderful changes during his "administration": "Things are not
as they were" (540.13), but even so succinct a summary allows for
a wide margin of interpretation, and Earwicker's statement of fact
is wonderfully equivocal. As such "thisorder" (540.19) implies
disorder   rather   than   order,   and   his   "politicoecomedy"
(540.26-27) is laughable rather than economically sound. The
usual boasts of public safety, public health, and public education,
the achievements of the solid bourgeois for the benefit of the solid
bourgeoisie, are all heard: "Thuggeries are reere as glovars' me-
tins, lepers lack, ignerants show beneath suspicion like the bitter-
halves of esculapuloids" (540.31-33). But his progress is dependent upon financial chicanery: "By fineounce and imposts I got and
grew and by grossscruple gat I grown outreachesly" (541.7-9),
and upon military conquest: "I wegschicked Duke Wellinghof to
reshockle Roy Shackleton: Walhalloo, Walhalloo, Walhalloo,
mourn in plein!" (541.21-22)—he sent soldiers like Wellington
to "shake up" the "king of the shekels," resulting in bloody battles
like Waterloo. His religion is surface, the building of churches,
"The chort of Nicholas Within was my guide and I raised a dome
on the wherewithouts of Michan" (541.4-5), but instead of
sackcloth and ashes, he is "rapt in neckloth and sashes" (542.34),
and religious persecution seems to have been as important as military intervention as a means toward financial conquest: "Paybads
floriners moved in hugheknots against us and I matt them, pepst to
papst, barthelemew: milreys (mark!) onfell, and (Luc!) I arose
Daniel in Leonden" (541.14-16).

In this manner the report of the nineteenth century on its material advances rambles on until Earwicker modulates from a politician delivering his state-of-the-union address to a landlord advertising his Victorian dwellings for rental:

> fair home overcrowded, tidy but very little furniture, respectable, whole family attends daily mass and is dead sick of bread and butter, sometime in the militia, mentally strained from reading work on German physics, shares closet with eight other dwellings, more than respectable, getting comfortable parish relief, wageearner freshly shaven from prison, highly respectable [etc.] [543.22-26].

Joyce here is reproducing, in Joycean form, a social worker's report (Shaun's *sales of work and social service*) of overcrowded living conditions in the slum areas of Victorian England—in this case, as Atherton has pointed out, B. Seebohm Rowntree's *Poverty*.[23] This sort of condemnation of imperialism's inability to provide prosperity at home is particularly effective because it marks one of the occasions in the *Wake* where Joyce does not use Ireland as the example of Britain's victimization, but includes the added irony of the victimizing of the English lower class (despite their highly vaunted claim to bourgeois "respectibility"). The peroration of Earwicker's defense is a parody of the Dublin Charter which awarded the city of Dublin to the citizens of Bristol, England, in 1172,[24] and Earwicker, the English conqueror, signs with the name of King Henry II, "Enwreak us wrecks" (545.23). As Joyce saw it, British expansion began with Henry's annexation of Ireland and reached its culmination in the nineteenth century, whose hero was Wellington. Wellington's famous cry of "Up guards and at 'em!" is thus echoed at the beginning of Earwicker's *apologia*, "Ubipop jay piped" (540.14), one of over three dozen such echoes in the *Wake* (7.35-36, 10.16, 18.36, 33.18, 41.16-17, 54.1, 60.15, 67.21, 69.19, 179.8, 187.13-14, 197.24, 257.33, 272.L, 303.13, 311.19-20, 317.16, 326.15-16, 338.32, 348.28, 366.27, 396.4, 446.30, 459.27, 487.4, 494.15, 516.15, 521.19, 536.33, 561.33, 596.24).

The word "progress," which for the nineteenth century and still in the early part of the twentieth century had an august sound, and even a magic strong enough to create "Crystal Palaces" and concrete-and-steel skyscrapers, to send missionaries across the globe, and ships of trade and railroad tracks along the same lines, and armies as well, had little appeal for Joyce. He was suspicious of the ideal of progress as a goal unto itself, without moral basis and a necessary respect for the development of history as an organic entity (no matter how nightmarish to the sensitive artist). The laissez-faire economy that has been seen to underlie the progress engendered by British imperialism, even in Joyce's dialectics, becomes an even greater theme as the pre-*ricorso* corpus of the *Wake* reaches its climax in chapter 16. During the two trials at the deepest nadir of Earwicker's nightmare (572-576), sex, religion, law, and finance are reviewed as perversion, hair-splitting, double talk, and chicanery, and result in Earwicker's final attempt to assert his sexual potency and his financial solvency. But just as the final coitus is a failure ("Humbo, lock your kekkle up! Anny, blow your wickle out! Tuck away the tablesheet! You never wet the tea!"— 585.30-31), so are Earwicker's finances. In the guise of an international cartelist, the sum total of his imperialistic parts, the hero is declared a bankrupt; he had once been successful and powerful, however, and his full career is reviewed:

> So childish pence took care of parents' pounds and many made money the way in the world where rushroads to riches crossed slums of lice and, the cause of it all, he forged himself ahead like a blazing urban-orb, brewing treble to drown grief, giving and taking mayom and tuam, playing milliards with his three golden balls, making party capital out of landed self-interest, light on a slavey but weighty on the bourse, our hugest commercial emporialist, with his sons booing home from afar and his daughters bridling up at his side. Finner! [589.3-11].

There is little doubt here either about his business ethics (*light on a slavery but weighty on the bourse*) or the *slums of lice* left in the wake of his economic "progress." Nor is there any doubt that his own children have been his undoing (*his sons booing home from afar and his daughters bridling up at his side*), as the younger generation overthrows the older in Joyce's cycle.

It is this last motif that is sounded in the next paragraph recounting the downhill road to bankruptcy. Riding high at first, *our hugest commercial emporialist* slowly begins to skid, the descent gathering momentum as the entire cast of characters emerges to push him down the slope:

> How did he bank it up, swank it up, the whaler in the punt, a guinea by a groat, his index on the balance and such wealth into the bargain, with the boguey which he snatched in the baggage coach ahead? Going forth on the prowl, master jackill, under night and creeping back, dog to hide, over morning. Humbly to fall and cheaply to rise, exposition of failures. Through Duffy's blunders and MacKenna's insurance for upper ten and lower five the band played on. As one generation tells another. Ofter the fall [589.12-20].

The Fall, the Flood, and the Crash; Adam, Noah, Humpty Dumpty, and the contemporary hero representing the fortunes of unscrupulous nineteenth-century financial dealings—these are the patterns apparent in Earwicker's sexual demise as the customers in his pub plague him, as his sons dog his steps, as the four old codgers hound him, as the temptresses taunt him, and as the archetypal pattern of Finnegan's fall from the ladder haunts him:

> First for a change of a seven days license he wandered out of his farmer's health and so lost his early parishlife. Then ('twas in fenland) occidentally of a sudden, six junelooking flamefaces straggled wild out of their turns through his parsonfired wicket, showing all shapes of striplings in sleepless tights. Promptly whomafter in undated times, very properly a dozen generations anterior to themselves, a main chanced to burst and misflooded his fortunes, wrothing foulplay over his fives' court and his fine poultryyard wherein were spared a just two of a feather in wading room only. Next, upon due reflotation, up started four hurrigan gales to smithereen his plateglass housewalls and the slate for accounts his keeper was cooking. Then came three boy buglehorners who counterbezzled and crossbugled him. Later on in the same evening two hussites absconded through a breach in his bylaws and left him, the infidels, to pay himself off in kind remembrances. Till, ultimatehim, fell the crowning barleystraw,

when an explosium of his distilleries deafadumped all his dry goods to
his most favoured sinflute and dropped him, what remains of a hep-
tark, leareyed and letterish, weeping worrybound on his bankrump
[589.20-590.3].

Thus one of the clearer accounts of Earwicker's sin in Phoenix
Park develops the motif of the economic bust of bourgeois capitalism: the micturating girls have sauntered off, the peeping Earwicker commences to masturbate (*to pay himself off in kind remem-
brances*), the sexual rise and fall mirroring the vagaries of the
Stock Exchange, resounding here in a rather definite fall.

Although the degree of Joyce's political preoccuaption with his
own time may remain rather slight, the extent to which he managed to preoccupy himself with society in general probably far exceeds the efforts of his more political contemporaries, many of
whom already appear dated after only a few decades. It becomes
safe to state, in fact, that Joyce managed to develop one of the best
balanced attitudes toward his own age in relation to the development of man and his society. Laszlo Moholy-Nagy, the Hungarian
artist whose revolutionary precepts in the plastic arts interestingly
paralleled Joyce's literary innovations, provides an intelligent analysis of Joyce's attitudes at the time (although it may be interpreted
to serve Moholy-Nagy's aims slightly better than Joyce's):

> One of the tragedies of our generation has been the forced belief in
> "today," in "progress," the stability of humanistic ideals. Joyce was
> not deceived by such camouflage. He knew man's timeless faults as
> well as his virtues. He had no illusions about potential duplications of
> barbarism. He stood for a totality of existence, of sex and spirit, man
> and woman; for the universal against the specialized; for the union
> of intellect and emotion; for blending history with forecast, fairy
> tale with science. With this he liberated himself from the restrictions
> imposed upon writers by Marxian theorists whose demand for
> adherence to the tactics of the party often neglected basic emotional
> concepts and human traits. . . . Joyce contained multitudes. And with
> these "multitudes", he paved the way to a related, space-time thinking
> on a larger scale than any writer had done before.[25]

Moholy-Nagy delineates the errors of political critics who attempt to tie Joyce down to a contemporary doctrine, who expect a contemporary writer to flash his sign ("Liberal," "Cynic," "Marxist") and to produce (if sufficiently "integrated" in his times) a work of art that can be reduced to an everyday slogan for everyday life. Joyce flew by that net also. He consciously insisted upon transcending such an approach, preferring to view his own age through a universal perspective that excludes neither the future nor the past (far more Marxian as such than many for whom Daiches would probably offer his convenient label). In the *Wake* this theme of timelessness is echoed and re-echoed: "Anna was, Livia is, Plurabelle's to be" (215.24); "For as Anna was at the beginning lives yet and will return after great deap sleap rerising" (277.12-14); "Since ancient was our living is in possible to be" (614.9-10). It was small praise offered Joyce by the correspondent in *Living Age* in 1934 who recounted the Moscow conference debate: "Though he may serve the bourgeoisie by his partial presentation of contemporary life and his failure to use his art for the revolutionary movement, still does he show the decay of the present system."[26]

There are critics still extant who continue to quote the once-clever platitude that the clock had stopped for James Joyce on June 16, 1904, probably because the idea either serves their own ends or simplifies the task of following the development of the artist through his mature years. The aphorism has lost its bite and certainly any veracity it might have once contained. More precisely, it was not a clock at all but an hourglass that served Joyce's approach to time: at its narrowest point it is June 16, 1904, when the sands reached a point at which past became present for Joyce and flowed into the future, like Anna Livia at the *Wake's* end passing between the North and South Walls before flowing out to sea. "I see them rising! Save me from those therrble prongs! Two more. Onetwo moremens more. So. Avelaval. My leaves have drifted from me. All. But one clings still. I'll bear it on me. To remind me of. Lff!" (628.4-7). The clock that someday must run down, as it does so

quickly for the writer whose concept is of ephemeral "today," gave
way for Joyce to an hourglass that is endlessly turned over again
and again, transforming monodimensional time into a polydimen-
sional kaleidoscope, the "collideorscape" (143.28) of *Finnegans
Wake*.

II: RELIGIOUS MYOPIA

"It has become a fashion," noted the outspoken Stanislaus Joyce,
piercing the web of silence and subterfuge woven by the Joycean
disciples, "to represent him [James Joyce] as a man pining for the
ancient Church he had abandoned, and at a loss for moral support
without the religion in which he was bred. Nothing could be far-
ther from the truth."[27] Although references to *Finnegans Wake* in
Professor Joyce's meager writings about his brother do not indicate
that he ever read the work (which Joyce sent to him in 1939, but
which he refused to accept), it is apparent that Stanislaus was a
most perceptive observer of Joyce's state of mind, and that he
needed no written testimony to understand the nature of Joyce's
religious doubts. It is from this understanding that he wrote: "I
am convinced that there was never any crisis of belief. The vigour
of life within him drove him out of the Church, that vigour of
life that is packed into the seven-hundred-odd quarto pages of
Ulysses."[28] He might well have added the six-hundred-odd pages
of the *Wake*.

For those who did not know Joyce personally—and for many of
those who have reminded us with nostalgia that they did—it is
Finnegans Wake, representing the last two decades of his thinking,
that exists as Joyce's final statement. Critical spotlights to date have
illumined only small niches of Joyce's literary cathedral, and these
efforts have been dimmed by the veils and miasmas beclouding an
accurate image. It is vital that these benign obstructions be removed—and shattered—for a true focus into Joyce's ideas. Such an
undertaking would most logically begin with a recollection of the
"*non-serviam*" Luciferism which the youthful Joyce proclaimed in
A Portrait, the familiar facts about his exile's existence, his break

with the Jesuits who educated him, his refusal to pray at his mother's deathbed (whether real or fictive, it was an aspect of Joyce's thinking), his long-standing denial of the sacrament of marriage, and the raising of his children outside the pale of the Church.

But the problem lies beyond mere lip service to religion or to apostasy, beyond the bent knee of submission or hurled invective of defiance. It is the problem of a spiritual deracination of Joyce's early beliefs, of a mind's freedom from or dependence upon those roots. Ellsworth Mason, in evaluating the complexity of these issues during the first years of *"non-serviam"* (Trieste, 1907–12), finds that Joyce's journalistic efforts at the time indicate various inconsistencies, hesitancies, and complications of thought and emotion. Mason contends that Joyce

> . . . is very much against the Church as an institution, against Vaticanism in politics, against the Church that smashed Parnell, and the roots of this attitude are twofold: the political gesture of Pope Adrian IV, the only English Pope, who gave Ireland to England; and the fact that throughout history, the Papacy had given not a single word of support to her most Catholic domain, Ireland, in her struggle with Black Protestants.[29]

These considerations are particularly important because of their relevancy to the situation in *Finnegans Wake,* since Pope Adrian IV (Nicholas Breakspear) figures prominently as the Mookse in the fable of the Mookse and the Gripes (152-59): "our once in only Bragspear" (152.32-33), "Adrian (that was the Mookse now's assumptinome)" (153.20). And Mason indicates that Joyce's attitudes toward the Church are essentially historical and humanitarian—or, more precisely, a humanitarian approach through a historical perspective. As such we see these attitudes pervade throughout the *Wake.*

The critics who have found more than mere complications in Joyce's religious renunciation are many; their opinions and evidence are varied. Magalaner and Kain summarize:

> Most critics agree with Gorman that Joyce's "Roman Catholicism is in his bones . . . he cannot rest until it is either removed or clarified. . . ."

Few, however, agree on what this means. Reading the story of Ste-
phen-Joyce's apostasy in *A Portrait* . . . Thomas Merton experiences a
strong impetus toward conversion *to* Catholicism. For each critic who
believes, like Elliot Paul, that Joyce enjoyed his status of nonbeliever,
there is another who insists upon the anguish that his lack of belief
caused Joyce. For each statement like Lloyd Morris' that Joyce may
have eagerly wished to return to Catholicism, there is a counterbal-
ancing argument, such as the one put forward by Morris Ernst. . . .[30]

The inadequacy of this sort of summary is that it attempts to deal in
concrete terms with questions of vague and abstract feelings; it
finds avowals where there are only implications, sees actual trends
where only waverings and inclinations exist. An examination of
the sources cited indicates the insufficiency of such a capsule. Merton, for example, admits that he is finding affirmation where the
author intended negation; pages 211 and 212 of *Seven Storey
Mountain* reveal the affirmation that is Merton's own, in contrast
to the renunciation that was Joyce's:

> And here is a strange thing. . . . I had tried to read *Portrait of the
> Artist* and had bogged down in the part about his spiritual crisis. . . .
> Strange to say . . . I reread *Portrait of the Artist* and was fascinated
> precisely by that part of the book, by the "Mission," by the priest's
> sermon on hell. What impressed me was not the fear of hell, but the
> expertness of the sermon. Now, instead of being repelled by the
> thought of such preaching—which was perhaps the author's intention
> —I was stimulated and edified by it.[31]

Merton continues by praising himself for his perverse reading
and Joyce for an artistic accuracy of portrayal. He was "fascinated
by the pictures of priests and Catholic life. . . . That, I am sure,
will strike many people as a strange thing indeed."[32] It is interesting to note how often Merton comments on the "strangeness"
of so incongruous an interpretation; he is keenly aware that there is
little justification in crediting Joyce with his own conversion. In
fact, Merton merely attests to the fact that his own inclinations
drove him to find in the accuracy of Joyce's depiction of the Jesuit
world that which he had been seeking. Yet Merton's strange mis-
use of Joyce's material finds sanction with Father William T.

Noon: "Why *must* one 'be amused by Thomas Merton's assertion
. . . that Joyce's *Ulysses* [*sic*] . . . was one of the influences
which brought him into . . . the Church'?"[33] Perhaps Father Noon
is quibbling over the term "amused"; certainly if Merton had chosen to emulate the horse after reading Swift, we might be amused,
but neither religious conversion nor bearing false witness is necessarily "amusing."

Whereas Merton's views must be discarded as pertaining to
Merton rather than to Joyce, the statements of Gorman, Ernst,
and Morris cannot be dismissed as easily, since they represent first-
hand accounts of interviews with Joyce. Morris Ernst, for example,
had asked Joyce *when* he left the Church, and reports Joyce's answer as, "That's for the Church to say."[34] The answer is clever and
flippant, and we have enough evidence from Richard Ellmann's
definitive biography of Joyce to know that he abhorred journalistic
prying into his life. Joyce is of course implying that the Church
makes its own decisions regarding those it considers heretical and
excommunicates, and he himself is not concerned with *when* the
Church acknowledges his apostasy. Ernst, however, interprets
Joyce's reply to mean that "inside himself he had never left the
Church, try as he might have."[35] He goes on to quote Judge Wool-
sey, to whom he repeated the conversation: "Maybe Joyce's inner
conflict as to Catholicism explains why the secondary streams of
the non-Catholics in the book [*Ulysses*] are penciled with more
clarity than are the inner thinkings of the Catholics."[36] And Ernst
wonders why this observation has never been commented on by
students of Joyce! Perhaps the answer is obvious: that Joyce as a
heretic concerns himself in *Ulysses* with other members of the
spiritual exile of which he was then a part. And perhaps Merton
has already provided an answer when he indicated with what success Joyce had in his previous work provided the primary penciling
of the thinking of the Irish Catholic.

Lloyd Morris's account of Joyce's religious conflicts is particularly perplexing; it is based on a single incident of unusual circum-
stance, involving an American cleric named Edwards who had re-

nounced his cure because of religious doubts. Morris had arranged
a large party to which he invited Joyce, Ford Madox Ford, and Edwards, who he assumed was an acquaintance of Joyce. But (as
Morris tells it, in the third person),

> . . . soon after Edwards' arrival, he [Morris] became aware that Joyce
> and Ford had deserted the party. He . . . found them irately pacing
> the garden path in the darkness. It developed that the presence of an
> unfrocked priest was an affront to their piety, and the venom of their
> indignation left Morris stupefied; he had not even suspected the pos-
> sibility of an affront to Joyce, the acknowledged apostate, and Ford,
> who publicly flouted the sacrament of marriage! The matter was
> somehow patched up, but Morris was to receive another shock when,
> a few days later, he entered a favorite restaurant and was summoned
> to a table where Joyce and Ford and Edwards were peaceably enjoy-
> ing luncheon. On Joyce's part, the double somersault of attitude im-
> plied no hypocrisy; but it expressed the profound insecurity to which
> he was always vulnerable.[37]

Actually, this incident—and we have only Morris' account of it—
suggests only Morris' profound naïveté; it was obviously a typically Joycean hoax which Joyce and cohort Ford perpetrated on their
innocent host, and which they later shared with Edwards at lunch.
A reader of Ellmann's biography would recognize the symptoms of
this sort of legpull (carried off with perfect *sang-froid*), as would
Oliver St. John Gogarty, who knew Joyce a good deal better than
did Morris, and who reminds us that Joyce was known to assume
"an air of very great gravity . . . when about to perpetrate a
joke."[38] A profusion of such "grave" jokes—in verbal form—fill
the pages of *Finnegans Wake*.

But Morris, who assumed Joyce to be in earnest, goes on to discuss Joyce's attitudes to religion, asserting that Joyce's

> . . . attitude to the faith of his youth was an affair of subjective,
> possibly subconscious, factors that threaded through the fabric of his
> superstitions and fantasies. Of this, the Jesuits who had educated him
> were vividly aware; whenever Joyce's precarious health ebbed in pro-
> tracted illness, two of their emissaries appeared at his door, and re-

mained to await an anticipated revocation of his apostasy under the imminence of death.[39]

This is of course a different sort of observation from the tale of Joyce and the unfrocked priest: here Morris attempts to treat the troubled state of Joyce's rebellion, and it seems valid on the basis of such glimpses into those disturbed feelings to assert that Joyce might well have become the victim of his own apostasy, that the image of the Jesuit hell presented in *A Portrait* may have remained vivid with the arrival of each duo of Jesuit emissaries. In this context it seems appropriate to quote a Joyce limerick regarding the subject of that highly colored version of Jesuit hell found in the *Portrait* sermon; from a letter to Ezra Pound, dated 9 April 1917:

> There once was a lounger named Stephen
> Whose youth was most odd and uneven.
> He throve on the smell
> Of a horrible hell
> That a Hottentot wouldn't believe in.[40]

But his apostasy remained just that, and he could hardly be considered responsible for the frightful night visitors who descended upon him. Acknowledging that it might have been a tenacity born of fear, Morris delineates the determination with which Joyce clung to his refusal to serve:

> He was bereft of certitude or the hope of it; troubled, anxious, despairing, confronted by the shards and rubble of all that the spirit of man had lived by. It is good to know that, when death came, he did not falter; that he met eternity or extinction without surrender.[41]

It is Herbert Gorman's quotation, however, that best presents a complete configuration of Joyce's "religiosity." As Joyce's authorized biographer Gorman is sanctified by the authority of Joyce's blue pencil; his words are the apparent gospel that Joyce wanted us to read. A full examination of the context of the quotation extracted by Magalaner and Kain, therefore, becomes important. The passage reads:

he [Stephen] has tried the prop of his religion and found it a thing that buckles beneath him. We must never lose touch with this thread of religion in Joyce's work for it is everywhere evident. The Roman Catholic tenets that formed the child's mind, that frightened the child's body into shaking fits of vomiting, have so permeated the mentality of the man that it is at the back of practically every thought and action. There are times when Joyce writes impartially but we feel that behind these impartial sentences there is a far from impartial man. In order to write so he must lift the scourge to his own back. Roman Catholicism is in his bones, in the beat of his blood, in the folds of his brain and he cannot rest until it is either removed or clarified. It is his misfortune that it may never be removed. It will pervert his nature (it does so in "Ulysses") but it is there, twisted out of all resemblance to itself even in the frankest passages. The vivid, highly-functioning mind of the Stephen Dedalus of "A Portrait of the Artist as a Young Man" is the mind of a Mediaeval Catholic.* If the same mind had been twisted to the other side of the line it would have been the intense visioning of a religiast.[42]

This in its full form is quite different from the ambiguous statement about Joyce's beliefs. It is a paraphrase of the religious upbringing Joyce had described in his *Portrait,* and it clearly considers the intensity of that religious education and the violence of the reaction to it, acknowledging Joyce's removal to a position antithetical to religion (while underscoring the precarious balance that might have sent him hurtling into its confines instead). Moreover it offers the reader of Joyce the gist of the religious problem which all of his work contains: we are told to look for a *removal* or *clarification* of Joyce's doubts, a search that particularly concerns the reader in *Finnegans Wake.*

Gorman exhibits a common tendency to equate Stephen Dedalus with James Joyce to a maximum degree, and to this Kevin Sullivan, in *Joyce among the Jesuits,*[43] offers an important corrective— perhaps excessively. A balanced attitude toward what is Joyce and what is fiction should be established in terms of *what happens to Stephen,* the elements of Joyce's narrative which the author has

---

* "middayevil down to his vegetable soul," comments Shaun (423.28).

chosen to present (whether autobiographical or fictive in origin). An adolescent James A. Joyce need not have emerged vomiting from a Jesuit sermon for the significance of Stephen's reaction to exist for us underscored by the mature Joyce's powerful narrative. Gorman's biographies of Joyce are also suspect because of the complex situation in which he found himself: as Joyce's chosen biographer he can be relied upon presumably to record what Joyce wanted recorded (whether fact or fiction—Richard Ellmann's very different sort of biography indicates painfully enough Gorman's committed errors and omitted facts), but even this separation is inaccurate when we realize Joyce's capacity to allow a vast degree of free rein to his biographer in areas presumably where Joyce felt such errors did not matter. Thus we are treated to a melange of supportable facts, half-truths, and fictions that Joyce thought politic to plant at the time, and errors of fact or interpretation committed by Gorman that Joyce did not consider worth correcting. The large Gorman quotation above, therefore, should best be read as the ideas of one more commentator who knew Joyce.

To the list of Merton, Ernst, Morris, and Gorman, Arland Ussher adds "the pronouncement of T. S. Eliot that Joyce is the most orthodox of writers."[44] But this need not detain us in a review of Joyce's religious heterodoxy since Eliot explains that "we are not concerned with the authors' *beliefs,* but with orthodoxy of sensibility and with the sense of tradition."[45] This sort of quoting out of context, as well as the acceptance of critical conclusions rather than the actual substance of an interview, obscures an examination of the already complex nature of Joyce's attitudes. But in contrast to these occasional bits of shoddy scholarship there does exist a body of critical material that attempts to prove with exegetical evidence the contention that Joyce experienced a religious reacceptance. Of those who attest to the essentially Catholic quality of Joyce's work, few agree on the actual Catholic nature of that work. Ussher, for example, claims that Joyce actually rejected Catholicism, but that his work remains Catholic despite—or even because of—this rejection:

Joyce proves himself, most truly, a Catholic—even if he could only exhibit the Catholic temper by rejecting the Catholic faith, as he knew it. . . . The "lapsed" Catholic has in fact peculiar advantages as a comic writer, since he is usually free from the perils of didacticism; and the famous "subtlety" of Jesuitism is near to the comic spirit.[46]

On the basis of Ussher's concept of the "lapsed" Catholic with a "joking" Jesuit spirit, it is interesting to recall Merton's statement on Joyce's Irish Catholicism: in the same paragraph in which he mentions Joyce's abandonment of the Irish Catholic Church, Merton described the Dublin air of "physical and spiritual slums"[47] that drove Joyce from the Church. It is the Dublin Jesuit strain of Catholicism that Merton believes Joyce primarily rebelled against, and yet it is that same strain that Ussher feels remained with Joyce.

The "fashionable" commentators against whom Stanislaus Joyce commits himself have had their day to a great extent and have vanished from the critical arena. They consisted of reputable men who had their own religious axes to grind, or nonliterary personages who had for a moment looked over Joyce's shoulder and had come to conclusions on the basis of inexact and incomplete evidence, or members of Joyce's own "coterie" who were at times overimpressed by monumental matters that they did not fully comprehend. Their disappearance can be attributed primarily to their preoccupation with Joyce's *personal* attitudes, rather than with evaluating the "religious" content of his finished work. Certainly the difficult terrain of *Finnegans Wake* detection frightened many of them away. The first of the several commentaries that have attempted to weigh the significance of *Finnegans Wake* in terms of Joyce's "Catholicism" appeared in 1929 while the *Wake* was still in progress. Thomas McGreevy, a member of the Joyce Paris circle, contributed to the *Exagmination* volume an article titled "The Catholic Element in Work in Progress," in which he maintained that it is the "Irish" vein of Joyce's Catholicism that can be found in *Ulysses* and the early drafts of the *Wake,* but is careful to avoid crediting the Dublin Jesuits as well. Irish Catholicism, and Joyce's Catholicism as such, McGreevy insists, is superior to the "pastiche

Catholicism of many fashionable critics in England."[48] He equates Joyce's broad concept of Catholicism with Dante's and insists that an "intelligent Irishman" has a religion which differs from that of "temporary Romanizers."[49]

Having redefined Catholicism, McGreevy manages to work Joyce easily into his scheme of things. But as part of an "exagmination" of Joyce's new work which concerns itself ostensibly with "The Catholic Element in Work in Progress," McGreevy's essay is a strange document to read through. It begins with a note on the relationship of reality to fantasy (p. 119), goes on to discuss Joyce's creation of a new language (pp. 119–20) and his sense of order in *Ulysses* and the unfinished new work (p. 120), and then mentions the influence of Dante's *Purgatorio* and Vico's philosophy (*ibid.*). Next McGreevy discusses the difference between "regular" Catholics and "temporary" Catholics already mentioned, the Irish-Catholic interest in phantoms and devils (p. 121), and an English-Catholic censuring of *Ulysses* (pp. 121–22). A discussion of *Ulysses* as an *Inferno* (pp. 122–24) is followed by a statement that the purgatorial aspects of the new work lie in its "transitional" language, the "politically purgatorial side" of H.C.E., and the fact that Joyce is in transition becoming an artist. McGreevy now predicts that Joyce will write a *Paradiso* eventually (p. 125), describes the Viconian cycles (*ibid.*), and finds delight in the wonderful characters who appear in *Work in Progress* (pp. 125–26). The article concludes with a mention of the satire and time-consciousness in *Ulysses* (pp. 126–27).

As a key to the Catholicism in the embryonic *Wake,* McGreevy's eight pages would be scant enough if they were *all* devoted to the subject, but all that McGreevy can actually offer is the bland insistence that if Joyce is not a Catholic to suit Catholics, then Catholicism will have to be redefined to include James Joyce. To this he adds an assertion that Joyce's use of hellish characters in *Ulysses* is concomitant with elements of Irish Catholicism and that the new work is a *Purgatorio* primarily because Joyce is inventing a new language of unusual beauty. To the defects of his slight exposition

McGreevy adds a single quotation from *Work in Progress* and does very little justice to it: "*In the name of the former and of the latter and of their holocaust.* The former is surely the Eternal, the latter the world and the holocaust the world consumed by fire as pre-ordained from eternity."[50] There is no real basis for such an explication since nothing in the text suggests its feasibility—and nothing is offered by McGreevy to support it. Actually, Joyce's symbol for the Holy Trinity is quite an irreverent—but wholly Irish—one, the brand name of a Dublin whiskey, John Jameson and Son: "Messrs Jhon Jhamieson and Song . . . of the twelve apostrophes" (126.4-7).* Here Joyce's parody serves to reiterate an aspect of the Viconian cycle, the *former* representing the last stage, the *latter* representing the new first stage, and the *holocaust* the present age of chaos from which the cycle begins anew. McGreevy's orthodox interpretation is especially weak when one considers the implications of the "Holy Ghost" as *holocaust;* here as elsewhere in the *Wake* Joyce's attitude is that "ein and twee were never worth three" (246.15).

Of those critics who insist that Joyce's work remained Catholic even if Joyce himself did not, L. A. G. Strong presents the most complete system of reasoning. He asserts that the anti-Catholic elements of *Ulysses* and the *Wake* are the desperate measures of a mind attempting in vain to rid itself of the "net" of religion, that the omnipresence of these elements acknowledges the superior strength of the Church's dominance over the mind's efforts to escape. It is Joyce's unconscious Catholicism (like Ussher's tag of "lapsed" Catholicism and McGreevy's brand of "regular" Catholicism) which Strong credits:

Joyce was brought up as a Catholic, and never escaped. . . . Over

---

* The Moslem deity, incidentally, seems to be still another brand of Irish whiskey, Old Bushmills. The Arabic word *Besmellah* ("In the name of Allah") is contained in "Bussmullah" (292.n3), "Bushmillah" (521.15), "Bismillafoulties" (357.4), and simply "Bushmills" (577.21).

Ulysses as over the earlier work broods the sense of sin, that terrific spiritual legacy which the Catholic Church irrevocably leaves her children. . . . The blasphemies . . . are the desperate gestures of a man who is doomed to accept . . . certain Last Things. . . . This is not to say that Joyce remained a Catholic writer. But he is always a theologian. He still sees the world in terms of the faith in which he was brought up, and his struggles attest its power. . . . Joyce's rage is a tribute to the hold of the Church on his unconscious mind. . . .[51]

It is with his "spiritual entrails," Strong insists, "if not with his intellect,"[52] that Joyce acknowledges Death, Judgment, Heaven, and Hell. The concept of "spiritual entrails" ironically echoes Merton's "spiritual slums" of Irish Catholicism, and the unconscious hold suggests Morris's emissaries at death's door. The issue then becomes involved with the Church's refusal to allow autoexcommunication (as Ernst's "when" question indicated). That Joyce was perpetually concerned with the Catholic world he knew is undeniable, that he was essentially interested in theological enigmas is obvious, but that a sense of sin is necessarily Catholic, or that a spiritual interest in man is necessarily religious, remain moot points. Although Strong believes that the writing of *Finnegans Wake* was "in the fullest sense a religious task,"[53] he does not define "fullest sense," leaving us to assume that he means the previously described "unconscious hold." Having already attested that Joyce's conscious efforts were to escape from the Catholicism of his youth, Strong certainly cannot expect us to believe that the "religious task" was consciously pro-Catholic. And when he adds that the *Wake* "is, in the original sense of the word, catholic: all-including: universal,"[54] he further vitiates his case since the Koran and the Upanishads and the Book of the Dead are in that sense also catholic (but hardly Christian), as are the *Iliad* and the *Odyssey* and the *Aeneid* and *Beowulf* (none of which is necessarily religious).

The one attempt made by Strong to find a conscious assertion in *Finnegans Wake* of the triumph of the Catholic Church concerns the events occurring on page 573 of the *Wake*. Strong insists that "the supremacy of Rome over the Protestant churches is roundly asserted."[55] Campbell and Robinson, in reviewing the events of that page, had already exclaimed, "In the end James Joyce remains the son of Rome!"[56] It becomes important, therefore, to examine the context of this passage.

The physical locale is the conjugal bed of the Earwickers. With startling suddenness it has been transformed into a world of perversion and defilement. Bereft of humor or poetic language, the suspicious sexual undertones of the *Wake* are shockingly announced in the most obvious and insipid terms—the terminology of the law courts. The realm of literary love conventions is parodied in humorless form; the subject matter is sex in its most perverted and pandered guises: rape, prostitution, procuring, incest, homosexuality, sodomy, and so forth. With minute detail the stark facts are reviewed until the criminal court action evolves into a civil court action over international financial dealings, and it soon becomes apparent that under the disguise of high finance and low morals Joyce is once again concerned with theological disputes.

The basis of the dispute, as Strong and Campbell and Robinson maintain, is the Anglican Church's demands for the recognition of the Thirty-nine Articles—sexually they are Earwicker's "thirtynine several manners" (573.20) and financially they are his "thirtynine years among holders of Pango stock" (574.27-28). Sexually he has "rendered himself impotent to consummate by subdolence" (573.22-23). Joyce's unfavorable disposition toward Anglicanism is apparent; he associates the religious movement with the political, with British imperialism: "the valuse of thine-to-mine articles . . . links unto chains . . . civil-to-civil imperious gallants into gells (Irish), bringing alliving stone allaughing down to grave clothnails and a league of archers, fools and lurchers under the rude rule of fumb" (283.10-20), and therefore with religious persecution in Ireland (in the Tale of Jarl van Hoother and the Prankquean and elsewhere); in the "story line" of the *Wake* this is represented by Earwicker's indiscretion in Phoenix Park: "my dudud dirtynine articles" (534.12). But this admission that the Anglican Church is impotent—as the Protestant Earwicker proves to be at this climactic moment—no more makes Joyce the son of Rome than it does of Jerusalem, or of Mecca, or of the Ganges. In the criminal court action the Roman Church is represented by "Sulla, an orthodox savage" who leads "a band of twelve mercenaries, the Sullivani" (573.6-7) and by "four excavators" named "Gregorious, Leo, Vitellius and Macdugalius" (573.8). Their names suggest Ireland and Rome (as well as the twelve apostles and the four evangelists), and they prove to be as depraved and as licentious as the rest of the participants in the case.

Had Strong or the authors of the *Skeleton Key* gone on to examine the civil court action as thoroughly as they did the criminal one, they might have found that the theological dispute assumes many interesting facets. Through the difficulty of the mock-trial terminology one discerns "Tangos, Limited" as representing the Roman Church, and "Pango, Limited" the Anglican. Tangos comprises a senior partner, identified as *Brerfuchs* (Br'er Fox), *Breyfawkes* (Guy Fawkes), and *Brakeforth* or *Breakfast* (Pope Adrian IV), and a junior partner: *Warren, Barren, Sparrem* and *Wharrem* at various instances. The *Skeleton Key* identifies the senior partnership with the Rome-Vienna-Madrid axis and the junior with Ireland.[57] Anglicanism is here suing the Roman Church for tithes due; they had been paid with a bad check (written by the senior partner). Ireland (in the person of Ann Doyle—the traditional "poor old woman"—the Shan Van Vocht, Dark Rosaleen, Kathleen ni Houlihan) wants to merge with *Monsignore Pepigi,* apparently a representative of Rome. The court rules that Anglicanism is dead ("no property in law can exist in a corpse"); that Rome has nothing to offer ("Pepigi's pact was pure piffle"); and that Ireland is out of luck ("Wharrem would whistle for the rhino"— 576.5-7). The churches of Rome and England will never reunite: "Will you, won't you, pango with Pepigi? Not for Nancy, how dare you do!" (576.7-8). So Ireland (Nancy-Ann) is abandoned still.

But if the Strong-Campbell-Robinson thesis that *Finnegans Wake* is a Catholic document is weak because it is based on a single debatable point, the same thesis proffered by Niall Montgomery is stronger because it is detailed and well-documented. Montgomery succeeds in doing what McGreevy set out to do several decades earlier; with the completed text and over a decade of post-publication scholarship at his disposal, he is able to determine the Catholic elements of the *Wake*. His announced intention is to prove "that Joyce is of the line and stature of Dante; that his art, too, is visionary . . . that the eyes blinded by its splendour and by its order are Irish and Catholic as Dante's were Italian and Catholic."[58] He does this by negating the heavy influence of "the Koran, the Rig-Vedas, the Book of the Dead and other religious codes" in order to stress that "the basic symbols are Catholic, with Irish overtones."[59] This contention is not worth disputing either, since Joyce sought to investigate mankind through history, sexual behavior, and religion, and although he employed as many religions as he had managed to study, he nonetheless basically employed the one religious school of thinking he knew best, Catholicism. Again this is not a valid test of acceptance or rejection.

Montgomery begins by pointing out the omnipresence of the concept of Original Sin in *Finnegans Wake,* finding twenty puns for St. Augustine's exclamation of *"O felix culpa!"*[60] What Montgomery fails to perceive is that Joyce is utilizing the Adam-Eve incident as myth, a myth that embodies man's feelings of sexual guilt. He employs Christian and Hebraic myths, as he does various Islamic, Hindu, pagan, and secular myths, as representative of mankind: he cuts across all religions and beliefs to include the entire realm of man in his universal guise. That the concept of Original Sin is prevalent among these myths is hardly accidental (any more than its use is piously Catholic): it is logically the most perfect mythical form for man's attitude toward his own sexual existence. It is as basic in the *Wake* as the Odysseus myth is basic in *Ulysses* and Daedalus-Icarus in *A Portrait.* This does not make *Finnegans Wake* any more Catholic than the previous works are made pagan by the Greek myths. Man's sexual existence did not begin with the publication of the Old Testament, and Joyce's application of the "happy fault" is not necessarily St. Augustine's. J. Mitchell Morse comments that

> Innocence and insight come from within, and he who will have one must forgo the other. This is the native quirk of our species. The original sin was intellectual curiosity, the quality that set Adam apart from the other animals. It alienated him from nature, which asks no questions and tells itself no lies. The peculiarly human quality is inherently sinful: to be fully human is to be cast out from grace.[61]

Morse therefore finds Joyce's use of the myth to be not only secular, but actually a negation of the Catholic principle.

Nor does Joyce's presentation of the Holy Trinity limit itself to a proper portrayal of the Catholic version: as has been indicated, the Trinity in the *Wake* is a bottle of Irish whiskey, but what is even more important is that it does not comprise a father, a son, and the interceding spirit of the father, but a father and his two sons. Joyce is concerned here with the trio of Isaac, Jacob, and Esau (Earwicker, Shem, and Shaun). His approach is again secular rather than spiritual (the only spirit content in Joyce's Trinity is alcoholic). Harry Levin identifies the trio: "When they [the sons] are Jacob and Esau . . . their father is the father of the Home Rule movement, Isaac Butt. A name to conjure with, John Jameson, is a potent symbol for this unholy trinity."[62]

As Levin implies, Joyce's logic supersedes Biblical logic in the *Wake*: he uses whatever material fits into his scheme of things no matter where he may find it, and he is willing to alter, deface, deform, subvert, and pervert without a qualm any material that may suit his ends. Joyce squares many a circle to wedge a square peg into a round hole. With that "meticulosity bordering on the insane" he scrambles Biblical text, as Morse indicates in his study of Joyce's treatment of the important Isaac-Jacob-Esau tale. Since Cain is Joyce's hero and Abel his bourgeois villain, we have a rather bizarre misreading of Genesis, and the Jacob whom Christians accept as a prefiguration of Christ is ironically also Shem, and therefore also Cain. As Morse proves: "Here we have an amalgamerging of the blessed Jacob with the cursed Cain—for were they not both types of the artist? Jacob 'sod pottage' (Genesis 25:29); Cain built the first city (Genesis 4:17); Shem 'sod town' (224)."[63] And in viewing this strange Shem-Cain-Jacob configuration, Morse adds: "But this directly opposes the orthodox view, which is that Esau is analogous to Cain, and Jacob to Abel."[64]

Along with the Trinity and Original Sin, Montgomery sees other Catholic aspects of *Finnegans Wake*: he finds the mirror imagery of the *Wake* a manifestation of man as made in God's image (pp. 439-40), and credits God with having created the polarity of good and evil which Joyce employs (p. 447). Such aspects are of course primarily a matter of Montgomery's interpretation: if he chooses to see divine inspiration in the split personality of the mirror-girl Issy, he puts himself in the position of necessarily having to defend vanity and sexual rivalry as the image of God. The dichotomy of good and evil is apparent in the *Wake,* but it is Montgomery who credits God with their creation, not Joyce (unless Montgomery intends supplementing his essay with documentation showing the hand of Joyce acknowledging the hand of God). Montgomery interprets Joyce's perspective as visionary and proclaims him a "seer" (p. 441), although this attribute too need not be considered the exclusive property of the Catholic artist. Nor is the use of the pun exclusively Catholic, although Montgomery cites Christ's pun on the building of the Church on the rock which is Peter (pp. 441-42).

Joyce's delight with Christ's pun is well known; it is echoed in the *Wake* in an allusion to the Last Supper: "for my thurifex, with Peter Roche, that frind of my boozum, leaning on my cubits" (449.15-17). Nevertheless one cannot help wondering how far removed Peter Roche is from the Nasty Roche of *A Portrait,* or about the extent to which a *frind of my boozum* is a drinking companion, the suggestion of an indelicate pun with "peter," and the further suggestion that rock here means the same sort of rocks that Molly Bloom mentions in *Ulysses* (used as an expletive obviously to mean testicles). In fact, "rocks" has this same meaning in various instances in the *Wake*: when the "rocks by the stream Oconee exaggerated themselse" (3.7)—the father engendering his progeny; and Shem's "yours till the rending of the rocks" (170.23-24).

Joyce no doubt admired the pun per se and admired Christ for punning, but certainly he sought to outdo Christ's pun with several thousands of his own (incorporating Christ's in the process):

> *the figure of a fellowchap in the wohly ghast, Popey O'Donoshough, the jesuneral of the russuates. The idolon exhibisces the seals of his orders: the starre of the Son of Heaven, the girtel of Izodella the Calottica, the cross of Michelides Apaleogos, the latchet of Jan of Nepomuk, the puffpuff and pompom of Powther and Pall, the great belt, band and bucklings of the Martyrology of Gorman. It is for the castomercies mudwake surveice. The victar* [349.18-25].

Here in a sequence from the Crimean War episode of "How Buckeley Shot the Russian General" Joyce characterizes the general as an Irish Pope, and a Jesuit at that, who is going to be shot; the war is once again given religious sanction (Peter and Paul punned with powder and ball), and here as elsewhere the irreverence of Joyce's puns suggests that as an artist he is rivaling not only the God of the Creation, but also the Christ Who Punned. As such he is seen toppling "the hoose that Joax pilled" (369.15).

Much of Montgomery's essay loses itself in circular reasoning and arbitrary deductions. He sees the "wake" motif as Catholic and the pagan Phoenix as Irish because of the "cases of the 'sacrifice' of a saviour by the Irish people" (p. 442). He decides that Earwicker is building a church at Chapelizod and scrambles the initials that represent Earwicker and Anna Livia into CHAPEL, the end result being a quest for the letters "HCE" in various disconnected words of the "Mass for the Dedication of a Church," until he arrives at the theory that "ALP is also the Blessed Virgin" (p. 444). If this is so, then Joyce's irony is again apparent since he has taken the trouble to reveal that his heroine and hero are both Protestants, "free kirk" (559.29) and "episcopalian" (559.26) respectively. Nor is the Virgin as instrumental in the framework of *Finnegans Wake* as Montgomery contends. Anna Livia is the archetypal Woman, and it is hardly inconsistent with her all-inclusiveness to find that she incorporates the *persona* of the Virgin among her masks. But her masks include Mohammed's wife Aysha: *"He Calls Me his Dual of Ayessha"* (105.19-20), her *aye* and *yes* recalling Molly's final promiscuous "yes" to life. And she is worshiped in a combined Christian-Moslem-Hindu form in the invocation to her "mamafesta" chapter: "In the name of Annah the Allmaziful, the Everliving, the Bringer of Plurabilities, haloed be her eve, her singtime sung, her rill be run, unhemmed as it is uneven!" (104.1-3).

Anna Livia, however, is bereft of the basic Catholic nature of the Virgin,* as Louis Gillet comments, since the "harmony, which Catholic piety expresses by the figures of mother and son as a Maternity which is sufficient in itself, Joyce sees rather as dependent upon men, an exclusively male mystery."[65] Montgomery mistakes the parts for the whole; the edifice that is in erection is something more than a Catholic chapel: it is a city, a wall, a tower, a fortress, a skyscraper. It may well contain a chapel *within* its confines—although it seems highly probable that the "chapel" in the *Wake* is a public convenience, not a place of worship. Many of what Montgomery finds as the Catholic elements in *Finnegans Wake* are its *catholic* elements, but it is fundamental to the understanding of Joyce's epic of contemporary man to realize that essentially he is describing modern Christian society, and for Joyce the roots of that

---

* It is Issy in fact who plays the part of the Blessed Virgin in the *Wake,* and what an irreligious part it is! Identified in her bedroom as "marygold to crown" (561.21) and "Mother of moth!" (561.27), she is invoked in exceedingly erotic terms, preceded by the basic warning: "Add lightest knot unto tiptition. O Charis! O Charissima! A more intriguant bambolina could one not colour up out of Boccuccia's Enameron. Would one but to do apart a lilybit her virginelles and, so, to breath, so, therebetween, behold, she had instant with her handmade as to graps the myth inmid the air" (561.22-26). The annunciation brought to Mary is described as: "I will to show herword in flesh. Approach not for ghost sake! It is dormition!" (561.27-28). Her predecessor, the Gerty MacDowell of *Ulysses,* lame, vain, and sexually curious as she was, is but a mild parody of the Blessed Virgin compared to Issy. Anyone searching the map of Ireland for "Knockmaree, Comty Mea" (186.25) seeks in vain; the direction is to the "Blessed" Issy, pregnant ("knocked up"), a successor to the "Cunty Kate" of the Circe scene in *Ulysses.*

society are Catholic, if only because it was from the basic Roman tree that the Protestant splinters were hewn.

The subtleties and erudition of Montgomery's essay seem to have changed the style of approach by critics eager to remake Joyce in the Church's image. No longer do they cry in ecstasy, "In the end James Joyce remains the son of Rome!" A closer devotion to chapter and verse becomes the method of exploration, and a series of hints, suggestions, asides, and innuendoes the method of statement. Even Robinson has since taken his lead from Montgomery, and his essay, "Hardest Crux Ever,"[66] is a tribute to the intricacies of *Finnegans Wake*, a cavern in which shouts of "Eureka!" soon fade into the endless expanse. Robinson's attempt to determine the significance of the choice of letters H, C, and E for the Joycean hero ("Why H.C.E.? Why not B.G.O., X.T.U., or any other combination of two consonants and a vowel to designate the male character dominating the *Wake*?" he asks[67]) arrives at the *"Hoc est enim corpus meum"* and *"Hic est enim calix sanguinis mei"* of the Catholic Mass.[68] The discovery is not an inaccurate one nor is it an insignificant one, although one may quibble along certain lines. Why H.C.E. instead of H.E.C.? or, better still, H.E.E.C.? The latter is not out of the question; there are many people with four names, and Joyce himself was transformed from a simple J.A.J. into James Augustine Aloysius Joyce by the Catholic Church and could have signed himself with the *sigla* J.A.A.J. How much more appropriate, therefore, that his hero be H.E.E.C.

That Earwicker personifies the crucified God of the Christian churches has long since been recognized and accepted. So does Leopold Bloom. And the H, the E's, and the C of the formula for the Transubstantiation obviously occurred to Joyce during the composition of the *Wake* and were employed by him as such. But in a list of 216 h.c.e.'s offered by Robinson in his essay, only *one* actually echoes the Mass pattern: "he is ee and no counter" (29.34), while a second at least has a possible "h.e.c." pattern: "How elster is he a called" (197.7-8). If Robinson's question about the *sigla* is not a rhetorical one, more of an answer than he provides can be found for him in evidence already common knowledge. The surname Earwicker derives from "earwig," the important *perce-oreille* that conjures up the surrogate of Persse O'Reilly for the hero. "Naw, yer maggers, aw war jist a cotchin on thon bluggy earwuggers" (31.10-11), says the surnameless H.C., and the name Earwicker was thus attached to him by the delighted monarch, pleased to find in his kingdom a "surtrusty bailiwick a turnpiker who is by turns a pikebailer no seldomer than an earwigger!" (31.26-28). The H for Humphrey is no less difficult because of the important key word designating Earwicker's guilt, "Hesitency" (35.20), also found in "hesitency" (82.30) and "HeCitEncy!" (421.23), plus a possible glance at the Humpty of Humpty Dumpty at this point. The intermediate C seems a bit more arbitrary. "Chimpden" seems to imply Earwicker's descent from the primates. A three-part construction could be understood in terms of H, the Cosmic Egg, Humpty Dumpty; C, the chimpanzee, man's predecessor; E, the man, *Homo sapiens,* Everybody. Another such construction could parallel the development of the Parent-Children-People transition which the *Skeleton Key* attaches to the first three books of the *Wake,* from King "Harold" (30.21) or "Duke Humphrey" (405.18) to "Childers" (535.34) or "Childeric" (4.32) to "Everybody" (32.19), "E'erawan" (46.1), "Eavybrolly" (315.20), "Ebblybally" (612.15), and so forth. (Without statedly intending to offset Robinson's H-C-E theory, Mabel P. Worthington has offered the possibility that the letters were chosen because of their significance in terms of "Host-Chalice-Eucharist"[69] —and this, with Robinson's *hoc-hic est enim corpus-calix* and Montgomery's HCE plus ALP equals CHAPEL, offers us an ecclesiastical trinity of possibilities.)

Among the subtleties of the apparently "orthodox" offerings of recent vintage are two volumes of different complexions, *Joyce and Aquinas* and *Joyce among the Jesuits.* The former, by Jesuit Father William T. Noon, is a work of analytical precision that attempts to weigh and evaluate the quantity and quality of Joyce's knowledge and use of St. Thomas Aquinas, and, except to remind us that Joyce remained faithful in his own fashion to the Divine Doctor throughout his literary career, there is no attempt on the part of Father Noon to make any judgment of Joyce's "Catholic residue." The latter volume, on the other hand, by layman Kevin Sullivan, purports to be only a biography of Joyce's schooling at the hands of the Society of Jesus, but Sullivan's sympathies shine through the thin veneer far too often for his study to be accepted as objective biography. What emerges in lieu of a study of Joyce is an apology for Jesuit education in Ireland during the nineteenth century. At every turn where he feels that Jesuits have been maligned, Sullivan takes it upon himself to vindicate the Order as a body and the individual Jesuit as a person.

Sullivan's most heroic efforts are in demolishing the "prejudices" of Joyce's official biographer, Herbert Gorman (and surely no one can accuse Gorman of having been subtle in stating the case against Catholicism), but although Gorman proves to be an easy whipping boy for Sullivan's tongue-lashings, others closer to the "facts" Sullivan seeks to present are not: against such formidable opponents as Joyce himself, Stanislaus Joyce, and J. F. Byrne, Sullivan is not quite so successful. The "facts" remain that at Clongowes Wood Joyce had the benefit of exceptional Jesuit instruction, but only for a scant handful of his early years; at Belvedere Joyce received only adequate schooling and excelled as a scholar; and at University College Joyce was exposed to a pitifully inadequate curriculum and had to find his "education" elsewhere during these important years. Sullivan would have Joyce be infinitely grateful for Clongowes Wood, thoroughly satisfied with Belvedere, and sympathetically understanding about U.C.D. The view that emerges from *Joyce among the Jesuits* is that if Joyce did not consider himself fortunate for what he received from the Jesuits, he was an ingrate, although Sullivan can never quite bring himself to admit that Joyce was not properly grateful.

Throughout the book Sullivan shows himself to be rather uncomfortable with his chosen subject, and only when he deals with Tom Kettle, Joyce's contemporary at U.C.D. and obviously a very different sort of fish, does he seem to be at ease, since Kettle never showed signs of being ungrateful to the Jesuits who educated him. But Kettle's meager talents were truncated by his early death in the Great War, while ingrate Joyce went on to write his highly charged chapters in the moral history of his country. Not to be overlooked, however, is Sullivan's comment that both Joyce and Kettle shared an "Irish Catholic sense of doom,"[70] the orthodoxy of which one would suppose to be somewhat questionable. An echo of the "doom sense" can also be heard in the introductory article by Brian Nolan to the James Joyce Special Number of *Envoy,* where Joyce is implicated again in "the sense of doom that is the heritage of the Irish Catholic."[71]

Considering the sort of book that *Joyce among the Jesuits* is, it might not be proper or necessary to quibble about small particulars, but Sullivan's explication of the "jesuit bark and bitter bite" phrase from the *Wake* (182.36) is nonetheless disconcerting. Having ascertained that *bark* can be medicinal in meaning here, he goes on to offer the interpretation that Joyce is paying homage to the Jesuits, rather than vilifying them:

> The man [Joyce] is remembering the Jesuits of his boyhood not as a contemptible breed (whose bark is worse than their bite) but as physicians of the soul who were concerned that the fevers of adolescence should not be soulcontracted into a chronic disease of life. They may have succeeded all too well. This bitter bite (in *Ulysses* "the agenbite of inwit"), under Jesuit medication, resulted in a form of spiritual cinchonism from which, it would appear, Joyce was never fully to recover.[72]

The operation was a success but the patient died, implies Sullivan, and expects his reader to believe that the patient was (and should have been) grateful. Even if one is satisfied with the explication of *bark, bitter bite* remains unequivocal. It is not surprising that both Sullivan and J. Mitchell Morse have chapters titled "Jesuit Bark and Bitter Bite" in their studies of Joyce's Catholicism, but the difference between the chapters is extraordinary.

In contrast to more dogmatic approaches one can find the view expressed by a supposedly "liberal" Catholic (American, of course) in *Commonweal,* where Sam Hynes, in commenting on "The Catholicism of James Joyce," contends: "And so Joyce (through Stephen) can make his compromise with Catholicism, rejecting its morality and employing it merely as a source of aesthetics, of symbols and of ritualistic structures. The result is Catholicism with the religion squeezed out."[73] This is certainly a liberal view from a Catholic layman in a Catholic publication no matter what its political shade may be. Yet, having allowed himself this heterodox an opinion, Professor Hynes seems unable to resist taking part of it back before his article is ended, and his final paragraph contains the surprising statement: "It is no glib paradox, then, to call Joyce a 'Catholic' writer in the same sense that Hopkins and Greene are Catholic."[74] In whatever sense that may be, Gerard Manley Hopkins and Graham Greene can hardly be accused of having squeezed their religion out of themselves to produce their "Catholicism." The only other "sense" in which Hopkins and Greene are mentioned elsewhere in Hynes's article is as converts to Catholicism, and no matter what Joyce was or wanted to be, he could never have been that.

Perhaps the most liberal attitude taken by a Catholic critic of Joyce's rebellion is displayed by Father Noon in his published address on "James Joyce and Catholicism."[75] Having given up on the apostate as regrettably lost to the Church, Father Noon actually goes on to question "the stress placed on original sin" in Joyce's *Wake,* and finds it "too emphatic." Moreover, he proceeds to comment on Joyce's "often called Catholic emphases, which seem to me to betray an un-Catholic, and, for the most part, an un-Christian understanding of the structure of reality, and of modern man's situation in his world." Finding that "a personal avowal of faith is absent from Joyce's work," Father Noon also underscores the "Joycean confusion of myth with theology," which he terms "perhaps, the most pervasive heresy of modern literature. I do believe it heavily qualifies the Catholic theological affirmations of Joyce in a secularist, pessimistic sense."[76]

Viewing Joyce from the vantage point of his own religion, the Catholic cleric, despite obvious personal sympathies with the ex-Catholic author, allows his clear evaluation of Joyce's position to become rather hazy at times. Having once accused Joyce of "pessimism," Father Noon adds that Joyce "fails to appreciate the goodness of man, fails to see, or, at least, to record what William Faulkner has called the 'compassion and sacrifice and endurance of man.'" (Critics of such divergent stress as Father Noon and David Daiches, not to mention Karl Radek, are equally concerned with Joyce's nonhumanitarianism.) But Father Noon, besides finding pessimism in Joyce, also comments that "much of Vico's optimism has come over into *Finnegans Wake*." This single comment, however, must be counterbalanced by the two previous negative judgments, to which can be added a laconic third: "Joyce despairs of man."[77] One wonders whether what Sullivan found as an "Irish Catholic sense of doom" has any direct relationship with the "despair" found by Father Noon.

A cogent example of the orthodox Irish inability as yet to swallow James Joyce with all his thorns can be found in the *Envoy* Special Number previously alluded to. In what one supposes to be an issue planned as an "appreciation" of the native Irish genius, an overwhelming pall can be discerned in which almost every contributor feels it necessary either to sneer at American scholars dissecting Joyce or to provide some sort of commentary on Joyce's Catholicism—usually both. A good deal of self-conscious "humor" is disseminated in an effort to make Joyce palatable, most of it tangential. Efforts to explain Joyce away are apparent throughout, but most particularly in the Brian Nolan introduction already mentioned:

> It seems to me that Joyce emerges, through curtains of salacity and blasphemy, as a truly fear-shaken Irish Catholic, rebelling not so much against the Church but against its near-schism Irish eccentricities, its pretence that there is only one Commandment, the vulgarity of its edifices, the shallowness and stupidity of many of its ministers.[78]

If enough such oblique and elliptical admissions are grafted together, there might not be enough left of the Catholic Church for orthodox Catholics to return Joyce to.

It is important, in the light of so much contradictory evidence, to reintroduce at this interval Herbert Gorman's assertion that Joyce's Catholic roots remained primarily medieval. There is actually little of "modern" Catholicism in the *Wake;* Joyce dredges deep into Church history (another nightmare underlying the Finnegan dreamwork), reviewing the concept of papal infallibility, the position of the Virgin in Catholic dogma, the teachings of the Jesuits, the indexing of prohibited books, the significant Filioque Controversy, and Church meddling in politics. The conversation with Joyce in Zurich recorded by Frank Budgen provides an interesting key:

> "What I can't understand," he said, "is, why do they boggle at the infallibility of the Pope if they can swallow all the rest." The Holy Roman Catholic Apostolic Church in its Irish form was a net he had flown by, but having won the freedom he needed, he could admire the Church as an institution going on its own way unperturbed in obedience to the law of its own being. "Look, Budgen," he said. "In the nineteenth century, in the full tide of rationalist positivism and equal democratic rights for everybody, it proclaims the dogma of the infallibility of the head of the Church and also that of the Immaculate Conception.[79]

The Popes who parade through the *Wake* are far from perfect: Adrian IV is of course the primary example of a Pope who misuses his powers for political purposes, and in the Mookse-Gripes fable Joyce caricatures Adrian IV with "vacticanated" ears (152.23) as a "dogmad Accanite" (158.3) who "could not all hear" (158.12-13). *Dogmad* not only implies "mad dog" and "dogmamad," but also "Goddam" when each syllable is reversed. Other Popes are added to Adrian in this scene: "clement, urban, eugenious and celestian in the formose of good grogory humours" (154.20-21) offers five papal names suggesting physical well-being under the influence of drink.

Joyce's attitude toward the Jesuits is mentioned by two of the *Exagmination* commentators, and they contradict each other. Mc-Greevy's assertion that Joyce retained basic Jesuitical teachings is countered by Robert McAlmon's statement that Joyce "damned intellectually the religious and metaphysical logics of Jesuitism, emphatically, and of Christianity as a whole, generally, for the effects they had on him and his race and his realization of what they have done to the emotions of people."[80] And, whereas McGreevy conditions his stress on Joyce's retention of Jesuitism by attributing it to an unconscious influence, McAlmon qualifies his negative by adding that "it probably was not his intent"[81] (although the term "realization" hardly suggests an "unconscious" condition).

But Joyce's attitude toward the Jesuitical practice of censorship is never equivocal: "—Ask my index, mund my achilles, swell my obolum, woshup my nase serene, answered the Mookse" (154.18-19). And much is made of official Catholic reaction to the works of James Joyce: "when Robber and Mumsell, the pulpic dictators, on the nudgment of their legal advisers, Messrs Codex and Podex, and under his own benefiction of their pastor Father Flammeus Falconer, boycotted him of all muttonsuet candles and rome-ruled stationery for any purpose" (185.1-5). Joyce here reviews the incidents relating to the ten-year campaign of attrition to have *Dubliners* published, the bickering with George Roberts (*Robbers*), and Maunsell and Co. (*Mumsell*), the burning of the manuscript by the moralistic Dublin printer John Falconer (*Flammeus Falconer*), and Joyce's constant suspicion that behind the scenes moved the unseen hand of the Catholic clergy (the Pope, the Index, the Code are condensed into *Codex* and *Podex**). Having announced his intention of damning Jesuit torpedoes and continuing his literary pursuits, Shem the Penman delivers his incantation in butchered Church Latin for making ink from his own excrement in order to write "over every square inch of the only fool-

---

* That both codex and podex have unpunned literal meanings does not mitigate the significance of these puns in context, but actually augments and diversifies them.

scap available, his own body" (185.35-36) and levels a final blast at Jesuits in general and their General Loyola in particular:

> on his last public misappearance, circling the square, for the deathfête of Saint Ignaceous Poisonivy, of the Fickle Crowd (hopon the sexth day of Hogsober, killim our king, layum low!) and brandishing his bellbearing stylo, the shining keyman of the wilds of change, if what is sauce for the zassy is souse for the zazimas [186.11-16].

Joyce will not let the Jesuits forget their infamous role in the destruction of Charles Stewart Parnell, and this passage re-echoes "Ivy Day in the Committee Room" and its reference to the death of the "uncrowned king" destroyed by clerical conspiracy and Irish narrow-mindedness.

Such Church intervention in Irish politics, rather than providing the "sacrificial king" that Montgomery conjures up, is interpreted by Joyce as having done the sacrificing, as the events of the Mookse-Gripes fable and Tangos-Pango trial indicate. The scheme of *Finnegans Wake* allows for a continuous amalgamation of incidents centered on the overrunning of Ireland by invaders on religious "missions." The theme of "holy war" is prevalent in the character of the Woman who engenders the conflict by inciting the sexual rivalry of the males; thus Anna Livia Plurabelle's surname contains the elements of *pia et pura bella.* Joyce depicts Shem as refusing to participate in such a war (although his attempts to win the affections of the flower girls belie his intentions of neutrality), even when it is the Easter Rebellion of the "mobbu . . . chanting the Gillooly chorus, from the Monster Book of Paltryattic Puetrie, *O pura e pia bella!* . . . in secular sinkalarum" (178.15-18). And the extent to which religious intervention is allied with political expansion, invasion, and exploitation becomes apparent when St. Patrick, destined to become the patron saint of Ireland, is himself identified with the stream of invaders: the coming of Patrick as a bishop to Ireland is characterized in the last chapter of the *Wake* in the same format in which the continental invaders arrived in the first chapter. There Mutt and Jute in dialogue form embodied the native interviewing the invaders, the Danes (*donsk*), Norse (*scowegian*), Angles (*anglease*), Saxons (*saxo*), and finally the Jute himself (16-18). The coming of Patrick to convert the Irish is paralleled with the coming of Strongbow in 1170 to conquer them:

> he landed in ourland's leinster of saved and solomnones for the twicehecame time, off Lipton's strongbowed launch the *Lady Eva,* in a tan soute of sails he converted it's nataves, name saints, young ordnands, maderaheads and old unguished P. T. Publikums, through the medium of znigznaks with sotiric zeal . . . (Gratings, Mr Dane!) . . . and showed em the celestine way to by his tristar and his flop hattrick and his perry humdrum dumb and numb nostrums that he larned in Hymbuktu, and that same galloroman cultous is very prevailend up to this windiest of landhavemiseries all over what was beforeaboots a land of nods [288.13-25].

The commingling here of the political invasion and the divine mission can be seen in the references to Strongbow (*strongbowed*), the leader of the invasion forces of Henry II; his Irish bride Eva (*Lady Eva*); his cohort Sir Tristram (*tristar*); as well as to the Danish ruler in Dublin in 1014, Sitric (*sotiric*); and to St. Patrick (*flop hattrick*), his shamrock (*tristar*), hymn (*Hymbuktu*), Roman Catholicism (*galloroman cultous*), soutane (*tan soute*), Paternoster (*perry nostrums*), and "Lord, have mercy!" (*landhavemiseries*). The Danish and Anglo-Norman invaders are strange bedfellows for the patron saint of Ireland, but Joyce is explicit in asserting that the bringing of Christianity to Ireland was not motivated by Christian kindness, but was an act of aggression—Cromwell and King Billy also came as future patron saints (Puritan and Anglican)—and, like other conquests, Patrick's was readily absorbed by the natives.

In the last book of the *Wake* Mutt and Jute have been transformed into Muta (the mutate) and Juva (the rejuvenated, the Java Man); history has come full circle as was foreshadowed in the beginning—"Mearmerge two races, swete and brack" (17.24)—and they stand on a similar hill watching St. Patrick land. A pagan Archdruid comes forth to interview the bearer of Christianity. "Ad Piabelle et Purabelle?" asks Muta; "At Winne, Woermann og

Sengs," answers Juva (610.21-22). Patrick's holy war results in the secular pleasures of victory for some, woe for others, and the spilling of blood for all. It is Patrick's defeat of the Archdruid that delineates a major aspect of Joyce's condemnation of the Catholic mind of his day: the Archdruid, strongly resembling the Irish metaphysician George Berkeley, represents profound philosophic thought, while Patrick is a simple-minded, hard-headed man of action. As the *Skeleton Key* explicates:

> St. Patrick . . . unable to follow the trend of the druid's transcendentalist argument, knows well enough how to give a popular reply. As the representative of the Rock of Peter he is the protagonist of effective action. He simply cuts the gloriously involved Gordian knot of metaphysics with a sharp, good-enough retort, and wins from the populace a triumphant cheer.[82]

The campaigning politician and military hero, St. Patrick is also referred to in this episode as the "Eurasian Generalissimo" (610.12-13), and the theme of imperialism-condoned-by-the-Church is once again underscored. The Crimean War episode (338-55) had fully developed the motif of imperialism, and this later section implicates Patrick; he represents the practicality and political schemings of the Church (as the Mookse did). Morse comments that the Mookse's brutality indicates "the persistence of Joyce's conviction that the church was not spiritual but anti-spiritual. The brother who stands for the church in *Finnegans Wake* is Esau, not Jacob. However . . . the mature Joyce rejected the spiritual as well as the political and social aspects of Christianity."[83] As the Inquisitors deduce from their interview with Yawn (addressed as "Mr Trickpat"): "Hood maketh not frere. The voice is the voice of jokeup, I fear. Are you imitation Roma now or Amor now" (487.21-23). The Church of Rome and Christian Love are antithetical; simply because it calls itself a church does not mean that it is spiritual.

At every instance in which the Roman Church alienated itself from its followers, at every schism in its history, and at various accusations of heresy,* Joyce the anti-Catholic pauses to identify. The Stephen who in the *Portrait* was concerned because Bruno had been "terribly burned" is the Joyce who is investigating Church history in *Finnegans Wake*. Rome's quarrel with the Irish Church is recorded in the Mookse-Gripes episode; the split with the Church of England makes up the Tangos-Pango affair; the schism that created the Greek Orthodox Church in 1054 is mentioned in the reference to its founder, "Michael, *vulgo* Cerularius" (573.4), and the issue that caused the schism is discussed in the Mookse-Gripes controversy:

> the acheporeoozers of his haggyown pneumax to synerethetise with the breadchestviousness of his sweeatovular ducose sofarfully the logger-thuds of his sakellaries were fond at variance with the synodals of his somepooliom and his babskissed nepogreasymost got the hoof from his philioquus [156.13-18].

* Professor Morse's chapter on John Scotus Erigena, "The Erigenal Sin: Irish John," coupled with his comments on St. Thomas Aquinas' early position as a heretic in "Art and Fortitude: Applied Aquinas," indicates something of the range of such inclusions of heretics and heresies in the *Wake*. Although a handful of the allusions listed below may be doubtful, most of them can be corroborated in the *Census* or *The Books at the Wake:*

Acacius: 160.12
Albigenses: 240.13, 350.31, 488.35
Arius: 75.2, 440.7, 530.18
Bruno: 117.12, 246.32, 287.24, 336.35, 369.8 (plus many others associated
    with Browne and Nolan)
Donatus: 563.18
Erigena: 4.36, 115.14
Gnostics: 170.11
Helvetius: 4.21
Huss: 267.5, 589.33
Jansen: 173.12
Luther: 21.30, 42.20, 71.27, 229.13, 263.n4, 536.36, 582.33
Marcion: 192.1
Monophysite: 156.11
Montanus: 478.31
Nestorians: 320.4
Pelagius: 182.3, 358.10, 525.7, 538.36
Socinus: 132.19
Toland: 601.34
Valentinus: 249.4, 289.28, 458.2

This difficult theological passage is paraphrased in the *Skeleton Key*:

> But though the Gripes had, time and time again, sought to teach his own flock how to trumpet forth the double meanings of his doctrines, his pastors were found to be at loggerheads and at variance with the constitutions of his provincial creed, and so he got the hoof; he having wished to follow the Eastern rather than the Roman interpretation of the relation of the Father and the Son to the Holy Ghost.[84]

The hounding of the Deist John Toland out of Dublin is celebrated in "Tolan, who farshook our showrs from Newer Aland" (601.34-35). The treatment by the Church of heretical groups and heretics is often commented upon: the St. Bartholomew's Day Massacre of Huguenots is mentioned as "Paybads floriners moved in hugheknots against us and I matt them, pepst to papst, barthelemew: milreys (mark!) onfell, and (Luc!) I arose Daniel in Leonden" (541.14-16). The presence of three of the Evangelists (*matt, mark, Luc;* and the fourth, John, may be the *eon* of *Leonden*) again lends Church sanction to the massacre.

The amassing of such textual evidence leads to a realization of the role of religion in *Finnegans Wake*. Although positive because of its dominance, it is nonetheless essentially negative in purpose: a criticism of orthodox religion, a bitter commentary on the role of the Church in world history, and a condemnation of the excesses committed in the name of orthodoxy. The "Mass" which Montgomery sees celebrated in the *Wake* is an "immense Black Mass" to Louis Gillet.[85] The "Last Blessing of the Mass" in the Yawn episode is interpreted by Hugh Kenner as a "garbled ceremonial" whose function

> . . . is not unlike that of the parody-mass performed by Buck Mulligan in the first section of *Ulysses*. In its perfunctory formularization, its melange of parish gossip, worldly wisdom, and completely un-supernatural motivations it epiphanizes both a corrupt clericalism and a verbalised and superficial culture playing with shells.[86]

The Trisagion Joyce interprets as "Haggis good, haggis strong, haggis never say die" (456.9); the Greek word for holy is evolved into the Scottish "porridge" because Shaun's religion (the religion of the bourgeois Christian) is primarily of the stomach. J. S. Atherton rightly calls this a "travesty," adding that "this is, of course, one of many quotations that would have to be ignored by anyone claiming to prove that Joyce was a devout Catholic treating the Mass with respect."[87] And yet Joyce greatly admired the Mass (for its dramatic stage values) as Stanislaus Joyce noted: "something of the pomp and ceremony with which the legend of Jesus is told impressed him profoundly."[88] There is much of pomp and ceremony in the *Wake*, it too tells many legends, and it is apparently Joyce's attempt to surpass previous attempts to write "bibles."

An exhaustive listing of blasphemies in *Finnegans Wake*, even those solely limited to Roman Catholic ecclesiastical material, can best be left to any *advocatus diaboli* of the future who cares to prosecute Joyce for his sins, but an easy index to such perversions of sacred words can be arrived at by reference to the "Index of Motifs" in Clive Hart's *Structure and Motif in Finnegans Wake*.[89] A calculated sampling, however, should be sufficient to exonerate Joyce of any intended piety in respect to the printed words of Catholic writ. The "holocaust" that seemed so innocent to Mc-Greevy, for example, can be found often in the *Wake*. Sins against all three persons of the Trinity are rampant: against the Father as dog ("Dodgfather"—482.1), as invert ("Lordy Daw and Lady Don"—496.2), as nonentity ("Cloudy father! Unsure! Nongood!"—500.19), as an avatar of previous gods ("oura vatars that arred in Himmal"—599.5); against the Son as dog ("Dodgson" —482.1), as an ichthyic-canine hybrid ("that former son of a kish"—164.11-12), as chandelier (Stephen smashes one in *Ulysses;* "Crystal elation"—528.9), as a sham minstrel ("bamboozelem mincethrill . . . christie"—515.28-29), as a heretic ("Jansens Chrest"—173.12), as a prime minister of England ("Llwyd Josus"—91.19); against the Holy Ghost as "holocaust" (419.9-10), "the haul it cost" (153.31-32), "their homely codes" (614.32), and "spirituous suncksters" (371.1)—containing suck, sunk, and gangster.

Familiar Jesuit mottoes are transformed by Joyce with a vengeance, so that *Laus Deo Semper* is used to identify God with Lucifer and a louse ("lousadoor"—107.36), while the initials LDS are scrambled to arrive at the symbols for pounds, shillings, and pence (*"L.S.D."*—107.2) in order to implicate the Roman Church in British imperialistic finances, as witness *"Ad majorem l.s.d.! Divi gloriam"* (418.4), where the Jesuit motto loses its *Deo* in favor of *Divi* (the devil and the dividing of money). The sexual and sadistic excesses of Jaun's sermon should be enough to convict the Church in Joyce's perspective, containing as it does such gems as the confusion of the "Order for the Burial of the Dead," by way of a Byron love lyric, into "Mades of ashens when you flirt" (436.32); an anal allusion in the *confiteor* (*mio colpo"*—455.27), elsewhere in a sexual-sadistic version ("May he colp, may he colp her, may he mixandmass colp her!"—238.21); and an obscene inclusion in the "Last Blessing of the Mass": "Bennydick hotfoots onimpudent stayers!" (469.23-24). Jaun ends his sermon with a military "Break ranks!" (469.26), a disrespectful "Fik yew!" (469.27), and, becoming the Holy Ghost, a jaunty "You watch my smoke" (469.27-28).

What else but complete conscious blasphemy can be understood from Joyce's parodies of religious material, unless there exists a dual standard by which "in-group" Catholics accept such desecration as the prerogative of the inner circle and practice an esoteric Catholicism denied to the ordinary Roman Catholic? How else can such brutal parodies be explained unless we accept Father Noon's realization that it is a foregone impossibility to attempt to "salvage" Joyce for the orthodox Roman Church? His version of the Paternoster alone is evidence of his accusation that God committed the original error (later condoned by Church council): "Ouhr Former who erred in having down to gibbous disdag our darling breed. And then the confisieur for the boob's indulligence As sunctioned for his salmenbog by the Councillors-om-Trent" (530.36-531.3). The prayer itself is merely a flatulent dissonance, a "farternoiser" (530.36), and God the Father is associated with

the executor of His Son: "Harrod's be the naun" (536.35), as
well as a London store. The Commandments on the lips of Jaun
evolve into: "First thou shalt not smile. Twice thou shalt not love.
Lust, thou shalt not commix idolatry" (433.22-23). And they are
not much holier from evangelist Mark's view:

> Bolt the grinden. Cave and can em. . . . Renove that bible. . . . Mind
> the Monks and their Grasps. Scrape your souls. Commit no miracles.
> Postpone no bills. Respect the uniform. . . . Hatenot havenots. Share
> the wealth and spoil the weal. Peg the pound to tom the devil. . . .
> Bottle your own. Love my label like myself. Earn before eating.
> Drudge after drink. Credit tomorrow. Follow my dealing. Fetch my
> price. Buy not from dives. Sell not to freund. Herenow chuck english
> and learn to pray plain. Lean on your lunch. No cods before Me.
> Practise preaching [579.8-22].

The Angelus, the Paternoster, the Confiteor, the Ten Commandments, the Last Blessing of the Mass—nothing is sacred in the
Wake that is the voice of orthodox religion. Joyce changes *secula
seculorum,* as Vivian Mercier notes, to "*Insomnia, somnia somni-
orum*" (193.29-30) and "circular circulatio" (427.7-8), which
"can be allowed to stand for all the thousands of such blasphemous
parodies in the book. Protestants may take note, for instance, of
two parodies of the Lord's Prayer, on pages 530-31 and 536."[90] No
religious work seems exempt from Joyce's mockery: the Old Testament and the New, the Koran as well as the Bible—as Atherton
proves, "Joyce's hostility to the Koran is shown in his reference to
sura III."[91] It is apparent that it is not just the Catholicism to
which he had reacted with fear and vomiting in his youth that is
his exclusive target now, but the foundations of all religion. Budgen again quotes Joyce on the subject, this time when asked why he
had brought up his children without religious training: "But what
do they expect me to do? . . . There are a hundred and twenty religions in the world. They can take their choice. I should never try
to hinder or dissuade them."[92] Joyce had obviously made his own
choice; the number of religions mocked in *Finnegans Wake* may
well total 120.

It is obvious that an attempt to interpret the misquotations and parodies in the *Wake* as an aspect of Joyce's eventual piety is naïve. The parody of his own childhood bit of doggerel:

> —*My God, alas, that dear olt tumtum home*
> *Whereof in youthfood port I preyed*
> *Amook the verdigrassy convict vallsall dazes.*
> *And cloitered for amourmeant in thy boosome shede!*
>
> [231.5-8]

is paraphrased by Campbell and Robinson as: "Then he traced a little poem about God who is our Home, the consolation and protection of our youth."[93] The limitation of this exegesis is pointed up by Edwin Berry Burgum:

> Here the meaning is certainly not religious nor mystical, but profane and scurrilous. "My God" is less a reference to deity than a profane expletive, the exasperated tone of which turns to boredom in the "tumtum". . . . Similarly, the bosom shade protecting the boy in the last line is also the shed in which he became acquainted with the bosom of girls.[94]

Professor Burgum might well have added that there exists a significant difference between *praying* and *preying,* while the word *cloitered* overlaps *clitoris* and *coitus* into a meaningful amalgam.

Joyce is derisive of the entire hierarchy from the God of the Catholic to the Catholic priest, not excluding the Catholic saints. Those saints who appear in the *Wake* are a pitifully inane group, from the hard-headed, vulgarly popular St. Patrick to the oddly mystic St. Kevin. In essence the bourgeois Patrick conceals traces of ascetic Kevin from himself (and appears all the more foolish for the strange dichotomy), but as the night progresses and the fusion of opposites intensifies, the Kevin-façade assumes greater importance. Toward dawn, in the final "ricorso" chapter, the hermit-priest floats out to an island in his *"altare cum balneo"* (605.8), his bathtub altar, and sits there in the cold Holy Water to contemplate. Joyce seems to consider him a "strong and perfect christian" (605.35-36), since he is isolated, out of harm's way, divorced from the Patrick "mission" of conversion and conquest. But St. Kevin exists only as an afterthought in this section in which night is already breaking and dawn disturbs the darkness of the dream. Shaun, as the ascetic saint, is becoming Shem-like, while the Shemish Archdruid is fused into Shaun's Patrick, a reversal of the night's shooting of the Russian General.

These saints give way to Earwicker's "catholic" attitude of accepting the world around him (in the hope of being accepted with all his sins, guilt, foibles, and folly by the world). It is not accidental, therefore, that the Earwicker Everyman is presented as a Protestant: as such he has Catholicism as his cultural heritage, as well as Judaism and earlier manifestations of man's spiritual existence. But he has rebelled against the excesses and perversions of Catholic policy and politics. This is not an acceptance of Protestant religious creeds—Joyce's rejection of the Thirty-nine Articles, for example, is obvious and final—but an acceptance of the "reformation" aspect of the movement.

Having arrived at this balance of his Catholic heritage through a Protestant impetus and a nonreligious attitude fused through a subject matter laden with religious material, Joyce could now present the dichotomies inherent in man through a perspective which realized his personal conflicts. In the *Wake* he concentrates on man's human foibles to a greater extent than on man's attributes (H.C.E.'s peccadillo in Phoenix Park, A.L.P.'s *pia et pura bella,* Shaun's hypocrisy, Shem's cowardice, Issy's sexual teasings) in an attempt to evaluate the totality of man unadorned by the warped mirror image of a creature modeled after its deity. Issy's mirror, like many other symbols in the *Wake,* reflects the numerous illusions beclouding man's real existence (illusions fostered throughout by the trappings of religion): Earwicker's grandiosity, Anna Livia's peace-making, Shaun's conviction that he is as talented as his brother, Shem's vanity with women, Issy's pretended innocence (or pretended sophistication). But reality discloses the hero to be "all glittering with the noblest of carriage" as well as a "bumpkin" and a "puny" (627.22-24) because he is "great in all things, in guilt and in glory" (627.23-24). Anna Livia engenders the "penisolate war" (3.6) among her children, but mollifies them after the battle by distributing gifts (210-12) and nursing the wounded like "floreflorence . . . lightandgayle" (360.2). Man replaces God in *Finnegans Wake,* and the cycles of life replace Christianity. Magalaner and Kain therefore conclude that for Joyce it is "not a question of conversion *to* anything but rather the greater difficulty of having to surrender one sanctuary, through conscience, without being able to replace it immediately with another. Not until middle age when he is able to erect his obscure Viconian citadel does Joyce truly resolve his problem."[95]

The significance of Giambattista Vico's philosophy of history in *Finnegans Wake* is too broad a subject to be covered here, but certainly the basic plan of the *Wake* owes its skeletal structure to the Neapolitan philosopher, although perhaps in no more vital a manner than *Ulysses* is indebted to Homer. But Joyce's treatment of the religious aspects of Vico's material is of significance here, especially since Vico himself uncomfortably straddled the tightrope between orthodoxy and near-heresy; it would not be surprising, therefore, to find that Joyce (who had no compunction about translating Homeric epic into Joycean mock epic) was delighting himself by pushing Vico from the precarious tightrope. Thomas Fitzmorris, writing in the *Catholic World,* attempts to salvage Vico for orthodoxy, but at the expense of James Joyce. He senses that Joyce's use of Vico strips the Catholic philosopher of his religious meaning:

> . . . the first, or Divine Age, in Vico is represented in *Finnegan's* [*sic*] *Wake* by the abstraction Birth, the Heroic Age by Maturity, the Human Age by Corruption, and the transitional period between cycles, which in Vico is dominated by the idea of Providence, is represented by the abstraction, Generation. . . . It is a significant distortion that, as Vico's cycles and [*sic*] with a stress on the beneficence of Providence, there is often an opposite suggestion in Joyce.[96]

If Providence is replaced by Generation, then Providence's beneficence may well be replaced by Joyce with the basic life force

which is the "beneficence" of rebirth. There is certainly no suggestion of malevolence in the *"ricorso"* chapter (as there had been in
the theological trials of the previous chapter); if anything, mankind waking from its dream of unconscious evil has assimilated
that evil into a proper, workable scheme of human behavior: Earwicker's sons have become reconciled within himself, and his in-
cestuous lust for his daughter disappears as he substitutes his wife
reborn as a young girl (627).

But Fitzmorris cannot reconcile the conflicting conglomeration
of materials assembled by Joyce as concomitant with the pious purpose of Vico's *Scienza Nuova:* "The political nursery rhyme, 'The
Frog He Would A-Wooing Go,' the fable of 'The Fox and the
Grapes,' Adam and Eve, Tristan and Isolde, Mutt and Jeff, Wellington, Guinness's Brewery: these suggest the range of often im-
pious reference employed."[97] Fitzmorris' list, apparently taken at
random, is accidentally a good cross section of the impiety in the
Wake: the wooing frog motif echoes the Church's "holy" crusade
of conquest; the fox and grapes fable is Joycean condemnation of
the Church as a Machiavellian fox (the Mookse); Adam and Eve
are used to translate the concept of Original Sin to that of Sexual
Guilt; Tristram and Iseult are a facet of that sexual guilt, introduc-
ing the theme of the old man (Mark) and his erotic desire for the
young girl; Mutt and Jeff are a translation of Bruno's concept of
the duality of opposites (in comic-strip scope); Wellington, the
hero on the white horse, symbolizing British imperialistic success,
is another older man preying upon a young girl, and is celebrated
by a phallic monument in Phoenix Park; and Guinness' Brewery,
just a stone's throw from St. Patrick's Cathedral, turns the water of
the Liffey nonmiraculously into the elixir of life. As such the brewery is a part of Joyce's theme of mock Communion in conjunction
with the other famous Dublin factory, the Jacobs Biscuit Company.
Fitzmorris, therefore, has ample reason to be concerned about
Joyce's use of Viconian cycles, which on one occasion in the *Wake*
are recorded as "a good clap, a fore marriage, a bad wake, tell
hell's well" (117.5-6).

The elusively equivocal Vico thus proves to be a valuable touchstone for testing Joyce's religious mettle. What emerges is Joyce's intention to replace religion with man's historical nightmare—a concoction of reality and illusion, history and myth. Man's religions are a part of that myth, and therefore of history, but all is fused through Joyce's artistic personality. The variety of Joyce's religious experiences remains conclusively negative, and it is no longer a question of apostasy or even atheism, as it is of actual antitheism. Should the God of the Roman Catholics—or some composite deity bridging all organized religions—actually exist, Joyce declares himself opposed and sits in judgment of Him. This theme of defiance, as Morse asserts, is repeated throughout the *Wake:* "the power, arrogance and corporate assurance of those who presume to speak for God, opposed by the intelligence, skepticism and lonely self-respect of the creative individual."[98] This "terrible indictment," he goes on to note, "amounts to a denial of God in the name of the human individual, who cannot live with Him; it is, in fact, the obverse of the Jesuit denial of the individual self in the name of God."[99]

Fortunately this "terrible indictment" is couched in the drollest of terms, tempered with cosmic laughter, verbal hoaxes, and assorted impractical jokes. The Stephen Dedalus who was so terribly self-serious has given way to a Shem—a "shemozzle" (177.5)—whom no one can take seriously, even himself. But the indictment is there—as is Joyce's final apostatic guffaw.

CHAPTER THREE

Comic Seriousness and Poetic Prose

As Shem and Shaun, the dual aspects of man's nature, constantly merge and "reamalgamerge" into each other; as Isobel, the Alice-girl, sees her image in her looking glass; so the twin muses of Comedy and Poetry are constantly fusing in the language of *Finnegans Wake*. Essentially they are dual characteristics of Joyce's "Revolution of the Word," which like most revolutionary aspects of the novel (the antithesis challenging the thesis) is actually a *romance* of the word—a synthesis of the comic with the poetic into a single entity of language. As it is often impossible to separate the meaning from the language in *Finnegans Wake*—its form being derived intrinsically from its content—it is equally impossible to segregate the humorous from the poetic. In an attempt to analyze the nature of the comedy and the qualities of the poetry in the *Wake*, it is important to do so primarily in terms of reuniting the dissected parts into its original unity—the synthesis which is the basis of Joyce's harmonic as well as intellectual balance. Its humor is basically verbal since Joyce's universal dream is poetically conceived in terms of "echoes" rather than "images"; it is a purblind-man's dream transliterated immediately upon perception into speech patterns capturing the many-leveled irrelevancies which dance about the central core of significance in each event.

This is not to imply that *Finnegans Wake* as a comic novel lacks its comedy of situations, but to impress that even its "slapstick" situations are delivered in terms of lingual gymnastics, words falling over each other in comic processions. The strong element of pantomime which, as Atherton indicated,[1] dominated much of Joyce's thinking in his conception of the *Wake*, is equally linguistic. His Harlequins and Columbines wear their splashed profusion of colors in a tumble of linguistic patterns of "rudd yellan gruebleen" (23.1), and like players in the early Catholic pageants they can be visualized in "their pinky limony creamy birnies and their turkiss indienne mauves" (215.20-21). Actually the pantomime is never *seen* in *Finnegans Wake;* it is there primarily because Joyce alludes to it:

> inseparable sisters, uncontrollable nighttalkers, Skertsiraizde with Donyahzade, who afterwards, when the robberers shot up the socialights, came down into the world as amusers and were staged by Madame Sudlow as Rosa and Lily Miskinguette in the pantalime that two pitts paythronosed, Miliodorus and Galathee [32.7-12].

The Gaiety Theatre on Dublin's King Street ("that king's treat house"—32.26) and its director, Michael Gunn ("game old Gunne. . . . He's duddandgunne"—25.21-24), are also mentioned. But essentially the pantomime as an art form exists in the *Wake* because Joyce characterizes it: "The piece was this: look at the lamps. The cast was thus: see under the clock. Ladies circle: cloaks may be left. Pit, prommer and parterre, standing room only" (33.10-12). These sentences describing the pantomime in chapter 9 are in themselves short and jerky, characteristic of the basic pantomime movement, and, like the actors for whom they serve as surrogates, they seem to wear one black sleeve and one white, one checkered leg and one striped, divided as they are down the middle.

But this is only a prologue to the larger pantomime scene, the children's play portion of the second book of *Finnegans Wake.* The mime re-enacted is the story of the Earwicker family presented as "The Mime of Mick, Nick and the Maggies." The play takes place at the "Feenichts Playhouse"; it is blessed by God and sponsored by the four old men, features the two brats, Shem and Shaun, and is taken from a temperance tract (Ballyhooley Blue Ribbon Army) as well as the German pre-Shakespearean version of the Hamlet story (*Der bestrafte Brudermord*):

> Every evening at lighting up o'clock sharp and until further notice in Feenichts Playhouse. (Bar and conveniences always open, Diddlem Club douncestears.) Entrancings: gads, a scrab; the quality, one large

Alicious, twinstreams, twinestraines, through alluring glass or alas in jumboland? (528.17-18)

For the Clearer of the Air from on high has spoken in tumbuldum tambaldam to his tembledim tombaldoom worrild and, moguphonoised by that phonemanon, the unhappitents of the earth have terrerumbled from firmament unto fundament and from tweedledeedumms down to twiddledeedees (258.20-24).

But if this could see with its backsight he'd be the grand old greeneyed lobster (249.2-3).

. . . it's mad nuts, son, for you when it's hatter's hares, mon, for me . . . (82.36-83.1).

shilling. Newly billed for each wickeday perfumance. Somndoze massinees. . . . With nightly redistribution of parts and players by the puppetry producer and daily dubbing of ghosters, with the benediction of the Holy Genesius Archimimus and under the distinguised patronage of their Elderships the Oldens from the four coroners of Findrias, Murias, Gorias and Falias . . . while the Caesar-in-Chief looks. On. Sennet. As played to the Adelphi by the Brothers Bratislavoff (Hyrcan and Haristobulus), after humpteen dumpteen revivals. Before all the King's Hoarsers with all the Queen's Mum. And wordloosed over seven seas crowdblast in cellelleneteutoslavzendlatinsoundscript. In four tubbloids. While fern may cald us until firn make cold. *The Mime of Mick, Nick and the Maggies,* adopted from the Ballymooney Bloodriddon Murther by Bluechin Blackdillain [219.1-20].

Joyce is presenting his pantomime not in action but in program form. His introduction, which plays upon the Humpty Dumpty story presented often as a mime by the Gaiety Theatre during Joyce's childhood, a key to the H.C.E. fall, gives way to a presentation of the list of characters: Mick (the Shaun character, the Archangel Michael) is called Chuff and referred to as "the fine frank fairhaired fellow of the fairytales" (220.12-13); Nick (the Shem figure, the devil) is called Glugg and is "the bold bad bleak boy of the storybooks" (219.24); Isobel is Izod, "a bewitching blonde who dimples delightfully" (220.7-8). Again Joyce is using the language of the pantomime bill to describe the stock characters who are masks for his universal figures. Hump (H.C.E.) is portrayed in the mime by "Mr Makeall Gone" (220.24), another reference to the Gaiety director.* Again Joyce uses the written con-

* The various names for Earwicker have their own necessary logic. When H.C.E. is designated as Michael Gunn (as he is here), the significance is that of his role as God the Father: *Makeall Gone* implies the Creator (who made everything) and the Destroyer (who will cause everything to disappear). A glance at some of the other Gunn-God parallels should corroborate this interpretation: *"Duddy Gunne"* (104.8) contains the colloquial form of Father (Daddy), but suggests also "dead and gone" (the crucified Christ, abandoned religion); "gunnfodder" (242.10) is God the Father as well as the sacrificed (canon fodder), an echo of the more literal and ecclesiastical "Canon Futter" (9.19-20); "Gonn the gawds" (257.34) and "Master's gunne" (531.4-5) further serve to indicate Earwicker's position as God, while "Diu! The has goning at gone" (598.9) multiplies the reference with French and Greek (*dieu, theo*).

ventions of such performances in lieu of the performance itself—this time he merely announces that "An argument follows" (222.21), and the brother-battle is on.

The pantomime is not the only nonverbal aspect of comedy that Joyce verbalizes in the *Wake;* its low brother, slapstick, is well portrayed in many of the jaunts of H. C. Earwicker. In many ways, Earwicker is something of a Chaplin figure, particularly in the "closing of the bar" scene (381-82). Once the pub has closed for the night, the radio that blared forth scantily disguised versions of the Earwicker peccadillo is silenced, and Earwicker can be seen stumbling about the darkened tavern, "cleaning up":

> when he found himself all alone by himself in his grand old handwedown pile after all of them had all gone off with themselves to their castles of mud, as best they cud, on footback . . . well, what do you think he did, sir, but, faix, he just went heeltapping through the winespilth and weevily popcorks that were kneedeep round his own right royal round rollicking toper's table, with his old Roderick Random pullon hat at a Lanty Lear cant on him . . . the body you'd pity him, the way the world is, poor he, the heart of Midleinster and the supereminent lord of them all, overwhelmed as he was with black ruin like a sponge out of water . . . thruming though all to himself with diversed tonguesed through his old tears and his ould plaised drawl, starkened by the most regal of belches, like a blurney Cashelmagh crooner that lerking Clare air, the blackberd's ballad *I've a terrible errible lot todue todie todue tootorribleday,* well, what did he go and do at all, His Most Exuberant Majesty King Roderick O'Conor but, arrah bedamnbut, he finalised by lowering his woolly throat with the wonderful midnight thirst was on him, as keen as mustard, he could not tell what he did ale, that bothered he was from head to tail, and, wishawishawish, leave it, what the Irish, boys, can do, if he did'nt go,

---

That both *Diu* and *The* have a missing letter suggests the lost phallus of the emasculated god, Osiris, as well as the Christ who disappeared from his tomb and was discovered to be "gone." The *Wake* significantly ends with the word "the," intended by Joyce to be an aspect of the cyclical pattern, the weakworded ending rising up again in the continued sentence at the beginning of the book. It is also a modulation from the strongest word in any language, the word for God, to the emasculated form which Joyce considered the weakest word in the English language.

sliggymaglooral reemyround and suck up, sure enough, like a Trojan, in some particular cases with the assistance of his venerated tongue, whatever surplus rotgut, sorra much, was left by the lazy lousers of maltknights and beerchurls in the different bottoms of the various different replenquished drinking utensils left there behind them on the premisses [380.34-381.35].

In drunken fashion, nursing a badly wounded ego after his bout with the twelve customers, Earwicker imagines himself the ancient king of Ireland; his thoughts, like a drunkard's words, repeat themselves, trip over themselves; he sings, weeps, burps, stumbles gingerly about, and then drinks up the dregs. And finally "he came acrash a crupper sort of a sate on accomondation and the very boxst in all his composs . . . on the flure of his feats and the feels of the fumes in the wakes of his ears our wineman from Barleyhome he just slumped to throne" (382.18-26).

It is this sort of verbal gymnastics worthy of "our Chorney Choplain" (351.13) that is a performance which can be termed a study in the ridiculous—and it is the "ridiculous" that Henry Fielding in his Preface to *Joseph Andrews* finds rooted in affectation. Fielding proceeds to define affectation as stemming from "one of these two causes, vanity or hypocrisy: for as vanity puts us on affecting false characters, in order to purchase applause; so hypocrisy sets us on an endeavour to avoid censure, by concealing our vices under an appearance of their opposite virtues."[2] This seems to characterize perfectly the comedy derived from Earwicker's situation in the *Wake:* his affectations stem from his attempt to boost his social standing. His situation in the tavern scene centers about his subterfuges concerning the incident in the park; he attempts to drown out speculation concerning his misdemeanor by turning on the radio—the customers have been bandying about a tale concerning a Norwegian Captain which smacks suspiciously of Earwicker's story—but the radio comics, Butt and Taff, only succeed in telling another story that reminds everyone of the Earwicker incident (337-55). To make matters worse, Earwicker arises to defend the Russian General who had been shot during the Butt-Taff skit, and again he further incriminates himself (355-59). No matter how many times he resorts to the radio to get him off the spot, Earwicker finds he is the subject again; he finally confesses—confesses to every sin imaginable (363-70)—and is soundly disparaged and beaten by the customers (371-80). His closing time boasting restores his ego through the affectations of vanity and hypocrisy. He is once again, in his drunken stupor, "old Roderick O'Conor Rex" (380.33).

If Earwicker's life is portrayed in terms of his guilty error (a comic situation), then Shem in contrast is comic in character. Unlike Earwicker, Shem does not perform a comic role in the *Wake* to the extent that his life is the travesty of propriety which Earwicker's is. Shem does not take himself seriously; paralleling Joyce himself he is aware that he is involved in a "funferall" (13.15) and lives his part not as the butt of the humor in the *Wake,* but as a humorous individual living out the logic of his life, aware of its absurdities without the Earwickerian quantity of vanity and hypocrisy. Shem is a caricature of a character (as a caricature of Stephen Dedalus) and is thus twice removed from reality. As such he sees himself as a character in a semiautobiographic novel and laughs at the image of himself: "young master Shemmy on his very first debouch at the very dawn of protohistory seeing himself such and such . . . dictited to of all his little brothron and sweestureens the first riddle of the universe: asking, when is a man not a man?" (169.20-170.5).

In burlesque fashion Joyce not only returns to his Stephen figure stranded at the age of twenty-two at the end of *Ulysses,* but actually recapitulates the autobiographical events of the *Portrait* and its successor. The opening sentence of *A Portrait of the Artist as a Young Man* ("Once upon a time and a very good time it was there was a moocow"—AP7) is echoed and parodied several times in the *Wake:* "Eins within a space and a wearywide space it wast ere wohned a Mookse" (152.18-19); "Once upon a drunk and a fairly good drunk it was" (453.20); "Once upon a grass and a hopping high grass it was (516.1-2); "once upon a wall and a hooghoog wall a was" (69.7). Joyce, then, is consciously parodying his own previous work, that young man's novel about his young self, and restating the themes of the *Portrait* in comic form as a basis for the material on which the new work is built. As such Joyce seems to have been conscious, as Daiches is, of the stages of a contemporary artist's development; he is parodying his "liberal" position in the first novel and the "cynical" position of his second in order to arrive at his "balanced" view of *Finnegans Wake*. It is characteristic of this reiteration of earlier material that Joyce magnifies the events of the first page of his *Portrait* into even larger proportions in the *Wake:* Stephen as a baby wets his bed ("When you wet the bed, first it is warm then it gets cold"—AP7). Jerry, the Shem figure as a child, breaks the continuity of his father's dream by crying in the night—"A cry off" (558.32)—and the anxious parents come to investigate. He has wet his bed in Stephen fashion: "And he has pipettishly bespilled himself from his foundingpen as illspent from inkinghorn" (563.5-6). This childish involuntary act already preshadows his career as a writer; it is significant that Joyce's last work is not only in itself in cyclical fashion, but this bedwetting occurring toward the end of the night's sleep reverts to the opening of the *Portrait*—Joyce's autobiographical work also makes a complete cycle.

A review of Stephen's life and character can be pieced together from the bits strewn throughout the *Wake,* particularly the portrait of Shem which constitutes the seventh chapter of the first book. Like Stephen, little Shem is sickly: "one generally, for luvvomony hoped or at any rate suspected among morticians that he would early turn out badly, develop hereditary pulmonary T.B." (172.11-13). He is terrified of thunder: "Tumult, son of Thunder, self exiled in upon his ego, a nightlong a shaking betwixtween white or reddr hawrors, noondayterrorised to skin and bone by an ineluctable phantom" (184.6-9). He spends his time as a young man strolling along with a companion boasting of his literary prowess: No one

ever nursed such a spoiled opinion of his monstrous marvellosity as did this mental and moral defective . . . who was known to grognt rather than gunnard upon one occasion, while drinking heavily of spirits to that interlocutor *a latere* and private privysuckatary he used to pal around with . . . Shem always blaspheming, so holy writ . . . that he was avoopf (parn me!) aware of no other shaggspick, other Shakhisbeard . . . if reams stood to reason and his lankalivline lasted he would wipe alley english spooker, multaphoniaksically spuking, off the face of the erse [177.15-178.7].

Like Stephen, Shem declares his *non serviam:* "Do you hold yourself then for some god in the manger, Shehohem, that you will neither serve not let serve, pray nor let pray?" (188.18-19); he is a tenor: "he squealed the topsquall . . . juice like a boyd . . . for fully five minutes, infinitely better that Baraton McGluckin" (180.5-8); he acknowledges his heritage from the Greeks and the Hebrews—"that greekenhearted yude!" (171.1)—and announces his exile from Ireland where he felt he was dying: "he would not throw himself in Liffey . . . he refused to saffrocake himself with a sod" (172.18-20). Shem is the prodigal son—"bumbosolom" (180.27)—who goes off to write "his usylessly unreadable Blue Book of Eccles, *édition de ténèbres*" (179.26-27) while teaching in the "beurlads scoel" (467.25)—"the beerlitz" (182.7)—in "his citadear of refuge" (62.1), Trieste.

Here he sees himself as "an Irish emigrant the wrong way out . . . an unfrillfrocked quackfriar, you (will you for the laugh of Scheekspair just help mine with the epithet?) semisemitic serendipitist, you (thanks, I think that describes you) Europasianised Afferyank!" (190.36-191.4). He has left the fine whiskey and good stout of Dublin to drink "some sort of a rhubarbarous maundarin yellagreen funkleblue windigut diodying applejack squeezed from sour grapefruice" (171.16-18), a liquor that smacks suspiciously of French *calvados* as well as the modern absinthe substitute, Pernod. When the First World War broke out—and when Ireland was in the throes of its bloodiest uprising against the English—Shem found himself in his Swiss exile, hiding from war and confined with his liquor and his writing implements:

Now it is notoriously known how on that suprisingly bludgeony Unity Sunday when the grand germogall allstar about was harrily the rage between our weltingtoms extraordinary and our pettythicks the mars halaisy and Irish eyes of welcome were smiling daggers down their backs, when the roth, vice and blause met the noyr blank and rogues and the grim white and cold bet the black fighting tans, categorically unimperatived by the maxims, a rank funk getting the better of him, the scut in a bad fit of pyjamas fled like a leveret for his bare lives. . . . kuskykorked himself up tight in his inkbattle house, badly the worse for boosegas, there to stay in afar for the life . . . he collapsed carefully under a bedtick from Schwitzer's . . . hemiparalysed by the tong warfare and all the schemozzle . . . his cheeks and trousers changing colour every time a gat croaked [176.19-177.7].

There are many such descriptions of Shem throughout *Finnegans Wake,* and with typically Joycean whimsy they contradict themselves with consistency. This is important if one assumes that autobiographically Joyce sees himself not only as the Shem figure, the artist, the nonconformist in the *Wake,* but also as the composite man, the synthesis of himself and his conformist brother with whom he forms the hero, H.C.E. It is usually the parallel of age—Shem as the writer often seen to be in his forties, "furtive-free yours of age" (173.7), and Earwicker as the father in his mid-fifties, "most frifty" (25.34)—that unites these two antagonists and indicates Joyce's identification with the element of humanity outside the nonconformist circle of aesthetes. In contrast, it appears to be eyesight that unites Shem with Anna Livia, the son complaining that he has "no sentiment secretions but weep cataracts for all me, Pain the Shamman" (192.22-23), while the mother intones: "I wisht I had better glances to peer to you"*
(626.34), again indicating that Joyce's identification is most highly universalized in terms of the All-Woman who remains eternal.[3]

But it is essentially Shem's preoccupation that Joyce is parodying in the *Wake.* Shem is writing a book—obviously the *Wake* itself —and it is in his many statements of purpose, descriptions of contents, and explanations of technique that Joyce proves himself to

---

* Both eyesight and age are investigated rather thoroughly in chapter 5.

be writing a parody of a parody. *Finnegans Wake* is a "meander-tale" (18.22) or "meanderthalltale" (19.25) in cyclical form, a "book of Doublends Jined" (20.15-16), which is a

> continuous present tense integument slowly unfolded all marryvoising moodmoulded cyclewheeling history (thereby, he said, reflecting from his own individual person life unlivable, transaccidentated through the slow fires of consciousness into a dividual chaos, perilous, potent, common to allflesh, human only, mortal) but with each word that would not pass away the squidself which he had squirtscreened from the crystalline world waned chagreenold and doriangrayer in its dudhud [186.1-8].

Here Joyce implies the use of the Viconian cycles in his *Wake;* he is presenting the unfolding panorama of continuous history through his use of representative individuals who are characteristic of himself. His process is a conscious one. All the material he collects is fused through his consciousness: it is the material that constitutes his antagonists, man divided in chaos against himself. His domain is the realm of humankind; his technique is complicated by the smokescreen that, like the squid, he squirts over the clear water —the ink of his art, which refuses to paint the story of man in terms of black and white but insists upon realizing the various shadings, the dual character of Wilde's golden Dorian and his distorted "Gray" image.

The language of the *Wake* is necessarily difficult, since Joyce is making his "bolderdash for lubberty of speech" (233.17-18), "letting punplays pass to ernest" (233.19-20); his is a universal slaughter of language, particularly of "pure undefallen engelsk" (233.33). As such he is attempting to "Find the frenge for frocks and translace it into shocks" (233.9)—getting the exact word in the language that would best fit the immediate purpose, as French would in the case of female fashion. As a melange of material collected at random from observations of life, *Finnegans Wake* is a shop of odds and ends forming a chaotic pattern:

> The warped flooring of the lair and soundconducting walls thereof, to say nothing of the uprights and imposts, were persianly literatured

with burst loveletters, telltale stories, stickyback snaps, doubtful eggshells, bouchers, flints, borers, puffers, amygdaloid almonds, rindless raisins [183.8-13]

(among other things, the "upright" Shaun and the "impost" Shem, the love letters of Stella and Swift which form the famous "letter" that recurs in the *Wake,* the telltale story of Earwicker's indiscretion, the broken bits of egg splattered after Humpty Dumpty's fall, mouthings, etc.);

alphybettyformed verbage, vivlical viasses, ompiter dictas, visus umbique, ahems and ahahs, imeffible tries at speech unasyllabled, you owe mes, eyoldhyms, fluefoul smut, fallen lucifers, vestas which had served, showered ornaments, borrowed brogues [183.13-17]

(varieties of written language, Vico's cyclical roads, pronouncements, threads in intricate patterns in all directions, asides, obscenities, the interrelation of individuals, the Biblical story of the fall of Satan, etc.);

reversibles jackets, blackeye lenses, family jars, falsehair shirts, Godforsaken scapulars, neverworn breeches, cutthroat ties, counterfeit franks, best intentions, curried notes, upset latten tintacks, unused mill and stumpling stones, twisted quills, painful digests, magnifying wineglasses, solid objects cast at goblins, once current puns, quashed quotatoes, messes of mottage, unquestionable issue papers, seedy ejaculations, limerick damns, crocodile tears, spilt ink, blasphematory spits, stale shestnuts [183.17-25].

A survey of articles of clothing uncovers the Earwicker family story of vanity and hypocrisy, and this leads into a survey of the aspects of lingual machinations which constitute the author's technique in the *Wake.*

Such epic listings of paraphernalia are keys to the contents of the book, the bits of broken colored glass that make up the kaleidoscope. They are but the raw material, the ingredients of this witch's caldron; it is how the glass is twisted and turned (how the brew is boiled) that makes it become the pattern that we discern in Joyce's *Wake.* Additional clues are readily available; from an objective view one can refuse to be taken in by Shem's portrait of the world around him, realizing that he is

> unconsciously explaining, for inkstands, with a meticulosity border-
> ing on the insane, the various meanings . . . and cuttlefishing every lie
> unshrinkable about all the other people in the story, leaving out, of
> course, foreconsciously, the simple worf and plague and poison they
> had cornered him about until there was not a snoozer among them
> but was utterly undeceived in the heel of the reel by the recital of the
> rigmarole [173.33-174.4].

It is this sort of objectivity, the presentation of the negative side of the artist's print of life, that characterizes Joyce's comic treatment of Shem the Penman. Joyce insists upon the necessary objectivity which permits an author to see life as the panorama around him and outside of himself, as well as the three-dimensional mirror in which he must view his juxtaposition to the panorama with equal objectivity. This allows Joyce to write a parody of himself and his artistic process with a detachment that is twice-removed. Joyce is Stephen Dedalus is Shem: Shem is a caricature of Stephen who is an exaggerated self-portrait of the young Joyce.

The author realizes that when his Shem wrote his book "he scrabbled and scratched and scriobbled and skrevened nameless shamelessness about everybody ever he met" (182.13-14). Is the book readable?

> That's the point of eschatology our book of kills reaches for now in
> soandso many counterpoint words. What can't be coded can be de-
> corded if an ear aye sieze what no eye ere grieved for. Now, the doc-
> trine obtains, we have occasioning cause causing effects and affects
> occasionally recausing altereffects. Or I will let me take it upon my-
> self to suggest to twist the penman's tale posterwise. The gist is the
> gist of Shaun but the hand is the hand of Sameas [482.33-483.4].

It is, if we approach it from both directions at once without pre-conceived notions. The rule might well be "ear before eye in order to see," but it has its exceptions, for at times the clue may be visu-ally lodged in the words on the printed page. The reader must think in terms of a manuscript divided against itself, for both the

Penman, Shem, and the Postman, Shaun, have left their mark upon the work: together, as a synthesis, they have produced this carefully balanced affair. The entire *Wake* parodies the Dedalus-Joyce family from the first page of *A Portrait*, where impressions of infancy are recorded, and may also prophetically bring Joyce's reader to his deathbed two years after the publication of *Finnegans Wake:* Anna Livia's dying words, "and is there one who understands me?" (627.14-15), an echo of younger Issy's plea in an amorous letter, "Can't you understand?" (459.22), may also have been Joyce's own. Eva Joyce, his sister, reports his dying words as "Does nobody understand?"[4] (Ellmann does not include these "last words," and I suspect that his apparent skepticism concerning their accuracy may well be justified.)

Joyce's self-portrait is caricature for an intensely serious purpose: he is interested in his last novel's stature as a view of life untinted by the perspective already declared in the earlier books. The perspective remains, but Joyce insists that it is objective despite the subjectivity of his autobiographic protagonist. Stephen as Shem is being sacrificed for the greater interests of the *Wake;* his sacrifice is being caricatured as well, and Shem emerges more maligned (and ennobled thereby) than maligning. But what constitutes parody on the specific level of burlesque becomes mock-heroic on the general level, and *Finnegans Wake* moves from the specific to the general to encompass all mankind, the character of Shem being only a facet of the personality of mankind. And whereas it is Earwicker who represents contemporary man (personifying generally Vico's "civil" era, while Shaun is its specific representative and as such is only a facet of the full character of his father), it is Finn MacCool, the legendary giant, who personifies man in his heroic age.

Much of the material of the first chapter (the introductory elements of the giant's wake which usher in H.C.E., his successor) revolves around the heroic figure of ancient Ireland, the fallen titan who is destined to wake when Ireland once again requires his services, as well as his stage counterpart, hod carrier Tim Finnegan, who re-enacts Finn's fall and resurrection in the Irish-American vaudeville ballad. The portions of *Finnegans Wake* that deal with Earwicker's heroic ancestor are written in mock-heroic language only duplicated during those portions of the novel in which either Earwicker or *his* deposer, Shaun, fancies himself the titanic hero: Earwicker's defense of the Russian General (355-58), Earwicker's self-defense rising up from the body of Yawn (534-54), and Shaun delivering his oration before the people (407-15). But neither the oligarch Earwicker nor the demagogue Shaun quite manages to recapture the titan's mighty lines.

The opening chapter contains much of the machinery necessary to construct a mock epic. It begins *in medias res*—"in midias reeds" (158.7)—with a small letter in the middle of a sentence; it echoes the introductory lines of the heroic epic, as well as the chorus of *The Frogs:* "What clashes here of wills gen wonts, ostrygods gaggin fishygods! Brékkek Kékkek Kékkek Kékkek" (4.1-2). This ushers in a paragraph dealing with the wars of the Dark Ages as well as the battle in heaven, and ends with the resurrection motif that foreshadows the events of Eden: "Phall if you but will, rise you must" (4.15-16). "Of the first was he to bare arms and a name: Wassaily Booslaeugh of Riesengeborg" (5.5-6) is another epical introduction to the hero, and it earmarks him as Adam the delver in the Garden of Eden, since Joyce is here parodying the gravedigger in *Hamlet* as he sports with the second clown:

> There is no ancient gentlemen but gardeners, ditchers,
>   and grave-makers; they hold up Adam's profession.
> *Second Clown.* Was he a gentleman?
> *Gravedigger.* 'A was the first that ever bore arms.
>   [V, i, 33-38]

The wake is under way; the keening is heard around the bier of the fallen titan, and the funeral feast is spread. "And the all gianed in with the shoutmost shoviality. Agog and magog and the round of them agrog" (6.18-19). Whiskey and stout are served: "With a bockalips of finisky fore his feet. And a barrowload of guenesis hoer his head" (6.26-27). The resurrection motif is sounded again: the whiskey will revive the hod carrier, and his "apocalyptic finish" will result in his "genesis" again. Much of this language echoes the Anglo-Saxon heroic poems: "rory end to the regginbrow was to be seen ringsome on the aquaface" (3.13-14) is a protracted tetrameter line with the first three stressed words alliterated; *regginbrow* and *aquaface* were probably intended as mock kennings for kingly brow and water.

But whether parodying *Beowulf* or the Bible, Joyce's technique invariably seems to involve verbal humor, "puns, quashed quotatoes, messes of mottage" (183.22-23). It is probably with the pun that Joyce does more to achieve his humorous linguistic effect than with any of the other aspects of his comic language.[5] Gillet finds the *Wake* "a linguistic jest, a sort of carnival, a grammatical mardi-gras, a philologist's good-humoured carouse" and cites his ancient precedent for the use of puns in a serious work: "In Homer, Ulysses, when the Cyclops asks his name, replies that he is named Outis, i.e. Noman. Now Ulysses in Greek is Odysseus, or Outis-Zeus (Noman joined to the name of the Deity)."[6] With the *Odyssey*, Shakespeare, and the New Testament (Christ's pun) corroborating the distinguished use of the "lowest form of wit," it remains only for Joyce to elevate the pun to heights of poetic fancy hitherto unknown. Joyce's puns usually have three levels of significance: as serious linguistic manipulations they allow the author to include various concepts, overlapping themes, and levels of meaning in compressed form; as humorous concoctions they grate against our dulled senses—they are the stumbling blocks that make us conscious of every step we take through the *Wake*; as a poetic device they are controlled by a rhythmic logic that creates individual sound patterns at once familiar in rhythm and new in sound. In a statement of the resurrection theme involving Finn Mac-Cool and his comic shadow, Tim Finnegan, Joyce intones: "Hohohoho, Mister Finn, you're going to be Mister Finnagain! Comeday morm and, O, you're vine! Sendday's eve and, ah, you're vinegar! Hahahaha, Mister Funn, you're going to be fined again!"

(5.9-12). Here basic sounds are repeated in logical fashion: *Finn* becomes *Funn* as well as *Finn again* (the titular pun of the work), while *vine* turns to *vinegar* (another transformation), and the *fine* we had first expected to hear is sounded again in the final sentence. *Comeday* and *Sendday* are both Sunday, of course (the Easter Sunday of Christ's resurrection parallels "a trying thirstay mournin" [6.14] preceding His crucifixion), while *Comeday* may also be Monday, giving us a full week's progression. The balance Joyce achieves through his language carries not only from *Finn* to *Funn* and *vine* to *vinegar* to *fined,* but is duplicated by his exclamations of *hohohoho* to *hahahaha* and *O* to *ah.*

The extent to which Joyce was capable of carrying an individual pun as a type of leitmotif throughout the *Wake* can be seen by tracing this particular Finn-again through several of its metamorphoses. Each time it changes it remains the Finn-Finnegan motif with a new concept tacked on to give it aptness in a particular situation or new dimension. At the wake, Finnegan's mourners are *thirstay,* so "Sobs they sighdid at Fillagain's chrissormiss wake" (6.14-15)—the hero's name becoming a call for refills; when the wife is again mourning her husband at a wake, she is a rather prissy woman and is seen "dragging the countryside in her train, finickin here and funickin there" (102.8-9)—Finn-Funn now transformed to fit this finicky Isis who is collecting the parts of Osiris' body (yet another resurrection myth) and is going up and down like a funicular cable-car ("Funiculi, Funicula"). (Her sexual indiscretions are apparent in the obscene pun in *funickin.*) When Anna Livia Plurabelle is seeking a title for her "mamafesta," she puns her initials into Lapp and finds a neighbor of the Lapps to be the Finns; the result is the comic title, *"Lapps for Finns This Funnycoon's Week"* (105.21). In toying with the Book of Kells and the amount of minute scholarship that has been spent in poring over that manuscript, Joyce echoes his own preoccupation with sound and sense: "here keen again and begin again to make soundsense and sensesound kin again" (121.14-16)—the wailing at the wake is combined with the resurrection. Since the Phoenix myth is a resurrection motif of rebirth out of destructive fire, as soon as it is mentioned Finnegan becomes "Flammagen's" (321.17). When Earwicker is being pursued and trounced during a series of athletic contests (again he is being hounded for his sin in the park), the last line of the "Ballad of Tim Finnegan" is re-echoed as "loss of fame from Wimmegame's fake" (375.16-17). While treating Earwicker's fall from grace because of his playing with women, Joyce is re-echoing the wake scene, since these athletic contests would remind a student of Homer of the funeral games at Achilles' cremation. And remembering T. S. Eliot's drowned man, Phlebas the Phoenician, Joyce triple-puns Finnegan and Phoenix as well into "Ashias unto fierce force fuming, temtem tamtam, the Phoenican wakes" (608.31-32).

These are just a handful of references to Finnegan and offer a partial indication of the various transformations a single pun will undergo in *Finnegans Wake,* each time adding a new layer of significance to an already established pattern. Often Joyce's technique calls for the creation of something that actually falls short of being a pun, but is merely an echo that can unearth a new level of meaning. "Rot a peck of pa's malt" (3.12-13) seems innocent enough: it refers to the brewing of liquor (the downfall of Finnegan and later of Earwicker in the tavern), and in this case is followed by "had Jhem or Shen brewed" (3.13), and the reference seems simply to be to Noah's drunkenness and the sin of his son, Ham. Occurring as it does on the first page of the *Wake,* however, it has an even greater significance, since it is an echo of "ring around the rosy" and describes the cyclical pattern of Vico's history and Joyce's novel; the rosy ring is also a rainbow, and the rest of the sentence reads: "by arclight and rory end to the regginbrow was to be seen ringsome on the aquaface" (3.13-14).

But with each page of *Finnegans Wake* offering hundreds of puns, it is hardly necessary to uncover indirect ones. Often puns that are easily discernible fail to provide a significance in their context until the reader becomes aware of their indirection. When the rainbow girls gush over Chuff (Shaun), calling him "Stainusless, young confessor" (237.11)—an obvious reference to Joyce's brother, Stanislaus—they comment, "You have not brought stinking members into the house of Amanti. Elleb Inam, Titep Notep, we name them to the Hall of Honour" (237.25-27). The setting is unmistakably Egyptian, but the subject is love. *Amanti* is Italian for lovers, but *the house of Amanti* is also a pun for the Egyptian *Amenti*, the Book of the Dead. Death and Love are synonymous in the Tristram Legend, particularly in Wagner's operatic version where the "love-death" aria begins *"Mild und leise"*—"locally known as Mildew Lisa" (40.17) or "mild aunt Liza" (388.4). The mock-Egyptian nonsense syllables *Elleb Inam, Titep Notep* add to the setting and assure that the *Amenti* significance is not overlooked, but they can also be read backward as *belle mani, petit peton*—beautiful hands, small feet—which Mason reminds us characterizes Joyce's brother, but which Kevin Sullivan credits as a characteristic of Joyce himself.[7]

The extent to which Joyce can control the poetic medium utilizing the pun for an artistic balance can be seen in such tightly constructed episodes as that of "Jarl van Hoother and the Prankquean" (21-23). The tale is told in a three-part form covering the three arrivals of the piratess at the castle of the jarl, yet the balance is disproportionate since the first states all the themes for the tale, the second is compressed for heightened action, and the third is expanded to include the new turns of events. The three events of the riddle provide the perfect balance, forming the frame for the story: "Mark the Wans, why do I am alook alike a poss of porterpease?" (21.18-19). *Mark the Wans* becomes "Mark the Twy" (22.5) and then the "Tris" (22.29), and the riddle asks about "two poss" and then "three" as it progresses. (In the third instance, *porter pease* splits from the monolithic *porterpease*.) When the jarl is first seen, he "had his burnt head high up in his lamphouse" (21.10)—he is the giant of Vico's first stage as well as the lighthouse on the Hill of Howth. But the second introduction to van Hoother finds him with "his baretholobruised heels drowned in his cellarmalt" (21.35)—prehistoric man having taken refuge in caves; Earwicker as a tavern-keeper is nursing bruises received during the religious massacre on St. Bartholomew's Day. And the third finds him with "his hurricane hips up to his pantrybox" (22.22-23)—man has become domesticated; the jarl is about to unleash his thunder and lightning. On one level of the tale, the jarl is Finn MacCool who lost his bride Grace to his aide Dermot: each time the prankquean arrives she is preceded by the interjection "be dermot" (21.14), "be redtom" (21.31), and "be dom ter" (22.18), suggesting that she is not only Grace O'Malley the piratess, but also the Grace of the Finn-Dermot story. She is announced by a series of changing expressions: the first time she "pulled a rosy one" (21.15-16), then she "nipped a paly one" (22.3), finally she "picked a blank" (22.27). Her riddle is changed from the simple "wit" (21.16) of the first visit to the comparative "she made her witter" (22.4), and finally the superlative "wittest" (22.28) foreshadows the culmination of her pranks. The final twist comes with van Hoother's response to each kidnaping; each time he has slammed the door in her face "Shut!" (21.20) and each time he has shouted after her (echoing "Come Back to My Erin") to "Stop deef stop come back to my earin stop" (21.23-24) and "Stop domb stop come back with my earring stop" (22.10). But each time the prankquean ran off with a twin, converting the first to the Anglican version of God as "the onesure allgood" and making him a "luderman" (21.30), while the second is "provorted" to the Puritan "onecertain allsecure" which makes him a "tristian" (22.16-17). But the simple slam of the door (*shut*) repeated in this simple form becomes the second of ten thunderclaps which punctuate the *Wake,* a one-hundred-letter-word for thunder.*

This sort of series of repetitions and changes not only occurs in individual episodes such as these, but is characteristic of the entire novel: words, numbers, motifs, and lines constantly crop up again and again, indicating an approach to the significance of a particular portion of the book or merely collecting for a definite final purpose. The most numerous recurrences of course are the designa-

---

* See Appendix for a fuller treatment of the Prankquean Tale.

tions for the hero and heroine: Humphrey Chimpden Earwicker and Anna Livia Plurabelle (as well as shortened versions of each name, and their initials—whether in the same order or anagrammed) can be found peeking through thousands of lines in the *Wake*, each time indicating that, if we have not realized so before, it is important to associate this particular character with the events being discussed or narrated. Even an innocuous "Hek" (411.18) in Shaun's speech discloses a reference to his father, while the double "f" in "Laffayette" (26.16) indicates that the Liffey—and consequently Anna Livia—is to be understood here.

The poetic value of recurring motifs is of singular importance in the *Wake,* a book that depends to a great extent upon sounds, sound patterns, and the balance of its components in both poetic texture and logical structure. The pun, therefore, like the series of otherwise meaningless sounds, provides one of the poetic bases of the book. The closing portion of Jaun's chapter supports the contention that Joyce can weave poetic stuff from the pun material on his loom. Shaun has been transformed into Jaun (the lover) who himself disintegrates into Haun (the ghost) to become Yawn (the exhausted body that decomposes in the next chapter to refertilize the banks of the Liffey as Osiris' body refertilized the banks of the Nile). Whatever hostility Joyce felt for his demagogue-turned-seducer now fades with the fading of the haunt; the farewell address delivered by the menstrual maidens is a tender poetic interlude, yet it does not fail to continue our awareness of the basic aspects of the plot:

> Life, it is true, will be a blank without you because avicuum's not there at all, to nomore cares from nomad knows, ere Molochy wars bring the devil era, a slip of the time between a date and a ghostmark, rived by darby's chilldays embers, spatched fun Juhn that dandyforth, from the night we are and feel and fade with to the yesterselves we tread to turnupon [473.6-11].

Such lines, actually nine tetrameter-pentameter lines, are a eulogy that reminds one of Anna Livia's farewell soliloquy at the end of the *Wake,* sounding an echo of "First we feel. Then we fall"

(627.11), which we will soon see again. The sense is certainly poetic: the cares of life having left Shaun; life compared to a brief letter—from the dateline to the postmark; even an echo of Hamlet's "undiscover'd country from whose bourn/ No traveller returns" can be heard. The puns themselves add levels of meaning to each line: the conceit of life as a letter is introduced as being *blank,* a vacuum (*avicuum*), and passing from one's date of birth until one's ghosthood. *Avicuum* returns us, however, to Vico and the cyclical theory: rebirth of the dead hero is forecast. Although we dread to turn back to yesterday's self, we are on a turning treadmill that will return us. Even the realm of Irish political history is accentuated since the *ante bellum in caelo* days implied in Moloch's war resulting in the era of Satan are also the wars fought by King Malachy II against the Danes, resulting eventually in the era of de Valera, when all invaders have been driven from Ireland. For relevance and richness, the Farewell to Haun seems capable of standing on its own merits.

A second case in point illustrates what Joyce can do with just the silent echo of a pun, where actually no pun really exists in the sense of tampering with language, and yet the dual sense upon which puns are based can be evoked. In the Mookse-Gripes fable, Nuvoletta attempts to attract the attention of the contesting "ecclesiasts," only to realize that they are incapable of heeding her temptation; she therefore dismisses her efforts as "mild's vapour moist" (157.23). The poetic echo here is of "love's labour's lost," yet the words Joyce chooses do not actually pun with the Shakespeare title. Nuvoletta's efforts are futile, and indeed her labors of love are lost, and the reader understands the implied meaning from the literary allusion, while the words go on by their own way to add secondary and tertiary meanings. As a cloud, Nuvoletta is vapor, and therefore moist. Literal sense would dictate that *mild's* reads *my,* but the omnipresence of Wagner's *Mild und leise* in the *Wake* adds the love-death aria to Nuvoletta-Isolde's song.

Adding additional weight and power to the poetic pun is Joyce's manipulation of various languages. The multilingual aspect of *Fin-*

negans Wake is readily explained as a facet of the dream technique of the novel: in attempting to record a significant cross section of Everyman dreaming in all time and all space (although firmly anchored in the psychological and social perspectives of contemporary thinking), Joyce feels free to choose from as many of the languages and dialects as are at his disposal. *Finnegans Wake* might well have been composed in unadorned contemporary English, the dream of Everyman understandably translated into a single language, the language at the individual dreamer's command, but Joyce is conscious that English itself is a hybrid and composed of fragments of many tongues—and not all of Indo-European ancestry—and that the "typical" Irishman is himself a cultural representative of more than one ethnic group. Foreign languages invade Joyce's *Wake* as foreigners had for centuries invaded his native land; they are just as readily assimilated and indeed add to the cultural composition of his book, providing an unlimited poetic possibility for his language.

One of the most language-conscious sections of *Finnegans Wake* occurs at the Mutt-Jute scene where early native-invader relationships are commented upon with a multilingual tongue. Mutt, the native, begins with an apology, "Scuse us" (16.5), which presents a root word as understandable to an Englishman as to an Italian. He then proceeds to determine the invader's language in order to converse: "You tollerday donsk? N. You tolkatiff scowegian? Nn. You spigotty anglease? Nnn. You phonio saxo? Nnnn. Clear all so! 'Tis a Jute. Let us swop hats and excheck a few strong verbs weak oach eather yapyazzard abast the blooty creeks" (16.5-9). Here Joyce is using root words of almost universal European character. The Jute's negative reply hardly needs more than the *n* sound to be interpreted by any European, other than a Greek, as a negative. The haphazard exchange of parts of languages through conversation is fundamental to the linguistic integration of two groups, and Mutt's indicates a philologist's awareness of the accident of language while conversing in a phonetic melange of syllables. (Nor is the name of Pigott in *spigotty* an accident, as subse-

quent uses of "Hasatency" and "hasitancy" [16.26,30] indicate;
Pigott had managed to get himself into quite a mess by his inability to spell his own language.)

The ensuing dialogue indicates that all is not amenable in the relations between native and conqueror; their battles are re-enacted simply by recording their language differences. There is a definite faultiness in their powers of communication; they mishear each other because of predispositions:

> Jute.—Are you jeff?
> Mutt.—Somehards.
> Jute.—But you are not jeffmute.
> Mutt.—Noho. Only an utterer.
> Jute.—Whoa? Whoat is the mutter with you?
> Mutt.—I became a stun a stummer.
> Jute.—What a hauhauhauhaudibble thing, to be cause! How, Mutt?
> Mutt.—Aput the buttle, surd.
> Jute.—Whose poddle? Wherein?
> Mutt.—The Inns of Dungtarf where Used awe to be he.
> Jute.—You that side your voise are almost inedible to me. Become a bitskin more wiseable, as if I were you [16.12-25].

This is of course nothing more than the comic dialogue between two burlesque buffoons and embodies the basis of their humor—mistaken understanding of what the other is saying. When Mutt says *stutterer* Jute hears "mutterer," while the audience hears "utterer." Jute replies with *mutter* meaning "matter," and Mutt tells him that his astonishment has made him mute (*stumm* in German) and a stammerer. Jute finds this horrible, finds Mutt inaudible, and finds the whole thing laughable. The battle between the native and the invader is the Battle of Clontarf in which the Irish defeated the Danes (A.D. 1014), but it is also the battle in Earwicker's tavern in which the native has been hit with a bottle of whiskey (*Used awe to be* is a transliterative reproduction of the Gaelic word of "the water of life"). *Bitskin* not only reproduces the mayhem of the fight but approximates the German words for "a little" and for "a mouthful."

The invader then offers to quiet Mutt with an offer of money: "Let me fore all your hasitancy cross your qualm with trink gilt. Here have sylvan coyne, a piece of oak. Ghinees hies good for you." He replies: "Louee, louee! How wooden I not know it, the intellible greytcloak of Cedric Silkyshag! Cead mealy faulty rices for one dabblin bar. Old grilsy growlsy! He was poached on in that eggtentical spot. Here where the liveries, Monomark" (16.29-17.1). The fact that the German word for a gratuity is *Trinkgeld* unearths another dual level of interpretation: money and drink are combined in forms from various languages—English guineas, French louis, German marks, and bars of Spanish doubloons in pieces of eight. We are also being told that Mutt and Jute are standing on the spot where Earwicker has committed (or will commit) his indiscretion, where the Liffey passes by.

Instances of other multilingual puns are numerous: the oft-discussed "Anna Livia Plurabelle" section is known to pun many hundreds of the rivers of the world throughout its pages:

> My hands are blawcauld between isker and suda like that piece of pattern chayney there, lying below. Or where is it? Lying beside the sedge I saw it. Hoangho, my sorrow, I've lost it! Aimihi! With that turbary water who could see? So near and yet so far! But O, gihon! I lovat a gabber. I could listen to maure and moravar again. Regn onder river. Flies do your float. Thick is the life for mere [213.4-10].

The two washerwomen (the banshees washing the blood from the shirts of the heroes) are gossiping about Anna Livia and her family while washing their dirty linen at opposite banks of the Liffey. A piece of laundry is washed away; they continue gossiping while the various rivers of the world flow by. In this same chapter, Anna's feeding the hero a ham sandwich is interpolated into three languages: "a shinkobread (hamjambo, bana?)" (199.19-20)—German, English, French.

In the tale of the Ondt and the Gracehoper, Joyce manages to interweave types of insects of every kind in many languages into the entomological fabric of his fable:

> The Gracehoper was always jigging ajog, hoppy on akkant of his joy-

icity, (he had a partner pair of findlestilts to supplant him), or, if not, he was always making ungraceful overtures to Floh and Luse and Bienie and Vespatilla to play pupa-pupa and pulicy-pulicy and langtennas. . . . He would of curse melissciously, by his fore feelhers, flexors, contractors, depressors and extensors [414.22-31].

A vast amount of entomological, as well as philological, knowledge is embedded in the fable; the four girls mentioned are names taken from various foreign words for various insects: *Floh* is flea in German, *Luse* (*lūs*) is Anglo-Saxon for louse, and so forth. Also, various philosophers find their way into the fable: *akkant, schoppinhour, leivnits, hegelstomes* (Hegel's tomes plus St. Thomas), and so forth. And to further the resurrection motif of the *Wake,* Joyce offers a "Chrysalmas" (416.26) which produces a host of butterflies in various languages: "smetterling of entymology" (417.4)— German, *Schmetterling;* "marypose" (417.28-29) —Spanish, *mariposa;* farfalling" (417.13)—Italian, *farfalla;* "Papylonian" (417.12)—French, *papillon;* all of them part of an international "batflea" (417.3).*

The secret of such a technique of interweaving word elements

---

* It is by a rather appropriate side door that entomology enters into the spirit of things in the *Wake.* The cosmological viewpoint allows us to see contemporary humanity as the insects scurrying over the body of the sleeping giant whose omphalos and environs is the metropolis of Dublin, although microcosmically they may be vermin in the Dreamer's bed: "Fleppety! Flippety! Fleapow!" (15.26-27). In fact, the Earwicker family is a buggy one, H. C. himself being an earwig, "earwigger" (31.28), Anna Livia an annalid worm, "analectual pygmyhop" (268.28-29) and "annywom" (475.21). The family can be found in their natural habitat at the end of the first chapter: "Shop Illicit, flourishing like a lordmajor or a buaboabaybohm, litting flop a deadlop (aloose!) to lee but lifting a bennbranch a yardalong (ivoeh!) on the breezy side (for showm!), the height of Brewster's chimpney and as broad below as Phineas Barnum; humphing his share of the showthers is senken on him he's such a grandfallar, with a pocked wife in pickle that's a flyfire and three lice nittle clinkers, two twilling bugs and one midgit pucelle" (29.1-8). Our archetypal grandfather is the Adam who has his grand fall, but (*O felix culpa!*) he has survived his fall from the tree like our primate ancestors, and like the butterfly (*farfalla*) has been resurrected from his earlier state. The archetypal woman is a tease as well as firefly, and her children are lice, nits, lightning bugs, midges, and fleas (French, *puce*), although they can pass as twin boys (German, *Zwilling*) and a maiden (French, *pucelle*). Note: Anoplura are the "true lice."

into a polyglottal pattern is explained by Gillet, who quotes Joyce's formula: "He told me about the language he had adopted in order to give his vocabulary the elasticity of sleep, to multiply the meaning of words, to permit the play of light and colour, and make of the sentence a rainbow in which each tiny drop is itself a many-hued prism."[8] In investigating this "unerring music, this ear, this sense of cadence and melody" in *Finnegans Wake,* Gillet comes to realize that the Joyce method actually involves an attempt to reproduce bits of lyric poetry throughout the book, that Joyce is as conscious of his poetic elements as any poet; he finds "pure vowels (and . . . a miraculous rhythm of iambics and anapests). . . . *For Camilla, Dromilla, Ludmilla, Mamilla, a bucket, a packet, a book and a pillow.*"[9] There are actually instances in the *Wake* in which Joyce indicates how a line should be read by interweaving the poetic key in the material he is using: "and all the livvylong night, the delldale dalppling night, the night of bluerybells, her flittaflute in tricky trochees (O carina! O carina!) wake him" (7.1-3). Both sound and image are evoked in this passage of thin flute-ocarina music, a dream quality dependent upon the presence of the eternal woman whose three names and initials are all present in the lines *and livvy bluerybells* and *dalppling,* as well as the "little heart" of *carina* (Anna Livia is later called "Miss Corrie Corriendo" [220.19], including a pun on the Greek word for "maiden"); and the trochaic rhythm dominates the music.*

Although almost all critics are quick to label *Finnegans Wake* "a great poem" (or some such safe, all-inclusive phrase), few have done much to interpret the poetry of the *Wake* as poetry. Frank Budgen notes that

> the cosmic viewpoint and the comic muse are old associates, but the presence of lyric inspiration in the alliance is rarer, perhaps unique, yet here they are in organic union in *Finnegans Wake.* I believe it was Joyce's aim to include every genre of poetic composition

---

* Clive Hart has noted that "throughout *Finnegans Wake* the spondee is associated with Shaun, the trochee with Anna or Issy, and, significantly, the pyrrhic with effete Shem" (*Structure and Motif,* p. 73 fn.).

in his book. I well remember him telling me with pleasure that his friend, James Stephens, had found all poetic elements blended in what at that time was called *Work in Progress.*[10]

The panorama of poetic genres employed in the *Wake* would not be difficult to uncover. In the various actual "poems" in the book —those sections of italicized verse incorporated in *Finnegans Wake*—Joyce shows his odd mastery of satiric verse and doggerel as he has indicated with his early broadsides, *The Holy Office* and *Gas from a Burner.* The ballad that Hosty made, "The Ballad of Persse O'Reilly" (44-47), for which Joyce provides musical notations, contains a four-line stanza usually of some sort of anapestic trimeter, the first two lines ending in feminine off-rhymes, while the last word of the quatrain is repeated and rhymed in a two-line chorus of anapestic dimeter:

> Here you heard of one Humpty Dumpty
> How he fell with a roll and a rumble
> And curled up like Lord Olofa Crumple
> By the butt of the Magazine Wall,
>   (Chorus) Of the Magazine Wall,
>   Hump, helmet and all?
>   [45.1-6]

Thirteen such stanzas make up the ballad, with an interjected line after every four stanzas and a final envoy of

> And not all the king's men nor his horses
> Will resurrect his corpus
> For there's no true spell in Connacht or hell
>   (bis) That's able to raise a Cain
>   [47.26-29]

Thus all the themes of the first two chapters concerning Earwicker's life (his conquest, his notoriety, his sin, his fall) are reviewed in this tavern-born ballad; the Humpty Dumpty myth provides the frame for this nursery rhyme, and the jostling verse form and bumbling rhymes provide the basis of this "popular" castigation of the hero.

As Hosty's verses cap the first two chapters which deal with Earwicker's rise and fall, a lament by the women at the wake caps the next two chapters which record the trial and jailing of the hero, his fall and resurrection. It is a lament that reflects both sorrow and the inevitable castigation; the verse form is varied, with two stanzas of four basic lines (only the first two of which rhyme), and the second stanza graced by an interjected chorus line after the first and second lines. Like many a paragraph in *Finnegans Wake*, each stanza is followed by a single coda word, a technique that reflects the *ricorso* motif of Viconian history—the book itself is in three basic parts followed by a single short *"ricorso"* chapter. The lament reads:

> *Sold him her lease of nineninenineetee,*
> *Tresses undresses so dyedyedaintee,*
> *Goo, the groot gudgeon, gulped it all.*
> *Hoo was the C.O.D.?*
>   Bum!
>
> *At Island Bridge she met her tide.*
> *Attabom, attabom, attabombomboom!*
> *The Fin had a flux and his Ebba a ride.*
> *Attabom, attabom, attabombomboom!*
> *We're all up to the years in hues and cribies.*
> *That's what she's done for wee!*
>   Woe!
>   [102.31-103.7]

The chorus line may well be a parody of the line in a French folksong concerning the execution of a chevalier of King Louis XIV who stood in the king's way by his refusal to share his beautiful wife with the monarch; the repetition of "rataplan, rataplan, rataplanplanplan" in the song echoes the drumroll at the execution.

The brother battle of Shem and Shaun is recorded in a victory song in *Finnegans Wake* following a football match between two Oxford colleges—a match that reflects the battle in heaven between St. Michael's heavenly host and the forces of the devil— "All Saints beat Belial! Mickil Goals to Nichil!" (175.5). The

song, of six long-lined rhymed couplets, again restates the basic
themes of the *Wake* and suggests the Viconian cycles:

> *In Nowhere has yet the Whole World taken*
> *part of himself for his Wife;*
> *By Nowhere have Poorparents been sentenced*
> *to Worms, Blood and Thunder for Life* . . .

and harkens back to Hosty's immortal ballad:

> *Till the four Shores of deff Tory Island*
> *let the douze dumm Eirewhiggs raille!*
> *Hirp! Hirp! for their Missed Understandings!*
> *chirps the Ballat of Perce-Oreille*
> [175.7-10, 25-28]

The next bit of doggerel is Shem's quatrain about the influence
of God and sex on his youth* (231.5-8), plus a five-stanza ballad,
each quatrain ending with "wather parted from the say," apparently in composition before the closing of Earwicker's pub and spaced
out over several pages (371.6-8, 18-20, 30-32; 372.25-27;
373.9-11), followed by a verse recording of the Tristram story
which opens the last chapter of the second book. This is a thirteen-
line monstrosity of uneven line length, all but the eleventh and
twelfth lines rhymed with "Mark." Serving as an introductory epi-
graph for the Tristram-Iseult chapter in which Earwicker lyrically
dreams of himself as Tristram, this bit of verse is as banal and
limping a piece of doggerel as one can imagine, but serves the function of reflecting the absurd, comic side of the medieval romance:
no sooner does old Earwicker embark upon his Tristram phantasy
of sexual prowess than the twelve customers sing out to remind
him what an old fool he is—he is cuckolded King Mark, not the
lover Tristram:

> —*Three quarks for Muster Mark!*
> *Sure he hasn't got much of a bark.* . . .
> *Fowls, up! Tristy's the spry young spark*
> *That'll tread her and wed her and bed her and red her*

* Commented on in chapter 2, Part II.

Without ever winking the tail of a feather
And that's how that chap's going to make his money
and mark!

[383.1-2, 11-14]

H.C.E. is being reminded of his sad role as the old man hood-winked by the young girl; the last line of this verse echoes an ear-lier American movie scenario of the "Daddy" Browning and "Peaches" scandal of the twenties: "that's how half the gels in town has got their bottom drars while grumpapar he's trying to hitch his braces on to his trars" (65.18-20). There, too, Joyce used comic rhyme in painful repetition to drill the distasteful circum-stances into Earwicker's drowsy unconscious. The use of the "ark" rhymes is as purposeful and significant as the "lead" rhymes in *The Merchant of Venice;* Joyce seems to be quite aware of the ad-vantages to which Shakespeare put poetic and musical interludes and denies himself none of the conventions that added to the Eliz-abethan's dramatic power.

As the chapter commences with a comic poem on Earwicker's folly as a Marked Tristram, so it ends with a hymn to Iseult la Belle (as such this chapter is a microcosm of the book itself). Here, in long unrhymed lines of free verse, Joyce manages to bal-ance the comic with the serious in poetic form. The language of the hymn suggests Walt Whitman in verse form and in an all-em-bracing bombast which talks of *"Nine hundred and ninetynine million pound sterling in the blueblack bowels of the bank of Ulster"* (398.32-33):

> *O, come all ye sweet nymphs of Dingle beach*
> *to cheer Brinabride queen from Sybil*
> *surfriding*
> *In her curragh of shells of daughter of pearl*
> *and her silverymonnblue mantle round her.*
> *Crown of the waters, brine on her brow,*
> *she'll dance them a jig and jilt them*
> *fairly.*
> *Yerra, why would she bide with Sig Sloomysides*
> *or the grogram grey barnacle gander?*

[399.3-10]

This poem announces the doom of old Mark-Earwicker (masquerading as young Tristram) and foreshadows the arrival (in Book Three) of the real swashbuckling lover, Jaun (Shaun as Don Juan-Tristram).

The next "poem" in the *Wake* comes at the end of the fable of the Ondt and the Gracehoper and repeats the various characteristics of the brother dichotomy. The poem is constructed of a series of closed couplets, pun-peppered and compounded of such brother situations as Castor and Pollux—*"Can castwhores pulladeftkiss if oldpollocks foresake 'em/ Or Culex feel etchy if Pulex don't wake him?"* (418.22-23)—and incorporates Joyce's comic pair composed of the Dublin booksellers, Browne and Nolan, who represent the theory of opposites advanced by Giordano Bruno (of Nola): *"Till Nolans go volants and Bruneyes come blue"* (418.31), a synthesis of the opposites. Delivered by the Gracehoper (poet Shem), these couplets end with Joyce's pained diatribe against the prosaic burgher:

> *Your feats end enormous, your volumes immense,*
> *(May the Graces I hoped for sing your Ondtship*
>   *song sense!),*
> *Your genus its worldwide, your spacest sublime!*
> *But, Holy Saltmartin, why can't you beat time?*
>   [419.5-8]

Other doggerel matter in *Finnegans Wake* consists of a handful of sprinkled stanzas serving as addenda for the ballads already cited: an acrostic of three lines alliterates H, C, and E (481.1-3); Earwicker cuckolded is again celebrated in lines rhyming with *"Marak"** (491.17)—a further twist on the misspelling that di-

---

* The transition from *Mark* to *Marak* (and *ark* to *arak*) again indicates the system of augmentation by which Joyce expands meaning in his work. Since old **Mark** cuckolded by nephew Tristram is also old Noah mocked by son Ham, the *ark* in *Mark* is apt. Noah's shame was caused by drunkenness, hence *arak*, the anise-liquor of the Near East. In this bit of verse Mark-Noah-Earwicker's misdemeanor is that *"He drapped has draraks an Mansianhase parak"* (491.18), indicating that he "dropped his drawers" (known as "bottom drars" in the Daddy Browning scene—65.18-19), but also that he drank a drop

vulges guilt; a new verse for Hosty's virulent ballad is offered (525.21-26); Shem and Shaun are synthesized in a three-line coda to the Gracehoper's poem (526.13-15); and Earwicker is once again laid to rest with a capping couplet:

> —*Day shirker four vanfloats he verdants market.*
> *High liquor made lust torpid dough hunt her orchid*
> [530.23-24]

It is not the selections of comic verse and doggerel sprinkled† throughout the *Wake* to provide a concise restatement of ideas, however, that primarily attests to the poetic value of the work. Joyce is interested in *Finnegans Wake* in a poetic texture that underlies the prose element. He has selected his language carefully and uses lyrical language for various poetic effects—effects integrated with the themes and characters.

The "Anna Livia Plurabelle" section is in itself a comic dialogue between two gossipy washerwomen, yet, in discussing the character and affairs of the most beautiful figure of the work, it manages to rise to many instances of lyrical heights foreshadowing the final rhapsodic soliloquy of the book. Anna Livia's death is already being mourned:

> Wait till the honeying of the lune, love! Die eve, little eve, die! We see that wonder in your eye. We'll meet again, we'll part once more. The spot I'll seek if the hour you'll find. My chart shines high where the blue milk's upset. Forgivemequick, I'm going! Bubye! And you, pluck your watch, forgetmenot. Your evenlode. So save to jurna's

---

(*drap* in Irish dialect) of arak (*raki* in Turkish). (Elsewhere, in a list of the first four months of the calendar, arak joins the homier gin, beer, and ale in "junipery or febrewery, marracks or alebrill"—15.35-36.) To compound his crime, *draracks* implies masturbation, since rocks are testicles in *Ulysses* and the *Wake;* elsewhere the onanistic act in the park (including the Three Soldiers who spy) is referred to as "dry yanks will visit old sod" (194.27).

† Two comic quatrains in the style of FitzGerald's Khayyam can be found in the *Wake* (122.11-13 and 368.24-26), the latter followed by a quatrain to the tune of "Casey Jones." For comments on the Near Eastern allusions, see my article on "Persian in *Finnegans Wake*," *Philological Quarterly*, XLIV, No. 1 (January, 1965), 100-9.

end! My sights are swimming thicker on me by the shadows to this place. I sow home slowly now by own way, moyvalley way. Towy I too, rathmine (215.3-11).

Already the river is flowing out to sea; the heroine's death has already occurred, is now occurring, will occur again at the final moments of the *Wake*. The short lines, bits of rhyme, and lyric lilt carry the river along as it flows out to sea. As the descending dusk that transforms the two women had several times already been anticipated—"Murk, his vales are darkling" (23.23) and

> shades began to glidder along the banks, greepsing, greepsing, duusk unto duusk, and it was as glooming as gloaming could be in the waste of all peacable worlds. . . . Oh, how it was duusk! From Vallee Maraia to Grasyaplaina, dormimust echo! Ah dew! Ah dew! It was so duusk that the tears of night began to fall, first by ones and twos, then by threes and fours, at last by fives and sixes of sevens, for the tired ones were wecking, as we weep now with them. *O! O! O! Par la pluie!* [158.7-24]

—so the "Die eve" poem anticipates Anna Livia's monologue:

> Ho hang! Hang ho! And the clash of our cries till we spring to be free. Auravoles, they says, never heed of your name! But I'm loothing them that's here and all I lothe. Loonely in me loneness. For all their faults. I am passing out. O bitter ending! I'll slip away before they're up. They'll never see. Nor know. Nor miss me [627.31-36].

The rhythms that dominate the earlier farewell to Anna Livia now return to echo that farewell; the short lines and breathless exclamations are echoes in our ears, making us feel that we have heard all this before, that Anna Livia's demise has occurred before. Throughout the *Wake* Joyce is poetically striving for the *déjà vu* experience to emphasize the Viconian continuity. Poetic echoes best serve his purpose; the memorable lines of poetry in the *Wake* reappear often to add to that strange sensation of having been here before.

Although definitions of poetry are not usually subjective—the basic elements of rhythm, meter, rhyme, alliteration, assonance, and so forth, having been objectively outlined—no one attitude toward Joyce's poetic medium can necessarily be universally arrived at; the novelist who is many things to many readers is as individually various as a poet. Margaret Schlauch sees Joyce's poetic language in terms of philological awareness, and finds that Joyce's linguistic variants "can easily be classified by a philologist as examples of reduplication, alliteration, assonance, primitive types of apophony, assimilation, dissimilation, sandhi variants and the like."[11] Harry Levin adds that the reader is "borne from one page to the next, not by the expository current of the prose, but by the harmonic relations of the language—phonetic, syntactic, or referential, as the case may be."[12] Joyce's philological consciousness of words, the shifts of meanings within words, their etymological significances and semantic discrepancies add to the levels of meaning made possible by his skillful handling of language. The philological handling of entomological minutiæ in the fable of the Ondt and Gracehoper is very much a case in point. In fact, when asked why he hates his literary brother, Shaun replies, "For his root language, if you ask me whys" (424.17), and the tenth thunderclap roaringly follows upon his answer, causing the comment: "The hundredlettered name again, last word of perfect language" (424.23-24). But Shaun brags that he too can perpetrate "Acomedy of letters!" (425.24).

Perhaps nowhere in the *Wake* is Joyce more adroit in his ability to apply his philological awareness than in the incidents dealing with the digging up of the famous letter in the midden heap by one Belinda Doran, better known as Biddy, the Earwicker hen. It all started when the "merest of bantlings observed a cold fowl behaviourising strangely on that fatal midden" (110.24-25). From here on Joyce rarely allows an ornithological pun to pass unplayed upon: "The bird in the case was Belinda of the Dorans, a more than quinquegintarian (Terziis prize with Serni medal, Cheepalizzy's Hane Exposition) and what she was scratching at the hour of klokking twelve" (111.5-8). This contains both the "cheep" and "cluck" of hen sounds, plus Chickenlittle, hen, and *Hahn*—German for a rooster. Joyce adds that, if the reader does not have the "poultriest notions" of what all this means, he may "pick a peck of kindlings yet from the sack of auld hensyne" (112.5-8).

The next paragraph begins "Lead, kindly fowl!" (112.9), and Joyce reminds us that he is parodying John Henry Newman, a "Cardinal."

> What bird has done yesterday man may do next year, be it fly, be it moult, be it hatch, be it agreement in the nest. For her socioscientific sense is sound as a bell, sir, her volucrine automutativeness right on normalcy: she knows, she just feels she was kind of born to lay and love eggs (trust her to propagate the species and hoosh her fluffballs safe through din and danger!); lastly but mostly, in her genesic field it is all game and no gammon; she is ladylike in everything she does and plays the gentleman's part every time [112.9-17].

Then follows the injunction, "Let us auspice it!" (112.18), and Joyce is aware that the word "auspicious" comes from the Latin where it originally had the meaning of looking at birds for signs in augury—it is this sort of fossil metaphor that delights Joyce. When he adds that "Ague will be rejuvenated" (112.20), the pun for egg is obvious and returns the motif to the Humpty Dumpty theme and the Egyptian Cosmic Egg, as well as the *Juva* (609.25) evolved from "Jute" (16.7). He predicts one step of "sublime incubation" for women and derides those "gloompourers who grouse that letters have never been quite their old selves again since that weird weekday in bleak Janiveer . . . when to the shock of both, Biddy Doran looked at literature" (112.21, 24-27). The verb *grouse* of Anglo-Saxon origin provides another pun for the noun *grouse* of Old French derivation, while *Janiveer* incorporates Chaucer's famous cock, Chanticleer, with Janus. In the next paragraph he reappears as part of the letter's author's "fallimineers" (112.33-34)—near family—and "Nuttings on her wilelife!" (113.3) reminds us that Nut is the Egyptian goddess who lays the Cosmic Egg.

In contrast to the philological approach to Joyce's language, Hugh Kenner tends to investigate the *Wake* in terms of its poetic rhetoric, noting that Joyce "sets up within each paragraph a drama of strophe, antistrophe, and parabasis turning on the interactions

of juxtaposed contexts, personae, and gestures." He examines Earwicker's stammered denial of guilt when confronted by the Cad
asking the time and finds that

> These phrases are items, not statements: items of talk. The tones of
> the Audenesque public-school man of action vibrating with embar-
> rassed friendship ("Shsh shake, co-comeraid!"), of the clean-living
> cricketer ("I have won straight"), of the challenged Tory ("I an [*sic*]
> woowoo willing to take my stand, sir"), of the correct Christian
> gentleman ("before the Great Taskmaster's (I lift my hat!)"), of the
> legal precisionist ("as of all such of said my immediate withdwell-
> ers"), of the reverberating orator ("every living sohole in every cor-
> ner whatsoever [*sic*] of this globe in general"), all these are so many
> juxtaposed aural observations organized with comprehending detach-
> ment. Character is elucidated by rapidly synthesizing the voices and
> locutions of many persons.[13]

This sort of Joycean rhetoric, as Kenner contends, can be found
in every paragraph of the *Wake,* especially in the speeches of Earwicker and Shaun; it punctuates Shaun's various guises throughout
the book. Joyce is capable of making his bourgeois hero sound like
the successful politician, the lover, *et al.* In fact, it is no far stretch
of interpretation to realize that good Shaun ironically embodies the
Seven Deadly Sins (perhaps in contrast to Shem's personification
of the Seven Lively Arts, rather than Cardinal Virtues). Shaun, as
the postman who steals the letter, is constantly jealous of his brother's literary talents and often boasts that he can do as well. His
envy drives him to belittle and deride Shem's literary efforts:

> Every dimmed letter in it is a copy and not a few of the silbils and
> wholly words I can show you in my Kingdom of Heaven. The
> lowquacity of him! With his threestar monothong! Thaw! The last
> word in stolentelling! And what's more rightdown lowbrown
> schisthematic robblemint! Yes. As he was rising my lather. Like you.
> And as I was plucking his gossybone. Like yea. He store the tale of
> me shur. Like yup. How's that for Shemese? [424.32-425.3].

And, as the schoolboy Kevin, Shaun had once before attempted to
outdo Shem (Dolph) in the letter-writing class, displaying the
same envy of Shem's success as an author (301).

Thus Envy and Pride are already obvious in the mouthings of the "good" brother; his pride is bristling in such statements as: "What I say is (and I am noen roehorn or culkilt permit me to tell you, if uninformed), I never spont it. Nor have I the ghuest of innation on me the way to. It is my rule so. . . . I am as plain as portable enveloped" (414.6-11). The arrogance of pride is well mixed in Shaun with false humility; his inability to conquer his brother intellectually galls him constantly, and he is quick to anger when confronted by Shem's superior intelligence. In the Lessons section Shem leads him a merry cerebral chase through geometry and logic while the dull-witted Kev-Shaun tries to follow the gist of Dolph-Shem's triangles and circles. When he finally becomes aware that the whole geometry lesson is nothing more than Dolph's clever leg-pulling (an obscene joke about their mother), it is not his desire to defend Anna Livia's sullied honor that leads him to beat Dolph, but his anger at having been the butt of his brother's roguish wit: "thur him no quartos!" he shouts, "quench his quill!" and "Spry him! call a bloodlekar!" (300.30-301.2). It is anger again which leads him in the Mime to beat Glugg-Shem— "Boo, you're through!" (247.12)—and shame him before the assembled Maggies.

In the fable of the Ondt and the Gracehoper, Shaun embodies the sin of Avarice. As in the La Fontaine fable, the Ondt (Dutch for "evil") hoards his food carefully and refuses his brother Gracehoper anything to eat during the cold foodless winter, and gloats: "Let him be Artalone the Weeps with his parisites peeling off him I'll be Highfee the Crackasider. Flunkey Footle furloughed foul, writing off his phoney, but Conte Carme makes the melody that mints the money. *Ad majorem l.s.d.! Divi gloriam*" (418.1-4). In words reminiscent of Joyce's brother's concern about the author's Paris friends and spurious efforts in writing the *Wake,* the Ondt delights in his money and in the Gracehoper's misfortunes. He interweaves the Jesuit motto with the signs for pounds, shillings, and pence, combining religion and money mania, providing God's sanction for his cardinal sin. The Ondt's avarice is also closely allied with his gluttony, and later, as Jaunty Jaun, Shaun's gluttony becomes a major facet of his personality. As a virtuous protector of the morality of the young schoolgirls, Jaun delivers himself of a sermon on maidenly virtues; but as he progresses he cannot keep his mind off food, and his Freudian slips are gastronomical:

> It's more important than air—I mean than eats—air (Oop, I never open momouth but I pack mefood in it) and promotes that natural emotion. Stamp out bad eggs. Why so many puddings prove disappointing, as Dietician says, in Creature Comforts Causeries, and why so much soup is so muck slop. If we could fatten on the elizabeetons we wouldn't have teeth like the hippopotamians [437.19-25].

Jaun's sermonizing concludes with an orgiastic gorging of food in which Joyce viciously parodies the Last Supper and the Eucharist; Jaun delights in his meal of cabbage and boiled Protestants and the last line of the Mass—*"Ite, Missa est"*—becomes "Eat a missal lest" (456.18).

It is also as Jaun that Shaun displays his Don Juanish lustfulness, but, whereas Shem is certainly sex conscious and obscene, Shaun adds a touch of sadism to his lust. In addressing the twenty-nine maidens he harps puritanically on their morals, finally plunging into an antisex tirade:

> I'll homeseek you, Luperca as sure as there's a palatine in Limerick and in striped conference here's how. Nerbu de Bios! If you twos goes to walk upon the railway, Gard, and I'll goad to beat behind the bush! See to it! Snip! It's up to you. I'll be hatsnatching harrier to hiding huries hinder hedge. Snap! I'll tear up your limpshades and lock all your trotters in the closet, I will, and cut your silkskin into garters. You'll give up your ask unbrodhel ways when I make you reely smart [444.35-445.7].

And finally Jaun becomes Yawn, the embodiment of Sloth; as if the huge feast has completely incapacitated him, he lies down on a hill and falls asleep. When the four inquisitors come to interrogate him, they find him there "rehearsing somewan's funeral" (477.9). They finally manage to get Yawn to talk, but his speech is slow and thick and hazy: "—Dream. Ona nonday I sleep. I dreamt of a somday. Of a wonday I shall wake. Ah! May he have now of here fearfilled me! Sinflowed, O sinflowed!" (481.7-9).

In this manner Avarice, Anger, Envy, Gluttony, Lust, Pride, and Sloth parade by in *Finnegans Wake* as aspects of Shaun the Post, and for each role Joyce fashions a rhetorical style comparable to Shaun's various guises. The sleepy monosyllables of Yawn's lethargy; the voluptuous mouthful of words for the gluttonous feasting, including the string of vowels and consonants indicating masticated food—"xoxxoxo" for cabbage (456.23); the long, panting clauses interrupted by short monosyllabic interjections for Jaun's sadistic lust; the short, snapping phrases of Kevin's anger; the verbosity of the Ondt's pride and envy: these characterize Joyce's handling of rhetorical language suited to each situation in the *Wake*.

In handling alliteration and assonance Joyce varies his language to fit the dual purpose of his comic-poetic variations. A principal example can be found in the *s* sounds that pervade throughout the *Wake*, recording the slithering of snakes in the grass and the swish of temptresses' skirts. Serpents and seductresses offer at least two parallels for Joyce—Eve in the Garden, Cleopatra and her asp, the latter heard hissing in a marginal comment to a reference to "Sire Jeallyous Seizer" (271.3): *"Cliopatria, thy hosies history"* (271.L), and the former at the genesis of the *Wake*: "past Eve and Adam's, from swerve of shore" (3.1). They form the "duo of druidesses" (271.4), the "sosie sesthers" (3.12).

A more innocent version of the temptation is attempted by the Issy maiden as "Nuvoletta in her lightdress, spunn of sisteen shimmers" (157.8), where the sixteen-year-old recalls the Eve depicted in the Sistine Chapel. Hers is obviously more flirtation than seduction, and the *l* sounds of *Nuvoletta in her lightdress* are light and ethereal and lilting, but soon take on the swishing sounds of her light nightdress made of shimmering stuff. This toning down of the temptress's seductiveness gives us the "Christine" side of Issy in contrast to her "Sally" personality in the mirror: not only is she a little cloud and a tender maiden of sixteen summers, but the Virgin as well as Eve. But, since her flirtations come to nought, she shrugs off the rebuff and comes to realize that there are many men in the world to tempt: "—I see, she sighed. There are menner" (158.5), and the sounds of her retreating skirts are echoed in her sigh and the soft fall of night: "The siss of the whisp of the sigh of the softzing at the stir of the ver grose O arundo of a long one in midias reeds: and shades began to glidder along the banks, greepsing, greepsing, duusk unto duusk" (158.6-9). Through the reeds flits the wind carrying calumny, the tale of the woman's seduction of the hero as here the reeds whisper the rumor that King Midas has ass's ears, and that all this is merely a single instant in a repeating cycle (*in medias res*) of such temptations. The *long one* is again the snake in the grass, known in the Cleopatra scene as "Lang Wang Wurm" (270.n2).

Elsewhere *l* sounds couple with *s* sounds as the gossip crosses and recrosses the river where the dirty linen is being washed, and the seduction of young Anna Livia provides conjecture for the washerwomen: "Letty Lerck's lafing light throw those laurals now on her daphdaph teasesong petrock" (203.29-31), and "She was just a young thin pale soft shy slim slip of a thing then, sauntering, by silvamoonlake" (202.26-28). The latter is re-echoed at the end of the *Wake* when Anna Livia describes her successor: "Just a whisk brisk sly spry spink spank sprint of a thing theresomere, saultering. Saltarella come to her own" (627.4-6), where again the lilting *l* sounds are close by: "I'm loothing them that's here and all I lothe. Loonely in me loneness" (627.33-34). And, just as the interrupted sentence continues on at the beginning of the book with serpentine sounds, so it commences at *Wake*'s end with "A way a lone a last a loved a long the" (628.15-16), Anna Livia letting on that she's "lilting on all the time" (627.21). There is a good possibility that a string of seven *s* alliteratives might imply the Persian New Year, when seven dishes whose names begin with the sound are served, most apparent in "sure, straight, slim, sturdy, serene, synthetical, swift" (596.32-33); this might be corroborated in the washerwomen scene where the *ruz* in "she ruz two feet hire" (204.2) could be intended to reveal *No Ruz,* the Persian New Year.

Serpent sounds are ubiquitous in any event in the *Wake,* as "Satyrdaysboost besets Phoebe's nearest" (583.19), and the temptresses reappear as "two hussites" (589.33) and as "your two cozes from Niece . . . surprised in an indecorous position" (608.7-9). Nor are the Three Soldiers immune from being considered snakes in the grass, sharing with the Two Girls the role of tempters; when the girls are the *two cozes,* the soldiers form the "Sigurd Sigerson Sphygmomanometer Society" (608.10); when they are "two drawpers assisters" (608.5-6), the soldiers are "three droopers assessors" (608.6). It is apparent that the military trio forms a "triplehydrad snake" (36.7), but most often the *s* sounds are feminine in context, conjuring up the duo: "two disappainted solicitresses" (90.16), a *"Pair of Sloppy Sluts"* (107.6), "saucicissters" (96.13), "Two Young Spinsters" (307.6-7), and "two stripping baremaids" (526.23).

The *s* sounds probably also suggest the sound of micturition, an act associated with the girls in the Park; thus we find that the *saucicissters* are "meeting waters most improper" (96.14). At another instance the "two scissymaidies" (192.2) are linked with the "bourgeoismeister, who thought to touch both himmels at the punt of his risen stiffstaff and how wishywashy sank the waters of his thought?" (191.35-192.1). This motif is of primary significance in the Prankquean Tale* where the *s* sounds of the urinating piratess are apparent in her riddle asking about "a poss of porterpease" (21.18-19). And the liquid *l* sounds of the more innocent temptress are included in many designations for the micturating maidens, known occasionally as "two lay payees" (480.1), immediately preceded by "Ess Ess. O ess" (479.36); they are also "one dilalah, Lupita Lorette" (67.33) and her "sister-in-love, Luperca Latouche" (67.36), who "stripped teasily" (68.1). See also: "Lili and Tutu" (52.3), *"the Misses O'Mollies"* (106.34), "lilithe

---

* See Appendix.

maidinettes" (241.4), "two lunar eclipses and its three saturnine settings" (264.4-5), "the liliens of the veldt, Nancy Nickies and Folletta Lajambe" (422.32-33), "Julie and Lulie at their parkiest" (502.24), "Lizzy and Lissy Mycock" (538.22)—linked with "hespermun" (538.23), a word containing *mun* (Irish, urine) and sperm, accounting for the confusion of masturbation and micturition in Earwicker's sin in the park. And finally there is a passage in which *s*'s and *l*'s and urination and sexual perversion and serpents are interwoven:

> the secret empire of the snake which it was on a point of our sutton down, how was it, Jimmy?—Who has sinnerettes to declare? Phiss! Touching our Phoenix Rangers' nuisance at the meeting of the waitresses, the daintylines, Elsies from Chelsies, the two legglegels in blooms, and those pest of parkies, twitch, thistle and charlock, were they for giving up their fogging trespasses by order which we foregathered he must be raw in cane sugar, the party, no, Jimmy MacCawthelock? Who trespass against me? Briss! [587.22-31].

Besides *Phiss* and *Briss,* the paragraph also contains "Hiss" (587.3), "Kiss" (587.5), and "Sish" (587.19).

It becomes apparent that the *l* sounds are best associated with the Biblical Lilith, apocryphal counterpart of Eve and thus a mirror image in the *Wake* to the young Eve, Issy. On the adult level, Lilith exists in the *Wake* as the wife of the sinister Magrath (obviously a Satan figure); they are thus negative counterparts to Anna Livia and H. C. Earwicker.[14] It is important that during the washerwomen's colloquy over the Earwicker laundry, Lily's drawers intrude, introduced by *l* sounds that echo Anna Livia's closing soliloquy: "longing loth and loathing longing" (204.26). "I can tell from here by their *eau de Colo* and the scent of her oder they're Mrs Magrath's," comments one of the laundresses (204.33-34).

> And here is her nubilee letters too. Ellis on quay in scarlet thread. Linked for the world on a flushcaloured field. Annan exe after to show they're not Laura Keown's. O, may the diabolo twisk your seifety pin! You child of Mammon, Kinsella's Lilith! Now who has been

tearing the leg of her drawars on her? Which leg is it? The one with the bells on it [205.7-13].

Only a glance at the opening of Anna Livia's last speech is enough to tie these themes together: "Soft morning, city! Lsp! I am leafy speafing. Lpf! Folty and folty all the nights have falled on to long my hair. Not a sound, falling. Lispn!" (619.20-22). Joyce's technique of providing sound patterns is sufficient to tie together divergent parts of the book into a coherent pattern in which Earwicker's sin in Phoenix Park involves the urinating girls who complement Eve and Lilith to Earwicker's Adam, and who indicate that all roads in the *Wake* lead back to the initial pair and the basic family, Issy and her mirror image dually reflecting Anna Livia and her own alter-image.

In contrast to the musical pairing of *l*'s and *s*'s, Joyce also offers a nonmusical pattern of sounds involving *p*'s and *q*'s, also indicating the girls in the park. The choice of these sounds probably has a lot less to do with their significance in Gaelic sound changes than with the dictum of propriety ("mind your *p*'s and *q*'s") against which all the characters in the *Wake* sin, and the urinary meaning of "pee," as well as the form of the two letters, both being yonic in shape with a small tail attached.* The Prankquean as such is a combined *p-q* female, most often seen in the *Wake* as a pair, the girls in the park: "a queen of pranks" (68.22), "the parkside pranks of quality queens" (394.27-28). During the Toucher "Thom" portion of the Yawn inquest, the girls are at their lascivious worst, and the *p*'s and *q*'s are thickly concentrated: after a "Pax and Quantum" reference (508.6), the question is "Like a skib leaked lintel the arbour leidend with . . . ?" (508.17-18)— with at least two urine references, *leaked* and *lintel* (since lentil is a pea). The answer comes back: "—Pamelas, peggylees, pollywollies, questuants, quaintaquilities, quickamerries" (508.19-20), evenly divided between *p*'s and *q*'s. The next question blends from

* At one instance the vagina is termed the *q* district ("the Cutey Strict"— 364.31).

s sounds into *p*'s and *q*'s, spelling them out quite succinctly and implicating Cleopatra, the temptress-cum-asp:

> —Concaving now convexly to the semidemihemispheres and, from the female angle, music minnestirring, were the subligate sisters, P. and Q., Clopatrick's cherierapest, *mutatis mutandis,* in pretty much the same pickle, the peach of all piedom, the quest of all quicks? [508.21-25]

and the answer in very much the same vein: "—Peequeen ourselves, the prettiest pickles of unmatchemable mute antes I ever bopeeped at, seesaw shallshee, since the town go went gonning on Pranksome Quaine" (508.26-28). Given this much encouragement, the interrogator goes on to hiss his next sexual question: "—Silks apeel and sulks alusty?" (508.29).

But this cluster is only a part of the whole, and many *p-q* combinations flow through the book, suggesting a theme rich but hitherto overlooked: "Questa and Puella, piquante and quoite, (this had a cold in her brain while that felt a sink in her summock, wit's wat, wot's wet)" (61.16-18); "dry puder for the Ill people and pinkun's pellets for all the Pale . . . her pinch to Anna Livia, that superfine pigtail to Cerisia Cerosia and quid rides to Titius, Caius and Sempronius . . . shot two queans . . . pause and quies, triple bill" (128.12-22)—Anna Livia strongly implicated here, while *p* and *q* are used in lieu of actual names, so that the two temptresses and the three soldiers are implied in *pause and quies, triple bill;* "Peena and Queena are duetting a giggle-for-giggle and the brideen Alannah is lost in her diamindwaiting" (377.18-20); "the gouty old galahat, with his peer of quinnyfears and his troad of thirstuns" (389.23-24); "a pair of pritty geallachers. —Quando? Quonda?" (502.13-15); "Mrs Pruny-Quetch" (550.32-33); "prunktqueen" (250.29); "a queen of Prancess" (312.22); "Peggy Quilty" (212.7); "P.P. Quemby" (536.6); and the definite identification with Anna Livia as "Panniquanne starts showing of her peequuliar talonts" (606.30). *P-q* becomes a leitmotif in the *Wake,* however, not just by dint of incorporation into proper names for the two seductresses or the single Prankquean figure, but in the very flow of language, as witness such instances in "the pees with their caps awry are quite as often as not taken for kews with their tails in their or are quite as often as not taken for pews with their tails in their mouths, thence your pristopher polombos, hence our Kat Kresbyterians" (119.35-120.2); "curly mequeues are of Mippa's moulding" (280.18); "A pushpull, qq; quiescence, pp; with extravent intervulve coupling" (314.19-20); "Mind your pughs and keaoghs" (349.3); "Pack pickets, pioghs and kughs" (350.17); "Nepos, Mnepos. Anumque, umque. Napoo. Queh? Quos?" (389.29-30); "Mint your peas! Coax your qyous!" (472.5-6); "—Pirce! Perce! Quick! Queck!" (491.25).

A handful of critics have cast an eye on the poetic effects of Joyce's language, stopping along the way between the labyrinth of explication and the tower of elucidation, commenting on occasional phrases and sentences. Nor could anyone actually expect any major attempt at an over-all commentary on *effect,* when the most serious problems remain in the area of exegesis, especially when the value of Joyce's poetic techniques exists in the pattern of "sound-sense" created, not in sound alone. In the early *Exagmination* Robert Sage tackles a sentence in Anna Livia Plurabelle:

> She was just a young thin pale soft shy slim slip of a thing then, sauntering, by silvamoonlake and he was a heavy trudging lurching lieabroad of a Curraghman, making his hay for whose sun to shine on, as tough as the oaktrees (peats be with them!) used to rustle that time down by the dykes of killing Kildare, for forstfellfoss with a plash across her [202.26-32].

Sage calls this "a sentence that is pool-like in its lucidity, that is supple and periodic," and goes on to analyze the poetic aspects of it:

> The sentence opens . . . with fifteen one-syllable words, the first eleven being accented, the twelfth and thirteenth hastening the rhythm through their lack of accent and the final two returning to long beats. Through this Joyce suggests the weakness and uncertainty of the stream at its commencement (girlhood). Then comes the stronger

three-syllable word *sauntering,* indicating development (adolescence) and leading by a short beat to the epitritus *silvamoonlake,* signifying full growth (maturity), the further associations with the latter stage being sylvan and the silver moon reflected in the lake. The male symbol is immediately introduced in the three ponderous trochees *heavy trudging lurching,* continuing to the molossus *forstfellfoss,* which balances *silvamoonlake* and suggests *first, forest, fell* and *waterfall,* the *foss* coming from the Scandinavian designation of waterfall. The latter part of the sentence, then, completes the introduction of the two symbols by describing the creation of the first cascade through the falling of the tree across the stream.[15]

It is this sort of word-by-word analysis that unearths the hidden beauties of Joyce's language in the *Wake,* the lilt of the string of opening monosyllables, the alliterative onomatopoeia of *forstfellfoss* (echoes of which build toward the grand restatement of chapter 8 in the last chapter: "fond Fuinn feels"—427.30; "felt the fall"—469.13; "fond floral fray"—471.27; and, finally, Anna Livia's "It's something fails us. First we feel. Then we fall"—627.11), the "luminous" sounds of *silvamoonlake,* and the comic undertones of the *heavy trudging lurching lieabroad of a Curraghman.* Whether for sheer lyricism, as in "Veil, volantine, valentine eyes" (20.34), or for comic sounds, as in the hollow echoing noises coming from the Egyptian dummy, "valiantine vaux of Venerable Val Vousdem" (439.17-18), Joyce can manipulate his alliteration of consonants and variations of vowels to create individually pertinent patterns of meaning.

Nor would a charge of poetic "formalism" be at all appropriate against Joyce in his *Wake,* as the analysis by Sage indicates: it is impossible to investigate Joyce's language without explicating meaning interwoven with that language. Form and content in the *Wake* are an interinvolved entity, with poetic patterns revealing ideas once those patterns are looked at closely, and Joyce's meaning engendering a type of language concomitant with the poetic form. It is only through the language in the sentence Sage investigates that one can learn that the Viking's seduction of the Irish nymph engenders the next generation of sons. Earwicker is colloquially "taking advantage of the girl" when he is "making hay while the sun shines," as is indicated by *his hay;* and *sun* suggests *son* in this context, thus *shine on* equals Shaun, Earwicker's chosen successor; but the brother conflict is never far from the surface as *oaktrees* conjures up Shem, *peats* indicating petrification from tree to stone, as well as the hope that peace will eventually be declared between them.

Thus it is through language as a medium of communication, heightened by musical intonations and strengthened by verbal intensity, that a basic series of interwoven myths and tales supplements a thin plot line to create a vast literary unit. "Prose" as hitherto defined could never sustain such a construction which defies the usual gravitational laws of prose composition: instead of the heavy base of plot material underlying a building toward unity and intensity, Joyce has constructed an inverted pyramid of a book, based on a delicate pinnacle but accumulating mass as it soars upward in cohesion and lyricism. This is apparent when Northrop Frye, in cataloguing the four basic types of fiction, acknowledges that *Ulysses* incorporates all four, while *Finnegans Wake* does as much and still adds "a fifth and quintessential form . . . traditionally associated with scriptures and sacred books!"[16]

Poetic variations are often of primary significance to Joyce's approach to his materials since so much depends upon maintaining a constant flow of many themes in an interrelated organization, with continuity dependent upon language and effect. In an investigation of several lines in the *Wake* William Troy notes:

> More often than not, Joyce begins with a regular metrical beat only to drop it suddenly for an effect of surprise: "Drop me the/sound of the/findhorn's/name, Mtu or Mti, sombogger was wisness." The first two feet are perfect dactyls, the third a spondee, and then the line seems to dissolve into prose. The predominant foot throughout the work, however, is the more lilting, caressing anapest because of its closer correspondence to theme and subject. . . . And if the anapest is used so often, it is because it is the inevitable movement for rendering the babbling and the bubbling of the "gossipaceous" Anna Livia that is the river of Time: "with a beck, with a spring, all her rillring-

lets shaking, rocks drops in her tachie, tramtokens in her hair, all waived to a point and then all inuendation."[11]

And in many such ways Anna Livia dominates the entire book, both in poetic measure and in structural balance. Her flowing style serves for much of the metrics of the *Wake*'s language, as Troy suggests, while her "mamafesta" chapter, the washerwomen chapter, and the final soliloquy are in many ways lyrical highlights in the *Wake,* and on a secondary level the similar lyricism of the younger Issy at various instances (the "pepette" letters, the farewell to Haun, and so forth) provides both a parallel and a counterpart.

A definite relationship exists, as I have already indicated, between the ideas and the structure of chapters 8 and 17, where the river-mother rises to prominence in her solo voice. The flow of language in these two sections exists in lyrical rises and falls, extending from the short lappings into longer waves as the river gathers momentum in her movement, as iambs and trochees give way to anapests and dactyls and short lines flow into longer ones; this can be noted in the oft-quoted

> Teems of times and happy returns. The seim anew. Ordovico or viricordo. Anna was, Livia is, Plurabelle's to be. Northmen's thing made southfolk's place but howmulty plurators made eachone in person? Latin me that, my trinity scholar, out of eure sanscreed into oure eryan! [215.22-27]

Troy comments that the last line of this passage is "capable of being analyzed as a quite acceptable example of the rare dactylic octometer—with a caesura after 'scholard,' " adding that the basic verse structure for the *Wake* is "established by the three-syllable foot, dactylic or anapestic, with its possibility of almost infinite variation within the line through the substitution of other shorter feet."[18] The sensation of fluvial augmentation can be felt as *Ordovico* becomes *or viricordo,* a two-part reversal followed by a three-part progression in which the first two contain two stresses and the third three, while the over-all patterns of the three parts include three beats (two stressed), four beats (two stressed), and finally five beats (three stressed). When echoed in the last section of the book, the rhythm has become decidedly regularized, with the same aspect of augmentation present: "Ardor vigor/ forders order./ Since ancient was/ our living is/ in possible to be" (614.9-10), where trochaic dimeter for two measures gives way to iambic dimeter for another two, to be followed by iambic trimeter. Joyce's poetic effects are rarely predictable, the poet apparently delighting in quickly tripping up his own metrics, and suddenly falling into rhymed verse, just as suddenly to leave a last line hanging or extend it into a completely new rhythm. Too much of significance is happening in the *Wake* for its language to be able to take on a monotonous consistency. Often a change in the poetic style of a paragraph indicates the introduction of a new motif or a new variant on the theme under consideration. Always Joyce works for an effective surprise to restartle the reader into a closer examination of the material being presented.

Joyce had mastered, as had Eliot, the style of heightened conversation in broken patterns to establish character (poetry as dramatic monologue), reveal psychological variations and inconsistencies in that character, and allow the reader to understand on several levels the significance of what is being said. In reply to the verse-question, "What bitter's love but yurning, what' sour lovemutch but a bref burning till shee that drawes dothe smoake retourne?" (143.29-30), where the jingle quality of the verse already implies frivolity, while the "swelling" lines (the second containing an added foot) and the change from two feminine rhymes to a truncated masculine one already indicate that the love in question is "out of joint," the answer maintains a flippant, feminine tone, often breaking into vindictiveness or lasciviousness or sentimentality or even apparently genuine tenderness:

> I know, pepette, of course, dear, but listen, precious! Thanks, pette, those are lovely, pitounette, delicious! But mind the wind, sweet! What exquisite hands you have, you angiol, if you didn't gnaw your nails, isn't it a wonder you're not achamed of me, you pig, you perfect little pigaleen! I'll nudge you in a minute! I bet you use her best Persian smear off her vanity table to make them look so rosetop glowstop no-

stop. I know her. Slight me, would she? For every got I care! Three creamings a day, the first during her shower and wipe off with tissue. Then after cleanup and of course before retiring [143.31-144.4].

The first two sentences, composed of short phrases in trios, are pure innocence and cloying coyness, and the third pretends to be the same, although somewhat foreshortened and already suspect in meaning: *mind the wind* may be a tender note of concern, but may also be a nasty personal comment. The next sentence attempts to re-establish the caressing tone in an iambic line ending in the extra unstressed syllable, *angiol,* but the second part of the sentence brings the viciousness into an obvious light with hard sounds and a masculine ending (*if you didn't gnaw your nails*), and, after another false tenderness (this time of contrition), the spondee *you pig* is completely brutal, to be modified again by the tenderer *you perfect little pigaleen. I'll nudge you in a minute* exists primarily as a threat and re-echoes the *n* sounds of the previous sentence's accusation, while accusation remains the dominant idea of the next sentence as well, this time modulated into a more gossipy, run-on form ending with the silly *rosetop glowstop nostop* (probably parodying Swinburne's epigram on Villon). The next three short ejaculations are classic examples of the dramatic monologue style of Browning, while the next two sentences lapse into advertisement style. What follows is a logical progression into run-on prose gossip, and Joyce has carried his techniques through various aspects of poetry, doggerel, and prose, his language at each instance indicating the surface and underlying sense.

Time and again in the *Wake* Joyce provides the signature by which his poetry is to be read. In analyzing the buried document he cautions that "to concentrate solely on the literal sense or even the psychological content of any document to the sore neglect of the enveloping facts themselves circumstantiating it is just as hurtful to *sound sense* (and let it be added to the truest taste)" (109.12-16). I have italicized *sound sense* because I feel that it becomes a poetic dictum for Joyce throughout his composition of *Finnegans Wake.* Without the envelope it is no letter, warns Joyce, form and content being intrinsically interrelated. What does Joyce's form actually achieve then? Again in his examination of the letter he notes: *"the Aranman ingperwhis through the hole of his hat,* indicating that the words which follow may be taken in any order desired, hole of Aran man the hat through the whispering his ho (here keen again and begin again to make soundsense and sensesound kin again)" (121.11-16). Later, we find: "wanamade singsigns to soundsense an yit he wanna git all his flesch nuemaid motts truly prural and plusible" (138.7-9)—the technique indicated is that of combining the musical with the prosaic, sound with sense, to produce words-made-flesh and flesh-made-words that are new and fresh in sound and both pure and multiple in meaning, adding levels of idea within a context that is nonetheless plausible.

> That's the point of eschatology our book of kills reaches for now [notes Joyce] in soandso many counterpoint words. What can't be coded can be decorded if an ear aye seize what no eye ere grieved for. Now, the doctrine obtains, we have occasioning cause causing effects and affects occasionally recausing altereffects. Or I will let me take it upon myself to suggest to twist the penman's tale posterwise [482.33-483.3].

In the Yawn investigation, the question thunders forth: "Can you not distinguish the sense, prain, from the sound, bray?" (522.29-30), and St. Patrick later suggests that we seek "the sound sense sympol in a weedwayedwold" (612.29). The Grace-hoper takes the word for the deed, commenting: *"Your feats end enormous, your volumes immense,/ (May the Graces I hoped for sing your Ondtship song sense!)"* (419.5-6).

It is perhaps dangerous to overstress the relationship of Joyce's book to musical form and technique, whose structure demands only that a composition have a logical relationship among its own parts—although *Finnegans Wake* certainly does have that. But the *Wake* is patterned so that the musical devices (the poetic language, the structural balance) are consistent primarily with the levels of meaning pertinent to individual portions. Joyce develops variations on his themes not for the sake of variation alone, but to reapply his ideas to new and inclusive situations, to broaden the theme itself as a structure composed intrinsically of its own variations. As difficult as it remains for the reader and the critic to derive even a single layer of meaning from every word in *Finnegans Wake,* it nonetheless becomes apparent with continued exegetical research that every word in it has been constructed for the primarily *literary* purpose of meaning rather than as mere musical abstraction. Hugh Kenner best manages to localize the interrelationship of sound and sense in *Finnegans Wake,* observing that

> Never did a book contain such virtuosity, such inventive, thorough, and minute exploitation of rhythm, gesture, association, song, oration, small talk, cliché, every—literally every—facet of discourse except substance. Yet never for a moment does Joyce's mind shift from his Dublin; its reality *was* in talk, and such is the leverage of his maturest double-writing that from phrase to phrase and from page to page a sense of that reality comes powerfully through.[19]

It becomes apparent, as Kenner implies, that the language of the Dublin streets and pubs—particularly the pubs—permeates *Finnegans Wake.* In fact, Joyce's use of that vernacular (of an English tongue in a Celtic mouth*) is the basis for the synthesis of poetry and comedy; the sound and sense one would associate with a Dublin bar brogue is the dominant linguistic element in *Finnegans Wake.* Joyce's twin muses of Comedy and Poetry are actually a pair of Celtic maidens plying their trades in the Dublin he knew at the turn of the century; they offer a language and a dialect that contemporary Irish playwrights like Synge, O'Casey, Robinson, and Johnston have exploited for both rich poetic qualities and rich comic delight. Himself well aware of the full extent of this interweaving of the linguistic and comic aspects of the Dubliner, Sean O'Casey commented to me that only an Irishman can understand *Finnegans Wake*—and he would have to be a Dubliner at that!

The opening lines of the portion of the *Wake* that Joyce re-

---

* A good deal more involved than this of course. To "Limba romena in Bucclis tuscada" (518.24-25) Joyce adds "Farcing gutterish" (518.25). See also "brain of the franks, hand of the christian, tongue of the north" (127.29-30) and "oyne of an oustman in skull of skand" (310.30).

corded offer the best example of the Dublin brogue exploited for its richness in both humor and melody: "Well, you know or don't you kennet or haven't I told you every telling has a taling and that's the he and the she of it. Look, look, the dusk is growing! My branches lofty are taking root. And my cold cher's gone ashley" (213.11-14). The repetitions, the interrogative statements, the long sigh of complaint, the exclamations of exasperation and weariness are elements of Joyce's colloquial expression. Part after part of the *Wake* falls easily into Irish dialect without the author's attempt to convert spellings or drop letters. It is the rhythm of Dublin speech that is recorded here, and the fact that the whole book is one long gossipy tale told at a hurried pace in a hushed tone behind the back of one's hand adds to the colloquial flavor of its composition. With what else but a brogue would these lines have their accuracy?

> Ah, but she was the queer old skeowsha anyhow, Anna Livia, trinkettoes! And sure he was the quare old buntz too, Dear Dirty Dumpling, foostherfather of fingalls and dotthergills. Gammer and gaffer we're all their gangsters. Hadn't he seven dams to wive him? And every dam had her seven crutches. And every crutch had its seven hues. And each hue had a differing cry. Sudds for me and supper for you and the doctor's bill for Joe John [215.12-18].

All one need do is read Ogden's translation of these lines into Basic English[20] to find them suddenly devoid of poetry and humor. Only by wagging his English tongue in his Celtic mouth does an Irishman produce such lyrical comedy.

Joyce, however, delighted in confusing the issue of his creation with a Jove-like whimsy and an unabashed fascination for leg-pulling, being resolutely an "artist" in the Gogartyan sense of the word—a jokester. Although the connotation of "leg-pulling" in modern art is usually highly suspect, some effort should be made to rescue the concept from becoming purely a pejorative: Joyce's "hoax" is a consummate work of literary art, logically constructed, carefully controlled, and aesthetically embellished. But it is not surprising that many readers and critics of serious mien have been unable to swallow "the hoax that joke bilked" (511.34). When an admirer managed to understand one level of meaning in a phrase, Joyce was quick to add a second, but when another admirer asked about levels of meaning, Joyce insisted "it's meant to make you laugh."[21] The seeming contradiction is resolved only when we understand that to Joyce the significance and the poetry and the humor of the book were inseparable, and he was quick to correct any impression that would insist upon only a single facet of his prismatic scheme of art.

CHAPTER FOUR

The Humphriad of that Fall and Rise

As a "novel" dealing with a vast cross section of the contemporary world, *Finnegans Wake* corresponds in various particulars with the many epics of other cultures and eras, and there are suggestions in the *Wake* that Joyce meant for a definite affinity between his work and the classical epics to be noted—with *Paradise Lost* primarily, and to a lesser extent with the *Divina Commedia,* the two Homeric works, the *Aeneid,* the *Chanson de Roland,* and *Beowulf.* Employing the familiar conventions prevalent in most instances in these epics, he often found that they naturally fitted with convenience into the framework of his *Wake,* and as often that they could be used in mock form to differentiate between the heroic material of classical epics and the nonheroic aspects of contemporary society. The familiar method of alternating and combining parallels and parodies, which had already reached a dazzling peak in *Ulysses,* is further exploited here, and a glance at the outline for a prose comic epic envisioned by Henry Fielding in his *Joseph Andrews* Preface over two hundred years ago, almost at the genesis of the English novel, indicates that such an ideal was probably close to Joyce's interests during the construction of *Finnegans Wake.*

The vast comic elements and the poetic prose language (both expanded and augmented since *Ulysses*) suggest the plausibility of an investigation of the use of epic conventions, of Joyce's acknowledgments to other epics and their creators, and of his attempts to telescope the history of mankind into a single multifaceted project through a contemporary perspective. Even if Joyce had not consciously sought to create a work that would generally be termed an epic, he must have been aware that the history of the form has witnessed the creation of both "authentic" (unconscious) and "literary" (conscious) efforts—the *Iliad, Odyssey,* and anonymous

Beowulf and *Chanson de Roland* classified in the former group; Virgil's, Dante's, and Milton's works in the latter. In these terms, the *Wake* is a literary epic, although there are significant implications in the text to indicate that Joyce's awareness of Jung's concept of the collective unconscious allowed him to anticipate the mysterious appearance in his masterpiece of elements of the natural epic.*

A basic list of various traits commonly associated with the epic is easily agreed upon: mythical, legendary, and historical materials usually underlie whatever plot exists; a tradition of oral recitation often pervades the work; and an element of monumental conflict —among the gods, between men and gods, among heroic mortals —seems vital to the epic scheme. A secondary consideration may well involve *types* of epics: the odyssey of search or discovery, the genesis of a new world, or heroic warfare. Joyce, an avid reader of the established primitive and literary epics of western civilization, must have been influenced by these characteristics, for he blends that which is history, that which is myth, and that which must be termed legend, in order to construct a timeless cosmos in which Finn MacCool, Eamon de Valera, and Kathleen ni Houlihan are contemporaries. Napoleon and Wellington are no more real in the *Wake* than Castor and Pollux, nor more historically accurate than Gog and Magog. The common denominator of prototype levels the legendary Cadmus, the mythical Bladud, and the literary Master Solness, all builders of cities.

Joyce is aware that no clear-cut distinction between history and legend can always be achieved: a literal acceptance of Biblical material makes it history, while the sceptic views it as legend. Joyce

---

* It is amusing to notice how many "literary" Irishmen have stepped forward since Joyce's death to claim a modest portion of responsibility for the material included in Joyce's "unconscious" epics. Many have claimed to have been the inspiration or the model for various episodes in Joyce's books or to have related the original story which Joyce wove into literature. Stanislaus Joyce has been primary in this area with three published works of diary, recollections, and *apologia,* followed by J. F. Byrne and of course Oliver Gogarty. Joyce himself preferred crediting his father as a source for several incidents. Without realizing it, these Irishmen have done much to make a "literary" epic into an "authentic" one.

accepts Cain as the first builder of the City of Man—"And that was how framm Sin fromm Son, acity arose" (94.18)—but he is equally aware that within his own lifetime Baron G. E. Haussmann was at work rebuilding parts of Paris: "This is the Hausman all paven and stoned, that cribbed the Cabin that never was owned" (205.34-36).* This fragment repeats the theme of citybuilding in terms of the oft-repeated rhyme of "The House That Jack Built," while Shem is Joyce's re-creation of Cain as the citybuilder: "He fould the fourd; they found the hurtled stones; they fell ill with the gravy duck: and he sod town with the roust of the meast" (224.5-7). The town that is being founded here is Dublin of course (Bailé átha Cliath, the Irish name for the city, means "Town of the Hurdle Ford"), and all references to the founding of cities and the building of towers and walls return us to this universal city in *Finnegans Wake*.

Joyce, then, is attempting to encompass a vast amount of historical and legendary material and fuse it through a timeless concept with the basic mythical patterns in order to create a work that deals essentially with what is universal.† His own narrative structure, on its most obvious literal level, concerns the story of his Chapelizod publican and family; this narrative forms the fictional details the author supplies. But the huge mass of amorphous material that underlies this iceberg cap of fiction is the accumulation of the many cultural levels of experience which give dimension in time and space to his localized series of events and personages.

Conscious of the "authentic" epic, the ancient work of folk origin, often of collated myths by several hands (although *Finnegans Wake* is the conscious product of a sophisticated mind, a calculated literary effort), Joyce is nonetheless striving to achieve a work that absorbs in its universality those aspects of the collective uncon-

---

* For further comments on the city-building theme see my note on "Anna Livia and the City Builder," *Notes and Queries,* VII, No. 9 (September, 1961), 352-53.

† A parallel in epic tradition between Joyce's Finnegan myth and Blake's Albion is traced by Northrop Frye ("Quest and Cycle in Finnegans Wake," *James Joyce Review,* I [February 2, 1957], 39-47).

scious that have a primitive basis for existence in our culture. The *Wake* is after all, as critics have frequently asserted, an aural book, and re-echoes often the facets of an oral recitation: it is the oration of an impersonal bard who sometimes surrenders his function to other commentators, like the pedantic Professor Jones, the narrator of the Mookse and Gripes fable and the Burrus-Caseous episode (149-68). The rhetorical devices of character speeches also add to the "aural" aspect of *Finnegans Wake,* and Joyce seems to envy the fresh naïveté with which the ancients could naturally approach the creation of an epic—the Icelandic *Eddas,* the Anglo-Saxon *Beowulf* and French *Roland,* the *Kalevala* of the Finns, and the *Iliad* and *Odyssey* of "Our homerole poet" (445.31-32)—so that he apparently seeks to reproduce the unconscious elements of presophisticated man in the *Wake.* Much of the first chapter of the *Wake,* therefore, is a reproduction of primitive sounds and qualities of early epical poems: "So, how idlers' wind turning pages on pages, as innocens with anaclete play popeye antipop, the leaves of the living in the boke of the deeds, annals of themselves timing the cycles of events grand and national, bring fassilwise to pass how" (13.29-32).

Nor are the elements of epic conflict missing from *Finnegans Wake.* "What clashes here of wills gen wonts, ostrygods gaggin fishygods!" (4.1-2), the epical introduction to the *Wake* announces. The haves against the have-nots comprise the economic struggle, the class war; one's *will* against one's *wants* forms the inner struggle of the individual; pagan Goths will be warring against each other, while those who worship other gods combat the God of the Christian (*fishygods*). This struggle in *Finnegans Wake* is primarily the same as that which concerns Milton in *Paradise Lost;** the difference between the two works is that Joyce has tampered with the *dramatis personae* of the events to arrive at a new central figure, the Adam whose fall creates Man, *"Père*

---

* Known in the *Wake* variously as "lost paladays" (69.10), *"paradox lust"* (263.L), "parroteyes list" (493.5), "Peredos Last" (610.34) and "paladays last" (615.25).

Adam" (124.34). Man, however, is the synthesis of this war in heaven, the synthesis of Shem and Shaun, who represent Lucifer and the Archangel Michael respectively—"mikealls or nicholists" (113.27) and "Mitchells *v.* Nicholls" (147.6). That union of the two sons happens both before and after the battle, of course: Earwicker is their father and combines the antithetical elements of both; the sons eventually are fused into the Earwicker figure, and that fusion may well suggest that the antithetical elements have finally been assimilated by the individual. The epic battle in heaven, however, concerns us throughout the work and is described in the introduction as:

> Where the Baddelaries partisans are still out to mathmaster Malachus Micgranes and the Verdons catapelting the camibalistics out of the Whoyteboyce of Hoodie Head. Assiegates and boomeringstroms. Sod's brood, be me fear! Sanglorians, save! Arms apeal with larms, appalling. Killykillkilly: a toll, a toll. What chance cuddleys, what cashels aired and ventilated! What bidimetoloves sinduced by what tegotetabsolvers! What true feeling for their's hayair with what strawng voice of false jiccup! O here here how hoth sprowled met the duskt the father of fornicationists but, (O my shining stars and body!) how hath fanespanned most high heaven the skysign of soft advertisement! [4.3-14]

The war in heaven is simultaneously taking place on earth as well; the pattern has been divinely fixed and repeats itself throughout life—the wars of religious fanaticism are being constantly fought and are reflections of the epic struggle among the angels. Joyce again accepts the convention of interweaving gods and men, angels and men, in the epical tapestry, but does so to the extent of having them lose their divine identities with the mortals who personify their actions on earth. The hooded "White Boys" spread religious violence in Ireland as a microcosmic re-enactment of the macrocosmic struggle in heaven; it is immaterial to Joyce whether they are followers of Michael or Old Nick—the sides have become confused with each other, and, like the Kilkenny cats, they have nothing left to show for their struggle but their tails.

The pattern becomes one of permanence and change; the regeneration that follows the wars is a sexual one rather than a religious resurrection: "The oaks of ald now they lie in peat yet elms leap where askes lay. Phall if you but will, rise you must: and none so soon either shall the pharce for the nunce come to a setdown secular phoenish" (4.14-17).

Although the *Wake* contains aspects of all three types of epic, it is essentially concerned with the creation myth. Joyce recognizes contemporary society as verging on chaos, a chaos from which, like Milton, he re-creates the world. After the statement of themes and "epical introduction" of the classic struggle, the "wake" motif is sounded: the battle in heaven is over, and the women wail for the dead, while the earth remains in chaos awaiting creation. But no sooner have the party of demons been "hurtleturtled out of heaven" (5.17-18) than the epic invocation is heard: "Stay us wherefore in our search for tighteousness, O Sustainer, what time we rise and when we take up to toothmick and before we lump down upown our leatherbed and in the night and at the fading of the stars!" (5.18-21). And suddenly we find ourselves in the midst of a bustling metropolis of our modern technological age; an epic listing of its characteristics is presented:

> the wallhall's horrors of rollsrights, carhacks, stonengens, kisstvanes, tramtrees, fargobawlers, autokinotons, hippohobbilies, streetfleets, tournintaxes, megaphoggs, circuses and wardsmoats and basilikerks and aeropagods and the hoyse and the jollybrool and the peeler in the coat and the mecklenburk bitch bite at his ear and the merlinburrow burrocks and his fore old porecourts, the bore the more [5.30-36].

The city is the Dublin Joyce knew, but it is also the Pandemonium built by the outcast angels. The world suddenly emerges full-grown (the ancient cities are incorporated into the building of the modern: Stonehenge is combined with engine to form *stonengens,* but it will someday return to stone again). This is Joyce's superfetation theme of one world burrowing on another, of a new world growing out of the old. And the city is the one Cain built, for since the fall from heaven and Adam's fall from grace are happening simultaneously—"so sore did abe ite ivvy's holired abbles" (5.29-30)—Satan and Cain find themselves building the same city, but only to find it fully built before them.

Creation in the *Wake* is a multileveled affair; actually it is the world which is being born and finally heralded as created in the *ricorso* chapter: "The old breeding bradsted culminwillth of natures" (593.12). But the creation myth has its microcosmic proportions as well as its macrocosmic: the birth of the world—"A hand from the cloud emerges, holding a chart expanded" (593.19)—is parallel to the building of the city and the erection of a wall and a tower. It is from this edifice that Tim Finnegan (like Ibsen's Bygmester Solness before him) falls: "(There was a wall of course in erection) Dimb! He stottered from the latter Damb! he was dud. Dumb! Mastabatoom, mastabadtomm" (6.9-11). Meanwhile, wave after wave of invaders are discovering, conquering, colonizing new lands, lands that had their own inhabitants and cultures, and each invasion of one civilization conquering another and merging its culture with the existing native culture re-echoes the superfetation theme. Sir Almeric Tristram arrives with Strongbow's forces in 1170 and settles in Dublin, founding Howth Castle: "Sir Tristram, violer d'amores, fr'over the short sea, had passencore rearrived from North Armorica on this side the scraggy isthmus of Europe Minor to wielderfight his penisolate war" (3.4-6); Jonathan Sawyer is simultaneously founding the city of Dublin in the state of Georgia (in Laurens County): "topsawyer's rocks by the stream Oconee exaggerated themselse to Laurens County's gorgios" (3.7-8); and St. Bridget is being created out of the goddess Brigit, while St. Patrick through baptism is creating Christians out of heathens: "avoice from afire bellowsed mishe mishe to tauftauf thuartpeatrick" (3.9-10), and Christ is creating the Church upon "the rock which is Peter."

All creation is therefore happening at once: the stone is hurled into the lake, and the successive waves of ripples are each a manifestation of the other; the growth of the individual repeats the growth of the species; the most minute event of creation reflects the major aspect of world creation that has already occurred, and nonetheless begins to build up a series of events (a snowballing of creation, invasion, founding, building, integrating) which will finally result in the one vast world-creation yet to come. The creation myth in the *Wake* is its major epical aspect in terms of scope and significance.

But although primarily an epic of the establishment of world order, *Finnegans Wake* may just as easily be interpreted in terms of its heroic warfare; the opening battle is just a foreshadowing of the heroic struggles that take place throughout the *Wake*. Joyce is dealing with man's wars of expansion and colonization, and he utilizes the Crimean War of the mid-nineteenth century as the prototype of such conflicts. He seems to select this particular war for several interesting reasons: because it was typical of imperialistic England's "necessary" conflagrations, because it was fought on the flimsiest of pretexts (England's concern for Turkey's rights violated by Russia's "aiding" Christians persecuted in that country), because so many Irishmen were conscripted to fight for England, and because the word "crime" is coincidentally incorporated into the name of the war.

Moreover, the Crimean War produced a genuine heroine, Florence Nightingale, the nurse who became more famous than any of the opposing generals because she wrought apparent miracles saving lives. After the battle is over, the radio in Earwicker's pub broadcasts an on-the-spot transcription of a nightingale's song (such broadcasts were apparently quite common in London during the thirties), but the bird's song is recognized by the customers to be Earwicker's guilty stammer: "(floflo floreflorence), sweetishsad lightandgayle, twittwin twosingwoolow" (360.2-3). Nurse Nightingale is instrumental in recording H.C.E.'s guilt because, as the single woman against the backdrop of men at war, she symbolized for Joyce the cause of the war—woman tempting man to strive for her protection and comfort. She subdivides here into the two temptresses, being both Florence Nightingale and her equally famous contemporary, Jenny Lind, the "Swedish nightingale." These two sing their *twosingwoolow,* a "wooing" song of "woe" to bring men "low." But they also return to heal the wounded, to mourn for their lovers, to piece together the body of Osiris, to bequeath to their children the attributes of the father. Miss Nightingale, wandering across the battlefield to tend to the wounded, echoes the role of the banshees in Celtic mythology—like the washerwomen of the final chapter of Book One of the *Wake,* they wash the blood from the raiment of the heroes *before* the battle (another aspect of the cyclical pattern). Florence Nightingale reappears in *Finnegans Wake* during a flood scene, and again she symbolizes the banshees at the river: "Flood's. The pinkman, the squeeze, the pint with the kick. Gaa. And then the punch to Gaelicise it. Fox. The lady with the lamp" (514.32-34). Here she is again the temptress who ruined the great man; she is Kitty O'Shea, Parnell's mistress, as the reference to *Fox,* one of Parnell's aliases in the affair, indicates.

The events of this "heroic warfare" in the *Wake* are hardly epical. Joyce has managed to reduce the Crimean War to the lowest level of absurdity: it is being broadcast by a pair of radio-video comedians named Butt and Taff, who eventually unite to become Buckley. It is Buckley who has the distinction of shooting the Russian General, and the episode depicts "How Burghley shuck the rackushant Germanon" (338.2-3). Actually, this fictitious bit of nonsense is an Irish pub tale concerning the mythical Buckley who spotted a Russian General in the process of defecating during a lull on the front lines. Although strongly tempted to shoot him, Buckley finds himself united by a common human bond with the general and desists until the general uses turf for toilet paper; it is then that the irate "budly shoots thon rising germinal" (354.34-35). This event becomes the deciding incident in Joyce's treatment of his "epic" battle, since the Russian General once again is the stuttering Earwicker, and he is once again beset by the soldiers and deposed by his sons. There is little doubt that Joyce here is commenting upon the stupidity of war, upon the common heritage that would ordinarily unify all mankind, regardless of country, until

the patriotic symbol is raised and the Irishman is once again goad-
ed into serving his oppressors and shooting his fellow man.

The events of the shooting of the general are, in addition, an
aspect of the Crucifixion: the Russian General is being sacrificed in
order to unite the antithetical elements of mankind, the Butt and
the Taff aspects of himself. But this Christ figure is far from a sinless man; he is the Earwicker who carries the entire burden of
man's guilt upon his back because he has *committed all sins.*
Joyce's implication here is that it is useless for a sinless man to assume mankind's guilt and die for those sins; the task requires the
composite sinner, and one by one Earwicker, Shem, and Shaun re-
enact the Crucifixion—Earwicker in the person of the Russian General, Shaun as Haun being interred (473), Shem as Glugg being
beaten by his brother at the end of the Mime when the dirge is
heard:

> Home all go. Halome. Blare no more ramsblares, oddmund barkes!
> And cease your fumings, kindalled bushies! And sherrigoldies yeas-
> symgnays; your wildeshaweshowe moves swiftly sterneward! For here
> the holy language. Soons to come. To pausse [256.11-15].

In echoes of *Cymbeline* and *The Tempest* (twilight is twilight,
whether Shakespearean or Celtic) the descendant of the great Irish
writers is laid to rest; the Hebrew word for peace (*shalom*) anticipates the Hebrew prayer for the dead, *kaddish*—"Kidoosh!"
(258.5)—and Shem's final "gttrdmmrng" (258.2).

Like all heroic warfare in *Finnegans Wake,* the Butt-Taff version of the Crimean War is merely another tavern brawl in Earwicker's Bristol* Bar—so named because it was to the city of Bristol that Henry II gave the charter for Dublin, causing all subsequent Irish wars for independence—and Earwicker as the general
is once again "crowned" with a "buttle" at the "Inns of Dungtarf
where Used awe to be he" (16.22). The radio war is being broadcast in the "Tavern" chapter, and it is when Earwicker rises to de-

---

* For pub-name dispute see chapter 1.

fend the fallen general that the real brawl takes place. The Crimean War, then, is merely a prelude to the real "heroic warfare" —a tavern brawl!—as it was merely a "reflection" of the epic struggle in heaven. No one affair of combat is any more important than another in the *Wake,* since they are essentially all the same war; no historical event is any more real than the fictional counterpart invented by Joyce or the legendary warfare recorded by epics and bibles.

As an epic of a search or voyage of discovery *Finnegans Wake* contains its parallel with the *Odyssey* and *Divina Commedia.* In its broadest pattern the *Wake* is a long night's groping for light and form; the *ricorso* episode brings the voyage of discovery to an end as dawn illumines the chaos, brings the world out of the void, and synthesizes the opposites into a coherent but still contradictory whole. The Odysseyan Everyman, who had by day wandered through the streets of Dublin in *Ulysses* in search of a son, a family, a home, repeats his odyssey in his nightmare; the search for himself becomes a quest for the assimilation of the antithetical elements of himself, a synthesis of sons Shem and Shaun. As Dante, Joyce wanders through the human purgatory he discovers on earth and comes to the realization that this earthly *purgatorio* is a composite of all aspects of heaven and hell; the historical, legendary, and mythical dead are present before him as they were for Dante in his wanderings through the strata of the three worlds. Joyce has destroyed that iron-bound stratification in the *Wake,* and seeks to combine all his personages into one universal man who can be neither damned nor blessed, since he is Everyman.

On the specific level, Joyce has created an odyssey story within the framework of the *Wake:* the fourth chapter of Book Two records the voyage of Tristram's ship bringing Iseult from Ireland. As such the voyage is sexual, as is Leopold Bloom's search for a family of his own in *Ulysses;* and, like Bloom, Earwicker is the universal aspect of his wife's lover. The voyage is Gulliver's to the land of the Houyhnhnms—"the whole yaghoodurt sweepstakings and all the horsepowers" (387.10-11). It is also Moses' Red Sea crossing—"and then there was the drowning of Pharoah and all his pedestrians and they were all completely drowned into the sea, the red sea" (387.25-27). The drowned man in the myth is Mark of Cornwall, destroyed by his nephew Tristram and his bride Iseult; as such he is also the Martin Cunningham of "Grace" and *Ulysses* whose real-life model was drowned off Kingstown: "and then poor Merkin Cornyngwham, the official out of the castle on pension, when he was completely drow ned off Erin Isles, at that time, suir knows, in the red sea and a lovely mourning paper and thank God, as Saman said, there were no more of him" (387.28-32). Other sea voyages are re-enacted by the Joycean bride-ship: Sir Roger Casement's landing by submarine near Dublin in 1916—"then there was the official landing of Lady Jales Casemate, in the year of the flood 1132 S.O.S." (387.22-23); the landing of the "Plymouth brethren" (389.1); the sailing of Noah's ark—"the Frankish floot of Noahsdobahs" (388.18-19)— and the Spanish Armada—"the Flemish armada, all scattered, and all officially drowned, there and then, on a lovely morning, after the universal flood, at about aleven thirtytwo was it?" (388.10-13). This Tristram voyage of discovery results in the sexual union of Tristram and Iseult: "whoever the gulpable, and whatever the pulpous was, the twooned togethered" (396.23-24).

As an epic, however, *Finnegans Wake* lacks two important classical elements: as poetic as Joyce's language is, its form is nonetheless that of prose; and as serious as Joyce's purpose is in the *Wake,* his subject matter is decidedly comic. This returns us to the specifications for a comic epic in prose set down by Henry Fielding in his Preface to *Joseph Andrews:*

> The EPIC, as well as the DRAMA, is divided into tragedy and comedy. HOMER, who was the father of this species of poetry, gave us a pattern of both these, though that of the latter kind is entirely lost; which Aristotle tells us, bore the same relation to comedy which his Iliad bears to tragedy. . . .
>
> And farther, as this poetry may be tragic or comic, I will not scruple to say it may be likewise either in verse or prose: for though it wants one

particular, which the critic enumerates in the constituent parts of an epic poem, namely metre; yet, when any kind of writing contains all its other parts, such as fable, action, characters, sentiments, and diction, and is deficient in metre only, it seems, I think, reasonable to refer to it to the epic. . . .[1]

Fielding, looking ahead, described the qualities of the new art form as it was developing under his pen, and as he expected it to develop thereafter. The history of the English novel, however, despite its varied characteristics and its attainment of a high level of sophistication, has rarely engendered the prose comic epic that Fielding predicted; as an art form the novel has developed away from the broad novels of epical significance, which the eighteenth century sought to produce, to highly specialized developments of a handful of characters and a small series of carefully analyzed events. With *Finnegans Wake,* as perhaps with his earlier *Ulysses,* Joyce seems to have attempted to write the culminating work embodying the varied aspects of the contemporary novel: symbolism and naturalism, the psychological as well as the sociological approach, the novel of character and the novel of prototypes.

That Joyce was an admirer of Fielding is apparent from parallels drawn from *Joseph Andrews* and *Finnegans Wake:* Joseph's parents, Gaffer and Gammer Andrews, become the epical parents of all of us in the *Wake*—"Gammer and gaffer we're all their gangsters" (215.14-15)—and Earwicker as the pub-keeper is given the generic name of innkeepers (his guilt and shame punned into it), "Burniface" (315.9), echoing the call for refreshments from the innkeeper in *Joseph Andrews: "Je voi* very well, *que tuta e pace,/*So send up dinner, good Boniface."[2] That Joyce was conscious of the epic as a form throughout the composition of *Finnegans Wake* is equally apparent from the vast list of classical epics sprinkled throughout the work. As he so often does, Joyce might well be hiding the hint that *Finnegans Wake* is to be viewed in terms of Fielding's definition in his references both to *Joseph Andrews* (in what other English novels is an inn so much the scene of

action as in these two?) and to the history of the world epic.*
The epic most significant in the *Wake* is *Paradise Lost* by "Mill-
town" (71.7), since the events of Earwicker's fall parallel those of
Adam in "Milton's Park" (96.10), and the cast of Joyce's epic fits
Milton's *dramatis personae*. But the fall of Dublin also parallels
the fall of Troy in the epics of "homeur" (34.12), and Joyce compares the battle for Troy and the funeral games following the
death of Achilles with the Easter Rising in Dublin:

> I want you, witness of this epic struggle, as yours so mine, to recon-
> struct for us, as briefly as you can, inexactly the same as a mind's eye
> view, how these funeral games, which have been poring over us
> through homer's kerryer pidgeons, massacreedoed as the holiname
> rally round took place [515.21-25].

This re-enactment of the *Iliad* follows upon Joyce's version of
Homer's other epic, and echoes of the *Odyssey* are heard in the
Wake as well: "nobodyatall with Wholyphamous" (73.9). Odysseus represents Everyman again for Joyce, especially since he embodies the ultimate negative side of Everyman when he declares
himself to be Noman: "Noeman's Woe, Hircups Emptybolly!"
(321.14-15). The H.C.E. of Here Comes Everybody is thus depicted in its converse as the Odysseyan Noman, the two sides of
Earwicker's universal personality. Some critical comparison has
been made between the two "blind poets" in reference to Joyce's
Ulysses, but what Joyce learned from the Greek epic poet in writing *Ulysses* is not discarded in the composition of *Finnegans
Wake.* In the earlier novel Joyce utilized Homeric parallels
throughout, as Stuart Gilbert's study has proved, emphasized, and
belabored, in instances where contemporary parallels were logical
with the ancient, or where—as in the case of his perfidious "Penel-

---

* It is interesting to note the comment of Howard Mumford Jones in his
Introduction to the Modern Library edition of *Joseph Andrews:* "I do not happen
to know whether James Joyce was an admirer of Fielding, but it is at least
remarkable that after two centuries the English novel in the case of *Ulysses*
should recur to a theory of fiction which is outlined in the preface to *Joseph
Andrews"* (p. xvii).

ope"—the parallels were ironic. The same technique can be found in the *Wake:* Earwicker is no more a heroic Ulysses than was Leopold Bloom, yet the struggles throughout remain as epic in proportion as those in Homer.

Other epics and epic writers are mentioned in the *Wake;* for example: "pious Eneas" (185.27), and a reference to the first line of the *Aeneid,* "If all the MacCrawls would only handle virgils like Armsworks, Limited!" (618.1-2), the implication being that Roman Catholics have been unable to write as great an epic about their basic myth—the Virgin—as had pagan Virgil; *MacCrawl* puns Finn MacCool and mackerel—the symbol of the fish of early Christianity. Dante figures throughout the *Wake* in various aspects: he has written the Catholic epic, "*Through Hell with the Papes* (mostly boys) by the divine comic Denti Alligator" (440.5-6), and was one of Joyce's favorite authors. Throughout the *Wake* Joyce calls upon the greatest of ancient poets to witness his epic: "Daunty, Gouty and Shopkeeper" (539.6), and "Suffoclose! Shikespower! Seudodanto! Anonymoses!" (47.19). But Dante, like the males in *Finnegans Wake,* is also the victim of a young girl's unwitting temptation; he had been tempted into the creation of an epic: "Still he'd be good tutor two in his big armschair lerningstoel and she be waxen in his hands. Turning up and fingering over the most dantellising peaches in the lingerous longerous book of the dark" (251.21-24).

The hero Roland is celebrated often in the *Wake,* since he is the prototype of the fallen hero, a man of epic stature, and since his friendship with Oliver becomes another parallel of the friendship motif that assimilates the antagonistic brothers:

> while olover his exculpatory features, as Roland rung, a wee dropeen of grief about to sillonise his jouejous, the ghost of resignation diffused a spectral appealingness, as a young man's drown o'er the fate of his waters may gloat, similar in origin and akkurat in effective to a beam of sunshine upon a coffin plate [56.15-19].

Echoing Byron, Joyce interweaves Roland with another epic figure, Finn's son, Ossian—"Rolando's deepen darblun Ossian roll"

(385.35-36)—into a pattern of epic figures which gives *Finnegans Wake* the appearance of a summation of epic literature. Joyce's use of myth allows him constantly to weld hero after hero into a single epical mold, and he draws from the literatures of many civilizations available to him.

It might be well to suggest in this connection that Joyce consciously attempted to create a "bible" of sorts from his contemporary summation of world myth, since the various bibles are in themselves epic summations of their cultures. This seems hardly unlikely when one realizes that the proof Mohammed offered to justify his contention that his Koran was divinely conceived was that no mortal man could have written such a work; he challenged any other mortal to duplicate the effort—and Joyce accepted the challenge. And, as Mohammed claimed that the Koran superseded the Old and New Testaments because he absorbed the older Bibles and surpassed them, so might Joyce claim the same for the *Wake*. Joyce's work obviously is based upon both Old and New Testament material as well as the Koran—the "alcohoran" (20.9-10)— and the Egyptian *Book of Amenti*—"the house of Amanti" (237.26), "our Amenti in the sixth sealed chapter of the going forth by black" (62.26-27).

Also present in the *Wake* can be found an acknowledgment of debt to Hindu religious material—"Bhagafat gaiters" (35.10)— and Confucian doctrine—"master Kung's doctrine of the meang" (108.11-12). Joyce's approach, as such, is intrinsically an aspect of the twentieth century: only through a realization of contemporary anthropological investigation could a concept of the basic myth underlying these various religious texts be postulated. Joyce fuses the material of these texts, arrives at his own version of a common denominator of mythical prototypes, and creates his synthetic "bible" of twentieth-century civilization. Joyce provides his own indications that the *Wake* is being constructed to rival the bibles of the world: Shem is creating "his farced epistol to the hibruws" (228.33-34), "a most moraculous jeeremyhead sindbook for all the peoples" (229.31-32). *Farced* and *jeer* indicate the comic tone

of the book, while *moraculous* contains the Gaelic word for ancient
(*mor*)—*culo* is gratuitous—and *hibruws* refers not only to
the Old Testament, but also to Joyce's select audience of high-
brows.

It is in the conscious use of epic conventions, however, that
Joyce indicates that his *Wake* is to be interpreted in the light of an
all-inclusive view of contemporary times as seen through the perspective of the ancient epics of other civilizations. The epic imita-
tions of the first chapter have already been discussed, but they are
only an opening clue to the epic conventions employed throughout
the work; in many instances Joyce will duplicate certain touches of
style or technique to enforce their significance upon the reader's
mind. The opening sentence of the *Wake* indicates that we are beginning the cycle of life in the middle, the last sentence of the
book ends without a final mark of punctuation and is meant to be
read directly into the first; and Joyce offers *"The Suspended Sentence"* (106.13-14) as a suggested title for Anna Livia's "mamafesta." The macrocosmic study of the establishment of world order
is being told from the middle, but at every instance within that
macrocosm the various component elements (like the microcosmic
incident of the life of one pub-keeper Earwicker) follow the pattern as well. This technique of duplicating in the miniature what
he is attempting in the entire structure carries over to Joyce's handling of the epic as a poetic convention in *Finnegans Wake*: not
only is the *Wake* itself to be viewed as a composite epic, but individual parts are minor epics of sorts within the larger framework.

Since several heroes occupy the same domain in the work, Joyce
indicates that each is deserving of an epic for himself. The actual
epic hero is Finn MacCool,* and therefore it is the first chapter,
dealing with the legendary giant, that is primarily written in epic
language; Earwicker as Finn's replacement is already a middle-
class sham hero, as is the Shaun-demagogue who deposes him. Earwicker is introduced in apologetically epic language; unlike Finn

---

* Finn in Joyce's epic is termed "a prince of the fingallian in a hiberniad of
hoolies" (138.10-11).

("Of the first was he to bare arms and a name: Wassaily Booslaeugh of Riesengeborg. His crest of huroldry, in vert with ancil-
lars, troublant, argent, a hegoak, poursuivant, horrid, horned"—
5.5-7), Earwicker is heralded forth at the opening of chapter 2
with:

> Now . . . concerning the genesis of Harold or Humphrey Chimpden's
> occupational agnomen (we are back in the presurnames prodromarith
> period, of course just when enos chalked halltraps) and discarding
> once for all those theories from older sources which would link him
> back with such pivotal ancestors as the Glues, the Gravys, the North-
> easts, the Ankers and the Earwickers of Sidlesham in the Hundred of
> Manhood or proclaim him offsprout of vikings who had founded wap-
> entake and seddled hem in Herrick or Eric, the best authenticated
> version, the Dumlat, read the Reading of Hofed-ben-Edar, has it that
> it was this way. We are told how in the beginning it came to pass
> that like cabbaging Cincinnatus the grand old gardener was saving
> daylight under his redwoodtree one sultry sabbath afternoon
> [30.1-14].

Although hardly ignominious, the presentation of Earwicker is
not the heroic trumpeting that sounded for the pagan hero, Finn.
This introduction is humble and Biblical: it presents Adam in the
garden (the Hill of Howth—*Ben Adair* in Celtic—is combined
with Eden), and the source is the Talmud (*Dumlat* read backward). He is compared with Cincinnatus, the Roman who twice
left his plow to fight for his country and twice returned to it; but
behind this humble figure stand the lusty Vikings who comprise
Earwicker's heritage ("discarded" heritages are not to be dismissed
in the *Wake*). The change from the first to the second signifies the
change from the divine age to the heroic age in Vico's cyclical pattern: the settling down of the giants to the agricultural life after
the voice of God in the thunderclap had driven them into the
caves, and their ungoverned sex under the skies is converted into
marriage and family.

The next stage is even less heroic, as the oligarch Earwicker is
upended by his son, the spokesman of the "people." Actually, this
is Shaun, the demagogue, but the Viconian situation is complicated

by Joyce's use of Bruno's concepts of antagonistic opposites: Earwicker has two sons, Shem and Shaun. It is Shem who destroys the old ruler: he embodies the three soldiers who have observed Earwicker's indiscretion in Phoenix Park ("some woodwards or regarders, who did not dare deny, the shomers, that they had, chin Ted, chin Tam, chinchin Taffyd, that day consumed their soul of the corn"—34.15-18); he is killer Cain as well as the Ham who observed his drunken father, Noah (that the soldiers were drunk identifies them again with Shem, whose drinking habits are legion: "he had gulfed down mmmmuch too mmmmany gourds of it retching off to almost as low withswillers"—171.19-20).

The son destroys the father when he has become aware of the Garden of Eden incident; he becomes his father's heir when he has become aware of sex—when he reaches puberty. This is Ham's sin, and in the *Wake* it becomes apparent at the dawn scene in which the parents have awakened to comfort little Jerry (Shem), who cries in the night when he wets his bed. Anna Livia comforts him, and Jerry, looking past her, sees his father standing naked in the doorway: "Gauze off heaven! Vision. Then. O, pluxty suddly, the sight entrancing!" (566.28-29).

It is this sight which leads into the lewd criminal court scene (572-74), and it is Shem's traumatic experience. As Glugg (the "Nick" of the Mime) he is beaten by his brother Chuff when during the games he has proven incapable of guessing the girls' riddles and lost their favor to Chuff (an odd instant of the victor adding injury to the vanquished's insult). The significance of this late beating becomes apparent from Glugg's baby-talk petulance when the girls scoff at his wounds: "Split the hvide and aye seize heaven! He knows for he's seen it in black and white through his eyetrompit trained upon jenny's and all that sort of thing which is dandymount to a clearobscure" (247.31-34). Shem knows the sexual secret because he has the intelligence to correlate his remembrance of his parents in the bedroom with what he has read in black and white, and he may well have reached puberty also; Shaun lacks the knowledge and the ability, and already resents what he does not understand and cannot accomplish.

In the situation in the *Wake,* the younger son displaces the older. Shaun has found the letter dug up by Biddy the hen; the letter was dictated to Shem by Anna Livia, and contains of course the sexual secret of life. With the letter Shem can replace his father, but Shaun steals the letter, and claims it as his own. He is Shaun the Post delivering the letter to the people; thus he is Richard Pigott (at this instant at least), forging the letter to destroy the true leader, Charles Parnell. Shaun succeeds and is heralded before the people in the opening chapter of "his" Book; he is Earwicker's chosen successor, however, although Anna Livia favored Shem. Here Joyce is utilizing the Jacob-Esau Biblical story for his own purposes in the *Wake;* he is toying with Biblical legend to suit his immediate purposes at any given point: Shem is Esau, "this Esuan Menschavik and the first till last alshemist" (185.34-35), when he is the older son deprived by the enterprising younger, and now an outcast; he is Jacob when he represents the deposer of the father, the cunning son, the mother's favorite, the villain who is Cain, Lucifer, Loki, even the Prometheus who rebelled against the gods:

> Shem is as short for Shemus as Jem is joky for Jacob. A few tough-necks are still getatable who pretend that aboriginally he was of respectable stemming (he was an outlex between the lines of Ragonar Blaubarb and Horrild Hairwire and an inlaw to Capt. the Hon. and Rev. Mr Bbyrdwood de Trop Blogg was among his most distant connections) but every honest to goodness man in the land of the space of today knows that his back life will not stand being written about in black and white [169.1-8].

The description of Shem which follows is hardly in keeping with the physical traits of an epic hero; twice removed from the heroic lineage of the great Finn, Shem is a freak. The "epic catalogue" of his

> bodily getup, it seems, included an adze of a skull, an eight of a larkseye, the whoel of a nose, one numb arm up a sleeve, fortytwo hairs

off his uncrown, eighteen to his mock lip, a trio of barbels from his megageg chin (sowman's son), the wrong shoulder higher than the right, all ears, an artificial tongue with a natural curl, not a foot to stand on, a handful of thumbs, a blind stomach, a deaf heart, a loose liver [etc.] [169.11-17].

This freakish Shem is a far cry from his popular brother, the contemporary epic hero. Proclaimed by the populace as the savior, Shaun is the embodiment of Earwicker's dream; if the father has somewhat fallen short of the epic hero, his dream representation of himself as his favorite son lacks nothing. In fact, the opening of Shaun's chapter (Book Three, chapter 1) is a minor epic in itself. Earwicker is finally in bed after the tavern brawl, and his dream is nothing less than Dante's *Divina Commedia:*

> And as I was jogging along in a dream as dozing I was dawdling, arrah, methought broadtone was heard and the creepers and the gliders and flivvers of the earth breath and the dancetongues of the woodfires and the hummers in their ground all vociferated echoating: Shaun! Shaun! Post the post! with a high voice and O, the higher on high the deeper and low, I heard him so! And lo, mescemed somewhat came of the noise and somewho might amove allmurk [404.3-10].

The epic hero is then introduced; items of his sartorial attire are enumerated in such a fashion as to indicate the convention of the putting on of armor in the Homeric and Virgilian epics:

> dressed like an earl in just the correct wear, in a classy mac Frieze o'coat of far suparior ruggedness, indigo braw, tracked and tramped, and an Irish ferrier collar, freeswinging with mereswin lacers from his shoulthern and thick welted brogues on him hammered to suit the scotsmost public and climate, iron heels and sparable soles, and his jacket of providence wellprovided woolies with a softrolling lisp of a lapel to it and great sealingwax buttons, a good helping bigger than the slots for them, of twentytwo carrot krasnapoppsky red and his invulnerable burlap whiskcoat and his popular choker, Tamagnum sette-and-forte and his loud boheem toy and the damasker's overshirt he sported inside, a starspangled zephyr with a decidedly surpliced crinklydoodle front [404.16-28].

As elegant as this apparel seems to be to the proud father, it is actually strictly a comic theater costume; Shaun is dressed like Sean the Post in Dion Boucicault's *Arrah-na-Pogue*. Here he represents the international politician. He has donned the political armor for every country and political occasion; he is able to vary his dialect to suit constituents everywhere, and his attire is composed of articles from every corner of the Empire. As such Shaun is not only the British demagogue attempting to appeal to the Welsh, Scots, and Irish (the Irish collar, the Welsh brogues—shoes and accent—the Scottish suit), but an American politico (*a starspangled zephyr*), a Russian (*krasnapoppsky red*), and an ecclesiast (*surpliced crinkly-doodle front*).

The epic describing of a hero's armor is a common device in *Finnegans Wake;* in the epic Crimean War scene, Earwicker as the Russian General is properly attired in "his raglanrock and his malakoiffed bulbsbyg and his varnashed roscians and his cardigans blousejagged and his scarlett manchokuffs and his treecoloured camiflag and his perikopendolous gaelstorms" (339.10-13). Joyce here has managed to pun into these articles of "armor" the names of three British commanders in the Crimean War, a Russian leader, and a fortification: Lord Raglan, the Earl of Cardigan, Sir James Yorke Scarlett, Prince Menchikov, and the Malakoff fort. (It is concomitant with Joyce's "cult of coincidences" that Raglan and Cardigan have given their names to such sartorial innovations as the raglan sleeve and the cardigan jacket and sweater.) The constant repetitions of articles of clothing through the *Wake* are aspects of Joyce's use of Carlyle's *Sartor Resartus* (of clothes as the surface coverings hiding the basic truth of the body), of Swift's *Tale of a Tub* (the coat which is willed by the father to his three theologically squabbling sons), and a reference to the Biblical Joseph, who owned a coat of many colors and was proficient in interpreting dreams. This theme of clothing becomes prominent in the tavern yarn of the Norwegian Captain and Kersse the Tailor, and the tale of the Prankquean and van Hoother.

Following his putting on of armor, we finally meet the epic hero himself. In the eyes of his father he is every inch the hero, and in the brogue of his father we hear him described:

> that young fellow looked the stuff, the Bel of Beaus' Walk, a prime card if ever was! Pep? Now without deceit it is hardly too much to say he was looking grand, so fired smart, in much more than his usual health. No mistaking that beamish brow! There was one for you that ne'er would nunch with good Duke Humphrey but would aight through the months without a sign of an err in hem and then, otherwise rounding, fourale to the lees of Traroe. Those jehovial oyeglances! The heart of the rool! And hit the hencoop. He was immense, topping swell for he was after having a great time of it [405.13-22].

This portrait of the hero is of course the jaundiced view of Earwicker identifying with his popular son, and it should be viewed in direct contrast with the author's "objective" view of H.C.E. In the sixth chapter of Book One, Joyce presents twelve riddles through which he identifies his *dramatis personae;* the first is a lengthy description of the central hero of the novel, and, despite the fact that the answer to the description is "Finn MacCool" (139.14), it becomes obvious that it is also Earwicker. Joyce has now compressed his epic hero with the bourgeois successor: as Everyman, Finn and H.C.E. have finally merged into a single individual, since enough time has now passed to allow us to render all the events of the first four chapters (dealing with Finnegan and Earwicker) into history and myth. What emerges is the single hero who retains some of the heroic aspects of the giant—"What secondtonone myther rector and maximost bridgesmaker was the first to rise taller through his beanstale than the bluegum buaboababbaun or the giganteous Wellingtonia Sequoia" (126.10-12)—but it is also "Dook Hookbackcrook" (127.17), the humble Earwicker. Joyce's portrait of our contemporary epic hero harks back to the Leopold Bloom of *Ulysses,* and the nonhero is characterized in the *Wake* as the typical burgher:

> business, reading newspaper, smoking cigar, arranging tumblers on

table, eating meals, pleasure, etcetera, etcetera, pleasure, eating meals, arranging tumblers on table, smoking cigar, reading newspaper, business; minerals, wash and brush up, local views, juju toffee, comic and birthdays cards; those were the days and he was their hero [127.20-25].

But in the minor epic of Shaun the "savior," Earwicker presents the hero he might have been had he, like Finn, lived in a heroic age; he imagines for his favorite son all the splendor he would have liked to have had for himself—a typically bourgeois reaction. Shaun is therefore depicted as the perfect hero of the epics, but since he is Shaun, the glutton, the description of the epic hero is followed by an epic feast. An encyclopedic listing of food follows, listing Shaun's daily meals: breakfast consists of "a bless us O blood and thirsthy orange, next, the half of a pint of becon with newled googs and a segment of riceplummy padding" etc. (405.32-34); then dinner: "half a pound of round steak, very rare, Blong's best from Portarlington's Butchery, with a side of riceypeasy and Corkshire alla mellonge and bacon with (a little mar pliche!) a pair of chops" (406.1-4), and so on through lunches and suppers and midnight snacks.

Having finished "gormandising and gourmeteering" (407.1-2), Shaun is now ready to speak to the people, and Earwicker launches into another epic introduction of his hero: "When lo (whish, O whish!) mesaw mestreamed, as the green to the gred was flew, was flown, through deafths of durkness greengrown deeper I heard a voice, the voce of Shaun, vote of the Irish, voise from afar" (407.11-14), and the epic boasting follows. Shaun apologizes with false humility that he is unworthy of the honor of being the Royal Mailman and discloses his envy of his brother, while patronizingly claiming that he feels sorry for the "game loser!" (408.29). His boasting is an unctuous collection of campaign promises; he advocates "no five hour factory life with insufficient emollient and industrial disabled for them that day o'gratises" (409.24-26), while he himself, the politician, is prevented from working by the fact that he is a cleric: "Forgive me, Shaun repeated from his liquid lipes, not what I wants to do a strike of work but it was condemned on me premitially by Hireark Books and Chiefoverseer Cooks in their Eusebian Concordant Homilies" (409.33-36). The Shauniad epic moves from his campaigning and apologetics to the tale of the Ondt and the Gracehoper, a further vilification of Shem, and the complete disintegration of the hero before he reappears in the next chapter as Jaunty Jaun.

The epic convention of cataloguing is another basic feature of *Finnegans Wake;* the list of hundreds of rivers in the Anna Livia Plurabelle section, the lists of items of clothing throughout—usually in groups of seven articles to comprise the Seven Mystic Sheaths*—"pouch, gloves, flask, bricket, kerchief, ring and amber-

---

* The primary listings of the seven articles are: "his goldtin spurs and his ironed dux and his quarterbrass woodyshoes and his magnate's gharters and his bangkok's best and goliar's goloshes and his pulluponeasyan wartrews" (8.18-21); "his broadginger hat and his civic chollar and his allabuff hemmed and his bullbraggin soxangloves and his ladbroke breeks and his cattegut bandolair and his furframed panuncular cumbottes" (22.34-23.1); "his caoutchouc kepi and great belt and hideinsacks and his blaufunx fustian and ironsides jackboots and Bhagafat gaiters and his rubberised inverness" (35.8-10); "his fourinhand bow, his elbaroom surtout, the refaced unmansionables of gingerine hue, the state slate umbrella, his gruff woolselywellesly with the finndrinn knopfs and the gauntlet" (52.25-28); "his raglanrock and his malakoiffed bulbsbyg and his varnashed roscians and his cardigans blousejagged and his scarlett manchokuffs and his treecoloured camiflag and his perikopendolous gaelstorms" (339.10-13); "with his old Roderick Random pullon hat at a Lanty Leary cant on him and Mike Brady's shirt and Greene's linnet collarbow and his Ghenter's gaunts and his Macclefield's swash and his readymade Reillys and his panpresturberian poncho" (381.11-15); "in his grey half a tall hat and his amber necklace and his crimson harness and his leathern jib and his cheapshein hairshirt and his scotobrit sash and his parapilagian gallowglasses" (387.3-6); "with his lolleywide towelhat and his hobbsy socks and his wisden's bosse and his norsery pinafore and his gentleman's grip and his playaboy's plunge and his flannelly feelyfooling" (584.15-18); "with her marchpane switch on, her necklace of almonds and her poirette Sundae dress with bracelets of honey and her cochineal hose with the caramel dancings, the briskly best from Bootiestown, with her suckingstaff of ivorymint" (235.33-236.1); "with her louisequean's broques and her culunder buzzle and her little bolero boa and all and two times twenty curlicornies for her headdress, specks on her eyeux, and spudds on horeilles and a circusfix riding her Parisienne's cockneze" (102.10-13); "wearing, besides stains, rents and patches, his fight shirt, straw braces, souwester and a policeman's corkscrew trowswers" (85.33-35); "this fancy-

ulla" (24.32-33), and "in his grey half a tall hat and his amber
necklace and his crimson harness and his leathern jib and his
cheapshein hairshirt and his scotobrit sash and his parapilagian gallowglasses" (387.3-6)—and the lists of titles for various occasions. The last group includes names that the American hog-caller
bellows at Earwicker through the prison-cell keyhole: *Firstnighter,
Informer, Old Fruit, Yellow Whigger, Wheatears, Goldy Geit,
Bogside Beauty"* etc. (71.10-11); titles for Anna Livia's "mamafesta": *The Augusta Angustissimost for Old Seabeastius' Salvation,
Rockabill Booby in the Wave Trough, Here's to the Relicts of All
Decencies, Anna Stessa's Rise to Notice"* etc. (104.5-8); lists of
children's games: *"Thom Thom the Thonderman, Put the Wind
up the Peeler, Hat in the Ring, Prisson your Pritchards and Play
Withers Team, Mikel on the Luckypig, Nickel in the Slot, Sheila
Harnett and her Cow"* etc. (176.1-3); and the list of essay titles
used by Kev and Dolph during their lessons: "Duty, the daughter
of discipline, the Great Fire at the South City Markets, Belief in
Giants and the Banshee, A Place for Everything and Everything in
its Place" etc. (306.15-18). These catalogues are an integral part
of the *Wake;* they serve the dual purposes of repeating the basic

---

dress nordic in shaved lamb breeches, child's kilts, bibby buntings and welling-
tons, with club, torc and headdress" (529.32-33); "Here is your shirt, the day
one, come back. The stock, your collar. Also your double brogues. A comforter
as well. And here your iverol and everthelest your umbr" (619.34-620.1); "in
topee, surcingle, solascarf and plaid, plus fours, puttees and bulldog boots"
(30.23-24); "budget, fullybigs, sporran, tie, tuft, tabard and bloody antichill
cloak" (99.11-12); and "pouch, gloves, flask, bricket, kerchief, ring and am-
berulla" (24.32-33). Also intended are the following (although they require
some stretching or squeezing to make seven): "With that so tiresome old milk-
less a ram, with his tiresome duty peck and his bronchial tubes, the tiresome
old hairyg orangogran beaver, in his tiresome old twennysixandsixpenny sheop-
ards plods drowsers and his thirtybobandninepenny tails plus toop!" (396.14-
18), "with a scrumptious cocked hat and three green, cheese and tangerine
trinity plumes on the right handle side of his amarellous head, a coat macfar-
lane (the kersssest cut, you understand?) a sponiard's digger at his ribs, (*Al-
faiate punxit*) an azulblu blowsheet for his blousebosom blossom and a dean's
crozier" (180.8-13), and "Catchmire stockings, libertyed garters, shoddyshoes,
quicked out with selver. Pennyfair caps on pinnyfore frocks and a ring on her
fomefing finger" (226.24-26).

themes in succinct form and of parodying contemporary song titles, slogans, epithets, and clichés and key words which are ban-
died about every day until they lose their significance and become
mere catch phrases. Joyce is rebelling against attempts at classification and pigeonholing. His characters remain elusive throughout; they exchange their masks with the utmost of abandon. They
represent essentials not particulars, prototypes not stereotypes.
Joyce's use of details, of minute characteristics, of clichés and song
titles, suggests the timelessness of the essential qualities of human
existence, as well as the immediacy of each age's "names" for
those qualities.

The epic characteristics already enumerated are all repeated
often in *Finnegans Wake*. The battles are numerous: the war in
heaven, the tavern brawl, the Crimean War, each is fought over
and over again, never the same twice. The initial struggle can be
compared with a later version:

> That it was wildfires night on all the bettygallaghers. Mickmichael's
> soords shrieking shrecks through the wilkinses and neckanicholas'
> toastingforks pricking prongs up the tunnybladders. Let there be fight?
> And there was. Foght. On the site of the Angel's, you said? Guinney's
> Gap, he said, between what they said and the pussykitties. In the
> middle of the garth, then? That they mushn't toucht it [90.9-15].

The war in heaven again dissolves into the battles of temptation in
the Garden of Eden, and yet a vast amount of time, the space between eons, has elapsed (*Guinney's Gap* re-echoes "ginnandgo
gap" [14.16] of the *Eddas*). Time is fluid: all wars are being
fought consecutively in time, as well as simultaneously, yet the gap
persists between wars. Earwicker is both the victor and the victim:
he has won the battle but is slain, he has been beaten but will be
resurrected:

> were he chief, count, general, fieldmarshal, prince, king or Myles the
> Slasher in his person, with a moliamordhar mansion in the Breffnian
> empire and a place of inauguration on the hill of Tullymongan, there
> had been real murder, of the rayheallach royghal raxacraxian variety,

the MacMahon chaps, it was, that had done him in. On the fidd of Verdor the rampart combatants had left him lion with his dexter handcoup wresterected in a pureede paumee bloody proper [99.24-31].

Man's fate in *Finnegans Wake* is to outlive his heroism; killed in the prime of his heroic life, the hero is resurrected to achieve old age and ignominy. Those who had been Tristrams become King Marks; like Arthur cuckolded by Lancelot and Guinevere, and like Finn cuckolded by Diarmait and Grainne, Earwicker lives too long to remain a hero.

As in the *Iliad,* the death of the hero calls forth the funeral games in the *Wake:* Earwicker's demise in the tavern scene is, in fact, accomplished through a series of athletic contests. Having already taken place as soon as the battle has begun, it is recorded in tomorrow's morning papers—on the sports page: "You'll read it tomorrow, marn, when the curds on the table. . . . Screamer caps and invented gommas, quoites puntlost, forced to farce! . . . One hyde, sack, hic! Two stick holst, Lucky! Finnish Make Goal!" (374.4-21). (The battle in heaven had already been described as a football match in Shem's chapter: "All Saints beat Belial! Mickil Goals to Nichil! Notpossible! Already?" [175.5-6], the last two words expressing the "reader's" dismay at the strange chronology of events.) As befits Joyce's time compression, these funeral games are also the cause of the hero's funeral; he himself is killed in the contests that are fought because of his death, and, in keeping with still another violation of chronological time, he is already reading about it in the sports section. This compression of time is inherent in the portmanteau words that describe the events; the shooting of the Russian General is again taking place, in a rugby match, in the morning papers: "Good for you, Richmond Rover! Scrum around, our side! Let him have another between the spindlers! A grand game! Dalymount's decisive. Don Gouverneur Buckley's in the Tara Tribune, sporting the insides of a Rhutian Jhanaral" (375.21-24).

Finnegans Wake (like the *Odyssey,* the *Aeneid,* the *Divina*

Commedia, and Joyce's *Ulysses*) also takes us down to Hades, on a journey into the underworld, where the dead heroes parade by. The vision of Pandemonium which we have already seen as modern Dublin (5.13-6.12) is magnified into many views of hell. After Earwicker's trial the epic fall and resurrection motif is heard: "The house of Atreox is fallen indeedust (Ilyam, Ilyum! Maeromor Mournomates!) averging on blight like the mundibanks of Fennyana, but deeds bounds going arise again" (55.3-5). And the drunken Earwicker goes off pub-crawling through seven Dublin taverns, taverns which are various versions of heaven and hell (and old Dublin pubs at that!): "to drink in the House of Blazes, the Parrot in Hell, the Orange Tree, the Glibt, the Sun, the Holy Lamb and, lapse not leashed, in Ramitdown's ship hotel" (63.22-25), the last an Egyptian tomb (the tomb of Rameses) which again echoes the Book of the Dead.

Earwicker is entombed as an Egyptian monarch, "first pharoah, Humpheres Cheops Exarchas" (62.20-21), Cheops, ark, and ship's hotel suggesting the method of burial employing a funeral ship. The *Amenti's* "Chapters of the Coming Forth by Day in the Underworld" is repeated in "the sixth sealed chapter of the going forth by black" (62.26-27). In imitation of Homer, Joyce describes his own exile in Trieste (which he likens to a journey into the underworld), as well as Earwicker's death: "For mine qvinne I thee giftake and bind my hosenband I thee halter. The wastobe land, a lottuse land, a luctuous land, Emeraldilluim" (62.10-12). Here the marriage vows are parodied as an approach to death, while shades of Eliot's "Waste Land," Homer's island of the lotus eaters, Lot's Sodom, and Ireland are combined to present Hades.

Actually, H.C.E. has been buried in Lough Neagh, "the Lake of Healing" in Northern Ireland, which thus becomes a symbol of resurrection. The healing lake returns the hero to life; the coffin in which he had been buried suddenly disappears: "The coffin, a triumph of the illusionist's art . . . had been removed from the hardware premises of Oetzmann and Nephew, a noted house of the gonemost west" (66.27-32), and Earwicker has descended into the underworld. The funeral pomp provides another catalogue of "Show coffins, winding sheets, goodbuy bierchepes, cinerary urns, liealoud blasses, snuffchests, poteentubbs, lacrimal vases" etc. (77.28-30). Earwicker is "buried burrowing in Gehinnon, to proliferate through all his Unterwealth" (78.9-10); his journey is made by "Coach, carriage, wheelbarrow, dungcart" (79.25-26)—a suggestion of the hen digging in the refuse pile (the Hebrew Gehenna, originally the valley of Hinnon where refuse was burned) again suggests the finding of the letter as a resurrection motif.

Hell is again seen as a series of Dublin pubs when Patrick brings Christianity (and consequently the Christian concept of heaven and hell): "Byrne's and Flamming's and Furniss's and Bill Hayses's and Ellishly Haught's, hoc . . . stiff or sober" (289.13-15). But the full-scale descent into the underworld does not take place in the *Wake* until the third chapter of Book Three. Shaun, as Yawn, lies exhausted on a hill in County Meath; the four judges arrive to question him, but as the interrogation proceeds Yawn disintegrates completely, and from the mound of his decomposed body rises a series of voices, resulting in the final voice, that of H.C.E. Under interrogation Yawn fondly remembers, "I used to be always overthere on the fourth day at my grandmother's place, Tear-nan-Ogre, my little grey home in the west" (479.1-2)—a reference to Tir-na-nOg, the land of eternal youth in Celtic mythology. And the ghostly voice from deep beneath Yawn's carcass is heard declaiming, "saouls to the dhaoul, do ye. Finnk. Fime. Fudd?" (499.17-19), a ghostly version of the Tim Finnegan vaudeville ballad: "Bad luck to your souls. D'ye think I'm dead?" This resurrection line Joyce renders elsewhere in Gaelic ("Anam muck an dhoul! Did ye drink me doornail?"— 24.15) and in Latin ("Animadiabolum, mene credidisti mortuum?"—74.8).

But Joyce need hardly have his protagonist descend into the underworld to bring forth his parade of dead heroes; the entire *Wake* is of course such a parade. The combatants in heaven, Napoleon and Wellington, the Irish defenders and foreign invaders, the

Crimean contestants, historic and mythological, all appear and reappear throughout the course of the flow of the book. Shem, while drunk at the Earwicker trial, conjures up "Helmingham Erchenwyne Rutter Egbert Crumwall Odin Maximus Esme Saxon Esa Vercingetorix Ethelwulf Rupprecht Ydwalla Bentley Osmund Dysart Yggdrasselmann" (88.21-23). Norse gods, Gallic defenders, Saxon kings, Roman emperors, German princes, Puritan invaders—and a healthy group of as yet unidentifiable personages— they provide another epic list of heroes marching through the underworld of Shem's drunken unconscious. But most significant are the initials of all their names, which spell HERE COMES EVERYBODY, and again the ghostly garner of heroes equals the totality of Earwicker himself.

Like many another epic *Finnegans Wake* contains a significant series of digressions; its plot line, like that of *Beowulf,* is rather thin, and actually more is discerned of its significance from the important digressions. Joyce is less concerned with the events than with the recording of these events, the various circumstances under which they are reported; his epic best resembles the epic events of the Fenian Cycle or the Tristram-Iseult saga (both of which are heavily drawn upon for the plot of the *Wake*), where many conflicting versions are available because of manuscript discrepancies. In this respect *Finnegans Wake* reverts to the "authentic" epic which accumulates its material with the passing of years. Like the mysterious letter found by the hen in the midden heap, it bears the ravages of time and tells its story in fragments; the important trial that attempts to get to the bottom of the epic event of Earwicker's fall is constantly being replayed, each time amassing new evidence on top of evidence already obscured. Never do the events wholly coincide, never is there a complete version of the important incident; each age interprets the significance of the epic fall in its own terms to satisfy its own needs and desires. In the short span of time that elapsed between the incident and the initial trial, many of the participants have already died: Peter Cloran (40.16), the scoundrel who divulged the news of the incident, has died in jail as Paul Horan (49.15)—born as St. Peter, he dies as St. Paul, representing the duality of self in the *Wake;* the Hosty who wrote the ballad has been drowned (quite probably in Lake Neagh) : "passed away painlessly after life's upsomdowns one hallowe'en night, ebrous and in the state of nature, propelled from Behind into the great Beyond by footblows coulinclouted upon his oyster" (49.23-26). Again in miniature fashion the fall has been repeated; Lucifer has once again been "booted" out of heaven.

But, despite the loss of the entire cast of principals, the trial takes place; substitutes for each of the accusers quickly appear— "by the coincidance of their contraries reamalgamerge in that identity of undiscernibles" (49.35-50.1)—and the trial goes on. The events are so thoroughly obscured that the trial begins to revolve around a false report of an encounter with a masked assailant (62-63), and finally the suggestion that Earwicker has been arrested for banging on his own door (64); the "authentic" version comes to light, and we now learn that Earwicker has put a lock on his gate to keep out donkeys, but has been locked in himself for his own protection (69). The series of reports on the happenings of the epic fall continues under a haze of time-obscured hearsay; there is never a single accurate account of the important occurrence. This handling of the material of the *Wake* attempts to present the contemporary epic as a version of the past as seen by the present; the nonheroic age retells the heroic story in its own versions. What Myles Dillon in his history of *Early Irish Literature* tells us about the Fenian Cycle applies equally well to *Finnegans Wake:*

> The temper of the Fenian Cycle might be characterized as romantic rather than epic. The heroic tradition is, for the most part, preserved not in the vivid narrative which brings the reader close to the action, but rather as the record of a glorious past, the fierce joy of paganism as it was remembered in a rather melancholy Christian present.[3]

It is significant that much of the story of Finn MacCool comes to us in a version in which a descendant is relating the tales of past heroism to St. Patrick (in *The Colloquy of the Old Men*), since one of the last significant incidents of the *Wake* is the arrival of St.

Patrick in A.D. 432 and his encounter with the Archdruid. Here the cyclical pattern again is obvious if we accept the possibility that the entire *Wake* is a romantic version of the heroic past (the age of Vico's giants), reported in chaotic fashion to Patrick (Vico's patriarch of the succeeding age).

These digressions are not the only Beowulfian aspects of *Finnegans Wake;* many instances in the *Wake* echo the alliterative verse form of Anglo-Saxon heroic poetry. Joyce often suggests a return to the heroic age with the sudden interjection of "that dark deed doer, this wellwilled wooer" into a passage concerning heroic warfare, celestial and terrestial:

> Arranked in their array and flocking for the fray on that old orangeray, Dolly Brae. For these are not on terms, they twain, bartrossers, since their baffle of Whatalose when Adam Leftus and the devil took our hindmost, gegifting her with his painapple, nor will not be atoned at all in fight to no finish, that dark deed doer, this wellwilled wooer, Jerkoff and Eatsoup, Yem or Yan, while felixed is who culpas does and harm's worth healing and Brune is bad French for Jour d'Anno. Tiggers and Tuggers they're all for tenzones. Bettlimbraves [246.25-33].

The Chuff-Glugg battle of the Mime is already over (but is of course also taking place, as well as *about to* take place), and the Eden incident has already been observed (*felixed is who culpas does*), the two events compressed into a single action. The word *painapple* refers both to the forbidden fruit and to the World War One euphemism for hand grenade, a pineapple. The brother dichotomy of Jacob and Esau (as well as the oriental principles of interlocked opposites, Yin and Yang) is evident from the day of their birth; *Jour d'Anno* not only implies the birth of the "twains," but reiterates the cause of the conflict—Anna Livia, the eternal woman. Joyce thus employed the alliterations of *arranked in their array and flocking for the fray* and *that dark deed doer, this wellwilled wooer* to suggest the heroic poetry of the Anglo-Saxon, as well as the Germanic prefix in *gegifting.*

During the tale of the Norwegian Captain, Joyce launches into many passages of alliteration, Beowulfian rhythms, and kennings. The setting throughout the tale is Viking and heroic—like the Prankquean, the Norse Captain sails three times into Dublin Bay, only to sail away without paying his tailor or his inn bills. The sacking of the mainland by the Scandinavian seamen is a frequent theme in the *Wake*—"Fuvver, that Skand, he was up in Norwood's sokaparlour, eating oceans of Voking's Blemish" (157.16-17)—and here the Norse Captain is again the guilty Earwicker:

> But old sporty, as endth lord, in ryehouse reigner, he nought feared crimp or cramp of shore sharks, plotsome to getsome. It was whol niet godthaab of errol Loritz off his Cape of Good Howthe and his trippertrice loretta lady, a maomette to his monetone, with twy twy twinky her stone hairpins, only not, if not, a queen of Prancess their telling tabled who was for his seeming a casket through the heavenly, nay, heart of the sweet (had he hows would he keep her as niece as a fiddle!) but in the mealtub it was wohl yeas sputsbargain what, rarer of recent, an occasional conformity, he, with Muggleton Muckers, alwagers allalong most certainly allowed, as pilerinnager's grace to petitionists of right, of the three blend cupstoomerries with their customed spirits, the Gill gob, the Burklley bump, the Wallisey wanderlook, having their ceilidhe gailydhe in his shaunty irish [312.17-30].

What begins as a Norse saga of seafaring soon dissolves into a theological dispute; the sailing of the Vikings for plunder is joined with the sailing of the Pilgrims (*pilerinnager's grace*) for safety from religious persecution. But, since all this is happening on several levels at once, such theologians as John Gill, George Berkeley, and John Wesley (*Gill, Burklley,* and *Wallisey*) are also the warriors Goll (slayer of Finn MacCool's father), the Buckley who shot the Russian General, and the Duke of Wellington—a merging of the mythical, the fictional, and the historical heroes. It is also significant that the first line of this paragraph (*But old sporty, as endth lord, in ryehouse reigner*) is a re-echo of the rhythms of the introduction of the epic hero Finnegan: "Bygmester Finnegan, of the Stuttering Hand, freemen's maurer" (4.18-19). The paragraph ends with an alliterative enumeration of twelve trades, cul-

minating significantly with that of the weaver, suggesting the
twelve apostles and the twelve customers present in Earwicker's
pub during the telling of the saga of the Norwegian Captain:
"Lorimers and leathersellers, skinners and salters, pewterers and
paperstainers, parishclerks, fletcherbowyers, girdlers, mercers,
cordwainers and first, and not last, the weavers" (312.35-313.1).
The sea battle that follows again evokes images of heroic verse: the
Norse Captain's ship is about to be overtaken, Earwicker is at the
cash register in his tavern, and Finnegan is about to fall again:
"Thus as count the costs of liquid courage, a bullyon gauger,
stowed stivers pengapung in bulk in hold (fight great finnence!
brayvoh, little bratton!) keen his kenning, the queriest of the crew,
with that fellow fearing for his own misshapes" (313.29-32).

The epic convention of repeating key phrases and stock epithets
is duplicated by Joyce in his use of recurring sounds in various individual ways in *Finnegans Wake*. Joyce's deployment of repeated
leitmotifs (of names, numbers, and sounds) is the binding element
of his narrative, and his use of catch phrases and rhythmic patterns
adroitly ties the various motifs together in the *Wake*. Ten one-
hundred-lettered words* depicting the roll of thunder that marks
the end of a stage of the cycle punctuate the book, each one fitting
into the particular series of events being narrated at the moment.
The first thunderclap is the basic fall motif: "bababadalgharagh-
takamminarronnkonnbronntonnerronntuonnthunntrovarrhounawn-
skawntoohoohoordenenthurnuk!" (3.15-17);⁴ the second is the
slamming of Jarl van Hoother's castle door (23.5-7);† the third
announces the ballad written by Hosty (44.20-21); the fourth
is an obscene rumble during the trial, suggesting the fall in
the park (90.31-33); the fifth is the babble of the gossipy letter
(113.9-11); the sixth is the slamming of the Earwicker door after
the children have come in from their play (257.27-28); the seventh records the din in the tavern as Earwicker's reputation takes a

---

* The tenth contains 101 letters, so that the totality consists of 1001 letters,
one for each of the Arabian nights.
† See Appendix.

fall and Finnegan is again heard toppling from his scaffold
(314.8-9); the eighth is the noise of radio static preceding the Crimean War broadcast, as well as the orgasm during the seduction of
Anna Livia (332.5-7); the ninth is Shaun's cough as he clears his
throat in preparation for the recounting of the Ondt-Gracehoper
fable (414.19-20); and the last follows soon after (424.20-22),
Shaun's angry rumble of abuse against Shem serving as the basic
thunderclap of destruction before the Cabalistic regeneration begins. The complete destruction of the established world order is
thus indicated as the end of the *sephiroth,* the blending of One and
Zero into the perfect union of Ten prefiguring the birth of a new
world.

In counterpoint to the thunderclaps are the chimes of the church
bells which during the night toll the hours throughout Earwicker's
dreams (a counterpoint of pagan and religious symbols, of the
heroic and the divine). Not as easily discernible as the hundred-
letter words, the bells are most distinctly heard in the "Anna Livia
Plurabelle" sequence (where many of the themes make their most
succinct statements), a chapter which Joyce wrote quite early in his
composition, and which underwent many series of corrections and
alterations. Here the bells toll for the Zurich spring festival with
which Joyce had become acquainted during his exile in the Swiss
city; as a rite of spring it evokes the resurrection motif of fertility:
"Pingpong! There's the Belle for Sexaloitez! And Concepta de
Send-us-pray! Pang! Wring out the clothes! Wring in the dew!"
(213.18-20). The feast of Sechselauten, during which the demon
of winter is burned, and the echo of the Tennysonian paean for the
coming of the new year are present in the washing of the dirty
clothes at the Liffey's public banks. Elsewhere Earwicker hears the
bells as he dreams of his incarceration: "Pinck poncks that bail for
seeks alicence where cumsceptres with scentaurs stay" (32.2-4).
And when the three soldiers who observed H.C.E.'s sin are tagged
as Kiplingesque British tommies preserving English markets in
China and India, the bells intone: "Peingpoeng! For saxonlootie!
. . . Thus contenters with santoys play" (58.24,32-33). The temp-

tresses lurk behind the sex lecture of the Lessons chapter as the bells announce: "ringrang, the chimes of sex appealing as conchitas with sentas stray" (268.2-3); and when the young girl dreams of the Flying Dutchman during the Norwegian Captain incident, the bell "pings saksalaisance that Concessas with Sinbads may (pong!)" (327.24-25), while "Bing bong! Saxlooter, for congesters are salders' prey" (379.7-8), later in the chapter, records the beating up of Earwicker, the Norse Captain, after the sea battle. Iseult, talking to her reflection in the looking glass—she is "Alicious, twinstreams twinestraines, through alluring glass or alas in jumboland" (528.17-18)—dreams of her lover while the church bells peal the night hours for the seventh time: "Ding dong! Where's your pal in silks alustre? . . . as Consuelas to Sonias may?" (528.18-19,25). The repetition of these phrases attests to the dream reality of converting external noises to fit the events of the particular episode of the dream; as the seven hours are chimed at accidental moments in the dream, Earwicker's subconscious converts them into the fabric of the dream's events.*

Equally important are the reiterations of the Viconian theme as they appear under their various guises, a motif sounded in the washerwomen's colloquy as "Teems of times and happy returns. The seim anew. Ordovico or viricordo. Anna was, Livia is, Plurabelle's to be" (215.22-24). Although parts of this four-sentence statement of theme are repeated often, the statement in its entirety

---

* I have limited my references here to the seven instances of this motif which I consider *primary* ones (full restatements of all significant parts of the motif), while secondary echoes can be heard in partial form in at least ten places: "this belles' alliance beyind Ill Sixty" (7.33); "Insects appalling; low hum clang sin!" (339.22); "pagne pogne" (344.22-23); "Bung! Bring forth your deed! Bang! Till is the right time. Bang!" (378.17-18); "the goattanned saxopeeler upshotdown chigs peel of him!" (441.33-34); "saxy luters" (492.14-15); "Silks apeel and sulks alusty?" (508.29); "Ring his mind, ye staples, (bonze!) . . . Sacks eleathury! Sacks eleathury! Bam!" (536.9-11); "Tix sixponce! Poum! Hool poll the bull? Fool pay the bill. Becups a can full. Peal, pull the bell!" (568.13-15); "Saxenslyke" (600.24); and "Skulksaloot!" (610.14). For a full treatment of this motif and complete lists of primary, secondary, and tertiary references, see Fritz Senn's "Some Zurich Allusions in *Finnegans Wake,*" *Analyst,* No. 19 (December, 1960), pp. 2-12.

does not reappear until Anna Livia's dying monologue. Echoes of its parts are scattered throughout, however: Mutt comments that "the same roturns" (18.5) when the Jute arrives early in the *Wake;* "Mammy was, Mimmy is, Minuscoline's to be. . . . The same renew" (226.14-17) is Iseult's grief at losing her lover, but she sagely realizes that there will be other men. "Hencetaking tides we haply return" (261.5) begins the history portion of the Night Lessons, and most of the statement appears in scattered form as the children study it: "For as Anna was at the beginning lives yet and will return. . . . We drames our dreams tell Bappy returns. And Sein annew. . . . of order and order's coming" (277.12-20). The wake scene during the interrogation of Yawn produces the destructive sense of the last thunderclap: "—Booms of bombs and heavy rethudders?—This aim to you!" (510.1-2). But it is Anna Liffey's final speech that produces the full restatement in its four Viconian parts; the significance of the reawakening is now present in Vico's formula: "Themes have thimes and habit reburns. To flame in you. Ardor vigor forders order. Since ancient was our living is in possible to be" (614.8-10). And the eternal woman adds a final "The sehm asnuh" (620.16) as a coda.

In this repetitive manner many of the concepts have their rhythmic leitmotifs recurring throughout; in many cases Joyce uses nursery rhymes, popular songs, and literary quotations as his epical echoes. "The House That Jack Built," for example, carries along with it the significance of the builder of the city, the Lucifer-Cain-Cadmus-Bygmester Solness characteristic of Finnegan and Earwicker and Shem: "This is the ffrinch that fire on the Bull that bang the flag of the Prooshious" (8.13-14) sounds the theme during the visit to the "Wellington Museum" as Kate displays the general's battle musket. When the reader, early in the *Wake,* pleads for a halt to the complicated proceedings, Joyce editorializes:

> In the ignorance that implies impression that knits knowledge that finds the nameform that whets the wits that convey contacts that sweeten sensation that drives desire that adheres to attachment that

dogs death that bitches birth that entails the ensuance of existentiality [18.24-28].

The implication here is that the growth of language mirrors the progress of man and his search for significance, that *Finnegans Wake* is an aspect of the growth of language, and, consequently, the reader's plea for a cessation is a regression to illiteracy. Joyce is allying himself, the artist, with the Master Builder as a builder in man's progress. Other such echoes include: *"His is the House that Malt Made"* (106.27), a reference to Earwicker's tavern; "This is the Hausman all paven and stoned, that cribbed the Cabin that never was owned that cocked his leg and hennad his Egg" (205.34-36), the city-building statement already mentioned; "that jackhouse that jerry built" (274.21-22), which identifies Shem as the builder, but denigrates the quality of the construction; "the house that juke built" (375.4), implying the family depravities of the Earwickers; "the mack that never forgave the ass" (476.26-27); and the most unrhythmic version:

> the fostermother of the first nancyfree that ran off after the trumpadour that mangled Moore's melodies and so upturned the tubshead of the stardaft journalwriter to inspire the prime finisher to fellhim the firtree out of which Cooper Funnymore planed the flat of the beerbarrel on which my grandydad's lustiest sat his seat of unwisdom with my tante's petted sister for the cause of his joy! [439.8-14]

Zeus's master-building of a mountain atop mountain to topple Cronos and the titans is recorded in "the ward of the wind that lightened the fire that lay in the wood that Jove bolt" (80.27-28), while Prometheus' defiance of Zeus in giving fire to man is incorporated in the same fragment. The Garden of Eden motif is chanted by the children during their studying as: "This is the glider that gladdened the girl that list to the wind that lifted the leaves that folded the fruit that hung on the tree that grew in the garden Gough gave" (271.25-29). In the tavern, Earwicker is described as being "the tout that pumped the stout that linked the lank that cold the sandy that nextdoored the rotter that rooked the rhymer that lapped at the hoose that Joax pilled" (369.13-15). Earwicker at his bar, Hosty writing the ballad, and Jesus establishing the Church are implied in this refrain.* The writing of the scurrilous ballad is re-echoed in the long passage during the early morning scene of Earwicker in bed; it records the reasons for the chaos and the destruction of the final age, and ends with "the ballad that Hosty made" (580.36). And the mourners at the wake review the reasons for Earwicker's sexual downfall: "—So this was the dope that woolied the cad that kinked the ruck that noised the rape that tried the sap that hugged the mort? —That legged in the hoax that joke bilked" (511.32-34).

Earwicker as the arriving conqueror is celebrated in the song "The Wild Man from Borneo," which reappears several times in the *Wake;* since the conqueror is still something of a barbarian, the history of Ireland consists of invasions by less cultured neighbors who are invariably absorbed into Irish culture. (A suggestion of Oscar Wilde is also to be gleaned from the use of the song, since Wilde plays an important part in the *Wake;* like Earwicker, Wilde had a fall and a famous trial; like Shem he was a writer, an extreme nonconformist, who eventually became somewhat reconciled with the bourgeois elements of those who "persecuted" him.) The song first appears in the Finn MacCool riddle: the fall of Finn, whose body forms the city of Dublin, is being re-enacted in the decline of the beautiful eighteenth-century city into a twentieth-cen-

---

* This last phrase is a good instance at which to examine the complex of possible puns. *Hoose* is most likely "house," of course, but may also be read as "hoax," "hose," "host," and possibly even a "hooch-boose" portmanteau of slang terms for whiskey. *Joax* has infinite possibilities: Jove, Jehovah, Ajax, Jacob, Job, John, Joyce, Jesus, Jones (the professor of the riddles chapter), Joe (the Earwicker's manservant), Jukes (the depraved family), *et al.* By adding the cumulative possibilities inherent in the other parodies of "The House That Jack Built" discernible in the *Wake,* a partial list of pun possibilities in this phrase includes: (1) the house that Jack built, (2) the house that God (Jove, Jehovah) built, (3) the house (temple) that Samson pulled (down), (4) the hoax that Jesus pulled, (5) the hoax that Joyce pulled, (6) the jokes that Joyce piled (up), (7) the horse that Ajax pulled, (8) the hooch-boose that the host (H.C.E.) spilled, (9) the host (H.C.E.) that Joyce built, (10) the hoax that the Holy Ghost played, etc. Fritz Senn suggests *Hose* (German, trousers) being pulled down.

tury slum: "the gleam of the glow of the shine of the sun through the dearth of the dirth on the blush of the brick of the viled ville of Barnehulme has dust turned to brown" (130.22-24). The actual use of the song for its conquest significance occurs at the end of the tale of the Norwegian Captain: the marauding rover has not only been beaten in the sea battle and captured (325), but converted to Christianity (326) and married to Anna Livia (328-329): "For the joy of the dew on the flower of the fleets on the fields of the foam of the waves of the seas of the wild main from Borneholm has jest come to crown" (331.34-36). Soon after, during the Butt-Taff version of the Crimean War, the echo of the *"waldmanns from Burnias seduced country clowns"* (345.4-5) is heard, as we are being reminded that the Russian General is none other than H.C.E. And the tavern chapter ends with the drunken demise of maligned Earwicker: having lapped up the dregs of wine and barleycorn, he falls to the floor in drunken slumber: "on the flure of his feats and the feels of the fumes in the wakes of his ears our wineman from Barleyhome he just slumped to throne" (382.24-26).

A final reference to the Earwickerian wild man from Borneo is found during the fable of the Ondt and the Gracehoper. Here the eight stages of the wild man's arrival are limited to four (the stages of the Viconian cycle): "The whool of the whaal in the wheel of the whorl of the Boubou from Bourneum has thus come to taon!" (415.7-8). More obscure echoes can be heard in "the brodar of the founder of the father of the finder of the pfander of the pfunder of the furst man in Ranelagh" (481.33-35) and "the firmness of the formous of the famous of the fumous of the first fog in Maidanvale?" (502.26-27). Even in these can be heard reverberations of the conquerors, both the *founder* and the *formous* (the Formorians, ancient settlers of Erinn, also seen in "Formoreans" [15.5] and "Fomor's in his Fin"—236.9); Oscar Wilde is also to be noted in *of the pfunder (De Profundis)*.

"The Man That Broke the Bank at Monte Carlo" is another vaudeville guise for H. C. Earwicker, since it concerns the popular acclamation granted a debonair gambler when he breaks the bank at the gambling casino, and the good graces with which he just as quickly loses all of his gains. During the second Earwicker trial (in which Shem and Shaun are somehow involved instead of their father), the hero is described as being "Like the crack that bruck the bank in Multifarnham" (90.24)—the famous Monaco casino overlapped with the Westmeath town of Multifarnham. One of the titles suggested for Anna Livia's manifesto is *"The Man That Made His Mother in the Marlborry Train"* (105.8-9). During the Night Lessons, Moses is being studied: "For the man that broke the ranks on Monte Sinjon" (274.1-2). Moses is here a parallel for Finnegan: atop Mount Sinai he too is a master builder, like Finnegan atop his ladder, since time past is time present: "That that is allruddy with us, ahead of schedule, which already is plan accomplished from and syne" (274.3-5). And during the Yawn episode the voice of Earwicker finally is heard from the heap announcing his innocence; he refers to himself as "The man what shocked his shanks at contey Carlow's" (538.28-29), a reference to the washerwoman's earlier suggestion that the gossip's "slur gave the stink to Carlow" (214.30). Again the Monte Carlo site of the gambler's fall is changed to an Irish location. Secondary echoes can be heard from *"the Man behind the Borrel"* (71.25-26), "the mauwe that blinks you blank is mostly Carbo" (232.2-3), and "Big Arthur flugged the field at Annie's courting" (514.6).

If the repetitive use of sounds, noises, leitmotifs, and titles is vital to the basic pattern of *Finnegans Wake,* then the use of the traditional riddle is crucial. Patterned after such diverse literary pieces as *Oedipus Tyrannus* and *Rumpelstiltskin,* riddles in *Finnegans Wake* underscore several of the most vital themes of the book: the Prankquean's riddle of "why do I am alook alike a poss of porterpease?" (21.18-19) concerns Bruno's concept of individual duality—the twins are as alike as two peas in a pod, yet they are distinct individuals mutually antagonistic to each other in all ways. That Earwicker in his dream hears the riddle as a call for "two pots of porter, please" (or "Piesporter") prevents the riddle from ever being answered.*

The bar call, in fact, becomes more distinct in later repetitions of the riddle, further obfuscating the problem of solving the riddle of identical features and dual minds. In the Lessons scene, where the riddle concerning the children logically should be most clearly stated, it is even closer to the call for drinks, as Earwicker in his dream moves even further away from solving the problem of his antagonistic sons—those facets of his own divided self. We hear calls for a "pint of porter place" (260.6) and a "glass of peel and pip for Mr Potter of Texas, please" (274.n3). As Earwicker's subconscious is obviously involved with his children in this part of the dream, too clear a statement of the riddle would necessitate a real grappling with this basic problem; his unconscious therefore pushes the riddle away from the problem to avoid any such coming-to-grips with it, and reiterates the calls for porter to relieve him of the responsibility.

A beginning of the solution of the problem is present in the version of the riddle asked Yawn by his interrogators: "For why do you lack a link of luck to poise a pont of perfect, peace?" (493.29-30). He is being told that his chance for perfect peace lies in his link with his opposite twin, that only through a synthesis of the antagonistic elements can a whole person emerge. Anna Livia in her soliloquy takes up the problem of her children, and also suggests a solution: they will have to swallow their pride and unite; they can no more stand on ceremony than could Mohammed when the mountain would not come to him: "If the Ming Tung no go bo to me homage me hamage kow bow tow to the Mong Tang. Ceremonialness to stand lowest place be! Saying: What'll you take to link to light a pike on porpoise, plaise?" (623.11-15). Anna Liffey as a river rephrases the riddle in terms of the fish living harmoniously in her charge; the Chinese dialect of the Mohammed parable indicates that the sort of humility preached by Confucius,

* See Appendix.

his doctrine of the "mean," and the principles of Yin and Yang are basic in reconciling the brothers despite their pride.

The Prankquean's riddle is an objective question regarding the brother relationship; the two riddles posed by Shem are subjective ones that reflect Joyce's thinking as a nonconforming artist. Shem's first question is asked early in life to his playmates—"when is a man not a man?" (170.5)—and he answers it himself, identifying himself with the man "that is not a man": "when he is a—yours till the rending of the rocks,—Sham" (170.23-24). The riddle is to Joyce's mind the logical sequel of the Oedipus sphinx riddle; accepting the Pythagorean concept of man as the measure of all things, Joyce becomes involved with the nature of man in *Finnegans Wake*. He is concerned with man as an artist divorcing himself from his class, country, and religion, refusing to serve. As such Shem sees himself as only a shadow of a man; and Shem is the sophisticated "hybrid" (169.9), while Shaun is the "natural" man who complies with nature and its institutions, a proper citizen.

We learn that Shem's

lowness creeped out first via foodstuffs. So low was he that he preferred Gibsen's teatime salmon tinned, as inexpensive as pleasing, to the plumpest roeheavy lax or the friskiest parr or smolt troutlet that ever was gaffed between Leixlip and Island Bridge and many was the time he repeated in his botulism that no junglegrown pineapple ever smacked like the whoppers you shook out of Ananias' cans [170.25-31].

Thus Shem is contrasted with the gorging, gluttonous Shaun; the "salmon" preference is important because it refers to the wisdom acquired by Finn MacCool when he ate of the legendary salmon. Shem is again the city dweller, the sophisticate educated with canned foods; he is a sham because he will not serve in the manly occupations of war and national allegiance. But the reverse implication in Shem's admission is that he is very much a man because of his sexual awareness—the "rending of rocks" equals procreation in the *Wake:* "nor had topsawyer's rocks by the stream Oconee exaggerated themselse to Laurens County's gorgios while they went doublin their mumper all the time" (3.6-9) also refers to Earwicker's begetting sons who will upend him, and hints at Joyce's own manhood in producing a son (Giorgio). Shem as an artist claims a sexual precocity, an earlier awareness of sex than is exhibited by his denser, morally inhibited brother; he claims his manhood early in life, announces as a child that he is certainly a *sham,* but only until puberty, only *till the rending of the rocks.*

The "when is a man not a man" riddle recurs several times during the book: this "first riddle of the universe" (170.4) is parodied later in the Mime chapter as "where was a hovel not a havel (the first rattle of his juniverse)" (231.1-2), mirroring Joyce's concern with the sanctity of the Catholic home; it follows his description of the progressively falling state of the Joyce household (as depicted by the decline of the Dedalus family in *A Portrait*). The home from which Joyce and Stephen escaped had ceased to be a haven and become a hovel, and Joyce sought to establish a real home of his own and raise his own family. The answer to the child's riddle about his household is, therefore, "while itch ish shome" (231.3-4). Unanswered, the question is again heard as a statement in "Here is a homelet not a hothel" (586.18), where home, hamlet, and Prince Hamlet are juxtaposed against hotel, house of God (Beth El), brothel, and hot Hell.

Conjunctively, Earwicker's defense of the Russian General deals with the problem of original sin, and Earwicker echoes Shem's riddle: "the farst wriggle from the ubivence, whereom is man, that old offender, nother man" (356.12-13). Having committed the initial sin, man has cut his umbilical cord, has wriggled out of the cocoon of Paradise, and must now fend for himself, must accept the reality of his own existence and his sin; he is a different man "wheile he is asame" (356.13-14). The female counterpart of the question is asked during Yawn's inquisition: "when is a maid nought a maid" (495.6)—when does a woman *really* lose her innocence? When a man "would go to anyposs length for her!" (495.6-7) comes the answer. The seduction motif comes full circle

and returns to man's seduction of the innocent woman, a reversal
of the Garden of Eden concept of woman's temptation of man.*
But this apparent contradiction is also accepted as part of the over-
all synthesis of opposites. Numerous instances of sex reversals
occur throughout *Finnegans Wake,* so that we never really learn
who is the tempter and who is the tempted, nor who is the male
and who is the female. Besides, the *he* who would *go to anyposs
length for her* can easily be interpreted as the serpent in the garden
—another Freudian symbol for masculine sexuality; the threefold
temptation therefore must be seen as Satan tempting Eve, Eve ca-
joling Adam, Adam seducing Eve.

The final repetition of the riddle occurs during the professor's
last glimpse at the scene before Anna Livia flows out to sea. Having reviewed Earwicker's indiscretion, he asks "The first and last
rittlerattle of the anniverse; when is a nam nought a nam"
(607.10-12). *Nam* as "man" backwards implies a synthesis of the
opposites: Man still is Man whether approached from his Shem
side or from his Shaun side. The answer this time is left hanging:
"whenas it is a. Watch! (607.12). *Watch* implies a vigil, the
watching during the wake: "It is their segnall for old Champel-
ysied to seek the shades of his retirement and for young Chappie-
lassies to tear a round and tease their partners lovesoftfun at Finnegan's Wake" (607.14-16). Earwicker, the champion of Chapelizod, is dead and in the Elysian fields; he has not yet been resurrected. The lassies of the town (Iseult in particular) have not
yet tempted their man. A man is therefore not a man in the state
between life and resurrection, between being born and being
tempted by woman into a sexual existence; again, he is not a man
while he is still a sexless sham. Joyce may well ask, "When is a
Pun not a Pun?" (307.2-3).

A second Shem-like riddle which offers a clue to Joyce's life and
attitude during the last twenty years of his exile's existence in Paris

* The problem is further compounded if we accept *anyposs length* as Oedipus
Rex, and the implication becomes irrefutable once it is noted that Joyce thus
doubly signs his allusion, with credits to both Sophocles and Sigmund Freud.

is "Was liffe worth leaving?" (230.25). This of course is a dual question: was life worth leaving? and was Dublin (the Liffey) worth leaving? It is also, of course, was life worth living? Since the answer is "Nej!" (230.25)—an apparent negative—we can infer from the question that Joyce regretted his exile from Ireland and the course of his life as well. What one must bear in mind is that it is Shem who is asking and answering the question; it was he who had previously asked: "What bitter's love but yurning, what' sour lovemutch but a bref burning till shee that drawes dothe smoake retourne?" (143.29-30). The later question, therefore, is the melancholy despair of the rejected lover (Shem having been abandoned for Shaun), as well as the despondent artist who has vowed to write the "jeeremyhead sindbook for all the peoples" (229.32), in which he intends to reveal the sins of his parents. Elsewhere the question reads "was Parish worth thette mess" (199.8-9)—Earwicker wondering about the outcome of his escapade (which, like Paris' seduction of "that miss," Helen, caused quite a stir),* and Joyce perhaps wondering about the years spent in Paris writing the *Wake*. In the Night Lessons, Issy's footnote asks: "Is love worse living?" (269.n1), a further indication of the dual nature of love. And, since the question reverts back to the theme of woman's temptation of man, an early reference to "that's what makes lifework leaving" (12.1-2) may provide a fuller understanding of the riddle:

> How bootifull and how truetowife of her, when strengly forebidden, to steal our historic presents from the past postpropheticals so as to will make us all lordy heirs and ladymaidesses of a pretty nice kettle of fruit. She is livving in our midst of debt and laffing through all plores for us (her birth is uncontrollable), with a naperon for her mask and her sabboes kickin arias (so sair! so solly!) if yous ask me and I saack you. Hou! Hou! Gricks may rise and Troysirs fall (there being two sights for ever a picture) for in the byways of high improvidence that's what makes lifework leaving and the world's a cell for citters to cit in. Let young wimman run away with the story and let

---

* Echoing Henry of Navarre's *"Paris vaut bien une messe."* Note that the king's answer is affirmative.

young min talk smooth behind the butteler's back. She knows her knight's duty while Luntum sleeps [11.29-12.5].

The riddle therefore can be seen to concern the question of whether the original sin was worth committing. Joyce incorporates St. Augustine's concept that the fortunate fall gave man a greater chance to achieve grace: he adds that the fruit of that sin (the birth of children and the growth of the race) justifies the woman's initiative in commencing the cycle of life. He justifies his concentration on the eternal woman as the focal point of his work, justifies Molly Bloom's all-embracing life lust in the face of Poldy's sexual ineffectiveness. While Bloom talks, Molly acts; while Bloom feels pangs of conscience over his clandestine letter-writing affair and *voyeur* glimpses at the seashore, Molly blithely hints at several dozen affairs. Hers is the avowal of the life principle that carries over into *Finnegans Wake:* while Earwicker torments himself over an insignificant indiscretion in the park (reduced to absurdity when seen "in actuality" as his relations with his wife), Anna Livia glories in the magnificence of her seduction:

> One time you'd stand fornenst me, fairly laughing, in your bark and tan billows of branches for to fan me coolly. And I'd lie as quiet as a moss. And one time you'd rush upon me, darkly roaring, like a great black shadow with a sheeny stare to perce me rawly. . . . And you were the pantymammy's Vulking Corsergoth. The invision of Indelond. And, by Thorror, you looked it! My lips went livid for from the joy of fear. Like almost now. How? How you said how you'd give me the keys of me heart. And we'd be married till delth to uspart. And though dev do espart [626.21-32].

So that whereas Earwicker envisions his sexual experience as a dreadful, sordid sin, Anna Livia sees hers as an epic seduction, as Leda seduced by the Zeus-swan. The numerous lovers of Molly Bloom's promiscuous life have been fused into a single Everyman figure; it is the woman, therefore, who is capable of singing the paean to life, as Anna Livia Plurabelle does.

Its all-inclusive attempt to present the scope and dimensions of human life establishes the *Wake* as a conscious effort to create an epic of the thought of twentieth-century humanity. Joyce transcends the boundaries of western culture to include aspects of other cultural patterns which have begun to become infused into the stream of contemporary thought during the past centuries; at once psychological and sociological, it is an epic of an era that has had its thinking shaped by Marx and Darwin, Freud and Frazer, Planck and Einstein. Joyce not only availed himself of the advances in various technological areas already made during his lifetime, but was equally capable of incorporating such prophetic experiments as the world-wide use of television (in public houses at that!) and the splitting of the atom, both of which figure prominently in the *Wake*. At many instances Earwicker's dream is visualized in his sleeping mind on a television screen: "Television kills telephony in brothers' broil. Our eyes demand their turn. Let them be seen!" (52.18-19). Elsewhere the marriage of the Norwegian Captain is seen in a cinematic newsreel: "With her banbax hoist from holder, zig for zag through pool and polder, cheap, cheap, cheap and Laughing Jack, all augurs scorenning, see the Bolche your pictures motion and Kitzy Kleinsuessmein eloping for that holm in Finn's Hotel Fiord, Nova Norening" (330.21-25). Conscious of the technological contrivances of the age, *Finnegans Wake* is at once a "fadograph of a yestern scene" (7.15), a "tolvtubular high fidelity daildialler, as modern as tomorrow afternoon and in appearance up to the minute . . . equipped with supershielded umbrella antennas for distance" (309.14-18), and a "nonday diary, this allnights newseryreel" (489.35).

The splitting of the atom is a vital point in *Finnegans Wake;* it occurs during the shooting of the Russian General (reported on the "up to the minute" radio presented to Earwicker by the customers at the tavern) and is an aspect of the destruction of the father by the son, the mysterious Buckley. Actually Joyce is not only anticipating the world-shaking explosion that shook Hiroshima six years after the publication of *Finnegans Wake,* but is explaining that even this modern phenomenon has occurred before:

The abnihilisation of the etym by the grisning of the grosning of the

grinder of the grunder of the first lord of Hurtreford expolodoto-
nates through Parsuralia with an ivanmorinthorrorumble fragorom-
boassity amidwhiches general uttermosts confussion are perceivable
moletons skaping with mulicules while coventry plumpkins fairlygo-
smotherthemselves in the Landaunelegants of Pinkadindy. Similar
scenatas are projectilised from Hullulullu, Bawlawayo, empyreal
Raum and mordern Atems [353.22-29].

This new explosion-detonation was heard in Eden when Adam
fell, and by the giants in God's thunderclap; it is all within the Viconian concept (*by the grisning of the grosning of the grinder of*
the grunder), the four stages of the cycle punctuated by the thunderclaps. This new thunder which "would split an atam"
(333.25) is expected to cap the realm of contemporary chaos.
Since Adam was first split into his many descendants, every new
annihilation of the atom is a repetition of the cycle of life. *Finne-*
gans Wake thus endeavors to summarize the redundant elements
of contemporary life, to boil down all the aspects of our civilization and its complex roots into a single environment that can be
analyzed: pagan Borneo, Imperial Rome, and modern Athens are
all present in the Dublin which is Joyce's world focus.

Like all expansive works that may vie for the title of epic, *Fin-*
negans Wake strives for scope and universality and attempts to
portray its own times in terms of timelessness. Joyce selected his
characters in terms of history, myth, and legend, and individualized
them in the light of the many prototypes available to him in world
literature. There is astonishingly little in the *Wake,* despite its
heavy reliance upon coincidence, that is accidental. With micro-
scopic accuracy Joyce hunted the "coincidental" element down to
its most basic root in repetitive, spiraling, evolving history, and relied upon his intimate knowledge of the Irish milieu (and particularly Dublin) for his "manufactured" coincidences.

The Phoenix Park setting for the Earwicker misdemeanor is a
case in point: whereas St. Stephen's Green exists in Dublin for Stephen Dedalus's convenient walks in *A Portrait,* the coincidence lies
in Joyce's choice in naming his hero; conversely, Phoenix Park exists, and is so called because of historic accident. Joyce need only

utilize the place for his purposes once he realized the significance of the resurrection motif in his epic fabric. In a letter to Harriet Shaw Weaver, dated 14 August 1927, Joyce comments: "As to 'Phoenix'. A viceroy who knew no Irish thought this was the word the Dublin people used and put up the mount of a phoenix in the park. The Irish was *fiunishgue*=clear water from a well of bright water there."[5] In the Fenian Cycle we learn that Finn (whose original name was Demne) received his name once he had eaten of the salmon of wisdom from the river, and was therefore termed "fair" or "white." The various linguistic accidents involved precede Joyce's tampering with language for his own purposes in the *Wake;* Joyce utilized the Anglo-Gaelic Fionn-Uisge-Phoenix pun as readily as he used Christ's pun—"thuartpeatrick" (3.10)—as it naturally fit his framework. Fionn is the legendary MacCool; Uisge is the river, Anna Livia (as well as the source for the English word, whiskey); together they are the rebirth motif of the Phoenix.

Perhaps, then, there remains only the necessity of defending *Finnegans Wake* from the too-easy assertion that it is mock-epic after all. It is as ill-fitting a term for the *Wake* as it is for *Don Quixote* or *Huckleberry Finn,* since all three achieve epic stature and grandeur by their scope, fullness of development, and all-inclusiveness in design. What Pope was able to do in *The Rape of the Lock* was *reduce* epic pretensions in his society to their basic absurdity; what Joyce sought to achieve was an augmented view of the basic elements in his material. He developed his figures as archetypes, as characters, and, on occasions when necessary to his design, as stereotypes. Each of the primary participants of the *Wake* is realized on all three levels, each exists allegorically, realistically, in exacting literalness, and in sketchy caricature. Every device chosen by Joyce earmarks the careful selection practiced by the artist to accumulate a totality of experience in an all-inclusive plan. The choice of the dream setting (perhaps a newly discovered source of psychological information for Freud and followers, but certainly an ageless source for poets and prophets for many civilizations) achieves for Joyce what it achieved for the creators of the *Divina Commedia,* the *Romance of the Rose, Pilgrim's Progress,* and *Piers Plowman:* a frame through which both the literal and the symbolic can harmoniously exist. The much-discussed question of "Who Is the Dreamer in *Finnegans Wake?*" seems easily answerable in the light of the epic material in the work. On the symbolic level it is of course Everyman dreaming the history of his existence; on the literal level it is Earwicker (*our* microcosmic Everyman) recounting in disguised form his misadventure in Phoenix Park; and on the creative level it is Joyce himself giving form to what he has experienced and learned and understood (in the same way in which the Demiurge, creating the universe, dreams away its cycles of evolution).

Having carried the modern novel to an ultimate point in *Ulysses* with a fusion of naturalistic and symbolic elements, Joyce goes even a step further in the *Wake* by creating a novel that defies definition as a novel while yet containing the basic story line. Having critically and judiciously consumed the existing literary epics available to our civilization, Joyce sets out to duplicate their most significant elements for his own age. Like the *Iliad,* the *Odyssey,* and the *Aeneid, Finnegans Wake* presents the most fabulous aspect of its age, while managing to reproduce its most natural aspects; like the *Divina Commedia* and *Paradise Lost,* it represents the morality of its age without moralizing; and like *Beowulf* and the *Chanson de Roland,* it holds a mirror to its times and shows the dual image of the age as it sees itself, as well as where the self-deception lies. In choosing his cumulative title for his many-sided work, Joyce arrived at *Finnegans Wake* because it signified the many levels of his epic: allegorically it was the awakening of the legendary giant, Finn MacCool; literally it was the wake for the hod carrier Tim Finnegan; and prophetically it was the arising of the "Finnegans" of the world. Within the confines of the *Wake* exists many an alternate title concomitant with its epic theme and treatment. Once such would be: "the humphriad of that fall and rise" (53.9).

CHAPTER FIVE

Not with a YES, *but a* THE

The creation of a prose comic epic of contemporary society necessitated for Joyce a consistent attitude toward the humanity which he sought to analyze in that epic. Whether we accept the David Daiches view that *Ulysses* is the product of a cynical mind or whether we find, as William York Tindall does, that the basis of a balanced view of mankind is already present in the earlier work, it is nonetheless important to determine Joyce's attitude toward humanity from the difficult accumulation of material that resulted in *Finnegans Wake*. At forty Joyce had completed *Ulysses* and embarked upon the new work; as Daiches views it, "Joyce's exile has been final: to the end he has denied any stake in the rejected world,"[1] yet Tindall insists that "*Ulysses* and *Finnegans Wake* have a social function; for modern man needs to be assured of his humanity."[2] Daiches has traced the development of Joyce's maturity, emphasizing the participation in world events that characterizes Stephen's position in *A Portrait* and remains only a secondary theme in *Ulysses;* the refusal to participate in the rejected world is therefore to be seen in the loss of Stephen in the *Wake*. Here the Daiches position seriously breaks down, for an investigation of the autobiographic elements of the *Wake* discloses that Joyce never more completely maintained his relationship with humanity than in the last novel.

The character of Shem the Penman has already been discussed: he is at once Joyce's self-portrait and self-caricature, a continuation of the Dedalus figure and a burlesque of him, the artist as seen by the author and as viewed by the world at large. We meet him at various times during the *Wake:* as the sensitive infant, Jerry; as the maligned child in the Mime, Glugg; as the clever student, Dolph; and finally as the penman, Shem. He is contrasted with his successful brother, Shaun, the bourgeois who taunts him and is jealous of him. As such, Shaun in many ways is Joyce's brother Stanislaus, and only recent documentation begins to fill in the lacunae of the relationship of James and Stanislaus Joyce.

The portraits* of James Joyce by his brother have raised many controversies since they began to appear in 1950. The close-knit web of silence concerning many of Joyce's personal activities which had been woven by the faithful (Gorman, Jolas, Budgen, *et al.*) seems to have been broken by the frank Stanislaus who saw Joyce as quite different from the sober man who occasionally drank a bottle of white wine in the evening. What is most important, the memoir-recollections frankly discussed the rift between Joyce and his brother, and several annotators have gone back to *Finnegans Wake* to find the very real conflict between the two brothers.

Richard Ellmann comments that

> James was extravagant in fancy and in finance, and the proceeds of Stanislaus's lessons often ended—after James, smiling and smoking a cigarette, had presented his latest need—in his brother's pocket. When James revamped in *Finnegans Wake* the fable of the dancing grasshopper and saving ant, he drew upon his experience with Stanislaus by letting the grasshopper carry the day.[3]

Joyce's Gracehoper in fact has "jingled through a jungle of love and debts" (416.8-9), while the Ondt is presented as a "weltall fellow, raumybult and ableboobied" who "bynear saw altitudinous wee a schelling in kopfers" (416.3-4). Nor can anyone who has read Stanislaus' admonitions to his brother concerning liquor and immorality, or his impatience with the difficulties of *Ulysses* and *Finnegans Wake,* fail to hear Stanislaus' voice issuing from the Ondt: "Grouscious me and scarab my sahul! What a bagateller it is! Libelulous! Inzanzarity! Pou! Pschla! Ptuh! What a zeit for the goths! vented the Ondt" (415.25-27), or hear him criticize Joyce's

---

* "James Joyce: A Memoir," also entitled *Recollections of James Joyce by His Brother,* trans. Ellsworth Mason (New York: James Joyce Society, 1950); *My Brother's Keeper* (1958); *The Dublin Diaries of Stanislaus Joyce,* ed. George Harris Healey (Ithaca, N.Y.: Cornell University Press, 1962).

Paris coterie: "Let him be Artalone the Weeps with his parisites peeling off him I'll be Highfee the Crackasider. Flunkey Footle furloughed foul, writing off his phoney" (418.1-3). But the Gracehoper forgives the Ondt's malice—Joyce sent Stanislaus a copy of *Finnegans Wake,* which was refused—and calling upon St. Martin, the patron of drunkards and reformed drunks, he laments the nonartistic nature of his brother: *"But, Holy Saltmartin, why can't you beat time?"* (419.8)

Ellmann goes on to note that

> Stanislaus could hardly have approved . . . of the brother theme in that book. Shem, who resembles James, is a penman, while his brother Shaun, modeled to some extent upon Stanislaus, is a postman; Shem is a tree and Shaun a stone. James of course had more in mind than his own fraternal relations, but these played their part too.[4]

It is significant that many other individuals serve as a model for Shaun: the Malachi Mulligan of *Ulysses* (Oliver St. John Gogarty) is once again the butt of Joyce's malice, the medical student taking his "varsatile examinations in the ologies" (468.2); and Eamon de Valera, the successful Irish politician who was born the same year as Joyce—*"It is Da Valorem's Dominical Brayers"* (342.11).* These two prototypes for Shaun are combined in the disintegration of Haun: "ere Molochy wars bring the devil era" (473.7-8), to add a third level of meaning to the phrase. Thus, rather than limit himself to a single antagonist for his hero, Joyce can use his nebulous, always-changing Shaun as a composite portrait of many antagonists, not least of whom is his brother, Stanislaus. In the footnotes written by Issy to the Lessons chapter one finds: "The stanidsglass effect, you could sugerly swear buttermilt would not melt down his dripping ducks" (277.n5). The contention that this is a nasty comment on the apparent innocence of the bourgeois brother is further strengthened by Stanislaus' own moral judgments of his brother in the three memoirs.

---

* Ruth von Phul states the case for J. F. Byrne, the Cranly of *A Portrait* ("Shaun in Brooklyn," *Analyst,* No. 16 [February, 1959], pp. 1-22).

During the Mime of Mick, Nick and the Maggies, the Rainbow Girls celebrate their sun god, the hero Shaun, with words of worship:

—Enchainted, dear sweet Stainusless, young confessor, dearer dearest, we herehear, aboutobloss, O coelicola, thee salutamt. Pattern of our unschoold, pageantmaster, deliverer of softmissives, round the world in forty mails, bag, belt and balmybeam, our barnaboy, our chepachap, with that pampipe in your putaway, gab borab, when you will be after doing all your sightseeing and soundhearing and smellsniffing and tastytasting and tenderumstouchings in all Daneygaul, send us, your adorables, thou overblaseed, a wise and letters play of all you can ceive, chief celtech chappy, from your holy post now you hast ascertained ceremonially our names. Unclean you art not. Outcaste thou are not. Leperstower, the karman's loki, has not blanched at our pollution and your intercourse at ninety legsplits does not defile. Untouchable is not the scarecrown is on you. You are pure. You are pure. You are in your puerity. You have not brought stinking members into the house of Amanti. Elleb Inam, Titep Notep, we name them to the Hall of Honour. Your head has been touched by the god Enel-Rah and your face has been brightened by the goddess Aruc-Ituc. Return, sainted youngling, and walk once more among us! The rains of Demani are masikal as of yere. And Baraza is all aflower. Siker of calmy days. As shiver as shower can be. Our breed and better class is in brood and bitter pass. Labbeycliath longs. But we're counting on the cluck. The Great Cackler comes again. Sweetstaker, Abel lord of all our haloease [237.11-35].

This is Joyce's most succinct statement about his brother, one which John Henry Raleigh finds to be "loving irony" of "the guilty forgiving the innocent."[5] And although Ellsworth Mason takes issue with Raleigh's black-and-white portrayal of the Joyce brothers, he nonetheless admits:

. . . [that] Joyce is using material from Stanislaus' life in this passage is undeniable. In addition to the pun on his name, we have "Elleb Inam, Titep Notep," which, spelled backwards as "Belle mani, petit peton," reflects the vanity about his hands and feet that Stanislaus actually had as a boy. The point is that Joyce is making dramatic use of his material, as always.[6]

Mason is accurate in realizing the numerous *double-entendres* in the flowergirls' paean to their sun god as they contribute to presenting Chuff's purity as a disguise for his sexual manifestations as a fertility god, but is rather hasty in dismissing Stanislaus from the position of prototype for the character. The biographical elements from Stanislaus' life are neither accidents nor whims;* Joyce is attempting once again to deal personally as well as objectively with the real problem is his own life. His relations with Stanislaus are important to him, and he deals with the brother conflict from apparent personal experience, working toward a synthesis which Stanislaus did not seem to welcome. Joyce continually allows Shem to swallow his pride and apologize to Shaun: "I can't say if it's the weight you strike me to the quick or that red mass I was looking at but at the present momentum, potential as I am, I'm seeing raying-bogeys rings round me. Honours to you and may you be commended for our exhibitiveness!" (304.5-11). The Gracehoper says:

> *I forgive you, grondt Ondt, said the Gracehoper, weeping,*
> *For their sukes of the sakes you are safe in whose keeping*
> [418.12-13],

as Joyce apparently intended to forgive Stanislaus for the years in which the younger brother remained estranged from the artist. Stanislaus notes: "Joyce then went to Paris, after which I saw him but rarely. I wrangled with him over *Finnegans Wake*, by correspondence and at different encounters in Paris, Salzburg, or Zurich."[7] Whether or not James Joyce had anything for which to forgive his brother, the symbol of his forgiveness has become apparent, and Stanislaus behaved as Shaun had done—he refused to forgive: "No, blank ye! So you think I have impulsivism?" (149.11) is the Shaun-Jones answer when he is asked if he would help Shem save his own soul. Stanislaus adds: "When *Finnegans Wake* was pub-

---

* Although Stephen Dedalus has the numerous siblings that Joyce himself had, his "predecessor," the Stephen Daedalus of *Stephen Hero*, had only a brother (Maurice) and a sister (Isabel). The Stephen-Maurice-Isabel trio are duplicated in the *Wake* by Jerry-Kevin-Isabel, as Joyce's work makes still another circle.

lished, on the author's fifty-eighth birthday [*sic*], my brother
wrote to me offering a copy in homage. I refused it." He adds:
"There is little need to tell how much regret this refusal has since
cost me—even less need when the uselessness of regret is
considered."[8] Perhaps this regret begins to suggest a reconciliatory
attitude on the personal level which Joyce had already anticipated
in the synthesis of Shem and Shaun in *Finnegans Wake*. Raleigh
comments:

> Certainly it would seem that each brother was in the nature of being a
> cross for the other to bear. Stanislaus was not being "holier than
> thou" when he dragged his reluctant brother from Italian barrooms
> and back to his wife and children, always, in the early days, on the
> verge of starvation. On the other hand, his attempt to dictate his
> brother's esthetic would seem to be presumptuous, and certainly, in
> purely psychological terms, a super-virtuous brother is a difficult thing
> to cope with. But wherever the burdens of guilt may fall, the moral
> would seem to be this: that it is infinitely easier for the guilty to for-
> give the innocent for the presumption of proffered guidance than it is
> for the innocent to forgive the guilty for not taking that guidance.[9]

Whether or not Stanislaus Joyce ever read a copy of the book he
had refused to accept, his memoir certainly anticipates the theme of
the antagonistic brothers in his brother's terms: he notes that in
writing about James he runs the risk of "playing the part of Cain
if I criticize and call a spade a spade."[10]

It is the character of Shem, however, which most concerns us
when investigating Joyce's actual participation in the portrait of
the world he saw around him. He viewed that world as torn between the antithetical aspects of the nature of contemporary man:
his proper, moralistic brother and his amoral, if not immoral, artistic self. He attempts to move away from the introspective hero
who began to wane in significance in *Ulysses* in order to concentrate on the nature of man around him, on the world in which he
played an atypical but important part as the nonconformist artist.
Joyce seeks to see beyond himself in portraying Shem, however;
his Stephen was only a particular type of artist reacting to a particular environment, and no matter how typical that interaction may

have been in his eyes, it had to be expanded to include every facet of the artist in every reaction to the hostile bourgeois world. Joyce is singularly aware that any sort of even division of all attributes to one type of man or the other is decidedly unreal; his purpose is to present these caricatures as two-dimensional facets of the nature of the single hero, of his Earwickerian Everyman who embodies both Shem and Shaun.

Whereas there is no single prototype for H.C.E., Shem and Shaun are based on nineteenth-century theatrical personages. Shaun is Dion Boucicault's Sean the Post; Shem is an equally two-dimensional stage-Irishman: they exist in the *Wake* primarily as they are seen by their society, the bourgeois world accepting its hero as the stage Sean of *Arrah-na-Pogue* and its artistic villain as a harmless Pigott as portrayed in the vulgar nineteenth century by Sir Charles Young's *Jim the Penman*. But behind the cardboard figure lurks the flesh-and-blood artist, the mature James Joyce, conscious of his own excesses as "the artist as a young man," conscious of the world's view of that artist, but peering out at the world with a new artistic objectivity from behind the eye-slits of the painted face of his literary "forger." Joyce is that forger in the dual sense of the word: as Stephen intended, he is here forging "in the smithy of my soul the uncreated conscience of my race" (AP 253). As the bourgeois world views it, Joyce has created a forgery of that world. Harry Levin sees the figure of Joyce playing his part behind Shem's façade:

> From Shem to Seumas to James is an easy modulation for Joyce, and there can be no doubt that the autobiographical interest of the book is centered upon this character, the black sheep of the family. In more than one passage Joyce seems to be announcing—in evasive jargon, to be sure—that he is Shem: "Immi ammi Semmi."[11]

The autobiographic aspects Joyce chooses to include in the *Wake* are important: they reflect the attitude of Joyce as an artist toward mankind and the world's attitude toward that artist; they are selected from the dual position of what Joyce thinks is important about his life and what the world chooses to highlight. From this

point of view, Shem himself is at work on the same project: "what
do you think Vulgariano did but study with stolen fruit how cutely
to copy all their various styles of signature so as one day to utter an
epical forged cheque on the public for his own private profit"
(181.14-17). Here is Shem, like Stephen, seeking the "signatures
of all things" (U 33) in order to write his epic, while the world
distrusts his methods and motives—they see him creating a forgery
while he sees himself forging with the hammer and anvil of his
artistry.

The chapter devoted exclusively to Shem the Penman is a mine
of information about Joyce himself. Even the initial caricature of
the grotesque Shem bears resemblances to Joyce: "fortytwo hairs
off his uncrown, eighteen to his mock lip, a trio of barbels from his
megageg chin (sowman's son) . . . all ears, an artificial tongue
with a natural curl" (169.13-16) suggest Joyce's thinning hairline,
sparse mustache, and slight chinbeard, his ear for language and the
style of his literary expression. A listing of his strange tastes in
food and drink is followed by his exile creed to become a "far-
soonerite" (171.4) and records his flight from Ireland and later
from war-affected Trieste (172). He becomes an exile and sends
for his brother to join him:

> He would not put fire to his cerebrum; he would not throw himself in
> Liffey; he would not explaud himself with pneumantics; he refused to
> saffrocake himself with a sod. With the foreign devil's leave the fraid
> born fraud diddled even death. *Anzi,* cabled (but shaking the worth
> out of his maulth: Guardacosta leporello? Szasas Kraicz!) from his
> Nearapoblican asylum to his jonathan for a brother [172.18-24].

Joyce then goes on to spoof (and explain) his literary methods
in an explanation of Shem's "unconsciously explaining, for ink-
stands, with a meticulosity bordering on the insane, the various
meanings of all the different foreign parts of speech he misused"
(173.33-36). Much is then made of Shem's cowardice as he parallels Joyce in avoiding both the Irish Insurrection and the First
World War, as he refuses to participate in the battles either in the
nation from which he had exiled himself or in the nation in which

he had sought refuge. The world thus views this double flight as cowardice, and Joyce interweaves the two struggles into a single combat:

> Now it is notoriously known how on that surprisingly bludgeony Unity Sunday when the grand germogall allstar bout was harrily the rage between our weltingtoms extraordinary and our pettythicks the marshalaisy and Irish eyes of welcome were smiling daggers down their backs, when the roth, vice and blause met the noyr blank and rogues and the grim white and cold bet the black fighting tans, categorically unimperatived by the maxims, a rank funk getting the better of him, the scut in a bad fit of pyjamas fled like a leveret for his bare lives [176.19-27].

Here a single word like *weltingtoms* unites the two wars: Wellington, the Dublin-born British leader, the British tommies, and "welt" as bruise and as the German word for world. The flags of the various combatants are the red, white, and blue of both France and England against the black, white, and red of Imperial Germany, while the Irish green, white, and gold fought against the British Black 'n' Tans. But here Joyce is punning his own wars into the European conflicts, for soon after he was fighting his own literary struggle against the bowdlerizing of his *Ulysses* by Samuel Roth, and the crusade in America by vice leagues against the book: thus, the *roth, vice and blause* of the American flag as well.

The campaign of slander against Joyce during the years in which he was trying to get *Dubliners* published, the hints of his cultivated depravities, the broadsides and letters he wrote, and the difficulties *Ulysses* experienced are all part of Shem's experiences as well:

> The answer, to do all the diddies in one dedal, would sound . . . he had flickered up and flinnered down into a drug and drunkery addict, growing megalomane of a loose past. This explains the litany of septuncial lettertrumpets honorific, highpitched, erudite, neoclassical, which he so loved as patricianly to manuscribe after his name. It would have diverted, if ever seen, the shuddersome spectacle of this semidemented zany amid the inspissated grime of his glaucous den making believe to read his usylessly unreadable Blue Book of Eccles, *édition de ténèbres,* (even yet sighs the Most Different, Dr Poinde-

jenk, authorised bowdler and censor, it can't be repeated!) turning
over three sheets at a wind, telling himself delightedly, no espellor
mor so, that every splurge on the vellum he blundered over was an
aisling vision more gorgeous than the one before [179.17-32].

Here again Joyce is capable of repeating the slanders against himself with tongue-in-cheek relish while castigating the slanderers,
censors, and literary pirates who maligned him. He ducks behind
Shem's comic mask and lets the pies be thrown into his face while
he reveals the Pagliacci tears hidden by the mask.

Such incidents as Joyce's participation in the Feis Ceoil singing
contest are slipped into the chapter on Shem: "he squealed the
topsquall . . . for fully five minutes, infinitely better than Baraton
McGluckin with a scrumptious cocked hat and three green, cheese
and tangerine trinity plumes on the right handle side of his amarellous head" (180.5-10). And the fanciful description of Shem as
an operatic tenor dissolves into a portrait of the pathetic clown
(somehow resembling a book, probably the first Paris edition of
Ulysses)—"but what with the murky light, the botchy print, the
tattered cover, the jigjagged page, the fumbling fingers, the fox-
trotting fleas, the lieabed lice" etc. (180.17-19).

Other Joyce works are mentioned in the chapter: his early book
of poems, "this chambermade music" (184.4), and his early
broadside, "a certain holy office" (190.14). His bad eyes ("The
simian has no sentiment secretions but weep cataracts for all me,
Pain the Shamman"—192.22-23), his famous black eyepatch ("a
blind of black sailcloth over its wan phwinshogue"—182.33-34),
and his fine tenor voice ("a plaintiff's tanner vuice"—182.22-23)
add to the portrait of James Joyce. But the highlight of the Shem
chapter is the self-portrait of Joyce as the poet of this doomed
world commenting on the destruction he has viewed in the world
during his lifetime, on the world's tribulations and his own:

Sniffer of carrion, premature gravedigger, seeker of the nest of evil in
the bosom of a good word, you, who sleep at our vigil and fast for
our feast, you with your dislocated reason, have cutely foretold, a
jophet in your own absence, by blind poring upon your many scalds

and burns and blisters, impetiginous sore and pustules, by the auspices of that raven cloud, your shade, and by the auguries of rooks in parlament, death with every disaster, the dynamitisation of colleagues, the reducing of records to ashes, the levelling of all customs by blazes, the return of a lot of sweetempered gunpowdered didst unto dudst but it never stphruck your mudhead's obtundity (O hell, here comes our funeral! O pest, I'll miss the post!) that the more carrots you chop, the more turnips you slit, the more murphies you peel, the more onions you cry over, the more bullbeef you butch, the more mutton you crackerhack, the more potherbs you pound, the fiercer the fire and the longer your spoon and the harder you gruel with more grease to your elbow the merrier fumes your new Irish stew [189.28-190.9].

A second episode bristling with autobiographic elements occurs in the Mime scene. Having failed to guess the three riddles and thus losing the affection of the Rainbow Girls to his "fine frank fairhaired" brother, Glugg denounces the sacraments of the Church (227), swears to pursue a program of exile, silence, and cunning (228), and becomes a writer (229). The book he writes is *Ulysses,* and Joyce lists a punned version of the chapters of his "Blue Book of Eccles": "Ukalepe. Loathers' leave. Had Days. Nemo in Patria. The Luncher Out. Skilly and Carubdish. A Wondering Wreck. From the Mermaids' Tavern. Bullyfamous. Naughtsycalves. Mother of Misery. Walpurgas Nackt" (229.13-16). The fallen state of the Joyce family is once again mentioned: "Ones propsperups treed, now stohong baroque" (230.35-36), and the young Joyce, having penned his erotic little poem to God, muses over the possibility of his failure as a poet: "who thought him a Fonar all, feastking of shellies by googling Lovvey, regally freytherem, eagelly plumed, and wasbut gumboil owrithy prods wretched some horsery megee plods coffin acid odarkery pluds dense floppens mugurdy" (231.11-15). He who would have been a Shelley or a Lovelace may find himself a poor journalistic doggerel writer like such nineteenth-century Irish and Irish-American writers as John Boyle O'Reilly (*gumboil owrithy*) or Thomas D'Arcy McGee (*some horsey megee*) or Kevin Izod O'-Doherty (*coffin acid odarkery*) or Denis Florence MacCarthy (*dense floppens mugurdy*).* He predicts that his literary work will be obscure and difficult to comprehend, but insists upon the inevitability and invincibility of communication among people (232); he will tamper with language—"making a bolderdash for lubberty of speech" (233.17-18)—even to the point of slaughtering language: "as raskly and as baskly as your cheesechalk cow cudd spanich" (233.34-35) is Joyce's version of the French expression: *"Il parle français comme une vache espagnole,"*† but his literary jesting will be in earnest, for he will only be "letting on he'd jest be japers and his tail cooked up" (233.3).

Other details from Joyce's life are strewn through the pages of the *Wake*. His exile is a dominant motif sounded time and again: "our Traveller remote, unfriended, from van Demon's Land" (56.20-21) is both Joyce exiled from Eamon de Valera's Ireland and Earwicker wandering through the underworld. Trieste, "his citadear of refuge . . . beyond the outraved gales of Atreeatic" (62.1-2), is also Priam's citadel of Troy (whose fall is a harbinger of the fall of the house of Atreus), as well as H. C. Earwicker's dear dirty Dublin. Later, during the second trial, Shaun muses over "those yarns yearning for that good one about why he left Dublin" (91.21-22), which he compares to Tir-na-nOg, the Celtic Elysium: "he skuld never ask to see sight or light of this world or the other world or any either world, of Tyre-nan-Og, as true as he was there in that jackabox that minute" (91.24-26). One of the twelve riddles refers to Shem as "a poor acheseyeld from Ailing" (148.33), a reference both to Joyce's exile and his aching eyes.‡

---

* The *Skeleton Key* calls them "Irish-American" (p. 148), but John V. Kelleher considers them Irish ("Notes on *Finnegans Wake* and *Ulysses,*" pp. 8-9). Actually all four were born in Ireland; MacCarthy died there, too, while O'Reilly died in the United States, McGee in Canada, and O'Doherty in Australia.

† Itself a pun on *Basque-vache.*

‡ Various members of the Earwicker family have weak eyes, but Shem in particular wears an eyepatch like Joyce's (although it is sometimes white and sometimes black). The patch does double duty in fact, serving also as a trouser patch (on the seat). References to weak eyes and the patch include:
One eyegonblack (16.29)

When an insignificant event in Joyce's life becomes magnified in importance to him, there is a good chance that it will somehow find its way into *Finnegans Wake*. A pair of trousers seems to have played such a role. While in Rome, Gorman reports, Joyce worked in a bank:

> It was a sedentary occupation; Joyce sat down all day; and it was not long before the rapidly thinning seat of his solitary pair of trousers became one of his major problems in the Holy City. Towards the end of his first month (and it was an extremely hot August) he was gloomily announcing to his brother in Trieste: "There are two great patches on the seat of my trousers so that I cannot leave off my coat in the office and sit stewing for hours."[12]

A second trouser reference in Gorman's biography is to a production in Zurich of *The Importance of Being Earnest,* but Gorman fails to mention that Joyce cabled Lloyd George, Prime Minister of England, about the affair. Harry Levin, however, notes that "when he cabled Lloyd George, who had other things on his mind during the first World War, re a pair of trousers and *The Importance of Being Earnest,* he was behaving like an aggrieved schoolboy unjustly pandied."[13] Perhaps Joyce realized that this was schoolboy behavior, for in the Lessons scene schoolboy Dolph notes in the margin: "*How matches metroosers?*" (280.L). And a reference to

---

the blink pitch (93.4)

his piteous onewinker (174.18-19)

a blind of black sailcloth over its wan phwinshogue (182.33-34)

blackeye lenses (183.17)

glass eyes for an eye (183.36)

Patch Whyte (223.17)

patchy the blank (379.9)

bedroom eyes, of most unhomy blue, (how weak we are, one and all!) (396.11-12)

blind as batflea (417.3)

blueygreen eyes a bit scummy developing a series of angry boils (443.36-444.1)

his blackguarded eye (464.12)

sore eynes (534.26)

fishy eyes (559.23)

I wisht I had better glances to peer to you through (626.34-35).

the earlier patched trouser seat in Rome is found during the Yawn inquest: "Have you forgotten poor Alby Sobrinos, Geoff, you blighter, identifiable by the necessary white patch on his rear?" (488.28-30).

No incident is too small or insignificant to become part of the patchwork of the *Wake;* Joyce himself walks through it in many guises and at various times, linking himself irrevocably with the world he has created in the *Wake,* and exists as a breathing part of that organism. He avenges himself on those he feels had wronged him: Sir Horace Rumbolt, the British Minister in Berne, who had ruled against him in the Zurich trouser affair, is not only the barber-hangman of *Ulysses,* but is an aspect of the evil Ondt in the *Wake*—"The Ondt was a weltall fellow, raumybult and abelboobied" (416.3).

His literary critics receive the same treatment. Rebecca West* is

* It may well appear that Miss West's function in the *Wake* is in excess of her actual significance to Joyce, but the references are numerous. Not only is she paralleled on one side with the Viking wench Ota, but she also has the name of an Ibsen heroine, the Rebecca West of *Rosmersholm,* which might have redeemed her somewhat in Joyce's estimation. Also, forty hats involve her with every other instance in which that magic number occurs in the *Wake;* while articles of clothing are important in the book, hats in particular are vital. In the invoking of Anna Livia at the end of chapter 4, we find her "dragging the countryside in her train, finickin here and funickin there, with her louisequean's brogues and her culunder buzzle and her little bolero boa and all and two times twenty curlicornies for her headdress, specks on her eyeux, and spudds on horeilles and a circusfix riding her Parisienne's cockneze" (102.8-13). The bare bottom (*culunder buzzle*) identifies Ota, the forty Parisian hats (*two times twenty curlicornies for her headdress, Parisienne's*) Miss West, while *headdress* may imply Hedda Gabler, and thus implicate another Ibsen heroine as well. Elsewhere, "a wife with folty barnets" (20.27-28) includes Miss West when *barnets* indicates bonnets rather than children; "Ulo Bubo selling foulty treepes" (243.24) is again the critic since *treepes* suggests toupees; "a jerry-hatted man of forty" (265.n2) masculinizes Miss West and identifies her ironically with author Shem (Jerry); "forty bonnets woman" (283.n1) is rather direct, as is "forty pins in her hood" (333.25). "And what do ye want trippings for when you've Paris inspire your hat?" asks Jaun (453.24-25). It becomes apparent that Joyce took Miss West "robecca or worse" (203.4-5) and married her into his involved framework for the *Wake.* (See Nathan Halper, "James Joyce and Rebecca West," *Partisan Review,* XVI [July, 1949], 761-63.)

celebrated in the *Wake* for having criticized *Ulysses* while hat-shopping in Paris: "and she sass her nach, chillybombom and forty bonnets, upon the altarstane" (552.29-30) presumably refers to a Viking lord's wife who sat naked on the altar of the church that her husband had desecrated in capture. Wyndham Lewis also had criticized *Ulysses* (for its time-consciousness), and Joyce divides his antagonistic brothers into time and space, with Lewis as a pro-totype of space-conscious Shaun. More specifically, Lewis is Shaun's alter ego, the pedantic Welsh professor: the time-space conflict is referred to as the "dime-cash" affair, and Lewis-Jones does not "hasitate to consult with and consequentially attempt at my disposale of the same dime-cash problem elsewhere naturalisti-cally of course, from the blinkpoint of so eminent a spatialist" (149.16-19). Jones goes on to relate the Mookse-Gripes fable—"Eins within a space and a wearywide space it wast" (152.18). Wyndham Lewis' name is often taken in vain in the *Wake:* "Nonsense! There was not very much windy Nous blowing at the given moment through the hat of Mr Melancholy Slow!" (56.28-30). Nor does his *Time and Western Man* fare much bet-ter: "that most improving of roundshows, *Spice and Westend Woman* (utterly exhausted before publication, indiapepper edition shortly) . . . an you could peep inside the cerebralised saucepan of this eer illwinded goodfornobody" (292.5-14).[14]

As Joyce tells us, "he scrabbled and scratched and scriobbled and skrevened nameless shamelessness about everybody ever he met" (182.13-14): the official biographies of himself he refers to as *"the Martyrology of Gorman"* (349.24). His mistress-wife, Nora Barnacle, is the "Highbosomheaving Missmisstress Morna of the allsweetheartening bridemuredemeanour!" (189.25-26), and he "barnacled up to the eyes when he repented after seven" (423.22-23) and married her in 1931. Gorman tells us in the bi-ography of Joyce that "Mrs. McCormick was affronted when Joyce refused to be psychoanalyzed by Dr. Jung,* a refusal, by the way,

---

* In his own guise Joyce commented on the event in a letter to Harriet Weaver in 1921: "A batch of people in Zurich persuaded themselves that I

that he made flatly and angrily."[15] And Joyce in the *Wake* adds his own explanation of this refusal. The following dialogue takes place between the interrogators and the spook voice from the exhausted body of Yawn:

> You have homosexual catheis of empathy between narcissism of the expert and steatopygic invertedness. Get yourself psychoanolised! —O, begor, I want no expert nursis symaphy from yours broons quadroons and I can psoakoonaloose myself any time I want (the fog follow you all!) without your interferences or any other pigeonstealer [522.30-36].

In terms of Joyce's psychology, the initials of the father appearing in *homosexual catheis of empathy* refer to the "Tiberiast duplex" (123.30-31), the deposing of the father by the Christ-Shaun. As Campbell and Robinson explain:

> Tiberius, Roman emperor, A.D. 14-37, at the time of the mission and crucifixion of Christ. As the living representative of the classical pantheon he was, so to speak, already superseded by the Christian theology still in microscopic germinal state. Joyce chooses this moment of history as symbolic of the supplanting of the father by the son. One also feels the play between "Oedipus complex" and "Tiberiast duplex."[16]

Duplex and *narcissism* refer again to the split between the brothers, the ambivalence of love and hate that binds them and eventually synthesizes their differences.

What Joyce refused from Jung personally he accepted from his books: the concept of the collective unconscious permeates *Finnegans Wake,* the history of the race lies dormant in the brain of Everyman-Earwicker and manifests itself in his epic dream. This is the "law of the jungerl" (268.n3), and Joyce, like Jung, is one of

---

was gradually going mad and actually endeavoured to induce me to enter a sanatorium where a certain Doctor Jung (the Swiss Tweedledum who is not to be confused with the Viennese Tweedledee, Dr Freud) amuses himself at the expense (in every sense of the word) of ladies and gentlemen who are troubled with bees in their bonnets" (*Letters,* p. 166). For an interview with Carl Jung on Joyce see Patricia Hutchins' *James Joyce's World* (London: Methuen and Co., 1957), pp. 180-84.

the "grisly old Sykos who have done our unsmiling bit on 'alices, when they were yung and easily freudened" (115.21-23); Joyce, like his schizoid Alice-Iseult heroine, records: "I will write down all your names in my gold pen and ink. Everyday, precious, while m'm'ry's leaves are falling deeply on my Jungfraud's Messongebook I will dream telepath posts dulcets on this isinglass stream (but don't tell him or I'll be the mort of him!)" (460.18-22). Joyce seems to object to the malice of practicing psychoanalysis (*Sykos, on 'alices*) on the individual, as committed by Morton Prince (*mort*) in his *Dissociation of a Personality,* but allows himself to psychoanalyze the entire race through the depiction of the sleeping mind of the individual.

As Earwicker dreams, he dreams the story of the development of mankind, his own life story in microcosm, the life of James Joyce as well. In review pass the scattered tidbits and incidents in Joyce's life, important enough to have marked themselves on his conscious mind (as they presumably have on Earwicker's unconscious); it is a parade of life and letters, of the young man who had expected to study medicine ("Then he went to Cecilia's treat on his solo to pick up Galen"—424.6-7) but decided instead to write ("Inkupot! He has encaust in the blood"—424.7-8). This "freak wanted to put his bilingual head intentionally through the *Ikish Tames*" (424.2-3), but found himself in Trieste where "he was capped out of beurlads scoel for the sin against the past participle" (467.24-25) and settled down to write "a (suppressed) book . . . long and limited" (356.19-21), following it with "the word in pregross" (284.21-22), "a warping process" (497.3). He is the man Jaun introduces to Aunt Julia as Dave (Shem): "Ah, he's very thoughtful and sympatrico that way is Brother Intelligentius, when he's not absintheminded, with his Paris addresse! He is, really. Holdhard till you'll ear him clicking his bull's bones!" (464.15-19). The initials of the father (*ear him clicking*) identify Shem as Earwicker's flesh and blood, and the Joyce who is Shem is also the Joyce who is Earwicker.

The extent of Joyce's identification with his people in the *Wake* is manifold. What Andrew Cass suggests concerning *Ulysses*—that the coincidence of Joyce's age toward the completion of *Ulysses* with that of Bloom's age of thirty-eight is a significant indication that the author identifies himself not only with Stephen but with the middle-aged wanderer[17]—is equally true of *Finnegans Wake:* Joyce sees himself allied with the stammering symbol of Everyman as well as with the articulate artist. The coincidence of age is again present in the *Wake.* One of the earliest references to age is to a "firewaterloover returted with such a vinesmelling fortytudor ages" (93.7-8)—Joyce was forty-two in 1924 when he had just begun work on what was to become *Finnegans Wake.* The final age reference is to "Fiftyseven" (620.4), the age at which Joyce published the completed *Wake* in 1939. It is significant that age references to a man in his forties are to Shem, while those to a man in his fifties are to Earwicker.* Joyce's kinship with his pathetic scribbler, Shem, is obvious, but of greater importance is Joyce's

---

* A comprehensive list of possible age references in the *Wake* should serve to support the contention that a definite logic was intended by Joyce. The list below is in order of appearance in the *Wake:*

50-54: if you can spot fifty I spy four more (10.31)
49-50: most frifty (25.34)
   45: about the middle of his forties (38.36-39.1)
40-44: Arcoforty, farfar (68.19)
   42: fortytudor ages (93.8)
 40's: in her fairly fat forties (99.8-9)
 40's: flatchested fortyish (109.3-4)
   43: furtivefree yours of age (173.7)
   42: fortytooth (177.26)
   44: full and forty Queasisanos (183.1-2)
 50's: fiffty odd Irish miles (208.26)
   40: a jerryhatted man of forty (265.n2)
   41: forfor furst (326.8)
 40's: the rolling forties (326.31)
   50: fiftyodd and fiftyeven years of age (380.14)
   49: maybe at 49 (410.15)
   56: well over or about fiftysix or so (443.22)
   50: a man of around fifty (506.34)
   52: his fiftytwo heirs of age (513.23)
   39: Nine dirty years mine age (535.29-30)
57-60: Fiftyseven and three (620.4-5).

kinship with the nonartist, with the Everyman who is his symbol of mankind, the composite of the bohemian and the burgher, the Earwicker who falls and is resurrected. As Joyce had so often signed Earwicker's name to his indiscretion, he also signs his own in a significant statement of mankind's guilt:

> The boyce voyce is still flautish and his mounth still wears that soldier's scarlet though the flaxafloyeds are peppered with salsedine. It is bycause of what he was ascend into his prisonce on account off. I whit it wel. Hence his deepraised words. Some day I may tell of his second storey. Mood! Mood! It looks like someone other bearing my burdens. I cannot let it. Kanes nought [536.21-27].

The Communicator (the radio announcer is also the seance medium) is Earwicker himself commenting on the sin committed presumably by someone else, but perfectly aware that he has been guilty of the same sin: as such it is Joyce commenting on man's guilt, but aware that he shares that guilt. He too, like Earwicker, is a descendant of Cain (*Kanes nought*).

The most obvious parallel between Joyce and Earwicker occurs during Jaun's harangue to the St. Bride's girls. The moralizer warns the girls against associating with a man who is obviously Earwicker, and describes him as

> a man in brown about town . . . picking up ideas, of well over or about fiftysix or so, pithecoid proportions, with perhops five foot eight, the usual XYZ type, R.C. Toc H, nothing but claret, not in the studbook by a long stortch, with a toothbrush moustache and jawcrockeries, *alias* grinner through collar, and of course no beard, meat and colmans suit, with tar's baggy slacks, obviously too roomy for him and springside boots, washing tie, Father Mathew's bridge pin, sipping some Wheatley's at Rhoss's on a barstool, with some pubpal of the Olaf Stout kidney, always trying to poorchase movables by hebdomedaries for to putt in a new house to loot, cigarette in his holder, with a good job and pension in Buinness's, what about our trip to Normandy style conversation, with an occasional they say that filmacoulored featured at the Mothrapurl skrene about Michan and his lost angeleens is corkyshows do morvaloos, blueygreen eyes a bit scummy developing a series of angry boils with certain references to the Deity, seeking relief in alcohol and so on, general omnibus character with a

dash of railwaybrain, stale cough and an occasional twinge of claudi-
cation, having his favourite fecundclass family of upwards of a decade, both harefoot and loadenbrogued, to boot and buy off, Imean
[443.20-444.5].

What is unusual about this portrait is that, while Shaun-Jaun is describing his own father as the culprit, he is also incriminating himself, since he bears many of his father's traits (*Michan* = Mick);
and Joyce here is describing Earwicker not only in terms of his own
appearance and his own life, but also in terms of his father, John
Stanislaus Joyce, the famous Simon Dedalus.

Not all the references can be ferreted out, but James Joyce is
represented by the propensity for wine exclusively, the age, the
trousers, the mustache, the constant moving about from house to
house during the Paris years, the vast amount of traveling throughout his life, the aching blue eyes, the cigarette holder, the reference
to the cinema which Joyce attempted to open in Dublin, and so
forth. But it is Joyce Senior who is the Roman Catholic (since Earwicker is an Anglican and James Joyce is a lapsed Catholic), who
was a man about town in Dublin, a natty dresser, the drinker of
stout with friends in Dublin pubs, who came from Cork and once
took young James on a trip to his home city (*corkyshows do mor-
valoos, quelquechose de merveilleuse*), and raised a huge family.
Buinness's unites Earwicker with both Joyces since it is the stout
that the pubkeeper sells in his pub, while John Stanislaus Joyce had
been "something in a distillery" (AP 241), and even Joyce himself had been offered a job at Guinness' when he finished at the
University.

Where Stephen so cleverly described Simon Dedalus in the *Portrait,* Shaun succeeds in doing the same for Earwicker here in the
Wake. The important difference is that Joyce has come to identify
himself as his father's son: the young artist who had rebelled
against his father's world now finds that, despite his rebelliousness,
he himself has a stake in that world. That John Joyce is very much
the prototype for Earwicker is indicated by Joyce in several letters.
Just after his father's death Joyce wrote to Miss Weaver (17 Janu-

ary 1932): "My father had an extraordinary affection for me. He was the silliest man I ever knew and yet cruelly shrewd. . . . Hundreds of pages and scores of characters in my books came from him." In a later note to Frank Budgen, dated 9 September 1937, he added: "The encounter between my father and a tramp (the basis of my book) actually took place at that part of the park."[18]

In the closing chapter of the *Wake* Joyce again intrudes to acknowledge his participation in the proceedings of his world; his landscape-describing professor (not to be confused with Shaun's apologist, Professor Jones, but an obvious manifestation of the author himself, first guiding the reader into the realm of dream in chapter 1 and now out again) recapitulates the history of mankind as it is being dreamed in the individual brain. In stating the scope of the dream's realm, the professor constantly asks "Why?" to each event, echoing the inquisitive method associated with Shem, whose solo chapter ended with the constantly reiterated "Quoiquoiquoiquoiquoiquoiquoiq!" (195.6)—a seven-part cyclical question returning into itself in the form of an exclamation. The professor's summation reads:

> You mean to see we have been hadding a sound night's sleep? You may so. It is just, it is just about to, it is just about to rolywholyover. Svapnasvap. Of all the stranger things that ever not even in the hundrund and badst pageans of unthowsent and wonst nice or in eddas and oddes bokes of tomb, dyke and hollow to be have happened! The untireties of lifesliving being the one substance of a streamsbecoming. Totalled in toldteld and teldtold in tittletell tattle. Why? Because, graced be Gad and all giddy gadgets, in whose words were the beginnings, there are two signs to turn to, the yest and the ist, the wright side and the wronged side, feeling aslip and wauking up, so an, so farth. Why? On the sourdsite we have the Moskiosk Djinpalast with its twin adjacencies, the bathouse and the bazaar, allahallahallah, and on the spontesite it is the alcovan and the rosegarden, boony noughty, all purapurthy. Why? One's apurr apuss a story about brid and breakfedes and parricombating and coushcouch but others is of tholes and oubworn buyings, dolings and chafferings in heat, contest and enmity. Why? Every talk has his stay, vidnis Shavarsanjiva-

na, and all-a-dreams perhapsing under lucksloop at last are through. Why? It is a sot of a swigswag, systomy dystomy, which everabody you ever anywhere at all doze. Why? Such me [597.1-22].

In the collective unconscious of each of us are unfolded the twice-told tales of mankind's evolution: they are the thousand-and-one-nights' exotic stories, each of which can be approached from all four sides, from every dimension, from the opposite aspects of right and wrong. But, Joyce explains, there is actually no *wrong* side, only the *right* and the *wronged*. The constant question being asked is, why is every dream an epic of the history of man, why does each one of us contain the mosaic of the entire pattern in the chaotic splinters that form our dreams?

The only answer the professor can offer is the equivocal *Such me* —this at once tells us that there is no answer, but that the answer again lies within each of us. The professor, like the book in which he is contained, shrugs off direct questions, but in his off-handed "Search me" it is indicated that the answers can be found if he is searched for them, echoed from "Sergo, search me" (186.33) to "Search me" (269.23). Essentially, however, it is self-identification, "such am I also," or, as the tailor's version has it, indicating that he too is cut from the same cloth: "Serge Mee, suit!" (322.17). The guilt of H.C.E. (*heat, contest and enmity*) is again shared by every one of us, and the author attaches his own signature to that guilt.

Whether an acceptance of the guilt of mankind is an acceptance of mankind remains a matter of individual interpretation; needless to say, there are basic riddles that remain in the *Wake* as insoluble, paradoxes that are accepted as reality despite their dichotomies. Any attempt to distill the essence of Joyce's "secret," as we have seen in the efforts of those who seek a religious or political pigeon-hole for that secret, risks reducing that essence into nothingness; in *Finnegans Wake* the critic can only hope to determine the directions Joyce's attitudes are indicating. That Earwicker's sins are visited upon his sons, that Shem and Shaun divide them between themselves and accept those which fit their own antagonistic per-

sonalities, that each absolves those sins within the rationale of his
own ideas, and that the opposites synthesize into a complete man
capable of bearing up under the burden of a tide of new events—
all this is a formula that can only be hinted at; only the pieces can
be found to fit together into such a pattern from suggestions in the
Wake. The vast significance of the synthesis motif throughout the
Wake is the strongest proof of such a supposition; it is Joyce's reliance upon the inevitable synthesis of opposites which most clearly
indicates that he is suggesting something more positive that a con-
tinual, single-leveled turning of Vico's cyclical wheel until that
wheel stops of its own inertia. But each clash of the antagonists
seems to result in a greater sharing of each other's qualities; with
each brush against one another more and more rubs off. Unlike the
Kilkenny cats who wear each other out until nothing but their tails
remains, Shem and Shaun become interlocked into a coalesced
unity.

In presenting Joyce's kaleidoscopic view of the melange of material that forms *Finnegans Wake,* riddle 9 notes that

> what is main and why tis twain, how one once meet melts in tother . . .
> all the rivals to allsea, shakeagain, O disaster! shakealose, Ah how
> starring! but Heng's got a bit of Horsa's nose and Jeff's got the signs
> of Ham round his mouth and the beau that spun beautiful pales as it
> palls" [143.18-24].

Here the brothers are "wrestless in the womb" (143.21) and
might just as likely come out into life opposite from what we know
they will be: Shem could just as easily be Shaun, and Shaun might
be Shem. The accident of their opposite natures is merely that, and
yet this accidental element facilitates their eventual synthesis. Hengest and Horsa, the Saxon brothers who led the initial invasion of
England, can easily be reversed in our minds without any loss of
significance: history has obliterated whatever differences may have
existed between them and united them as a single entity in our
minds. The brother conflict gives birth to its own synthesis; whereas we can read the line to mean that Hengest is biting his brother's
nose in anger, we can also read it to mean that Hengest's nose re-

sembles Horsa's. Similarly, Japhet may well be taking a bite of ham (or of his brother, Ham), but as brothers they have similar mouths. They are just as easily Mutt and Jeff, the comic-strip characters who are equally unlike each other and interchangeable. The key to this synthesis is the reduction in magnitude of the favored brother: only when Shaun has been cut down to size (reduced from his father's emulation of the favorite in Book Three) does synthesis set in. Book Four represents a "real" view of the future as contrasted with Earwicker's "wishful" view in the previous book; only when Earwicker's unconscious allows him to realize that his *beau* (Shaun as his desired self) is only half *beautiful* (the other half necessarily being the undesired artist aspect of himself) can he arrive at a reconciliation of his own antagonistic elements.

The battle of the brothers revolves about Shem's willingness to forgive (although he feels it is he who has been wronged) and Shaun's refusal to forgive. The eleventh riddle asks Shaun if he will help Shem save his soul (should Shem finally show a willingness to do so); it is Shaun's Professor Jones who repeatedly provides the negative answer, although his classic examples invariably backfire: in the episode of the Mookse and the Gripes, both antagonists prove impotent when tempted by Nuvoletta, and the maiden who here represents reconciliation goes off to search elsewhere— *"Why, why, why! Weh, O weh! I'se so silly to be flowing but I no canna stay!"* (159.17-18)—to reappear as Margareen (a synthetic product!) flirting now with Burrus and Caseous. When the dairy boys show themselves as pigheaded as their ecclesiastic predecessors, the synthesis girl, "A cleopatrician in her own right she at once complicates the position while Burrus and Caseous are contending for her misstery by implicating herself with an elusive Antonius" (166.34-167.1). Antonius (A) is the apex of the triangle whose base is formed by the opposite corners of Burrus (B) and Caseous (C); he represents the synthesis of Shem and Shaun in the same manner that the conflict between Cassius and Brutus resulted in the rise of Mark Antony, and the melting of butter and cheese will result in an amorphous amalgam of the two.

But Shaun, like Belshazzar—or "Ballshossers" (146.13)—cannot read his own handwriting on the wall and continues to withhold salvation from his brother. His final refusal, however, contains its own element of synthesis as he displays a strong consciousness of the reality and inevitability of such an amalgamation:

> if he came to my preach, a proud pursebroken ranger, when the heavens were welling the spite of their spout, to beg for a bite in our bark *Noisdanger,* would meself and Mac Jeffet, four-in-hand, foot him out?—ay!—were he my own breastbrother, my doubled withd love and my singlebiassed hate, were we bread by the same fire and signed with the same salt, had we tapped from the same master and robbed the same till, were we tucked in the one bed and bit by the one flea, homogallant and hemycapnoise, bum and dingo, jack by churl, though it broke my heart to pray it, still I'd fear I'd hate to say! [168.3-12]

The very use of the conditional (*were he my own breastbrother*) indicates that Shaun must eventually relent; Shem *is* his own breastbrother, and Shaun must eventually realize himself his brother's keeper. Several Freudian slips give him away: by referring to his alter ego as *Mac Jeffet* (Japhet) and denying his erring brother (Ham), he forces us to conclude that he is the Biblical Shem (and as such identifies himself by the coincidence of names with Joyce's Shem). We can reasonably assume that he will eventually allow Ham onto the Ark, and that as the Ondt he will spare the Gracehoper a bite to eat (*to beg for a bite in our bark*)—his bark is obviously worse than his bite.

Toward the close of the Mime of Mick, Nick and the Maggies, Joyce reconciles the antagonists of the battle of heaven: the Glugg-Chuff fight is over, and the father has called the children in to go to bed (253); the "bold bad bleak boy" has been beaten (as Lucifer had been), and the prayer for the dead has been said over his corpse (as the children say their bedtime prayers). But in the dark of their common bedroom Shem and Shaun are indistinguishable from each other, and, like the tree and stone of the end of the washerwomen's scene, they merge into each other in the darkness:

"Who were Shem and Shaun the living sons or daughters of? Night now! Tell me, tell me, tell me, elm! Night night! Telmetale of stem or stone. Beside the rivering waters of, hitherandthithering waters of. Night!" (216.1-5). Here in the Mime scene the Archangel and the fallen angel are equally clothed from discerning eyes, and in Biblical echoes Joyce indicates that the opposites inevitably become reconciled:

> And let Nek Nekulon extol Mak Makal and let him say unto him: Immi ammi Semmi. And shall not Babel be with Lebab? And he war. And he shall open his mouth and answer: I hear, O Ismael, how they laud is only as my loud is one. If Nekulon shall be havonfalled surely Makal haven hevens. Go to, letus extell Makal, yea, let us exceedingly extell. Though you have lien amung your posspots my excellency is over Ismael. Great is him whom is over Ismael and he shall mekanek of Mak Nakulon. And he deed [258.10-18].

In the dark the devil and his heavenly adversary lose themselves in each other. *Babel* realizes that he is actually a reversed form of *Lebab; extoll* and *expell* are joined in *extell:* it is Michael who is being both praised as the defender of heaven and thrown down into hell as Satan. The Hebrew chant of *Shema Israel, Adonoi Elohenu, Adonoi Echod*—the Lord is God, the Lord is One— forms the basis for reconciling the opposites of Shem-Nick and Shaun-Mick into one: they again became an entity of *mekanek* (Mick-Nick neck-and-neck) and *Mak Nakulon*. But once again Joyce indicates that he can use a single word to mean two things: *And they war* indicates that Mick and Nick *were* merged and that Mick and Nick were still at *war.*

The conclusion of the next episode enlarges the theme of reconciliation and synthesis: once again Shem (Dolph) has managed to enrage his brother into violence, and once again Shaun (Kev) is forgiven for the blow he struck (304). Shaun finally accepts the truce: "I'm only out for celebridging over the guilt of the gap in your hiscitendency. You are a hundred thousand times welcome, old wortsampler, hellbeit you're just about as culpable as my woolfell merger would be. . . . And if you're not you're bloater's kipper may I never curse again on that pint I took of Jamesons" (305.8-17). Here the parental guilt it shared by the sons, as Shaun admits in citing the word of guilt (*hiscitendency*), since it is the revelation of that guilt by Dolph that earns him the blow. Awareness carries with it implication, and Dolph's geometrical outlining of the sexual union of the parents involves him in Original Sin. Once Kev has understood the drift of Dolph's diagramming—"So analytical plausible! And be the powers of Moll Kelly, neighbour topsowyer, it will be a lozenge to me all my lauffe" (299.26-29) —he too must share that guilt. Acknowledging that Cain's hypothesis is correct, Abel reminds Cain that he is Abel's keeper: Joyce's version of the Biblical material effects a reconciliation on the basis of awareness (insight instead of innocence) and nonviolence. Shaun finally forgives Shem for the sin of being correct, as Cissy Caffrey had forgiven Stephen the insult (U 566); the significant difference is that in the *Wake* the insulted and the injurer are the same person, and the forgiveness is granted after the injury. Shaun's awareness of the interdependence of the brothers manifests itself also in Shaun's pedantic marginal note: *"The Twofold Truth and the Conjunctive Appetites of Oppositional Orexes"* (305.L). With the full sexual awareness of both brothers accomplished, they now go forth into the world as men: "Item, mizpah ends" (306.7). The period of fructification begins, and Shem need no longer consider himself a sham.

When we next meet the brothers they are a pair of radio comics named Butt and Taff, and they are engaged in presenting their skit of How Buckley Shot the Russian General. The element of combativeness is decidedly lessened if not totally absent, but whereas Taff remains the impartial observer of the Crimean battle for the most part, Butt is identified with Buckley engaged in cutting down the father. The events are broadcast in dialogue form as Butt and Taff discuss the proceedings; but toward the end of the broadcast —at the moment of the Russian General's demise—the two comics become one: "BUTT and TAFF" (354.7), uniting to dethrone their father. As Butt reminds us, Earwicker falls as Finn MacCool

fell: "Shurenoff! Life Faun MacGhoul!" (354.5-6)—*MacGhoul*
combines MacCool and Goll, the slayer of Finn's father, Cumhal,
who in turn was slain by Finn—while Finn in turn was slain by
the followers of Goll. The merging of these ancient enemies
tightens the merger of Butt and Taff in the succeeding line. This
amalgamation had in itself been anticipated just prior to the fatal
blow which killed the Russian General: at zero hour, the television
screen (Joyce's "radio" adding the dimension of visual image in
dreamlike fashion) had gone dark, and as happened during the
dusk of the washerwomen's colloquy and the darkness of the children's bedroom, the two brothers had become indistinguishable:
*"In the heliotropical noughttime following a fade of transformed
Tuff and, pending its viseversion, a metenergic reglow of beaming
Batt, the bairdboard bombardment screen, if tastefully taut gurani-
um satin, tends to teleframe and step up to the charge of a light
barricade"* (349.6-10). In successive stages the individual Butt and
individual Taff are first confused as Batt and Tuff and eventually
synthesized as the combined Butt-Taff. For a crowning touch, Butt
and Taff sneak in later during the tavern brawl; each has had the
duplicated consonant at the end of his name knocked off, and each
is reversed, but there they are nonetheless: "Every tub here spucks
his own fat" (378.26-27).

Thus Joyce stresses the interdependence of the antagonistic
brothers. Butt needs Taff to help him deliver the *coup de grâce* to
the Russian General; it is only when the sons have united that they
succeed in upending their father. As strong as their hostility has
been, and as opposite as they are from each other, they necessarily
become aware of their interdependence: it is Shem who is building
castles in the air, and Shaun who is furnishing foundations under
them. As much as Shem flaunts his voluntary exile—"would we
go back there now for sounds, pillings and sense? would we now
for annas and annas? . . . not for a dinar! not for jo!"
(169.24-170.3)—he nonetheless laments his absence: "Was liffe
worth leaving? Nej!" (230.25). As much as Shaun mocks Shem's
literary prowess—"Every dimmed letter in it is a copy and not a

few of the silbils and wholly words I can show you in my King-dom of Heaven. The lowquacity of him!" (424.32-34)—he none-theless attempts to emulate his brother's writing: "He store the tale of me shur. Like yup. How's that for Shemese?" (425.2-3). Anna Livia, in fact, in her dying monologue, adds: "But there's a great poet in you too" (619.31-32). Having favored Shem against Earwicker's favoring Shaun, the magnanimous mother bestows this final tribute to her other son. This stress on creativity, on which Shem bases his detachment and Shaun his envy, is characteristic of Joyce's *apologia pro vita sua:* reconciliation seems dependent upon the artist's willingness to share his creative inspiration and the willingness of the bourgeois to accept the significance of that inspi-ration.

That Joyce adopted his concept of the synthesis of opposites from Giordano Bruno of Nola is apparent by the numerous refer-ences to the Italian philosopher sprinkled throughout the *Wake:* Bruno himself is split in two to form Browne and Nolan, another set of pseudonyms for Shem and Shaun, which again synthesize them in terms of literary creations when Browne and Nolan, the Dublin stationers, are implicated. They appear as the "overspoiled priest Mr Browne . . . in his secondary personality as a Nolan" (38.25-28) who passes on the cad's wife's gossip about Earwick-er's indiscretion in Phoenix Park. Scores of other instances repeat the dichotomy until Yawn finally confesses that he and his brother are interdependent and inseparable:

> —Dearly beloved brethren: Bruno and Nola, leymon bogholders and stationary lifepartners off orangey Saint Nessau Street, were explain-ing its avicendas all round each other ere yesterweek out of Ibn Sen and Ipanzussch. When himupon Nola Bruno monopolises his egobru-no most unwillingly seses by the mortal powers alionola equal and opposite brunoipso, *id est,* eternally provoking alio opposite equally as provoked as Bruno at being eternally opposed by Nola. Poor omni-boose, singalow singelearum: so is he! [488.4-12]

The disintegrating Yawn displays many of his brother's traits, and at times his voice is that of Shem. Bruno is an individual split against himself, reflecting his other self, being his other self when he least suspects; Yawn acknowledges here the permanent exclusiveness of the two which equals their permanent unity. He goes on to refer to Shem as "Cabler" (488.28)—uncertain now which of the brothers is Cain and which is Abel. As Coulson Turnbull, commenting on Bruno, explains:

> we find him anticipating the doctrines of Goethe and Darwin. Speaking of the soul, he taught that nothing in the universe is lost, everything is in a state of transformation; therefore body and soul, spirit and matter, are equally eternal. The body may dissolve, but becomes transformed; the soul transmigrates, and, drawing around itself atom to atom, it reconstructs for itself a new body. The spirit which animates and moves all things is One. Everything differentiates according to the different forms and bodies in which it operates. Some animate things are inferior by reason of the meanness of the body in which they operate, others are superior through the richness of the same.[19]

Yawn is Joyce's name for Shaun's disintegrating body: it has blocked his attainment of the richness of soul which his artist brother as "mystic" has presumably achieved. Now that the body is dissolving, Shem's soul begins to appear through the mist of the decomposition. The transition appears final in the last book of the *Wake:* the *ricorso* presents the reality of the future after Earwicker's inflated image of his favorite son has been detected. The "angelic" Shaun, whose potential has been thwarted by his father's bourgeois ideals, now returns as St. Kevin: he has adopted the guise of his brother and allowed his own angelic nature to transform him from the crass burgher to the ascetic saint. He sits in a cold altar-tub of water on his lonely island and contemplates; he is "leaving all the messy messy to look after our douche douche, the miracles, death and life are these" (605.1-3). He combines Shem's quest for the mystic experience with Shaun's undefiled naïveté; it is he who is now doing penance and expiating his father's sin. Giordano Bruno in the *Wake* is, therefore, still Stephen Dedalus' Bruno: he is at once the "terrible heretic" and the "terribly burned" (AP 249)—the "wright" and the "wronged" (597.11).

J. S. Atherton notes that the uniting of Butt and Taff, *"desprot slave wager and foeman feodal unsheckled, now one and the same person"* (354.7-8), is an example of Bruno's synthesis of opposites:

> Butt and Taff begin as a couple of cross-talk comedians and end as one person. For Joyce this seems to have been a personification of the dialectic theory according to which the ultimate truth, although perhaps unobtainable, is to be sought for in the interaction of opposites. To most moderns the idea will probably suggest Karl Marx. For Joyce it was associated with Giordano Bruno. . . .[20]

The coincidence of Marx and Bruno on the interaction of opposites parallels the coincidence of Marx and Vico on the four stages of societal development; in each case Joyce seems to have derived his own versions of the contemporary aspects of the Italian philosophers as Marx had derived his dialectics from Hegel. And it becomes important in attempting to determine Joyce's attitude toward his fellow man to realize the actual political context in which, despite his essential indifference toward ephemeral political movements and slogans, he nonetheless viewed mankind's twentieth-century environment. Joyce garnered from Vico and Bruno (and many another political and psychological thinker) that which he felt would aid his insight into man—contemporary and future man. The political climate of *Finnegans Wake* owes as much to fundamental Marxian dialectics as its psychological climate is dependent upon Freud and Jung and its evolutionary structure determined by Darwin. There is no reason to assume that Joyce was a Marxist, but it is important to realize that Joyce was aware of the various political aspects of contemporary society spotlighted by Marx's sociological perspective. Whether he arrived at the disintegration of contemporary society by Marxian dialectics or by classical concepts of cyclical history, the verdict in the *Wake* remains that the phoenix of our modern world is plunging toward its destruction in order to achieve its rebirth. The approach undertaken in the *Wake* is nonetheless that of the social philosopher, and Marx's interest in "changing" the world is reflected in Joyce's work.

The unique problem presented by Ireland to its world-enlight-
ened writer cannot be overstressed: as a backward nation seriously
divorced from the flow of European culture, Ireland disturbed
even the youthful student who saw in attempts to revive the Gaelic
language and diffuse the Celtic Twilight a reactionary force that
would further prevent her from taking her place in the twentieth-
century array of nations. He realized that the Ireland of the twentieth century was still in the process of undergoing its nationalistic
revolution—a step in the ladder of political evolution which Europe had taken during the previous century—and like his Marx-
conscious contemporary, Sean O'Casey, Joyce did not permit his
concern for his country to deter him from the realization that the
nationalist movement of the 1916 insurrection was essentially reactionary and the Civil War of 1921-22 detrimental to the political
development of the new nation. Ireland was just undergoing its
bourgeois revolution and was almost a century behind the Europe
with which Joyce realized he must finally associate himself. But
whereas *Ulysses* is a view of that bourgeois revolution of nineteenth-century liberalism affecting Dublin—as Mann's *Der
Zauberberg* and its Settembrini character form a similar view of
Europe at the beginning of the century—*Finnegans Wake* again
marks a step forward in political evolution. Here the germ of a
proletarian class begins to arise; Harry Slochower notes that "the
proletarianized petty bourgeois Earwicker is to fuse all polarities,
natural and human, conscious and subconscious."[21] That Joyce was
aware of the necessity of the rise of such a class in Ireland, before
that nation could begin to become a cultural and political part of
Europe, is obvious from his own comment in a letter to Stanislaus
written early in his exile years: he notes that despite his realization
that the nationalistic Sinn Fein policy is inevitable in Ireland, the
important part of any revolutionary struggle there is the rise of a
proletarian class: "Of course, I see that its success would be to substitute Irish for English capital, but no one, I suppose, denies that
capitalism is a stage of progress. The Irish proletariat has yet to be
created."[22] Such class consciousness is far too contemporary to be

considered Viconian; it indicates a fundamental awareness of scientific socialism.

In essence the *dramatis personae* of the *Wake* are indeed common men. Despite Earwicker's middle-class pretensions as a small businessman, the lowly pub-keeper is definitely being proletarianized: he is the "birth of an otion that was breeder to sweatoslaves, as mysterbolder, forced in their waste" (309.12-13), and behind him stands the shadow of Tim Finnegan, about whom the song notes: "to rise in the world he carried a hod." Shaun, despite his claim to be carrier of the Royal Mail—"Or for royal, Am for Mail, R.M.D." (404.30)—is nothing more than a foot-sore letter carrier: "How all too unwordy am I, a mere mailman of peace, a poor loust hastehater of the first degree" (408.10-11). And the exalted artist, Shem? A penman, a scribe, a scribbler at other people's dictation; in a parody of *Hamlet,* "His jymes is out of job, would sit and write. . . . Copies" (181.29-33). Shaun and Shem as the radio comics, Butt and Taff, we are reminded, are *"desprot slave wager and foeman feodal unsheckled"* (354.7-8), and Joyce reminds us that, as Marx has stated, the petty bourgeois is destined to become a part of the proletariat, so that the wage slave and the foreman essentially are *"now one and the same person"* (354.8). They too, the oligarch sons, become part of the common people, become Finnegans carrying their hods up the ladder. That the political Judgment Day in *Finnegans Wake* has a definite Marxian tinge can be seen from Shem's statement at the second trial "that the thorntree of sheol might ramify up his Sheofon to the lux apointlex but he would go good to him suntime marx my word fort" (83.8-10)—the blowing of the Hebrew ram's horn (*Sheofon, ramify*) on the Day of Atonement will herald forth a dawn (*suntime*) when the Finnegans will rise to their appointed role (*lux apointlex*), as Marx predicted; the upending of the father by Shem will usher forth the rule of the sons (*suntime*).

If Joyce is finding parallels in Marx to support the Bruno concept of an eventual synthesis of opposites, he is doing so in order to emphasize the positive aspect of his use of Viconian cycles for the stages of mankind's development. But Vico himself remains something of an enigma in the *Wake:* like Bruno he was a controversial figure with a controversial doctrine that straddled precariously the fences of heterodoxy. His contemporary supporter, Thomas J. Fitzmorris, finds that "since nations have, according to Vico, a *common nature* and go through similar experiences, each cycle in effect gives man another chance to improve himself in the light of history."²³ Fitzmorris therefore sees a spiral pattern to Vico's cycles, but fails to note any such pattern in *Finnegans Wake;* Harry Levin, however, insists that critics "may take what consolation they can from Vico's bland belief that the cycles continue to spiral upwards and onwards. A long-range optimism is reflected in the provisional title, *Work in Progress.* Mankind, viewed under the aspect of eternity, is 'a human pest cycling (pist!) and recycling (past!).' "²⁴

What Levin finds in the provisional title can also be found in the final one, and Magalaner and Kain remind us that Maria Jolas "finds in the missing apostrophe of the title a cautionary admonition to the powers that be. Finnegans (the small men of our world) do eventually Wake—and Joyce is here warning of the coming day of judgment."²⁵ Although one may well be suspicious about the twentieth-century concept of progress in Joyce's work, it is nonetheless apparent that he was concerned in the *Wake* with the progress of mankind, that he thought in terms of the world as a work in progress and his epic as a work concerned with man's progress. The cycle that approaches its end in the *Wake* evokes a positive image, although Joyce allows neither for a black-and-white controversy nor for a black-or-white solution; he reminds us in the "new" portrait of Earwicker in the last chapter that it may well be a case "of a pfan coalding the keddle mickwhite" (596.32). The twins will obviously awaken this morning to find that the messotint in their room of Michael combating Satan is as static as before the night's cataclysm: in essence the antagonists have become synthesized into a work or art. Anna Livia reconciles the victor and the vanquished in her final words of farewell: "Let besoms be bosuns. It's Phoenix, dear. And the flame is, hear! Let's our joornee saintomichael make it. Since the lausafire has lost and the book of the depth is. Closed. Come! Step out of your shell! Hold up you free fing! Yes. We've light enough" (621.1-5). Since *laus* is both German for louse and Latin for praise, Lucifer is both the louse-of-fire and the praise-of-fire (Prometheus providing fire for mankind); it is Lucifer's hellfires which light St. Michael on his journey—again a coalescence of the antagonists.

Edwin Burgum analyzes Joyce's use of Vico in the *Wake* and underscores Joyce's translation of the Italian philosopher's scheme of history into contemporary terms; Burgum concedes that Joyce

> . . . was too good and too modern a novelist to be content with writing mere allegory. He sought to humanize Vico's abstractions, and found in Jung a method which seemed to him to avoid the necessity of sacrificing our ordinary demand for characterization. Since Jung believed that the history of the race remains as a deposit in the unconscious of each individual, to expose the unconscious of a single contemporary tavern keeper would present in acceptable fictive form the history of the race as Vico saw it.[26]

Joyce's view of the cyclical pattern of historical repetition, therefore, moves beyond Vico and incorporates Vico into the pattern. Vico echoes the classical four ages as Marx echoes Vico's four cycles; Vico and Jung dovetail, as Burgum has here noted, into a further extension of the cyclical spiral. The Earwicker who appears in the final chapter is the Jungian dreamer tossed free from the Viconian merry-go-round; whether Vico allowed for a progression, as Levin contended, or kept the earthly cycle on an even keel, as Wilson maintained,[27] Joyce nonetheless spins his hero free from his primeval guilt: "when no crane in Elga is heard; upout to speak this lay; without links, without impediments, with gygantogyres, with freeflawforms" (596.22-24)—the guilty stutter associated with H.C.E. is gone, although an afterthought reminds us that he is still far from perfect in this new eon: he "stoatters some" (596.27). It is, Joyce tells us, "as Jambudvispa Vipra foresaw of him; the last half versicle repurchasing his pawned word . . . sure, straight, slim, sturdy, serene, synthetical, swift" (596.29-33). Giambattista Vico and the Sanskrit *Jambu Dvipa,* the "great continent inhabited by man,"[28] foreshadow the new era; the seven alliterated attributes of the new man include the process of synthesis undergone to reconcile the opposite elements within him.

Joyce is envisioning in his *ricorso* a leveling off of man's whirl through history at a juncture where he can take stock and reappraise; there is no definite insistence upon an achieved perfection as such, as much as there is an indication of a higher attainment in man's spiral toward that perfection in the foreseeable future. The Muta and Juva who stand on the brink of the new eon discuss the possibility that retrogression might set in, that the cycles might well return us to where we had started and begin again without any consciousness of past development. Muta outlines the four stages of the past as mankind has experienced them: "So that when we shall have acquired unification we shall pass on to diversity and when we shall have passed on to diversity we shall have acquired the instinct of combat and when we shall have acquired the instinct of combat we shall pass back to the spirit of appeasement?" (610.23-27). Muta's doubt concerning the achievement of peace in the new stage of man's civilization is answered by Juva (the new generation growing up from the mutation of past generations): "By the light of the bright reason which daysends to us from the high" (610.28-29). And the final combat of *Finnegans Wake* is allowed to ensue, as we move toward the spirit of appeasement.

An outline of Joyce's short *ricorso* chapter supports the contention that the cycles of the *Wake* arrive at a high plateau of evolutionary development foreshadowing the perfectibility of man. The opening pages present the new eon of the new cycle in terms of Hindu and Buddhist philosophy; here is the day of judgment "to the cowld owld sowls that are in the domnatory of Defmut after the night" (593.20-21), and yet also a political revolution, "Calling all downs to dayne. Array! Surrection!" (593.2-3). The night of conflicting opposites is ended; Shem and Shaun have been

turned topsy-turvy ("the night of the carrying of the word of
Nuahs and the night of making Mehs to cuddle up in a coddlepot
—593.21-23), and the synthesis is another mock-Egyptian divinity
—"Pu Nuseht, lord of risings in the yonderworld" (593.23)—
who is simply "the sun up" read backward. In an echo of the familiar advertisement already found in *Ulysses* (U 77-78) we hear:
"Guld modning, have yous viewsed Piers' aube?" (593.9); the
morning ritual of washing with Pears' soap is compressed with a
view of Persse O'Reilly's dawn, as the victim of Hosty's scurrilous
ballad is cleansed of his night's sins. The hen who had found the
letter in the midden heap and revealed the night's secrets is once
again out in the yard: "Let shrill their duan Gallus, han, and she,
hou the Sassqueehenna, makes ducksruns at crooked"
(594.29-31).

The product of the Shaun-Shem synthesis in the morning's light
results in a realization of what Shem had predicted when person-
ified during the night as Mercius: "all that has been done has yet
to be done and done again, when's day's woe, and lo, you're
doomed, joyday dawns and, la, you dominate" (194.10-12). His
soliloquy had been introduced by the statement: "He points the
deathbone and the quick are still" (193.29), and concluded with:
"He lifts the lifewand and the dumb speak" (195.5). At the end
of the Lessons, a childish drawing at the bottom of the lefthand
side of the page shows a pair of gnawed crossed bones (which also
look like eating utensils), representing, according to the *Skeleton
Key*, the duality of love and death—the *x* that represents a kiss at
the bottom of a letter and the cross that represents Christ's
death.[29]* The final pedantic marginal note reads: *"Balance of the
factual by the theoric Boox and Coox, Amallagamated"* (308.L)—
the unification of the opposites in sexual terms. The crossbone implements are also the deathbone and lifewand—in Joyce's own
word they are "crossbuns" (308.n2)—and hark back to Mercius'
two statements; these statements of life and death are repeated in

* Clive Hart, who makes a point of seeing both the forest *and* the trees, adds
a significant shade of meaning to the *x* (*Structure and Motif*, p. 205).

the opening of the *ricorso* episode: "Death banes and the quick quoke. But life wends and the dombs spake! Whake?" (595.1-3). The conflicting principles represented by Shem and Shaun during the night are resolved into the resurrection of the cabalistic formula of Life and Beauty; one cannot but feel that the Shem principle has somewhat triumphed in the synthesis, that Mercius' prediction of domination in the new era has been realized: "to me unseen blusher in an obscene coalhole, the cubilibum of your secret sigh, dweller in the downandoutermost where voice only of the dead may come, because ye left from me, because ye laughed on me, because, O me lonly son, ye are forgetting me!, that our turfbrown mummy is acoming, alpilla, beltilla, ciltilla, deltilla" (194.17-23). As the flow of the "giddygaddy, grannyma, gossipaceous Anna Livia" (195.3-4) closes the chapter dealing with Shem the Penman, so does she also end the final chapter and the entire *Wake* (619-28).

The professor now begins his last tour of the unconscious landscape as dawn begins to break in upon the dreamer's consciousness. The theme is set by his reference to "Geoglyphy's twentynine ways to say goodbett" (595.7-8), and goes on to describe the landscape around him in a catalogue of the items he sees; this returns us to the first such listing at the beginning of the *Wake* (5-6), where we gazed at the brink of the unconscious to view the world scene. Here the first dawn image of the world scene is perceived:

> For korps, for streamfish, for confects, for bullyoungs, for smearsassage, for patates, for steaked pig, for men, for limericks, for waterfowls, for wagsfools, for louts, for cold airs, for late trams, for curries, for curlews, for leekses, for orphalines, for tunnygulls, for clear goldways, for lungfortes, for moonyhaunts, for fairmoneys, for coffins, for tantrums, for armaurs, for waglugs, for rogues comings, for sly goings, for larksmathes, for homdsmeethes, for quailsmeathes, kilalooly [595.10-17].

This strange collection is at once the landscape of Ireland, the landscape of the world, the rubbish heap of the past found on the dawn of the new day: as Jute had noticed during his first view of

the new land at the beginning of *Finnegans Wake:* "he dumptied the wholeborrow of rubbages on to soil here" (17.4-5). The
night's deposit is the scattered bits of Humpty Dumpty's splattered
sins upon which the new world will have to build again: "Kilt by
kelt shell kithagain with kinagain" (594.3-4).

The cock of dawn crows, announcing the fourth stage of Vico's
cycle. Earwicker is the new man rising above sin: he is Dagda, the
chief Irish divinity—"in full dogdhis; sod on a fall; pat" (596.2)
—as well as Patrick; his resurrection parallels Christ's as well as
Finn's predicted rearising: "the hundering blundering dunderfun-
der of plundersundered manhood; behold, he returns; renascenent;
fincarnate; still foretold around the hearthside; at matin a fact;
hailed chimers' ersekind; foe purmanant, fum in his mow; awike
in wave risurging into chrest; *victis poenis hesternis*" (596.2-7).
His resurrection is nonetheless sexual and has gone through the
four stages of Viconian evolution, but he is still the familiar hero,
Earwicker (*hailed chimers' ersekind*), although he is now devoid
of his classic guilt. It is in his mind that the history of mankind has
left its residue, and his significant dream has been signed and acknowledged by the author's important "Such me" (597.22). But
all of this is part of the myth of world creation as "through the
windr of a wondr in a wildr is a weltr as a wirbl of a warbl is a
world" (597.28-29).

Another aspect of coalesced opposites is introduced with a repetition of the Hindu concept of the lotus growing from the navel of
Vishnu as he dreams the entire universe into being: "Padma,
brighter and sweetster, this flower that bells, it is our hour or risings. Tickle, tickle. Lotus spray" (598.12-14). The union of East
and West becomes an important aspect of the reconciliation of opposites, "In that european end meets Ind" (598.15-16), as echoed
in the opening *Sandhyas!* repetitions of the chapter. This union is
again reflected in the unity of space and time now represented by
the All-Father and the All-Mother—"the old man of the sea and
the old woman in the sky . . . Father Times and Mother Spacies"
(599.34-600.3). A transition of opposites from Shem and Shaun

to their unified relationship in Earwicker and Anna Livia is an important aspect of the sanity of dawn countering the night's inver-
sions: themes of incest (Earwicker's lust for his daughter, the
"niece" Iseult; the brothers battling for Izod-Margareen-Nuvolet-
ta); homosexuality (Earwicker's adulation of Shaun; Shaun's sus-
picions concerning Shem); impotence (the unsuccessful union of
the Earwickers during the early morning hours—581.18-19); and
the horrible perversions of the Honophrius criminal court trial
(572.21-573.32). These Freudian overtones of the censored
dream have been obliterated with the coming of dawn; the reconciliation of opposites is further magnified by the cemented relationship between husband and wife once the guilty dream has been
forgotten. Yet it is important not to overlook that this dawn episode is not real dawn as much as it is the dawn anticipated in the
dream: to awaken from the guilty dream and censor its connotations from the mind is one thing; to expiate the sins of the dream
within the dream itself is another. The former would imply con-
secutive nonspiraling cycles: the dream is likely to recur just as
guiltfully on any succeeding night; the latter recognizes the end of
guilt within the framework of guilt: there is the permanent possibility of guiltless man maturing toward perfectibility.

The sexual potency of the parents now becomes accepted; they
are responsible for "the regenerations of the incarnations of the
emanations of the apparentations" (600.8-10) and engender the
composite son, "Keavn!" (601.18). This saint-priest's arrival is
heralded by the menstrual schoolgirls: and all the bells of the
Catholic churches of Dublin "clangalied" (601.20). The names of
the churches, however, are changed into feminine forms: "S. Wil-
helmina's, S. Gardenia's, S. Phibia's, S. Veslandrua's, S. Clarinda's
. . . S. Thomassabbess's and . . . S. Loellisotoelles!" (601.21-28).
Not only has Kevin's gender been neutralized (he is the first born
now of the new era, born without Original Sin and consequently
without any apparent sex), but the forecast of Anna Livia's final
monologue is present in this emphasis on the All-Woman. The last
two churches in the listing are puns on Sts. Thomas à Becket and

Lawrence O'Toole, the antagonistic clergy who experienced different treatment during the reign of King Henry II—Becket being murdered in Canterbury while O'Toole was being made Bishop of Dublin by the conquering Anglo-Normans. Their careers make them prototypes of the antagonistic brothers in the *Wake,* first seen in "with larrons o'toolers clittering up and tombles a'buckets clottering down" (5.3-4). Now their unequal treatment, their mutual hostility, and even their sexual existences have been neutralized by the coming of the new dawn. They combine to become the new hermit, the "strong and perfect christian" (605.35-36).

The introduction of the saint results in a recapitulation of the themes of the *Wake;* all the night's adventures are reintroduced as part of the morning's events. The church bells are ringing for morning mass (they are also the twenty-nine "belles" pealing for their hero, Kevin); the air is once again thick with ecclesiastic sounds: "the engine of the load with haled morries full of crates" (604.10-11); breakfast is being served: "with that smeoil like a grace of backoning over his egglips of the sunsoonshine" (603.1-2); Shaun, the postman, who is delivering the morning mail ("Bring us this days our maily bag!"—603.7-8), seems as lecherous as ever ("A dweam of dose innocent dirly dirls. Keavn! Keavn!"—601.17-18), and the children are playing their games before breakfast ("Batch is for Baker who baxters our bread"—603.6-7). The morning newspaper is being read at the table: "the Durban Gazette, firstcoming issue" (602.19-20). And the news once again concerns the Earwicker incident in Phoenix Park of the previous night:

> From a collispendent. Any were. Deemsday. Bosse of Upper and Lower Byggotstrade, Ciwareke, may he live for river! The Games funeral at Valleytemple. Saturnights pomps, exhabiting that corricatore of a harss, revealled by Oscur Camerad. The last of Dutch Schulds, perhumps. Pipe in Dream Cluse. Uncovers Pub History. The Outrage, at Length. Affected Mob Follows in Religious Sullivence. Rinvention of vestiges by which they drugged the buddhy [602.20-27].

Just when it appeared that the night's colossal sin had been obliterated by the dawn, the dreaming Earwicker finds himself at the breakfast table confronted by the screaming headlines of his night's dream. Finn is dead; the funeral games are reported; Earwicker (*Ciwareke*) is being hailed as the conqueror. But the cad with the pipe has once again heard of the Phoenix Park affair, and investigations are under way; the twelve Sullivans of the court trial (573) are looking into it, and H.C.E. is on the verge of being discovered in the newspaper's text (*exhabiting the corricatore of a harss*), as his initials are embedded in reverse order. But salvation is on the way since Kevin has appeared and rows his "*altare cum balneo*" (605.8) into the lake at "Glendalough-le-vert" (605.11) to sit in the cold water and expiate his father's sin: "he meditated continuously with seraphic ardour the primal sacrament of baptism or the regeneration of all man by affusion of water" (606.10-12). Glendalough, in the Wicklow Hills, is not only the site of St. Kevin's hermitage, but also the source of the waters of the Liffey; thus Kevin is discovering for himself the secret of the mother which Dolph had attempted to reveal to him in the Night Lessons: "amiddel of meeting waters of river Yssia and Essia river" (605.12-13). "Yee"* (606.12) is his cry as he sits down in the cold water, immersing himself in the sexual secret of the parents. It is Anna Livia Plurabelle's secret which climaxes the dawn of the *ricorso;* hers is "the feminiairity which breathes content" (606.22-23).

The twilight tour of the consciousness continues on into its last moments as the wake is anticipated; the last riddle of the universe is asked (607.10-12), and the apparent answer is the resurrection of the legendary giant: "the week of wakes is out and over; as a wick weak woking from ennemberable Ashias unto fierce force

---

* Kevin's final *Yee* is a cross between Molly Bloom's final *yes* and Anna Livia's final *the*. A significant echo from *Stephen Hero:* "There are some people in this island who sing a hymn called 'Washed in the blood of the Lamb' by way of easing the religious impulse. Perhaps it's a question of [impulse] diet but I would prefer to wash in rice-water. Yeow! what a notion!" (SH 190).

fuming, temtem tamtam, the Phoenican wakes" (608.30-32). The invocation to dawn is sounded: "Passing. One. We are passing. Two. From sleep we are passing. Three. Into the wikeawades warld from sleep we are passing. Four. Come, hours, be ours!" (608.33-35), and the new dawn finds Muta and Juva on the hill overlooking Dublin Bay (609-10), as they announce the arrival of St. Patrick and his meeting with the Celtic Archdruid (611-12). The debate takes place before the reigning King Lughaire, who expresses Joyce's whimsical confidence concerning the outcome of the new era: "He has help his crewn on the burkeley buy but he has holf his crown on the Eurasian Generalissimo" (610.11-13). The king has placed equal bets on both opponents, and the future is assured.

The reality of Patrick's direct slicing of the Gordian Knot of the Archdruid's involved metaphysics parallels the morning sun's breaking through the druidical murkiness of the night's dream. The transition of morning breaking finds the world newly created: "A spathe of calyptrous glume involucrumines the perinanthean Amenta: fungoalgaceous muscafilicial graminopalmular planteon; of increasing, livivorous, feelful thinkamalinks" (613.17-19)—the first monocelled items of geological existence are beginning to take shape as the earth spins into being out of chaos. H.C.E. and A.L.P. awaken; the antagonism of opposites (Shem and Shaun, morning and evening) has been reconciled, "Health, chalce, endnessnessessity! Arrive, likkypuggers, in a poke! The folgor of the frightfools is olympically optimominous; there is bound to be a lovleg day for mirrages in the open; Murnane and Aveling are undertoken to berry that ortchert" (613.27-31), and the dirty linen of history that had been washed throughout the night (the Earwicker laundry washed by the banshees at the banks of the Liffey until nightfall) has been returned from the laundry clean and white, as the various themes find their morning expression:

> Mopsus or Gracchus, all your horodities will incessantlament be coming back from the Annone Wishwashwhose, Ormepierre Lodge, Doone of the Drumes, blanches bountifully and nightsend made up,

every article lathering leaving several rinsings so as each rinse results
with a dapperent rolle, cuffs for meek and chokers for sheek and a
kink in the pacts for namby. Forbeer, forbear! For nought that is
has bane. In mournenslaund. Themes have thimes and habit reburns.
To flame in you. Ardor vigor forders order. Since ancient was our living is in possible to be. Delivered as. Caffirs and culls and onceagain
overalls, the fittest surviva lives that blued, iorn and storridge can
make them. Whichus all claims. Clean [614.1-12].

The Earwicker who awakens this morning is cleansed of his
guilt by the laws of natural selection; the Darwinian principle (*the
fittest surviva lives*) had been sounded earlier in the *ricorso* as the
girls surround the hero: "they coroll in caroll round Botany Bay"
(601.16-17). Earwicker and Anna Livia are now "anastomosically
assimilated" (615.5), in sharp contrast to their unsuccessful union
during the early hours before dawn: "Humperfeldt and Anunska,
wedded now evermore in annastomoses by a ground plan of the
placehunter, whiskered beau and donahbella. Totumvir and esqui-
meena, who so shall separate fetters to new desire, repeals an act
of union to unite in bonds of schismacy" (585.22-26). When husband and wife awaken from the sleep induced by liquor (*whiskered
beau*) and drugs (*donahbella*), they sit down to breakfast: "when
cup, platter and pot come piping hot, as sure as herself pits hen to
paper and there's scribings scrawled on eggs" (615.9-10). The
final edition of the letter dug up by Biddy now appears on the
breakfast table as the morning mail.

The letter of course reviews the entire dream, but the news is
now quite good: the weather for the new era seems to be fine—
"Yon clouds will soon disappear looking forwards at a fine day"
(615.17-18). The guilty dreamer's sins have been washed away—
"When he woke up in a sweat besidus it was to pardon him"
(615.22-23)—and the whole guilt was nothing but a pantomime:
"but he daydreamsed we had a lovelyt face for a pulltomine"
(615.24). The brothers have been reconciled, "Tomothy and Lor-
can, the bucket Toolers, both are Timsons now they've changed
their characticuls during their blackout" (617.12-14), and the letter ends with a notice concerning Earwicker's resurrection from the

dream world of the dead: "Hence we've lived in two worlds. He is
another he what stays under the himp of holth. The herewaker of
our hamefame is his real namesame who will get himself up and
erect, confident and heroic when but, young as of old, for my daily
comfreshenall, a wee one woos" (619.11-15). And as the final
postscript is written to her letter, Anna Livia commences her elegy
to the sea, acknowledging responsibility for the letter and the secret of life; from the plateau reached at the dawn of this chapter
the new cycle of life begins to rise anew. It is with the mother of
mankind that the new dawn reaches its climax.

Joyce views man's possibilities in the new stage of development
foreshadowed in *Finnegans Wake* through his mock-serious perspective, thus discouraging optimistic attempts to codify his attitude under a single black-or-white classification. Yet there are
many indications, no matter how oblique, which serve to remind
the reader of Joyce's basic acceptance of the history of mankind,
the development of man to his present state, and the possibility of
great advances in man's future development. His facetious comparison of man and fowl—"What bird had done yesterday man may
do next year, be it fly, be it moult, be it hatch, be it agreement in
the nest" (112.9-11)—marks Joyce's expectation of a pacifistic future, a future governed by the "spirit of appeasement." After the
Glugg-Chuff mime-battle, Joyce discourses on "the coming man,
the future woman, the food that is to build, what he with fifteen
years will do, the ring in her mouth of joyous guard, stars astir and
stirabout. A palashe for hirs, a saucy for hers and ladlelike spoons
for the wonner" (246.11-15). This sort of affirmation recurs in
several instances, taking various forms and guises, whether in
terms of the polarity of the fixity of stars and the feeding of children (*stars astir and stirabout*) or in terms of the polarity of the
seasons in nature and the rebuilding of cities: "We will not say it
shall not be, this passing of order and order's coming, but in the
herbest country and in the country around Blath as in that city self
of legionds they look for its being ever yet" (277.18-22). And
later, during the tavern scene, Earwicker denounces those who can

only see the hog in man's makeup and insists that "when booboob brutals and cautiouses only aims at the oggog hogs in the humand, then . . . I'll tall tale tell croon paysecurers, sowill nuggets and nippers, that thash on me stumpen blows the gaff off mombition and thit thides or marse makes a good dayle to be shattat" (366.25-30). He contends that if Brutus and Cassius (Shem and Shaun) insist upon presenting the brutality of man in their internal conflict, he would just as soon be Caesar sacrificed on the Ides of March.

During the fable of the Ondt and the Gracehoper, the devil-may-care artist (Shem-Gracehoper) is spending his time composing a work which is to be called *"Ho, Time Timeagen, Wake!"* (415.15). He adds that

> if sciencium (what's what) can mute uns nought, 'a thought, abought the Great Sommboddy within the Omniboss, perhops an artsaccord (hoot's hoot) might sing ums tumtim abutt the Little Newbuddies that ring his panch. A high old tide for the barheated publics and the whole day as gratiis! Fudder and lighting for ally looty, any filly in a fog, for O'Cronione lags acrumbling in his sands but his sunsunsuns still tumble on [415.15-22].

The Gracehoper expresses his disillusion concerning the existence of a Divine Being (now that science has brought religious speculation to nought), and is turning his song toward mankind (the nobodies who are to have a new existence); Cronos, like John Brown's body, lies dead in his grave, but his sons (Zeus, mankind) have taken over the future. Here Joyce is celebrating the possibility of art as the impetus in perfecting man; it is Shaun's potentiality as a writer (turning his useless envy into actual productivity) which Shem recognizes as the hope of their reconciliation (*artsaccord*), and the Gracehoper's final plea to his Ondt brother is of course: *"why can't you beat time?"* (419.8).

The Finnegans (Maria Jolas' "small men of our world") are very much the heroes of *Finnegans Wake;* they wait in the shadows of their hero's dream world in anticipation of dawn, in hopes of fulfillment and liberation and recognition. At the disintegration

of Haun which ends the two chapters of public adulation for the
bourgeois leader, they celebrate the wake of the fallen hero and
still anticipate the arrival of the real leader, who arrives at the
opening of the *ricorso* chapter—"The leader, the leader! Securest
jubilends albas Temoram. Clogan slogan. Quake up, dim dusky,
wook doom for husky!" (593.13-15)—heralding the new age.
The eulogy to Haun is preceded by Joyce's portrait of these waiting Finnegans:

> Numerous are those who, nay, there are a dozen of folks still un-
> claimed by the death angel in this country of ours today, humble indi-
> visibles in this grand continuum, overlorded by fate and interlarded
> with accidence, who, while there are hours and days, will fervently
> pray to the spirit above that they may never depart this earth of theirs
> till in his long run from that place where the day begins, ere he re-
> tourneys postexilic, on that day that belongs to joyful Ireland, the peo-
> ple that is of all time, the old old oldest, the young young youngest,
> after decades of longsuffering and decennia of brief glory, to mind us
> of what was when and to matter us of the withering of our ways, their
> Janyouare Fibyouare wins true from Sylvester (only Walker himself is
> like Waltzer, whimsicalissimo they go murmurand) comes marching
> ahome on the summer crust of the flagway [472.28-473.5].

The Irish tradition that for centuries repeated that the giant Finn
MacCool only slept awaiting the hour that Ireland needed him underlies this passage; its contemporary analogue of Parnell as not
dead but waiting to be called in Ireland's hour of need (U 105)
provides the political motif for the *Wake*. Here again the Irish
people are presented as downtrodden and waiting for salvation,
but an earthly salvation in political terms. The end of the eulogy to
Haun forecasts the dawn of the *ricorso*: "Work your progress!
Hold to! Now! Win out, ye divil ye! The silent cock shall crow at
last. The west shall shake the east awake. Walk while ye have the
night for morn, lightbreakfastbringer, morroweth whereon every
past shall full fost sleep. Amain" (473.21-25).

Joyce does not appear to delude himself concerning the future
being engendered during his own lifetime; there is no sense of re-

trogression from the present wasteland to a romantic, orderly, comprehensible past. He depicts the future of mankind as intricately involved with the technical advances of the new century, with industrialism and contemporary politics. There is no sentimentality in *Finnegans Wake* attached to the classical attitudes of the past; when the four doddering old men falter and fumble their way through an attempt to unearth the material of past history and the secret of life from the disintegrated Yawn, they are quickly scrapped for a modern young brain trust who employ twentieth-century methods to get results (528). The quartet of ancient religionists have become quite effete in their efforts and are derided as four old ladies—"Mattahah! Marahah! Luahah! Joahanahanahana!" (554.10)—and laughed into oblivion. Nor does Joyce harbor any illusions concerning the saintliness of mankind; his representative of Everyman is guilt-ridden, his All-Woman is something of a Janus figure luring men to war and making peace, his "saint" (Shaun) is a hypocrite, and his hero-self (Shem) is a scoundrel. Joyce's reacceptance of mankind in *Finnegans Wake,* therefore, allows for no conditions: he refuses to love mankind *despite* faults, but insists upon accepting mankind as human because of these faults.

This is the mankind with which the sensitive, rebellious exile-artist chose to ally himself during his mature years; this is the cast of his epic portrait of his age as he felt himself living it. Joyce himself concedes that only through an alliance with mankind can the artist progress to a full realization of the significance of his work as an artist; his "Securest jubilends albas Temoram" (593.13-14) at the opening of the *ricorso* quotes St. Augustine's *securus iudicat orbis terrarum,* acknowledging that "the calm judgment of the world is that those men cannot be good who in any part of the world cut themselves off from the rest of the world."

It is impossible at this point to say what the future contains for *Finnegans Wake,* except to predict a library shelf of scholarly works which will probably be the only one to rival Shakespeare's. But it seems fairly certain that the bugaboo of Joyce's morbid cynicism has been laid to rest for good, and that whatever else it may turn out to be (all things to all critics), the scope and wit and warmth of Joyce's view of the world he knew and lived in and fought in will survive the morbidity and cynicism of his times, which fallaciously saw in James Joyce an image of itself. Joyce jiggled the kaleidoscopic mirror in the face of his age until he made it dance and sing and laugh. As chronicler of his times, he also took for himself the function of prophet, and although a bard, he was not above being a sociologist. And it is in this multiple capacity that he undertook to create the comic epic of contemporary man.

OBEDIENTIA·CIVIUM·URBIS·FELICITAS

". . . a Pair of Sloppy Sluts plainly Showing all the Unmentionability"
(107.6-7).

Reprinted from *The Early Christians* by Michael Gough, with
permission of Thames and Hudson.

" . . . flick off that hvide aske, big head!" (302.8).

Demonstration of Pun Possibilities in the Tale of Jarl van Hoother

Appearing as it does in the first chapter of *Finnegans Wake,* the portion usually referred to as The Tale of Jarl van Hoother and the Prankquean (21.5-23.15) provides a clear statement of several of James Joyce's basic themes in the *Wake:* the periodic invasions of Ireland which result in the assimilation of the successful invader by the conquered; religious attempts to convert the Irish; the role of the woman as destroyer and seductress, resulting in the necessary compromise by the male; and the sons as opposite facets of the father's personality. On the literal level of the book's "plot" the tale once again involves the guilty pub-keeper, H. C. Earwicker, in an encounter that reveals his sexual indiscretions, his blustering denials of guilt (which further incriminate him), and a significant hint of his sexual impotence. Earlier tales, legends, myths, and historical events underlie the story line, particularly the encounter of privateer Grace O'Malley with the Earl of Howth, and the love triangle involving Dermot, Grania, and Finn MacCool (incorporating also the Tristram-Iseult-King Mark story, as well as the Flying Dutchman yarn). Also foreshadowed is the later tale of Kersse the Tailor and the Norwegian Captain (311-332).

Of the two most important echoes of Irish "history" and legend, the stories of Grace O'Malley and Grania and Dermot, the latter certainly seems more basic to the concepts of the tale, while the former does little more than provide a frame for Joyce's version. There are many stories associated with the female piratess who sailed for Queen Elizabeth I and had a checkered career, a long lifetime alternating "crime" and respectability, and an apparently bad end. But Joyce is most concerned with a rumor that she had been involved in the kidnaping of the son of the Earl of Howth after her anger had been aroused by the refusal of the Earl, preoccupied with his dinner, to grant her a welcome in his castle. One version even insists that the ransom exacted was an insistence that the castle doors be left open during mealtimes. Joyce's rewriting of this material concerns the Prankquean arriving three times at the Jarl's castle, each time catching the gentleman unaware, each time asking a riddle, and—upon the Jarl's inability to answer it—each time kidnaping a child, until the third visit results in a concession from the furious Jarl. The form of the tale is therefore obviously a fairy story, involving the three-part repetition of a riddle, with modifications of the riddle resulting in a resolution of conflict. Riddles are numerous in the *Wake* (chapter 6 is devoted to a dozen of them; chapter 9 depends again on a three-part version, this time of a three-part riddle) and are as important in Joyce's book as they are throughout Irish mythology.

The versions of the Grania-Dermot-Finn story are numerous and only a perusal of an authoritative survey of Irish mythology can give the many nuances from this tale of the Fenian Cycle which offer allusions in Joyce's work. The basic elements of concern in the Prankquean-van Hoother yarn, however, seem to be these: in his middle age (or whatever constitutes middle age for a giant who lived two hundred years) Finn MacCool chooses (or is convinced) to marry. The selected Grania is of royal lineage and accepts (or is compelled to accept) Finn's proposal. At a banquet to celebrate the betrothal Grania falls in love with Dermot, Finn's most trusted aide (because of his irresistible "love spots" or any one of several supernatural factors). It is to Dermot's credit that in most versions he attempts to remain loyal to his leader, but again either supernatural factors are introduced or a choice is presented to him with both possibilities being distasteful, and eloping with Grania the lesser of the two evils—some versions even credit Dermot with asking a riddle or proposing a task for the seductress, but Grania always proves the master of such situations. In any event, they elope with a small contingent loyal to Dermot, after drugging

Finn and his followers. Finn gives chase but never succeeds in trapping the lovers (there are many adventures, many years of pursuit, many close escapes, but always ingenuity and/or supernatural powers prevail for the escaping pair). Most versions even insist that many years elapse before Dermot permits the elopement to be consummated, but whether immediately or eventually the temptress always wins. Finn eventually concedes defeat, declares a truce, and in some versions even invites Dermot to join him on a boar hunt—which proves fatal to Dermot (Finn either deliberately or inadvertently failing to save his successful rival from death). The two versions of the coda to the story offer us a choice of believing that Grania remained faithful to the memory of Dermot forever or eventually married old Finn and proved a loyal wife to him. For Joyce the elements of the temptress baiting the old man, the riddle or task presented, the "elopement" with the younger male, and the old man's concession seem to be paramount.

It is the riddle which most piques the old Jarl and which figures as the key to the tale; it has several alternate meanings, each one adding a new layer of significance to the tale in particular and the *Wake* in general. In its initial form it reads, "Why do I am alook alike a poss of porterpease?" On its simplest level it asks the question of the duality of opposites, since the hero's twin sons are asking why do we look like two peas in a pod (but are really as different as day and night)? The riddle relationship to the "plot" of the book is that heard by Earwicker in his drunken sleep after his pub had closed: he hears a call for "pots of porter, please" or even for "Piessporter" (38.5). These are the two levels of meaning that most commentators have contented themselves with, but several others also suggest themselves. A complement to the twins' version of the riddle is the echo of the nursery rhyme of "peas porridge hot, peas porridge cold," which suggests in the Joycean scheme the Biblical pair of opposite sons, Jacob and Esau, the latter having sold his birthright for a "pottage of lentils" (Genesis 25:29-34). The call for porter occurs often in the *Wake* (see listing below), and several commentators believe that in the story line of the publican and his family, the name is actually Porter (as it is in the early morning scene in chapter 16) rather than Earwicker. The use of "Porter" is not nearly as universal in the book; it merely delineates Earwicker's function of carrying drinks to his customers, and probably stems as well from the porter who hears the knocking at the gate in *Macbeth*. This knocking at the door further suggests the invader seeking to gain entrance into Ireland, so that Earwicker as defender is also a customs official or policeman asking to see "passports, please." This is supported only two pages later in the phrase "Poppypap's a passport out" (25.5), which in turn also reiterates Earwicker's drunken sleep when, having drunk all the dregs in his closed pub, "in the wakes of his ears our wineman from Barleyhome he just slumped to throne" (382.25-26).

But a most important fifth version of the riddle should not be overlooked: the Prankquean, arriving at the Jarl's castle in quest of sanctuary, asks permission to use the Jarl's toilet facilities, to "pass water, please"; when rebuffed, she made her "wit [witter, wittest]" on the doorstep and then she "rain, rain, rain." The extent to which the motif of urinating is vital in the *Wake* can be neither underestimated nor ignored without a resultant loss that would leave only an incomplete impression of Joyce's basic ideas. Along with probably every other body function, sexual and eliminative, urination looms even larger here than in *Ulysses*. Those who had difficulty accepting in print such aspects of natural existence as Leopold Bloom's pleasures in defecating in the Calypso chapter, the flatulent peroration to the Sirens chapter, the wealth of such activities real and imagined in the Circe nightmare, and the three urinations—Stephen's on the beach, the communal one of Stephen and Bloom under the stars in the Ithaca scene, and Molly's visit to the chamber pot during the Penelope portion—will find no respite when Bloom's day is turned into Earwicker's night. But the vast element of distortion that Joyce allowed himself in *Finnegans Wake* (the riddle is a minute example) eliminates the prudish and the squeamish with all others uninitiated in the vast subtleties which are the prizes for delvers into the realm often labeled obscure or obscene. Nowhere in the *Wake* are the body functions to which all flesh is heir (and from which most conscious minds are screened) very far from the surface. Of these the urinary process is certainly second in importance to the sexual, although Joyce allows no real distinction between the two.

His interest is often in the *dual* function and the oddity of a coalescence of opposites; in the same way in which hands serve equally for taking as well as giving, and lips move in natural modulation from smile to frown, from kiss to snarl, Earwicker's genitals serve him doubly. It is almost impossible to decide whether van Hoother is urinating or masturbating when he is "laying cold hands on himself";* the phrase itself is more apt in expressing masturbation, but much internal evidence in the tale points to urination. Similarly, in chapter 11, where we see Earwicker in his tavern surroundings, we can speculate whether his outdoor visit was for relief of excess bladder deposits or sexual frustrations. In either event Taff seems to be informing him that his "flup is unbu . . ." (341.2), the word itself remaining tactfully unbuttoned, this observation recalling Ham, the son of Noah, who mocked his father's nakedness. Although defecation is the dominant idea of this chapter (the pun on the verb is most apparent in "how bulkily he shat the Ructions gunorrhal" [192.2-3] and "buckly shuit Rosensharonals" [620.4]—the General's name appears at one instance as *"Pugger old Pumpey O'Dungaschiff"*—350.6-7), micturition provides at least a dozen allusions (see listing below for pages 309 through 382).

By an all-too-easy association the urine motif is linked with the female principle in the *Wake:* as Anna Livia represents the river Liffey and all rivers, she is the flow of life from the rain of birth to the emptying into the sea which is death. Biologically, urine is a result of metamorphosis and urinating a form of elimination, as fluid changes from potable liquids in channelized flow through the body into the waste product of which the body rids itself. Since, however, the process that begins with the intake of liquids and

---

* Ecclesiastically, of course, he is ordaining himself.

ends with its elimination is not a single one but repetitive, a second principle is introduced: if the river-flow through the land and the urine-flow through the body are synonymous with the life-flow, the drinking process (like the rain falling in the Wicklow hills in the *Wake*) is representative of birth and resurrection. This principle is attached to the male protagonist, the imbiber Earwicker, who partakes of the whiskey that is the water of life (if only in its Gaelic etymology). While the female exists as eternal flow, the male is subject to death and must be revived, as Finn and Finnegan and Dionysus and Osiris and Christ are. In the ultimate pattern Anna Livia also "dies" at the end of *Finnegans Wake,* but it is a single action that is continuous, as the dying sentence that ends the book is resurrected at the beginning. In contrast cowardly Earwicker dies a thousand deaths and enjoys an equal number of resurrections.

To return to the urination-masturbation configuration: whereas in real life they remain separate acts that cannot biologically be performed simultaneously, in Joyce's scheme they become almost interchangeable for Earwicker. The deeper significance is certainly the onanistic one, representing as it does Earwicker's sexual guilt and his loneliness, the act foreshadowing the unsuccessful sexual union enacted in the early morning hours in chapter 16—coming as it does in consequence of being awakened by Jerry's bed-wetting trauma (563.1-6)—so that urinating becomes a rationalization for the masturbating Earwicker. Thus the indiscretion in Phoenix Park can be interpreted in various ways depending upon the varying degrees of severity of guilt. On the most innocent level we have Earwicker (like his infant son) obeying the simplest of nature's calls: wandering through the park he feels the need to relieve himself and takes advantage of the darkness, the natural surroundings, and the supposed isolation. He is observed by the two girls who, through embarrassment or malicious mirth, snicker at him. Their snickering attracts the attention of the three soldiers who find the larger tableau of two girls laughing at a middle-aged man urinating in the park even funnier, and consider it a story worth telling.

Alternately, what the girls may well have seen was Earwicker masturbating (the socially more serious misdemeanor and the juicier story for the soldiers to retell), in which case Earwicker's defense is to insist that he was actually urinating (accepting the lesser crime when accused of the greater). This can be further complicated—and it often is—into Earwicker's purposeful self-exhibition before the girls, an erotic act containing all the frustrations of onanism, or into voyeurism, implying that it was the girls who were urinating (in Prankqueanish fashion) and Earwicker peeping: this is suggested by references to the Dublin crest which is purported to depict two maidens gingerly lifting their skirts to step over a puddle. In no case, however, except in the hero's guilty imagination, can anything more serious (any act of sexual aggression) be attributed to the pathetic publican. That something actually happened in the park is undeniable, but the degree of difference between man's actual state of guilt and the dimensions of his guilt feelings are purposefully exaggerated by Joyce. In any event, urinating—whether the committed act or as a rationalization or guilty alibi for masturbating—remains important, and the Tale of Jarl van Hoother expands in significance when viewed as a retelling of the peccadillo in Phoenix Park.*

As a review of the park script, the tale is both myth retold and a new scenario all its own. The hero remains the familiar H.C.E., that singular hero, now known as Jarl van (or von) Hoother (the Earl of Howth; Van der Decken, the Flying Dutchman; van Hou-

---

* It has been a source of unnecessary frustration to *Wake* analysts that such self-contained and apparently lucid portions of the *Wake* as the Prankquean Tale do not offer golden keys unlocking the exegetical mysteries. Such segments as these can be regarded by the logic that governs the pattern of dreams to be at the furthest remove from the *real* source of the dreamer's disturbance. That they are by nature transparent narratives means that they are the most disguised versions of Earwicker's sin, and indeed the Jarl is more sinned against than sinning. It has often been tempting to me to read this tale in reverse, as a photographic negative: the Prankquean as Earwicker, van and von Hoother as the two temptresses, or the *jiminies* as the temptresses, paralleling the *jinnies* of the Museyroom portion. In any event, I suspect that the events of the tale are purposely tangential to the event which nonexistently stands for THE event in Phoenix Park.

ten's cocoa—the last for reasons best known to Joyce and William York Tindall). The Prankquean in this case is equally singular, although she represents the two temptresses (the mother-daughter pair, Anna Livia and Issy; the two parts of Issy's conflicting egos) and is both the legendary Grania (Grainne, Grace) and the historical Grace O'Malley (Grainne O'Malley). By kidnaping the twins in alternate succession, she is re-enacting the apocryphal event of the privateer's vengeful raid on Howth Castle; by thumbing her nose at the raging, aging, impotent Jarl, she is re-enacting Grania's love-flight from Finn. Each time she arrives at the castle she takes the cantankerous Jarl by surprise (the Earl was at dinner when the piratess called; Finn and his cohorts were drugged when Grania ran off with Dermot). But Joyce creates substitutes for eating and drinking (although both of these are quite important in the *Wake*, the first primarily linked with Shaun, the second with Earwicker and Shem). At the first call van Hoother "had his burnt head high up in his lamphouse, laying cold hands on himself"; at the second he "had his baretholobruised heels drowned in his cellarmalt, shaking warm hands with himself"; at the third he "had his hurricane hips up to his pantrybox, ruminating in his holdfour stomachs." It is apparently his action at the moment which preoccupies his attention, resulting in his unawareness of her arrival. The last action of the three most suggests eating (the Earl's preoccupation); the middle instance most suggests drinking (Finn's distraction); but the first is innocent of both of these socially acceptable pursuits. All three, however, strongly invoke sexual images: the expression *laying cold hands on himself*, the erotic phallic symbol of *lamphouse* with *burnt head*, the word *hips*, and the vaguely suggestive *pantrybox*, which seems to be something other than just a place where foodstuffs are stored. All these connote masturbation, while component elements also support the milder suspicion that the good Jarl was doing nothing more monumental than relieving himself, a necessary adjunct to his drinking: the drowning of the second instance and the hurricane of the third both presuppose a goodly amount of liquid.

But while Jarl van Hoother is performing the composite eating-drinking-urinating-masturbating act, what is the Prankquean up to? Like the female pirate that she is, she arrives by sea and departs in haste the same way. For Joyce such a flight over water becomes "raining," an easy surrogate for urinating, and a hyperbole at that, to keep pace with the exaggerated retelling of the events. And the "wit" that she makes before the "dour" is not only her clever, sphinxlike riddle before the surly Jarl, but the insulting act of urinating in front of his door (a typical prankish gesture befitting the setting of the Beltane or Samhain fire festivals—"and fireland was ablaze"—the evenings preceding All Souls' and All Saints'). Again the same ambiguities are implied: Earwicker either masturbating or micturating, or Earwicker spying at the urinating temptresses. In any case the parallels with legendary and historical events are important only when superimposed upon the basic "original sin" motif of Earwicker's nocturnal fall in Phoenix Park: "O foenix culprit!" (23.16).

The early morning scene in the penultimate chapter of the *Wake* has already been mentioned in relation to the Prankquean-van Hoother Tale, but the importance of the urinating-masturbating theme merits a closer look at the parallels. In this cinematic scene at dawn, the Porters (the Earwickers' family name in the film version) are awakened by Jerry's crying. They hurry to the children's room to learn that he had "pipettishly bespilled himself from his foundingpen as illspent from inkinghorn" (563.5-6). This involuntary bed-wetting forecasts a literary future for Shem, who, we have learned during the Shem chapter, makes "synthetic ink" from his feces, "for his own end out of his wit's waste" (185.7-8):

> when the call comes, he shall produce nichthemerically from his unheavenly body a no uncertain quantity of obscene matter not protected by copriright . . . bedung to him, with this double dye, brought to blood heat, gallic acid on iron ore, through the bowels of his misery, flashly, faithly, nastily, appropriately, this Esuan Menschavik and the first till last alshemist wrote over every square inch of the only foolscap available, his own body [185.28-36].

But Shem's "Latin" incantation for making the synthetic ink is interrupted by such comments as "highly prosy, crap in his hand, sorry!" and "did a piss, says he was dejected, asks to be exonerated" (185.17-18, 23)—the latter suggesting Earwicker's courtroom plea. Here again defecation and urination prove dually significant, and the word *pipettishly* adds the sexual connotation, since it is most often associated with the lascivious alter ego of Issy in her correspondence with her "lover" or her other self, as witness her letter (457-461): "pet" (457.25), "pettest" (458.4), "Pip pet" (459.25); as well as an earlier letter (143-148); "pepette" (143.31), "pette" (143.32), "Peppt" (144.17), "pettest" (145.8), "pippy" (146.33), *"pipetta mia"* (147.33).

The awakened bed-wetter is comforted by his mother, while his groggy, disgruntled father stands naked in the doorway. Despite Mrs. Porter's admonition in her own "pig-latin" that he may be seen by the child (*"—Vidu, porkego! Ili vi rigardas"*—566.26), Mr. Porter is seen by Jerry (as Ham sees Noah's nakedness), who comes to understand the significance of his father's erection: "first futherer with drawn brand . . . That crag! Those hullocks! . . . a stark pointing pole . . . the dunleary obelisk . . . the Wellington memorial . . . O my big bagbone! . . . a buntingcap of so a pinky on the point . . . standard royal when broken on roofstaff" (566.24-567.10). To the modern psychologist this might well represent the sort of trauma that will warp the child; to Joyce it meant, like all knowledge hidden from the uninitiated, a source of awareness for the precocious child which leads to an understanding beyond that of his compeers. For Earwicker, who has exposed the secret to his heir, it means the end of his sexual reign. The coition that takes place once the children are again asleep ("The galleonman jovial on his bucky brown nightmare. . . . her lamp was all askew and a trumbly wick-in-her"—583.8-9, 30-31) merely amuses the wife ("it tickled her innings to consort pitch at kicksolock in the morm"—584.2-3), since she is apparently accustomed to a better performance these days than her husband's ("Magrath he's my pegger. . . . He'll win your toss. . . . He's posh. I lob him"

—584.5-8). Even the Earwickers' hen crows with derision at Mr. Porter's efforts: "the hen in the doran's shantyqueer began in a kikkery key to laugh it off" (584.20-22). When dawn thus "repeals an act of union" (585.25)—the metaphor changing from cricket to Irish politics—the husband is enjoined to "Withdraw your member! Closure" (585.26-27), and the sad fact is revealed that Mr. Porter "never wet the tea!" (585.31). The predictable irony is that the aging man who pursues young girls (the image of his own daughter disguised as the niece-of-his-in-law) is in actuality a cuckold and a sexual has-been.

Many echoes of aspects of van Hoother's tale are prevalent throughout the *Wake,* especially sounding the theme of either the male or female urinating. The basic riddle of *Mark the Wans, why do I am alook alike a poss of porterpease?* occurs in several forms: "How do you do that lack a lock and pass the poker, please?" (224.14-15); "Moke the Wanst, whye doe we aime alike a pose of poeter peaced?" (372.4-5); "wheer would his aluck alight or boss of both appease" (417.7); "For why do you lack a link of luck to poise a pont of perfect, peace?" (493.29-30); and "What'll you take to link to light a pike on porpoise, plaise?" (623.14-15). Secondary echoes are heard in such phrases as "pint of porter place" (260.6), "pip for Mr Potter of Texas, please" (274.n3), and "the pint of porter" (511.19), while tertiary soundings may include "trickle triss, please" (96.15), "Whose porter? Which pair?" (187.15-16), "tome to Tindertarten, pease" (191.21), "a potion a peace, a piece aportion, a lepel alip, alup a lap" (397.18-19), and "to pose three shielings Peter's pelf" (520.14). Other references to the liquid consumed and eliminated are found in "Piessporter" (38.5), "boomarpoorter on his brain" (327.33-34), "he dropped his Bass's to P flat" (492.3), and to wine, porter, and ale may be added champagne: "peepair of hideseeks" (462.10).

A particularly large group of words punned with such urine substitutes as "peas," "peace," and "poss" are found throughout the *Wake* (as witness their significance in the quotations already used as well as in the group below):

ptee . . . peteet peas [19.1-2]
possing of the showers [51.2]
And both as like as a duel of lentils? Peacisely [89.4]
plight pledged peace [94.7]
widowpeace upon Dublin Wall [101.18]
Peamengro [171.29]
pious Eneas [185.27]
poing her pee [204.12]
posspots [258.16]
spilleth peas [267.11]
possetpot [294.31]
trying to make keek peep [296.13]
pond's apeace [301.n1]
hot peas [363.27]
peace peace perfectpeace [364.20]
peaces pea to Wedmore [391.27]
sweetpea time [392.25-26]
clister of peas, soppositorily petty [406.19]
pease Pod pluse [412.31]
petween peas [432.9]
Peace in Plenty [440.10]
your pease again was a taste tooth psalty [456.4]
Poss, myster [466.30]
Mint your peas [472.5-6]
anyposs length [495.6]
this leggy peggy spelt pea [496.19]
peacies [496.32]
pppease [571.21]
peascod [578.8]
old missness wipethemdry . . . as proud as a peahen [578.19-20]
A lintil pea [625.23]

Other puns involve expressions for urine and urinating, particularly vulgarizations and the familiar euphemisms employed for the
benefit of children:

wee peep, see . . . see peegee [6.31-32]
preealittle [10.32]
peewee [11.10]
peewee o'er the saltings [17.20]
pispigliando [38.14]

pisononse . . . the wetter is pest [39.14]
peese [50.5]
cockaleak and cappapee [58.25]
Szpissmas [101.28]
Spissially [113.16]
piscines [127.35]
polerpasse [128.25]
Pissasphaltium [157.2]
piscivore [171.8]
Fanny Urinia [171.28]
inspissated [179.25]
did a piss [185.23]
wious pish [189.1]
Domine vopiscus [193.31]
peihos piped [205.32]
pistania [206.31]
passe of him [207.14]
pay [207.14]
pison plague [212.24]
Euro pra nobis [228.26]
Pull the boughpee to see how we sleep [248.18-19]
pitssched . . . against our seawall [254.1-2]
Elpis, thou fountain of the greeces [267.4]
There was a sweet hopeful culled Cis [267.L]
pizdrool [287.31]
Pee for Pride [296.5]
Like pah, I peh [296.28]
I'll pass out if the screw spliss his strut [296.n2]
bistrispissing [302.6-7]
Fore auld they wauld to pree [336.10]
pitschobed [339.5]
wee engrish, one long blue streak, jisty and pithy [351.8-9]
Some Poddy pitted in [361.15]
trisspass through minxmingled hair [363.26]
Irish prisscess [396.8]
Piscisvendolor [408.36]
he made a cat with a peep [420.6-7]
shoepisser pluvious [451.36]
bissing will behind the curtain [467.6-7]
p.p. [467.33]
Trickspissers vill be pairsecluded [503.29]

an early peepee period [533.26]
pisoved [548.10]
Haveandholdpp [571.29]
Urania [583.16]
Panniquanne starts showing of her peequuliar talonts [606.30]

wee, wee [57.13]
wee [103.6]
wetbed confession [188.1]
The wee taste the water left [212.25]
he was weeting [223.36]
Mahamewetma [297.30]
nowet badder [298.22]
their wetting [314.33]
for a wee [354.9]
weeter to wee [354.34]
Wee, wee, that long alancey one [360.34]
wetting with the bimblebeaks [416.10]
golden violents wetting [461.17-18]
wee wiping womanahoussy [578.32]
our weewee mother [598.34]
this lad wetting his widdle [620.22-23]
cara weeseed [625.24]

meeting waters most improper [96.14]
she had never cessed at waking malters among the jemassons [229.22-23]
they made whole waters [312.4]
mouths making water [386.11]
making wind and water [391.17]
May he me no voida water [415.34]
on the makewater [420.7]
the mingling of our meeting waters [446.14]
Water *non* to be discharged [586.5]

Allusions to Tom Moore's "The Meeting of the Waters" echo the association that occurs to Bloom in *Ulysses* as he passes Moore's statue on College Green: "He crossed under Tommy Moore's roguish finger. They did right to put him up over a urinal: meeting of the waters" (U 151). Another urinary allusion is also carried over from *Ulysses* into the *Wake:* the postcard that Denis

Breen received with the succinct message: "U.P.: up" (U 147) be-comes: "Ah well, sure, that's the way (up) and it so happened there was poor Matt Gregory (up), their pater familias, and (up) the others and now really and (up) truly they were four dear old heladies" (386.12-15).

Other variations on the micturition motif include the Irish word for urine, "mun" (251.4), also seen in "hespermun" (538.23); the Persian *shash* in "Shasser"* (494.20); Japanese *shoben* in "Shoebenacaddie" (200.23); and the Latin word† already seen in "minxmingled hair" (363.26), but also available in "your dirty minx" (80.30); *"Miction"* (106.19); "micturious mites" (166.28); "micture" (184.22); *"mixto"* (185.24); "Minxy Cun-ningham" (95.9)—it should be remembered that Martin Cunning-ham "drowned" (387.28, 393.5); "comminxed" (139.11); *"minxit"* (185.21); "Minxing marrage" (196.24); "Aminxt" (222.32); *"Minxy was a Manxmaid"* (433.19); and "a minx from the Isle of Woman" (496.8-9). The two *minxing minx* are of course the temptresses, the "two quitewhite villagettes who hear show of themselves so gigglesomes minxt the follyages" (8.3-4), who in reality are merely the maidens seen on the Dublin coat of arms discreetly and daintily lifting their skirt hems ever so slightly: "helts her skelts up the casuaway the flasht instinct she herds if a tinkle of tunder" (227.5-6). One identification of the two young ladies cites a pair of eighteenth-century beauties named Elizabeth and Maria Gunning, transformed by Joyce into

> Elsebett and Marryetta Gunning, H 2 o, by that noblesse of leechers at his Saxontannery with motto in Wwalshe's ffrenchllatin: O'Neill saw Queen Molly's pants: and much admired engraving, meaning complet manly parts during alleged recent act of our chief mergey margey magistrades, five itches above the kneecap, as required by stat-

---

* Identified as the Belshazzar who saw the handwriting on the wall, Joyce's "Bill Shasser's Shotshrift writing academy" (494.20-21) involves more than wall-writing. Shasser, apparently a relative of the Pisser Burke of *Ulysses*, is urinating and defecating against that same wall. See also "Sish" (587.19).

† The children urinate and defecate before going to bed: "they do ming no merder" (259.5).

ues. V.I.C.5.6. If you won't release me stop to please me up the leg of me [495.25-32].

The last phrase suggests another urination theme found in various instances in the *Wake* as: "he make peace in his preaches and play with esteem" (225.6-7) and *"Prisson your Pritchards and Play Withers Team"* (176.2, *errata;* see p. 633), variations of the children's chant of "piss up your leg and play with the steam."

To these references may also be added: "had bourst a blabber" (224.18-19), "bladey well pessovered" (553.8), "emptybloddy" (324.11), "fly fly flurtation" (352.7), "privet stationery" (412.27), "Nupiter Privius" (390.22-23), "frish uov in urinal" (407.17), "look before you leak" (433.34), "his silenced bladder" (467.20), and "Proserpronette whose slit satchel spilleth peas" (267.11). Thus it becomes apparent that in hundreds of instances Joyce is "alluding to the whole in the wall" (90.21-22), advising the reader: "when you're done push the chain" (278.n5).

In the light of this mass of evidence on the all-important theme of urination, an analysis of the Tale of Jarl van Hoother and the Prankquean is offered below in terms of the pun-possibilities apparent. Some of the suggestions will seem obvious, others farfetched and absurd, while gaps exist where either the word seems to be worth taking on face value or any feasible explanation is beyond me; the reader is invited to consider such lacunae as blanks for his own "possibilities."* I have in one instance at least avoided the obvious: underscoring the various phallic words (*lamphouse, nail, lance, pike,* and so forth), since the above text should serve to make them more than apparent already.

It was of a night, late, lang time agone, in an auldstane eld,

	long	ago	old stone elm
	lag	gone	elder
		agon	stained hero (*held*)
			eld (fire, Nor.)

---

* Mr. L. A. Wiggin, whose analysis of the first thunderword has already appeared in the *James Joyce Review,* has kindly offered some "possibilities" for the second one, which appear here.

when Adam was delvin and his madameen spinning watersilts, when
"When Adam   dwelling   little madam   silk
   Delved"   delving   Mrs. Adam (Eve)   silt
                 deviling   dam, dame
                 Delvin   mad *spinnen* (mad, Ger.)
                 drunk (of wine)   "Madamina" (*Don Giovanni*)
                 elfin   *amener* (to lead, Fr.)

mulk mountynotty man was everybully and the first leal
much mountain not-a-man   everybody   real
most mounting   bully   loyal
hulk   **naughty**   bull   little
mulct   **knotty**   lisle
bulk mountebank
Battle of Montenotte
      notte (night, It.)

ribberrobber that ever had her ainway everybuddy to his lovesaking eyes
river-robber (pirate)   own way everybody   lovesick
river-rover (sailor)   one way   buddy   love-seeking
rib-robber (Eve)   rain   bud   love-sake
joker-thief   anal   Butt   love-making
                                   love's aching
                     "great searching eyes"
                         (*Ulysses*)

and everybilly lived alove with everybiddy else, and Jarl van Hoother
   everybody   in love   everybody   Earl of Howth
   King Billy   alone   **C. J.** van Houten's
      billy goat   above   Biddy the hen   **cocoa**
      bill, pike   beloved   bid   Bartholomew Vanhomrigh
                              Johannes de Doper (John
                              the Baptist, Dutch)
                              Hut (hat, Ger.)

had his burnt head high up in his lamphouse, laying cold hands on
      burned   lighthouse   (masturbation)
      burnished   lampoon   (suicide)
      blunt

himself. And his two little jiminies, cousins of ourn,
                    Gemini   sin   ours
                    jinni   cozened   our own
                    Jimmy   *unser*
                               iron

Tristopher and Hilary, were kickaheeling their dummy on the oil
Christopher   kicking   doll
(Hotspur and Prince Hal) kneeling   servant
 taufe (baptize, Ger.) kicking their mute
"In tristitia hilaris, in   heels   sister
hilaritate tristis"—   tummy
  Bruno

cloth flure of his homerigh, castle and earthenhouse. And, be
 floor   home   Erse
 flue   Homeric   hen house
 flore   home rule   earthy
 Flur (fields, Vanhomrigh
  Ger.) Humphrey Chimpden Earwicker
     ri (king, Irish)
     Heinrich, Henry

dermot, who come to the keep of his inn only the niece-of-his-in-law,
Dermot, Diarmuid   kip, brothel   (female non-blood
bedammit   custody sin   relative)
by the word   guard   nice **sin**
       key
        innkeep

the prankquean. And the prankquean pulled a rosy one and made **her**
 queen of pranks   (plucked a rose: urinated)
  slut, wench   paled **rosary** maid
 Pranke (paw, Ger.)   *poule* (whore, Fr.)
         arroser (to water, Fr.)
      (made a joke)

wit foreninst the dour. And she lit up and fireland was ablaze.
wet in front of door   was aglow Ireland aflame
joke before   dour, sour, *lit* (bed, land of fire blasé
riddle against   sullen   Fr.) ire, anger
 foreign   doer
 forene *dur* (hard, Fr.)
  (unite,
  Nor.)
 fornenst (opposite, Ir.)

And spoke she to the dour in her petty perusienne: Mark the Wans,

	petit Parisian,-enne	King Mark
	pretty perusings	one, once
	pettish, peevish	wan
(Prussian,	Persian, Peruvian)	first
	ruse, prank	the Swan

why do I am alook alike a poss of porterpease? And that was how

look   like   pot of porter, please
look-alike   peas in a pod
          pot of pottage
          mess of pottage
          peas porridge hot
          passports
          pass water
          posse (to be able, Lat.)
              Piesporter
              Mr. Porter (H.C.E.)

the skirtmisshes began. But the dour handworded her grace in

skirmishes   answered   Grainne
skirt   she-he   *antworden*, Dutch
   misses   handiwork
   mishe (I am, Irish)   hand-to-mouth   her grace,
   Moses
Misch-Masch—Lewis Carroll

dootch nossow: Shut! So her grace o'malice kidsnapped up the

Dutch   now so   close   Grace O'Malley   kidnapped
douche Nassau shite   malicious   snapped up
douce   nor' sou' *Schutt* (rubbish,   Alice   snatched
douse   Norse   Ger.)
the duchess

jiminy Tristopher and into the shandy westerness she rain, rain, rain.

              shady   wilderness   ran
              merry   west   rann
              schande   rain
              (shame, Ger.)   reigned
              chanty   waste
              shindy
      Tristram Shandy—Laurence Sterne

And Jarl van Hoother warlessed after her with soft dovesgall:

warred	dove's call
watered	Donegal gall, bitter
wailed	dark stranger (Irish)
warbled	Swift?
warison	Saints Columcille & Gall
wirelessed	

Stop deef stop come back to my earin stop. But she swaradid to him:

deaf	Erin	swore
thief	erring	did swear
	hearing	sword
"Come Back to Erin"		*svare* (answer,
	earstopper	Norse)
		svara (voice,
		Sanskrit)
		war

Unlikelihud. And there was a brannewail that same sabboath night

unlikelihood	banshee wail	sabbath
unlikely head	brand new wail	sobbeth
hud (skin, Norse)	brain wave	Saboath
	brand ale	boat
	brennen (burn, Ger.)	Boat Night
	Brangäne	oath
	Bran (Finn's dog)	both

of falling angles somewhere in Erio. And the prankquean

angels	Eire
Angles	air, aria
shooting stars	eerie
	rio (river, Sp.)
	(Eros, Erin, Erebus, Erinys?)
	Erewhon—Samuel Butler

went for her forty years' walk in Tourlemonde and she washed the

30-years' war	tour the world	cleansed
40 days of rain	world tower	baptized
(Numbers 14:33)	turley whale	wished
	lemon	
	leman, lover	
	Mund (mouth, Ger.)	
	Mond (moon, Ger.)	
	onde (wave, Fr.)	

blessings of the lovespots off the jiminy with soap sulliver

blushings	(Dermot)		soap suds
wounds (Fr.)	pots		saddle soap
	venereal disease		Sullivan
			sully
			soul
			liver
			Gulliver's Travels—Swift
			Oliver (Cromwell)

suddles and she had her four owlers masters for to tauch him his

subtle		old	teach history
sudlen (to dirty, Ger.)		wise	touch
sud (south, Fr.)		owler, smuggler	torture
	4 Master Annalists		*tauchen*
	4 Evangelists		(to dip, Ger.)
		howlers	*Tau* (dew, Ger.)
		Aule	

tickles and she converted him to the onesure allgood and he became

tricks	converted		Almighty God
merriments	distorted	unsure	all-in-one
catechism	cavorted		omniscient
canticles	consorted	one-for-all	
testicles	conveyed		

a luderman. So then she started to rain and to rain and, be redtom,

Lutheran	pour	Dermot
lewder man	run	Atum
ladder man	terrain	soldier
Leute, Mann	Touraine	*beredt* (talkative, Ger.)
laundryman		
lawndamaun		
(lout, Irish slang)		
lud (bleach, Nor.)		
ludere (to play, Lat.)		
Luder (scoundrel, Ger.)		

she was back again at Jarl van Hoother's in a brace of samers and

pair	doubles
embrace	summers
	Samhain*
	Same (semen, Ger.)

* For a tale involving supernatural events and a kidnaping on Samhain Eve, see W. B. Yeats's "Red Hanrahan."

the jiminy with her in her pinafrond, lace at night, at another time.
　　　　　　　　　　　　pinafore　　late
　　　　　　　　　　frond pinned in front
　　　　　　　　　　　(Eve's fig leaf)

And where did she come but to the bar of his bristolry. And Jarl
　　　　　　　　　　　　　　　inn　　　　　Bristol
　　　　　　　　　　　　　　sandbar　　　bristle
　　　　　　　　　　　　　　　　　　　　history
　　　　　　　　　　　　　　　hybris

von Hoother had his baretholobruised heels drowned in his
van　　　　　　　　　　bare-thole-bruised　　　down
　　　　　　　　　　　Achilles' heel
　　　　　　　　　　Bartholomew
　　　　　　　St. Bartholomew's Day Massacre

cellarmalt, shaking warm hands with himself and the jimminy Hilary
cell　　　　　　　　　　　　　　　　　　　　　　Sunny Jim
cellar vault　　　　　　　　　　　　　　　　　　　St. Hilary
　　　malt liquor
　　　　alt
　　larme (tear, Fr.)
　　Larm (noise, Ger.)
c'est la morte

and the dummy in their first infancy were below on the tearsheet,
　　　　　　　　　　　　　　fancy　　　bellow　　　　torn sheet
　　　　　　　　　　　　　　　　　　　blow　　　crying sheet
　　　　　　　　　　　　　　　　　　　be low　　Doll Tearsheet

wringing and coughing, like brodar and histher. And the prankquean
ringing　　　coffin　　　　brother　　sister
wrangling　　　　　　　　*Bruder*　　Hester, Esther
　　　　　　　　　　　　brood　　　hiss
　　　　　　　　　　　　brooder　　hysteria
　　　　　　　　Brodhar—slew Brian　history
　　　　　　　　　　　Boru

nipped a paly one and lit up again and redcocks flew flackering
drank a nip of pale ale   aglow   cocks   flying
plucked a white rose   coxcomb   flocking
Napoleon   red cocks (slang) clucking
  Apollo   redcoats   flickering
  the English Pale   (pagan fire festival)
  Apollyon

from the hillcombs. And she made her witter before the wicked,
    coxcombs   wittier   evil, cruel
    welcomes   wetter   wicket
    ills   *wieder* (again, Ger.)
    ilk

saying: Mark the Twy, why do I am alook alike two poss of
                two, twin, twain   trespass
                second
      Mark Twain

porterpease? And: Shut! says the wicked, handwording her
                            handling
                            answering

madesty. So her madesty a forethought set down a jiminy and
majesty   malice   a-forethought
modesty   Prometheus
madness
  Esther
D'Este

took up a jiminy and all the lilipath ways to Woeman's Land she
                 lily pathways   No Man's Land
                 lilypad   Woman's
                 Lilliput   Roman's
                 Lilith   sad

rain, rain, rain. And Jarl von Hoother bleethered atter her
                      bleated   after
                      blustered   at her
                      blasted   otter
                      blasphemed
                      blithered
                      Blätter (leaves, Ger.)

with a loud finegale: Stop domb stop come back with my earring
    lewd fine gale   dumb, mute   Erin
        Fingal   damn   hearing
        Finn MacCool *dom* (stupid, Dutch)   earwig
        Finnegan   herring
        fin   Mayerling
        fair stranger
        (Irish)

stop. But the prankquean swaradid: Am liking it. And there
was a wild old grannewwail that laurency night of starshootings
        Wilde   grand new wail   larceny   falling stars
           granny   St. Lawrence O'Toole Stella
           Grainne   Laurence Sterne
           Grana Uaile   "Larry McHale"—Charles Lever

somewhere in Erio. And the prankquean went for her forty years'
        Erewhon

walk in Turnlemeem and she punched the curses of cromcruwell
           leman, lover   *crucis*   cruel Cromwell
        turn *même*   crosses   Cromwell's crew
        pantomime—Punch and Judy   cruises
        Turm (tower, Ger.)   crisis
        Tür (door, Ger.)
        Tor (gate, Ger.)
        René-Joseph de Tournemine
        tourmaline

with the nail of a top into the jiminy and she had her four
        top of a nail

larksical monitrix to touch him his tears and she provorted
lexical   monitors   teach him to cry   converted
larcenous monkey tricks   history   perverted
lachrymose   *triste*   provoked
larks   one-in-three   proved
    sickle meretrix
    cycle
lackadaisical

him to the onecertain allsecure and he became a tristian. So
   omniscient omnipotent   sad Christian
   uncertain Lord Protector   Tristan
   once-certain *secour*
    all-so-sure

then she started raining, raining, and in a pair of changers,
           2 interchangeables
            changelings

be dom ter, she was back again at Jarl von Hoother's and the
 Dermot
 damn to her
  thrice (Lat.)

Larryhill with her under her abromette. And why would she halt
Hilary   apron
larrikin   umbrella
 hell   Abraham
St. Lawrence O'Toole *abromado* (foggy, Sp.)

at all if not by the ward of his mansionhome of another nice lace
     guard   Mansion House   night late
     wall   *maison*
          man

for the third charm? And Jarl von Hoother had his hurricane hips
    time   hurricane lamps
    term

up to his pantrybox, ruminating in his holdfour stomachs
     sentry box chewing his cud old four stomachs
     bread box pondering   aches
     Bantry Bay rummaging
     Santry
     Pandora's box
     Pan (pan—)

(Dare! O dare!), and the jiminy Toughertrees and the dummy were
dear oh dear   Tristopher
hard, severe   tough tree
there   Tophet three
give (Lat.)

```
belove on the watercloth, kissing and spitting, roguing and
in love        oil cloth                        rogue
beloved        water closet                     rough
below                                           rouge
                                       Arrah-na-Pogue—
                                          Boucicault


poghuing, like knavepaltry and naivebride and in their second infancy.
kissing        paltry knave      navel bridal           second childhood
poking         nave                                     Second Coming
puking         naive
               St. Patrick and St. Brigid


And the prankquean picked a blank and lit out and the valleys lay
                   plucked a white rose
                   drew a blank


twinkling. And she made her wittest in front of the arkway of trihump,
twin                     wittiest              Arch of Triumph
                         wettest               ark        three humps
                         whitest               aqua       trump
                         test                      Humpty Dumpty


asking: Mark the Tris, why do I am alook alike three poss of
               three, third                      trespass
               sad
               thryst
               thrice


porter pease? But that was how the skirtmishes endupped.
                                   skirts       upended
                                   skirmishes   ended
                                                ended up
                                                   dropped
                                                   duped


For like the campbells acoming with a fork lance of lightning,
               bells coming              foreglance
               belles acumen
          "The Campbells Are Coming"
```

Jarl von Hoother Boanerges himself, the old | terror of the dames,
 sons of thunder, | terror of the Danes,
 Sts. James & John | Brian Boru
 bone urges | bearer of the flames
 boa | women
 Boru | queens

came hip hop handihap out through the | pikeopened arkway of his
 hippity-hop | forced open darkway
 hip hip hurray | unbuttoned
 hip   handy | fish
   hops handicapped | capon
   haphazard

three shuttoned castles, in his | broadginger hat and his civic
three-shuttered | Broadbrim (Quaker)
three-towered | Broad Church
three-buttoned trousers | gingerbread
   setoon (pillar, Pers.)
   Sutton | The Seven Articles of Clothing:
   shat-on
the Dublin coat of arms

chollar and his allabuff | hemmed and his bullbraggin
 collar   cuffs | ballbearings
  choler   all a-buff, naked | bragging
gingery-choleric buffoon | brogans
   aleph, beth, ghimel | brogues
   à la boeuf | papal bull
     hemmen (inhibit, | Balbriggan
          Ger.) | brigand
     Hemd (shirt, Ger.)

soxangloves and his ladbroke breeks and his | cattegut bandolair
socks and gloves   breeches | cat   bandoleer
sex and love   broke wind | catgut   lair
Anglo-Saxons   Pembroke bricks | Catholic O'Leary's band
     Ragnar Lodbrok | Catechism   air
 | categorical *dolor*
 | (pain, Sp.)
 | cattegat
 | *gut* (good, Ger.)

and his furframed   panuncular cumbottes like a rudd   yellan
        farframed   avuncular culottes   red   yellow
    fur (thief, Lat.)   pantaloon cummerbunds   rude   yelling
    fremd (strange,   pantalette cumbrance   ruddy *élan*
           Ger.)   Pan   *bottes*
                                      (boots, Fr.)

gruebleen   orangeman in his violet   indignation, to the whole
blue green   Ulsterman   vile   indignation   hole
gruesome   orangutang   violent   indigo
true blue   orange   Indian nation
groveling   *rang* (color, Pers.)   dig
  bleeding
grübeln (to ponder, Ger.)
grue (turn from with disgust, Ir.)

Seven Colors of the Rainbow

longth of the strength of his bowman's bill. And he clopped his
long   strong   archer   pike, lance   clapped
length   strength   bow
                         bau (build, Ger.)
                    Isa Bowman
          Strongbow, Earl of Pembroke

rude hand to his eacy hitch and he ordurd and his thick spch spck
red   easy hatch   ordered in   speech
right   itch   ordure   spoke
                ici (here, Fr.)   odor   speak
                icy   endured   *spucken*
                E.C.H.   *ord* (word, Swed.) (to spit, Ger.)

for her to shut up shop, dappy. And the duppy shot the shutter clup
            shut dummy   dummy shut   clapper shut
            stop pappy   puppy   shutter up
            sharp dopey   opener   thunderclap
                dap (to steal,   club
                     slang)   clap (slang)
                dapi (pool, O. Norse)
                    "Polly Put the Kettle On"
          "Yet up he rose and donn'd his clothes"—Ophelia's song

(Perkodhuskurunbarggruauyagokgorlayorgromgremmitghundhurthrumat-

perk	husk	barge, boat agok: struggle

mit, with

kod:	scrotum
cod:	kurun: running, vagina layer

gruau: porridge, semen

hund: hundred

hurth: hearth

barg (lightning, Pers.)

ru: rue

current

yago: hunt yore

math:

Iago gore grom: man, penis   destruction

grom (thunder, Rus.)

grem: woman, vagina

One-hundred-lettered word for thunder:

hunaradidillifaititillibumullunukkunun!)   And they all drank free.

thunder dilly tit lib: free   *kennen,* know   made free

una: together Tilly mull: demolish

rad: afraid ill bum: din   "And they all drank tea"

rad (river, Pers.) bum: arse

bomull (cotton-wool, Nor.)

Id   *fait,* made   nuk: destruction, nucleus

For one man in his armour was a fat match always for any girls

armour   fair match   girl's

armor   fat chance

ardor

Arms and the Man—Shaw

"Arma virumque"—Virgil

"Eleven men well armed will certainly subdue one single man in
his shirt"—Swift

under shurts. And that was the first peace of illiterative

undershirts   piece   alliterative

skirts   piss   illiterate

shorts   ill-lit

sheets

Schurz (apron, Ger.)

porthery in all the flamend floody flatuous world. How kirssy the tiler

poetry	flaming flooded flat	Kersse the Tailor
pottery	flamen bloody fat	Tilly the Toiler
porter	flame-end fatuous	Phil the Fluter
port	*Flamand,* Flemish flatulent	Teddy the Tiler
	flamant (flamingo, Fr.)	cursed till

made a sweet unclose to the Narwhealian captol. Saw fore shalt
    suit of clothes   Norwegian   Captain so   forth
    sweet finish   narwhale   capitol soar
    Swede uncle   Noah   *caput* foresaw
    sweat exposure   wheel   *kaput* seafare
        heal   cap
        Tim Healy

            "As thou sows so shalt
                thou reap"
   "Therefore shall a man leave . . ." (Gen. 2:24)

thou sea. Betoun ye and be. The prankquean was to hold her
   see between you and me
   be   between "Y" and "B"
   "C" return   see
   "Z" *béton* (concrete, Fr.)
      town

dummyship and the jimminies was to keep the peacewave and van
position   keep the peace
custody   rule the waves
Dampfschiff (steamboat, Ger.)   hold back her urine
ghost ship
pirate ship
demi-chapeau (half-a-hat)

Hoother was to git the wind up. Thus the hearsomeness of the
        get the wind up   obedience,
        provide wind   *gehorsam*
        break wind   fearsomeness
     open the window   handsomeness
          windup   Herr Solness
                  hearse
                  arse

burger felicitates the whole of the polis.
citizen,   hold   city,
burgher   hole   *polis*
burglar   whale   police
bugger   all   piss
                    poles
"Obedienta civium urbis felicitas"—Dublin's motto

Notes

CHAPTER 1

1. Joseph Campbell and Henry Morton Robinson, *A Skeleton Key to Finnegans Wake* (New York: Harcourt, Brace and Co., 1944). Adaline Glasheen, *A Census of Finnegans Wake* (Evanston, Ill.: Northwestern University Press, 1956). Frances Motz Boldereff, *Reading Finnegans Wake* (Woodward, Penn.: Classic Nonfiction Library, 1959). James S. Atherton, *The Books at the Wake* (New York: Viking Press, 1960). J. Mitchell Morse, *The Sympathetic Alien* (New York: New York University Press, 1959). Matthew J. C. Hodgart and Mabel P. Worthington, *Song in the Works of James Joyce* (New York: Columbia University Press, 1959). Clive Hart, *Structure and Motif in Finnegans Wake* (Evanston, Ill.: Northwestern University Press, 1962); *A Concordance to Finnegans Wake* (Minneapolis: University of Minnesota Press, 1963).

2. William York Tindall, *A Reader's Guide to James Joyce* (New York: Noonday Press, 1959), p. 237.

3. Glasheen, *A Census of Finnegans Wake;* Campbell and Robinson, *A Skeleton Key;* and Tindall, *A Reader's Guide to James Joyce.*

4. Harry Levin, *James Joyce* (Norfolk, Conn.: New Directions, 1960), p. 146; Edmund Wilson, "The Dream of H. C. Earwicker," in *James Joyce: Two Decades of Criticism,* ed. Seon Givens (New York: Vanguard Press, 1948), p. 324.

5. Richard Ellmann, *James Joyce* (New York: Oxford University Press, 1959), p. 734.

6. Levin, *James Joyce,* p. 146.

7. Edmund Wilson, "H. C. Earwicker and Family," *New Republic* (June 20, 1939), pp. 203-6; and "The Dream of H. C. Earwicker," *New Republic* (July 12, 1939), pp. 270-74. The name was subsequently altered from "Maggie" to "Ann" by the time these two essays appeared under the latter title in *Two Decades of Criticism* and Wilson's *The Wound and the Bow.*

8. Morton Prince, *The Dissociation of a Personality* (New York: Longmans, Green and Co., 1905).

9. Glasheen, *A Census of Finnegans Wake,* pp. xxv-xxvii.

10. Stuart Gilbert (ed.), *Letters of James Joyce* (New York: Viking Press, 1957), p. 208.

11. Glasheen, *A Census of Finnegans Wake*, p. 35.

12. *Letters*, p. 220.

13. Campbell and Robinson, *A Skeleton Key*, p. 255.

14. *Ibid.*, p. 349.

15. Matthew J. C. Hodgart, "Earliest Sections of *Finnegans Wake*," *James Joyce Review*, I (February 2, 1957), 8.

16. Glasheen, *A Census of Finnegans Wake*, p. 134.

17. Adaline Glasheen, "Out of My Census," *Analyst*, No. 17 (1959), p. 11.

18. *Letters*, p. 220.

19. Hart, *Structure and Motif*, p. 130.

20. *Ibid.*

21. Campbell and Robinson, *A Skeleton Key*, p. 219.

22. Hart, *Structure and Motif*, p. 130.

23. J. Mitchell Morse, "Cain, Abel and Joyce," *ELH*, XXII (March, 1955), 48-60; also appears as chap. iv in *The Sympathetic Alien*.

24. For a dissenting opinion on this disclosure, see Hart, *Structure and Motif*, p. 80.

25. Campbell and Robinson, *A Skeleton Key*, p. 252.

26. *Ibid.*

27. William York Tindall, *The Joyce Country* (University Park: Pennsylvania State University Press, 1960), p. 148.

28. *Letters*, p. 396.

29. *Ibid.*, p. 258.

30. Glasheen, *A Census of Finnegans Wake*, p. 83.

31. Campbell and Robinson, *A Skeleton Key*, p. 271.

32. *Letters*, p. 279.

33. *Ibid.*, p. 281.

34. *Ibid.*, p. 249.

CHAPTER 2

1. Levin, *James Joyce*, p. 140.

2. Louis Gillet, "Stele for James Joyce," in *A James Joyce Yearbook*, ed. Maria Jolas (Paris: Transition Press, 1949), pp. 41-42.

3. Ellmann, *James Joyce*, pp. 707-8.

4. *Letters*, p. 277.

5. *Ibid.*, p. 367.

6. Levin, *James Joyce*, p. 197.

7. Glasheen, *A Census of Finnegans Wake*, pp. 73-74.

8. *Ibid.*, p. 123.

9. Ellmann, *James Joyce,* pp. 15-16.

10. Hugh Kenner, *Dublin's Joyce* (London: Chatto and Windus, 1955), pp. 357-59.

11. Stanislaus Joyce, "James Joyce: A Memoir," trans. Felix Giovanelli, *Hudson Review,* II (Winter, 1950), 497.

12. Helmut Bonheim has an interesting note on "'Tory' in 'Finnegans Wake,'" *Notes and Queries,* VIII, No. 9 (September, 1961), 349-50.

13. Herbert Gorman, *James Joyce* (New York: Rinehart and Co., 1948), p. 183.

14. *Ibid.*, fn.

15. David Daiches, *The Novel and the Modern World* (Chicago: University of Chicago Press, 1939), pp. 102-3.

16. *Ibid.*, p. 103.

17. "A Communist on Joyce," *Living Age,* CCCXLVII (November, 1934), 268.

18. Daiches, *The Novel and the Modern World,* p. 103.

19. "A Communist on Joyce," p. 269.

20. Gorman, *James Joyce,* p. 183.

21. S. Joyce, "James Joyce: A Memoir," p. 488.

22. Sidney Alexander, "Bloomsday in Italy," *Reporter,* XXIV, No. 8 (April 13, 1961), 38.

23. James S. Atherton, "'Finnegans Wake' and 'Poverty,'" *Times Literary Supplement* (November 23, 1951), p. 749.

24. John V. Kelleher, "Notes on *Finnegans Wake* and *Ulysses,*" *Analyst,* No. 10 (March, 1956), pp. 3-4.

25. Laszlo Moholy-Nagy, *Vision in Motion* (Chicago: Paul Theobald, 1947), pp. 345-46.

26. "A Communist on Joyce," p. 269.

27. S. Joyce, *My Brother's Keeper* (New York: Viking Press, 1958), p. 130.

28. *Ibid.*

29. Ellsworth Mason, "James Joyce's Shrill Note—The *Piccolo della Sera* Articles," *Twentieth Century Literature,* II (October, 1956), 118.

30. Marvin Magalaner and Richard M. Kain, *Joyce: The Man, the Work, the Reputation* (New York: New York University Press, 1956), pp. 37-38.

31. Thomas Merton, *Seven Storey Mountain* (New York: Harcourt, Brace and Co., 1948), p. 211.

32. *Ibid.*, p. 212.

33. William T. Noon, S. J., *Joyce and Aquinas* (New Haven, Conn.: Yale University Press, 1957), p. 99 fn. 9.

34. Morris L. Ernst, *The Best Is Yet* (New York: Harper and Bros., 1945), p. 118.

35. *Ibid.*

36. *Ibid.*

37. Lloyd Morris, *A Threshold in the Sun* (New York: Harper and Bros., 1943), p. 244.

38. Oliver St. John Gogarty, "They Think They Know Joyce," *Saturday Review of Literature,* XXXIII (March 18, 1950), 8.

39. Morris, *A Threshold in the Sun,* p. 243.

40. *Letters,* p. 102.

41. Morris, *A Threshold in the Sun,* p. 245.

42. Herbert Gorman, *James Joyce: His First Forty Years* (B. W. Huebsch and Viking Press, 1924), pp. 74-75.

43. Kevin Sullivan, *Joyce among the Jesuits* (New York: Columbia University Press, 1958).

44. Arland Ussher, "James Joyce: Doubting Thomist and Joking Jesuit," *Three Great Irishmen* (New York: Devin-Adair Co., 1953), p. 155 fn. 2.

45. T. S. Eliot, *After Strange Gods* (London: Faber and Faber, 1934), p. 38.

46. Ussher, *Three Great Irishmen,* p. 129.

47. Merton, *Seven Storey Mountain,* p. 212.

48. Thomas McGreevy, "The Catholic Element in Work in Progress," in *An Exagmination of James Joyce* (Norfolk, Conn.: New Directions, n.d.), p. 121.

49. *Ibid.*

50. *Ibid.,* p. 124.

51. L. A. G. Strong, *The Sacred River* (New York: Pellegrini and Cudahy, 1951), pp. 11-12.

52. *Ibid.,* p. 11.

53. *Ibid.,* p. 152.

54. *Ibid.,* p. 156.

55. *Ibid.,* p. 11 fn.

56. Campbell and Robinson, *A Skeleton Key,* p. 331 fn.

57. *Ibid.,* p. 333.

58. Montgomery, "The Pervigilium Phoenicis," p. 438.

59. *Ibid.*

60. *Ibid.,* pp. 438-39, 446, 470-71.

61. Morse, *The Sympathetic Alien,* p. 50.

62. Levin, *James Joyce*, p. 161.

63. Morse, *The Sympathetic Alien*, p. 64.

64. *Ibid.*, p. 65.

65. Louis Gillet, "Joyce's Testament: *Finnegans Wake*," *Quarterly Review of Literature*, I (Winter, 1944), 91.

66. Henry Morton Robinson, "Hardest Crux Ever," in *A James Joyce Miscellany*, 2nd ser., ed. Marvin Magalaner (Carbondale, Ill.: Southern Illinois University Press, 1959), pp. 195-207.

67. *Ibid.*, p. 196.

68. *Ibid.*, p. 206.

69. Mabel P. Worthington, "Joyce's ULYSSES ('Ithaca')," *Explicator*, XXI (January, 1963), item 37.

70. Sullivan, *Joyce among the Jesuits*, p. 179.

71. Brian Nolan, "A Bash in the Tunnel," *Envoy*, V (April, 1951), 11.

72. Sullivan, *Joyce among the Jesuits*, pp. 106-7.

73. Hynes, "The Catholicism of James Joyce," p. 488.

74. *Ibid.*, p. 489.

75. William T. Noon, "James Joyce and Catholicism," *James Joyce Review*, I (December 15, 1957), 3-14.

76. *Ibid.*, pp. 11, 14.

77. *Ibid.*

78. Nolan, "A Bash in the Tunnel," p. 10.

79. Frank Budgen, "Further Recollections of James Joyce," *Partisan Review*, XXIII (Fall, 1956), 532.

80. Robert McAlmon, "Mr. Joyce Directs an Irish Word Ballet," in *Exagmination*, p. 106.

81. *Ibid.*

82. Campbell and Robinson, *A Skeleton Key*, p. 348.

83. Morse, *The Sympathetic Alien*, p. 60.

84. Campbell and Robinson, *A Skeleton Key*, p. 115.

85. Gillet, "Joyce's Testament," p. 90.

86. Kenner, *Dublin's Joyce*, p. 353.

87. Atherton, *The Books at the Wake*, p. 185.

88. S. Joyce, *My Brother's Keeper*, p. 130.

89. Hart, *Structure and Motif*, pp. 211 ff.

90. Vivian H. S. Mercier, "James Joyce and an Irish Tradition," in *Society and Self in the Novel*, ed. Mark Schorer (New York: Columbia University Press, 1956), p. 89; a later version appears as "Joyce and the Irish Tradition of Parody" in Professor Mercier's excellent *The Irish Comic Tradition* (Oxford: Oxford University Press, 1962).

91. Atherton, *The Books at the Wake*, p. 203.
92. Budgen, "Further Recollections," p. 533.
93. Campbell and Robinson, *A Skeleton Key*, p. 148.
94. Edwin Berry Burgum, *The Novel and the World's Dilemma* (New York: Oxford University Press, 1947), p. 118.
95. Magalaner and Kain, *Joyce*, p. 40.
96. Thomas J. Fitzmorris, "Vico Adamant and Some Pillars of Salt," *Catholic World*, CLVI (February, 1943), 576.
97. *Ibid.*
98. Morse, *The Sympathetic Alien*, p. 80.
99. *Ibid.*

CHAPTER 3

1. James S. Atherton, *"Finnegans Wake*: 'The Gist of the Pantomime,' " *Accent*, XV (Winter, 1955), 14-26.
2. Henry Fielding, *Joseph Andrews* (New York: Modern Library, 1950), p. xxxvi.
3. See Robert Bierman, "Streameress Mastress to the Sea," *Modern Fiction Studies*, II (May, 1956), 79-80.
4. Quoted in W. R. Rodgers, "Joyce's Wake," *Explorations*, V (June, 1955), 22.
5. Comments on Joyce's punning are most extensive in Noon's chapter, "The Root Language of Shem," in *Joyce and Aquinas*, pp. 144-60, and in Hart's chapter, "Art of Panning," in *Structure and Motif*, pp. 31-38. Additional comments can be found in William York Tindall, *The Literary Symbol* (New York: Columbia University Press, 1955), p. 206; Levin, *James Joyce*, p. 185; Magalaner and Kain, *Joyce*, pp. 236-37.
6. Louis Gillet, "Mr. James Joyce and his New Novel," *Transition*, XXI (March, 1932), 268.
7. Ellsworth Mason, "Mr. Stanislaus Joyce and John Henry Raleigh," *Modern Language Notes*, LXX (March, 1955), 188 fn. 5; Sullivan, *Joyce among the Jesuits*, p. 114.
8. Gillet, "Stele for James Joyce," p. 35.
9. Gillet, "Joyce's Testament," p. 97.
10. Frank Budgen, "Joyce's Chapters of Going Forth By Day," in *Two Decades of Criticism*, p. 347.
11. Margaret Schlauch, "The Language of James Joyce," *Science and Society*, III (Fall, 1939), 485.
12. Levin, *James Joyce*, p. 184.
13. Kenner, *Dublin's Joyce*, pp. 305-6.

14. Glasheen, *A Census of Finnegans Wake*, p. 74.

15. Robert Sage, "Before *Ulysses*—and After," in *Exagmination*, pp. 167-68.

16. Northrop Frye, *Anatomy of Criticism* (Princeton, N.J.: Princeton University Press, 1957), p. 314. For a commentary on the preoccupation of Irish writers with the creation of a sacred book, see Herbert Howarth, *The Irish Writers, 1880-1940* (London: Rockliff, 1958).

17. William Troy, "Notes on *Finnegans Wake*," in *Two Decades of Criticism*, p. 304.

18. *Ibid.*, pp. 303-4.

19. Kenner, *Dublin's Joyce*, p. 304.

20. C. K. Ogden, quoted by Levin, *James Joyce*, pp. 196-97.

21. Ellmann, *James Joyce*, pp. 720, 716.

CHAPTER 4

1. Fielding, *Joseph Andrews*, pp. xxxi-xxxii.

2. *Ibid.*, p. 134.

3. Miles Dillon, *Early Irish Literature* (Chicago: University of Chicago Press, 1948), p. 34.

4. For an analysis of the initial thunderword, see Lawrence A. Wiggin, "The First Thunderword," *James Joyce Review*, III (February, 1959), 56-59.

5. *Letters*, p. 258.

CHAPTER 5

1. Daiches, *The Novel and the Modern World*, p. 103.

2. William York Tindall, *James Joyce* (New York: Charles Scribner's Sons, 1950), p. 104.

3. Richard Ellmann, "The Grasshopper and the Ant—Notes on James Joyce and his brother, Stanislaus," *Reporter*, XIII (December 1, 1955), 36.

4. *Ibid.*, p. 37.

5. John Henry Raleigh, " 'My Brother's Keeper'—Stanislaus Joyce and 'Finnegans Wake,' " *Modern Language Notes*, LXVIII (February, 1953), 109-10.

6. Mason, "Mr. Stanislaus Joyce and John Henry Raleigh," p. 188 fn. 5.

7. S. Joyce, "James Joyce: A Memoir," p. 512.

8. *Ibid.*, p. 514.

9. Raleigh, " 'My Brother's Keeper,' " p. 110.

10. S. Joyce, "James Joyce: A Memoir," p. 485.

11. Levin, *James Joyce*, pp. 161-62.

12. Gorman, *James Joyce*, p. 163.

13. Levin, *James Joyce*, pp. 54-55.

14. Geoffrey Wagner, "Wyndham Lewis and James Joyce: A Study in Controversy," *South Atlantic Quarterly*, LVI (January, 1957), 57-66.

15. Gorman, *James Joyce*, p. 264.

16. Campbell and Robinson, *A Skeleton Key*, p. 105 fn. 17.

17. Andrew Cass, "Sprakin Sea Djoytsch?" *Irish Times* (April 26, 1957), p. 6.

18. *Letters*, pp. 312, 396.

19. Coulson Turnbull, *Life and Teachings of Giordano Bruno, Philosopher, Martyr, Mystic, 1548-1600* (San Diego, Calif.: The Gnostic Press, 1913), p. 39.

20. James S. Atherton, "Lewis Carroll and *Finnegans Wake*," *English Studies*, XXXIII (February, 1952), p. 6.

21. Harry Slochower, *No Voice Is Wholly Lost* (New York: Creative Age Press, 1945), p. 246.

22. Quoted by Vivian Mercier, "Dublin Under the Joyces," in *Two Decades of Criticism*, p. 288.

23. *Fitzmorris*, "Vico Adamant," p. 570.

24. Levin, *James Joyce*, p. 145.

25. Magalaner and Kain, *Joyce*, p. 275.

26. Burgum, *The Novel and the World's Dilemma*, p. 112.

27. Levin, *James Joyce*, p. 145; Wilson, "The Dream of H. C. Earwicker," p. 326.

28. Campbell and Robinson, *A Skeleton Key*, p. 342 fn. 10.

29. *Ibid.*, p. 341 fn. 6.

A Selected Finnegans Wake *Bibliography*

The following list, although a fragment of the material available about *Finnegans Wake,* is a sampling of the important books and substantial articles on the subject in English. An almost complete bibliography (at least through 1963) is now available in Robert H. Deming's *A Bibliography of James Joyce Studies* (Lawrence, Kan.: University of Kansas Libraries, 1964); in particular, consult pp. 49-68, 136-163. Since March, 1962, a newsletter devoted exclusively to the *Wake* has been appearing regularly, now at the rate of six issues a year: *A Wake Newslitter,* edited by Clive Hart and Fritz Senn. The *James Joyce Quarterly,* edited by Thomas F. Staley, has been in progress since the fall of 1963.

BOOKS

Atherton, James S. *The Books at the Wake.* New York: Viking Press, 1960.

Beckett, Samuel, *et al. Our Exagmination Round his Factification for Incamination of Work in Progress.* Paris: Shakespeare and Co., 1929.

Boldereff, Frances Motz. *Reading Finnegans Wake.* Woodward, Conn.: Classic Nonfiction Library, 1959.

Bonheim, Helmut. *Joyce's Benefictions.* Berkeley, Los Angeles: University of California Press, 1964.

Campbell, Joseph and Henry Morton Robinson. *A Skeleton Key to Finnegans Wake.* New York: Harcourt, Brace and Co., 1944.

Connolly, Thomas E. *Scribbledehobble: The Ur-Workbook for Finnegans Wake.* Evanston, Ill.: Northwestern University Press, 1961.

Ellmann, Richard. *James Joyce.* New York: Oxford University Press, 1959.

Gilbert, Stuart (ed.). *The Letters of James Joyce.* New York: Viking Press, 1957.

Glasheen, Adaline. *A Second Census of Finnegans Wake: An Index of the Characters and Their Roles.* Evanston, Ill.: Northwestern University Press, 1963.

Hart, Clive. *A Concordance to Finnegans Wake.* Minneapolis: University of Minnesota Press, 1963.

————. *Structure and Motif in Finnegans Wake.* Evanston, Ill.: Northwestern University Press, 1962.

Hayman, David. *A First-Draft Version of Finnegans Wake.* Austin: University of Texas Press, 1963.

Higginson, Fred H. *Anna Livia Plurabelle: The Making of a Chapter.* Minneapolis: University of Minnesota Press, 1960.

Hodgart, Matthew J. C. and Mabel P. Worthington. *Song in the Works of James Joyce.* New York: Columbia University Press, 1959.

Kenner, Hugh. *Dublin's Joyce.* Bloomington, Ill.: Indiana University Press, 1956.

Levin, Harry. *James Joyce: A Critical Introduction.* Norfolk, Conn.: New Directions, 1960.

Litz, A. Walton. *The Art of James Joyce: Method and Design in Ulysses and Finnegans Wake.* New York: Oxford University Press, 1961.

Magalaner, Marvin and Richard M. Kain. *Joyce: The Man, the Work, the Reputation.* New York: New York University Press, 1956.

Morse, J. Mitchell. *The Sympathetic Alien: James Joyce and Catholicism.* New York: New York University Press, 1959.

Noon, William T., S. J. *Joyce and Aquinas.* New Haven, Conn.: Yale University Press, 1957.

Spoerri, James Fuller. *Finnegans Wake by James Joyce: A Check List.* Evanston, Ill.; Northwestern University Library, 1953.

Tindall, William York. *A Reader's Guide to James Joyce.* New York: Noonday Press, 1959.

———. *James Joyce: His Way of Interpreting the Modern World.* New York: Scribner's, 1959.

ARTICLES

Atherton, James S. "*Finnegans Wake:* 'The Gist of the Pantomime,' " *Accent,* XV (Winter, 1956), 14-26.

Beechhold, Henry F. "Finn MacCool and *Finnegans Wake,*" *James Joyce Review,* II (June, 1958), 3-12.

Begnal, Michael H. "The Prankquean in *Finnegans Wake,*" *James Joyce Quarterly,* I (Spring, 1964), 14-18.

Benstock, Bernard. "Americana in *Finnegans Wake,*" *Bucknell Review,* XII (March, 1964), 64-81.

———. "Persian in *Finnegans Wake,*" *Philological Quarterly,* XLIV (January, 1965), 100-9.

Bishop, John Peale. "Finnegans Wake," *Southern Review,* V (Winter, 1940), 439-52.

Bogan, Louise. "Proteus, or Vico's Road," *Nation,* CLXVIII (May 6, 1939), 533-35.

Budgen, Frank. "Joyce's Chapter on Going Forth By Day," *James Joyce: Two Decades of Criticism,* ed. Seon Givens. New York: Vanguard Press, 1948; pp. 343-67.

Burgum, Edwin Berry. "The Paradox of Scepticism in *Finnegans Wake," The Novel and the World's Dilemma.* New York: Oxford University Press, 1947.

Campbell, Joseph. "Finnegan the Wake," *Two Decades of Criticism;* pp. 368-89.

Carlson, Marvin. "Henrik Ibsen and *Finnegans Wake," Comparative Literature,* XII (Winter, 1960), 133-41.

Chase, Richard V. "*Finnegans Wake:* An Anthropological Study," *American Scholar,* XIII (Autumn, 1944), 418-26.

Coleman, Elliott. "Heliotropical Noughttime: Light and Color in *Finnegans Wake," Texas Quarterly* (Winter, 1961), 162-77.

Dolmatch, Theodore B. "Notes and Queries Concerning the Revisions in *Finnegans Wake," Modern Language Quarterly,* XVI (June, 1955), 142-48.

Frye, Northrop. "Quest and Cycle in *Finnegans Wake," James Joyce Review,* I (February, 1947), 39-47.

Gillet, Louis. "Joyce's Testament: *Finnegans Wake," Quarterly Review of Literature,* I (Winter, 1944), 87-99.

Glasheen, Adaline. "*Finnegans Wake* and the Girls from Boston, Mass.," *Hudson Review,* VII (Spring, 1954), 89-96.

———. "The Strange Cold Fowl in *Finnegans Wake," Spectrum,* VI (Spring, 1961), 38-64.

———. "Part of What the Thunder Said in *Finnegans Wake," Analyst,* No. 23 (November, 1964), 1-29.

Graham, Philip Lamar, Philip B. Sullivan, and G. F. Richter. "Mind Your Hats Goan In!: Notes on the Museyroom Episode of *Finnegans Wake," Analyst,* No. 21 (July, 1962), 1-21.

———. "Mind Your Hats Goan In!" Part II, *Analyst,* No. 22 (October, 1962), 1-24.

Halper, Nathan. "James Joyce and the Russian General," *Partisan Review,* XVIII (July-August, 1951), 424-31.

Hayman, David. "Dramatic Motion in *Finnegans Wake," Texas Studies in English,* XXXVII (1958), 155-76.

———. "From *Finnegans Wake:* A Sentence in Progress," *PMLA,* LXXIII (March, 1958), 136-54.

———. "Tristan and Isolde in *Finnegans Wake:* A Study of the Sources and Evolution of a Theme," *Comparative Literature Studies,* I, No. 2 (1964), 93-112.

Hill, Archibald A. "A Philologist Looks at *Finnegans Wake*," *Virginia Quarterly Review*, VX (Autumn, 1939), 650-56.

Hodgart, Matthew J. C. "Work in Progress," *Cambridge Journal*, VI (October, 1952), 23-39.

———. "The Earliest Sections of *Finnegans Wake*," *James Joyce Review*, I (February, 1957), 3-18.

Jarell, Mackie L. "Swiftiana in *Finnegans Wake*," *ELH*, XXVI (June, 1959), 271-94.

Johnston, Denis. "Clarify Begins At: The Non-Information of *Finnegans Wake*," *Massachusetts Review*, V (Winter, 1964), 357-64.

Kelleher, John V. "Notes on *Finnegans Wake* and *Ulysses*," *Analyst*, No. 10 (1956), 1-9.

———. "Notes on *Finnegans Wake*," *Analyst*, No. 12 (1957), 9-15.

———. "Notes on *Finnegans Wake*," *Analyst*, No. 15 (March, 1958), 9-16.

Magalaner, Marvin, "The Myth of Man: Joyce's *Finnegans Wake*," *University of Kansas City Review*, XVI (Summer, 1950), 265-77.

McLuhan, Herbert M. "Radio & TV vs. the ABCED-minded," *Explorations*, V (June, 1955), 12-18.

Montgomery, Niall. "The Pervigilium Phoenicis," *New Mexico Quarterly*, XXIII (Winter, 1953), 437-72.

Peery, William. "Shakhisbeard at Finnegans Wake," *Texas University Studies in English*, XXX (1951), 243-57.

Robinson, Henry Morton. "Hardest Crux Ever," *A James Joyce Miscellany*, 2nd series; ed. Marvin Magalaner. Carbondale: Southern Illinois University Press, 1959; pp. 195-208.

Schlauch, Margaret. "The Language of James Joyce," *Science and Society*, III (Fall, 1939), 482-97.

Semmler, Clement. "Notes on the Themes and Language of 'Finnegans Wake,'" *For the Uncanny Man*. Melbourne: F. W. Cheshire, 1963.

Senn, Fritz. "Some Zurich Allusions in *Finnegans Wake*," *Analyst*, No. 19 (December, 1960), 1-23.

Strong, L. A. G. "Symbols, Words, and *Finnegans Wake*," *Irish Writing*, No. 1 (1946), 101-13.

Thompson, Francis J. "A Portrait of the Artist Asleep," *Western Review*, XIV (Summer, 1950), 245-53.

Thompson, W. I. "The Language of *Finnegans Wake*," *Sewanee Review*, LXXII (January, 1964), 78-90.

Troy, William. "Notes on *Finnegans Wake*," *Two Decades of Criticism*; pp. 302-18.

Von Phul, Ruth. "Who Sleeps at Finnegans Wake?" *James Joyce Review,* I (February, 1957), 27-38.

———. "Shaun in Brooklyn," *Analyst,* No. 16 (February, 1959), 1-22.

Wagner, Geoffrey. "Wyndham Lewis and James Joyce: A Study in Controversy," *South Atlantic Quarterly,* LVI (January, 1957), 57-66.

Wiggin, L. A. "The First Thunderword," *James Joyce Review,* III (February, 1959), 56-59.

Wilder, Thornton. "Giordano Bruno's Last Meal in *Finnegans Wake,*" *Hudson Review,* XVI (Spring, 1963), 74-79.

Wilson, Edmund. "The Dream of H. C. Earwicker," *Two Decades of Criticism;* pp. 319-42.

Worthington, Mabel P. "Nursery Rhymes in *Finnegans Wake,*" *Journal of American Folklore,* LXX (January-March, 1957), 37-48.

Index

A.B.C., 19, 19–20n, 28
Age, 31–32, 118, 233, 235
Anglicanism: and H.C.E., 22, 48, 80, 85, 104, 235; mentioned, 62, 80, 81, 96, 98, 104, 128
Anna Livia, 7, 9, 10, 19, 23, 24, 26, 26–27n, 38, 43, 67, 85–86, 95, 104, 105, 118, 122, 129, 134n, 135, 141–42, 146, 149, 151–52, 153, 157, 183, 196, 200, 206–7, 211, 244, 249, 253, 255, 257, 260, 271–72
Autobiographical elements, 12, 16, 32, 47, 74–75, 115–22, 127, 207–8, 209–10, 215, 216–37

Biblical references, 9, 10, 11, 13, 14, 16, 19, 21, 23, 24, 29–32, 39, 49, 65, 82, 83–84, 85, 97, 102, 106, 120, 123, 125, 126, 134n, 140–41n, 148, 151, 152, 166, 167–68, 169–70, 174–75, 177, 181, 182, 183, 185, 190, 192, 195, 196, 201, 202, 203n, 205, 209, 213, 231, 234, 239, 240, 241, 242, 244, 249, 250, 269, 271, 276, 283, 286, 287, 289, 290, 291
Blasphemy, 78, 79, 92, 93, 99–103, 106, 147
British imperialism, 34, 57–66, 69, 80, 97, 101, 106, 171, 185, 199
British liberalism, 56–57, 60–66
Bruno, Giordano: theory of the conflict and reconciliation of opposites, 12–13, 15–21, 21–23, 26–28, 29, 46, 48, 49, 50, 51, 61, 84, 97, 103, 106, 108, 110, 118, 119, 122, 137, 140, 145–48, 155–56, 168, 173, 174, 178, 182–83, 187, 195, 199, 205–7, 209, 218–21, 222, 231, 237–46, 248–53, 254–56, 258, 267, 269, 284

Cad (and Magrath), 9, 16, 17, 21, 37, 38–39, 145, 151, 257, 276

Catholicism: schisms, 8n, 80–81, 93, 97–99; Irish, 48, 53, 69, 71, 76–77, 79, 80–81, 82, 85, 90, 92–93, 95, 98; Joyce's attitudes toward, 56, 57, 68–69, 73, 75, 78, 79, 83, 91, 93–104, 106, 107, 226; Church involvement in politics, 69, 81, 93, 95, 96, 97, 99, 104; Jesuits, 69, 70, 72, 73, 74–76, 85, 88–90, 93, 94–95, 101, 107; Joyce's position as a Catholic, 70–71, 78–79, 79–80; Joyce's "unconscious" Catholic residue, 71, 74, 75–76, 78–79, 91, 94; "medieval," 74, 93; the mass, 87–88, 99, 100, 101, 102; "liberal" Catholic attitudes toward Joyce, 90–92
Character: augmentation of, 19–21, 25–28, 30, 37, 47, 140–41n, 214
Cities: founding and building of. See Creation myth
Coincidences, 23–25, 30, 35, 47, 171, 185, 195, 213–14, 232, 240
Comedy: slapstick, 108–15; of character, 115–22; pantomime, 111–13, 259. See also Doggerel; Verbal humor
Constables: 16, 37–38
Creation myth, 25, 43, 85, 86, 165, 166, 169–71, 180, 199, 201, 202, 205, 254, 258, 260
Critics: Joyce's attitudes toward, 7, 229–30

Dante. See under Epic literature
Doggerel, 49, 103, 136–41, 159. See also Poetic techniques
Dramatic monologue, 158–59. See also Poetic techniques
Dream structure, 8, 38, 38–40, 64, 93, 104, 106, 108, 116, 131, 174, 199, 200, 205–6, 211, 214, 231, 232,